COMPUTER BOOK SERIES FROM IDG

PageMaker® 6 For Macs®
For Dummies,® 2nd Edition

Cheat Sheet

D1311713

Type Size and Leading

To Do This:	Press This:
Increase to next larger type size in menu	⌘+Shift+period
Decrease to next smaller type size in menu	⌘+Shift+comma
Increase type size 1 point	⌘+Option+Shift+period
Decrease type size 1 point	⌘+Option+Shift+comma
Change to Auto leading	⌘+Shift+A
Return to 100% width	⌘+Shift+X

Kerning

To Do This:	Press This:
Kern text together $\frac{1}{25}$ em space	⌘+Delete
Kern text apart $\frac{1}{25}$ em space	⌘+Shift+Delete
Kern text together $\frac{1}{100}$ em space	Option+Delete
Kern text apart $\frac{1}{100}$ em space	Option+Shift+Delete
Clear all kerning	⌘+Option+K
Remove tracking	⌘+Shift+Q

Alignment (Justification)

To Do This:	Press This:
Flush left	⌘+Shift+L
Flush right	⌘+Shift+R
Center	⌘+Shift+C
Justify	⌘+Shift+J
Force justify	⌘+Shift+F

Type Style

To Do This:	Press This:
Plain	⌘+Shift+spacebar
Bold	⌘+Shift+B
Italic	⌘+Shift+I
Underline	⌘+Shift+U
Outline	⌘+Shift+D
Shadow	⌘+Shift+W
Strikethru	⌘+Shift+slash (/)
Reverse	⌘+Shift+V
Superscript	⌘+Shift+plus
Subscript	⌘+Shift+minus
All caps	⌘+Shift+K
Small caps	⌘+Shift+H

Special Characters

To Do This:	Press This:
Open curly quote	Option+left bracket ([)
Single open quote	Option+right bracket (])
Close curly quote	Option+Shift+left bracket ([)
Apostrophe/close single quote	Option+Shift+right bracket (])
Bullet	Option+8
Nonbreaking space	Option+spacebar
Thin space	⌘+Shift+T
En space	⌘+Shift+N
Em space	⌘+Shift+M
Discretionary hyphen	⌘+hyphen
Nonbreaking hyphen	⌘+Option+hyphen
En dash	Option+hyphen
Em dash	Shift+Option+hyphen
Nonbreaking slash	⌘+Option+slash (/)
Line break	Shift+Return
Copyright symbol	Option+G
Trademark symbol	Option+2
Registered symbol	Option+R
Automatic page number	⌘+Option+P

. . . For Dummies: #1 Computer Book Series for Beginners

COMPUTER
BOOK SERIES
FROM IDG

PageMaker® 6 For Macs® For Dummies,® 2nd Edition

Cheat Sheet

Getting Around

To Do This:	Press This:
Zoom to 100%	⌘+1
Zoom to 200%	⌘+2
Fit in window	⌘+0
Zoom to 50%	⌘+5
Toggle between 100% and Fit in Window	⌘+Option+click
Toggle between 200% and 100%	⌘+Option+Shift+click
Magnify beyond 400%	Drag around area with Zoom tool
Scroll with hand cursor	Option+drag with any tool but Zoom tool
Go to previous page (or two-page spread)	⌘+Shift+Tab
Go to next page (or two-page spread)	⌘+Tab

Toolbox Shortcuts

	Tool:	Press This:
↖	Arrow tool	Shift+F1
T	Text tool	Shift+F2
○	Ellipse tool	Shift+F3
□	Rectangle tool	Shift+F4
╱	Line tool	Shift+F5
├	Perpendicular Line tool	Shift+F6
⬡	Polygon tool	Shift+F7
⌕	Zoom tool	Shift+F8
↻	Rotate tool	Shift+F9
⌗	Crop tool	Shift+F10
	Toggle between Arrow tool and last tool used	⌘+spacebar

Commands

To Choose This Command:	Press This:
Place	⌘+D
Print	⌘+P
Save	⌘+S
Undo	⌘+Z
Send Backward	⌘+9
Bring Forward	⌘+8
Send to Back	⌘+B
Send to Front	⌘+F
Group	⌘+G
Ungroup	⌘+U
Align	⌘+4
Close document	⌘+W
Toggle between Story Editor and Layout view	⌘+E
Snap to Rulers	⌘+Shift+Y
Snap to Guides	⌘+Shift+G

IDG
BOOKS
WORLDWIDE

. . . For Dummies: #1 Computer Book Series for Beginners

References for the Rest of Us!®

COMPUTER BOOK SERIES FROM IDG

Are you intimidated and confused by computers? Do you find that traditional manuals are overloaded with technical details you'll never use? Do your friends and family always call you to fix simple problems on their PCs? Then the . . . *For Dummies®* computer book series from IDG Books Worldwide is for you.

. . . *For Dummies* books are written for those frustrated computer users who know they aren't really dumb but find that PC hardware, software, and indeed the unique vocabulary of computing make them feel helpless. . . . *For Dummies* books use a lighthearted approach, a down-to-earth style, and even cartoons and humorous icons to diffuse computer novices' fears and build their confidence. Lighthearted but not lightweight, these books are a perfect survival guide for anyone forced to use a computer.

> *"I like my copy so much I told friends; now they bought copies."*
>
> **Irene C., Orwell, Ohio**

> *"Quick, concise, nontechnical, and humorous."*
>
> **Jay A., Elburn, Illinois**

> *"Thanks, I needed this book. Now I can sleep at night."*
>
> **Robin F., British Columbia, Canada**

Already, hundreds of thousands of satisfied readers agree. They have made . . . *For Dummies* books the **#1 introductory level computer book series** and have written asking for more. So, if you're looking for the most fun and easy way to learn about computers, look to . . . *For Dummies* books to give you a helping hand.

IDG BOOKS WORLDWIDE™

PAGEMAKER® 6
FOR MACS® FOR DUMMIES®

2ND EDITION

PAGEMAKER® 6
FOR MACS® FOR DUMMIES®

2ND EDITION

**by Galen Gruman
and Deke McClelland**

**Revised by
Julie King**

IDG Books Worldwide, Inc.
An International Data Group Company

Foster City, CA ♦ Chicago, IL ♦ Indianapolis, IN ♦ Braintree, MA ♦ Dallas, TX

PageMaker® 6 For Macs® For Dummies®, 2nd Edition

Published by
IDG Books Worldwide, Inc.
An International Data Group Company
919 E. Hillsdale Blvd.
Suite 400
Foster City, CA 94404

Library of Congress Catalog Card No.: 95-81443

ISBN: 1-56884-616-9

Printed in the United States of America

10 9 8 7 6 5 4 3 2 1

2B/QT/QR/ZW

Distributed in the United States by IDG Books Worldwide, Inc.

Distributed by Macmillan Canada for Canada; by Computer and Technical Books for the Caribbean Basin; by Contemporanea de Ediciones for Venezuela; by Distribuidora Cuspide for Argentina; by CITEC for Brazil; by Ediciones ZETA S.C.R. Ltda. for Peru; by Editorial Limusa SA for Mexico; by Transworld Publishers Limited in the United Kingdom and Europe; by Al-Maiman Publishers & Distributors for Saudi Arabia; by Simron Pty. Ltd. for South Africa; by IDG Communications (HK) Ltd. for Hong Kong; by Toppan Company Ltd. for Japan; by Addison Wesley Publishing Company for Korea; by Longman Singapore Publishers Ltd. for Singapore, Malaysia, Thailand, and Indonesia; by Unalis Corporation for Taiwan; by WS Computer Publishing Company, Inc. for the Philippines; by WoodsLane Pty. Ltd. for Australia; by WoodsLane Enterprises Ltd. for New Zealand.

For general information on IDG Books Worldwide's books in the U.S., please call our Consumer Customer Service department at 800-762-2974. For reseller information, including discounts and premium sales, please call our Reseller Customer Service department at 800-434-3422.

For information on where to purchase IDG Books Worldwide's books outside the U.S., contact IDG Books Worldwide at 415-655-3021 or fax 415-655-3295.

For information on translations, contact Marc Jeffrey Mikulich, Director, Foreign & Subsidiary Rights, at IDG Books Worldwide, 415-655-3018 or fax 415-655-3295.

For sales inquiries and special prices for bulk quantities, write to the address above or call IDG Books Worldwide at 415-655-3200.

For information on using IDG Books Worldwide's books in the classroom, or ordering examination copies, contact Jim Kelly at 800-434-2086.

For authorization to photocopy items for corporate, personal, or educational use, please contact Copyright Clearance Center, 222 Rosewood Drive, Danvers, MA 01923, or fax 508-750-4470.

 is a trademark under exclusive license to IDG Books Worldwide, Inc., from International Data Group, Inc.

About the Authors

Galen Gruman

An executive editor at *Macworld* and a frequent reviewer of desktop publishing software for *InfoWorld,* Galen Gruman was an early adopter of desktop publishing in professional magazine production.

Galen's honors include being a finalist in the Computer Press Awards for best computer-oriented news story in a general-interest publication (1986) and a winner for best in-depth technical feature in the American Society of Business Press Editors Awards (1993), which he shared with Lon Poole and Arne Hurty of *Macworld.* He was president of the Computer Press Association from 1992 to 1994.

Galen is also the author of *PageMaker 5 For Macs For Dummies* and coauthor, with Barbara Assadi, of the critically praised *QuarkXPress 3.1 for Windows Designer Handbook* and *Macworld QuarkXPress 3.2/3.3 Bible.*

Deke McClelland

Deke is the author of more than 30 books about desktop publishing and graphics programs for the Mac and Windows including IDG's best-selling *Macworld Photoshop 3 Bible, CorelDRAW! 6 For Dummies, Photoshop 3 For Macs For Dummies,* and *Macworld FreeHand 4 Bible.*

He is also contributing editor to *Macworld* magazine and frequently pops up in *Publish* and *PC World.* He received the Ben Franklin award for the Best Computer Book in 1989 and won prestigious Computer Press Awards in 1990, 1992, and 1994. When he isn't writing, he hosts the television series Digital Gurus for the Jones Computer Network. In his few minutes of spare time, Deke lives with his wife and aging cat in Boulder, Colorado.

Welcome to the world of IDG Books Worldwide.

IDG Books Worldwide, Inc., is a subsidiary of International Data Group, the world's largest publisher of computer-related information and the leading global provider of information services on information technology. IDG was founded more than 25 years ago and now employs more than 7,700 people worldwide. IDG publishes more than 250 computer publications in 67 countries (see listing below). More than 70 million people read one or more IDG publications each month.

Launched in 1990, IDG Books Worldwide is today the #1 publisher of best-selling computer books in the United States. We are proud to have received 8 awards from the Computer Press Association in recognition of editorial excellence and three from Computer Currents' First Annual Readers' Choice Awards, and our best-selling ...*For Dummies*® series has more than 19 million copies in print with translations in 28 languages. IDG Books Worldwide, through a joint venture with IDG's Hi-Tech Beijing, became the first U.S. publisher to publish a computer book in the People's Republic of China. In record time, IDG Books Worldwide has become the first choice for millions of readers around the world who want to learn how to better manage their businesses.

Our mission is simple: Every one of our books is designed to bring extra value and skill-building instructions to the reader. Our books are written by experts who understand and care about our readers. The knowledge base of our editorial staff comes from years of experience in publishing, education, and journalism — experience which we use to produce books for the '90s. In short, we care about books, so we attract the best people. We devote special attention to details such as audience, interior design, use of icons, and illustrations. And because we use an efficient process of authoring, editing, and desktop publishing our books electronically, we can spend more time ensuring superior content and spend less time on the technicalities of making books.

You can count on our commitment to deliver high-quality books at competitive prices on topics you want to read about. At IDG Books Worldwide, we continue in the IDG tradition of delivering quality for more than 25 years. You'll find no better book on a subject than one from IDG Books Worldwide.

John J. Kilcullen

John Kilcullen
President and CEO
IDG Books Worldwide, Inc.

Acknowledgments

Deke and Galen thank Julie King for doing a super job in revising this edition of our *PageMaker 6 For Macs For Dummies* book. Julie is a long-time editor at IDG Books Worldwide with a big fan club of happy authors. In this edition, she has added her personal charm and knowledge about PageMaker 6, helping us get this book into your hands as fast as possible with the information you need to make the most of the latest PageMaker version. Thanks, Julie!

The authors would like to acknowledge Project Editor Jennifer Wallis and all the other great folks at IDG Books Worldwide, Inc. whose hard work and talent helped make this book a reality.

(The Publisher would like to give special thanks to Patrick J. McGovern, without whom this book would not have been possible.)

Credits

**Senior Vice President
and Publisher**
Milissa L. Koloski

Associate Publisher
Diane Graves Steele

Brand Manager
Judith A. Taylor

Editorial Managers
Kristin A. Cocks
Mary Corder

Product Development Manager
Mary Bednarek

Editorial Executive Assistant
Richard Graves

Editorial Assistants
Constance Carlisle
Chris Collins
Kevin Spencer

Acquisitions Assistant
Gareth Hancock

Production Director
Beth Jenkins

Production Assistant
Jacalyn L. Pennywell

**Supervisor of
Project Coordination**
Cindy L. Phipps

Supervisor of Page Layout
Kathie S. Schnorr

Production Systems Specialist
Steve Peake

Pre-Press Coordination
Tony Augsburger
Patricia R. Reynolds
Theresa Sánchez-Baker

Media/Archive Coordination
Leslie Popplewell
Michael Wilkey

Associate Project Editor
Jennifer Wallis

Copy Editor
Kelly Ewing

Technical Reviewer
David Marbaugh

Project Coordinator
Valery Bourke

Graphic Coordination
Shelley Lea
Gina Scott
Carla Radzikinas

Production Page Layout
E. Shawn Aylsworth
Kerri Cornell
Todd Klemme
Jill Lyttle
Jane Martin
Kate Snell
Michael Sullivan

Proofreaders
Joel Draper
Christine Meloy Beck
Gwenette Gaddis
Dwight Ramsey
Carl Saff
Robert Springer

Indexer
David Heiret

Cover Design
Kavish + Kavish

Contents at a Glance

Cartoons at a Glance

By Rich Tennant

page 7

page 213

page 200

page 297

page 59

page 151

page 106

page 36

page 325

page 341

Table of Contents

Introduction

· ·

Desktop publishing began with PageMaker on the Apple Macintosh computer. In fact, many argue that PageMaker and desktop publishing were the single most important force in the Mac's early success.

Despite having loads of competition over the years, PageMaker has managed to remain a leading desktop publishing program, thanks to a surprisingly straight-forward design. The program works exactly like traditional paste-up pages and layout tools, except without the wax and X-acto knives. Over the years, PageMaker has grown to be a lot more than an electronic galley-waxer, though. It provides the tools you need to make your words attractive, to integrate images and photos with your prose, and to put together a whole document — whether it's a 1-page ad, a 16-page employee newsletter, a 30-page annual report, a 100-page technical manual, or a 350-page book. In fact, the very book you're reading was created using PageMaker.

Why a Book . . . For Dummies?

Gee, all those types of documents and just one little program. Well, not so little — in fact, PageMaker is stuffed with features and tools. You won't need most of them on any one given project, and you'll probably be able to live your life without using a third of them. So how do you know which tools you need for a particular kind of document and which you can leave to that whiz-bang artist down the hall who produces 3-D posters? The answers to all your questions — well, a couple of them anyway — as well as a few questions you never thought to ask are revealed in the pages that follow.

This book shows you how to create the kinds of documents that most people need to produce. The real fancy stuff is best left to those who do that kind of work all day, and they can read someone else's book. This book is for you: the person who has more to do than just use PageMaker.

About This Book

You can approach this book from several perspectives, depending on how you learn:

✔ If you're a reader — as in, you *like* to read, which you must if you're reading the introduction — you can follow the book from cover to cover, building up your expertise as you progress.

✔ If you're looking for a reference to how something works, but you're not interested in sitting by a roaring fire, reading chapter after chapter, flip to the back of the book and look up the topic in the index. The kind of indexes provided in . . . *For Dummies* books makes it easy to find the information you need.

✔ If you have already used PageMaker but want some tips on how to accomplish a certain task or some information on the new stuff in Version 6, scan the pages and read the paragraphs marked by the little margin icons — like the one next to this paragraph. The icons, as explained shortly, point out tidbits of information that will make you a more efficient and effective PageMaker user.

✔ If you're looking for water-cooler talk to impress your friends and neighbors, check out Part VI, which is full of trivia and factoids about PageMaker. You may even be able to take advantage of a few of these golden nuggets when you get back to your desk.

No matter which way you read the book, enjoy it. (That's an order!) Desktop publishing is a creative experience. It's often fun, but it's just as frequently frenetic and even frustrating. When it's not so fun, take a break, read a chapter, learn a neat trick, and then go back to your project better equipped and a little more relaxed.

How to Use This Book

To make sure that you understand what we're talking about, this book uses several conventions to indicate what you're supposed to type, which menus you're supposed to use, and which keys you're supposed to press.

If we describe a message you see on-screen or something you type, it looks like this:

Type **Bill** and then press the Return key.

Menu commands are listed like this:

File⇨Print

This instruction means that you choose the File menu at the top of the PageMaker window and then choose the Print command in the menu.

Keyboard shortcuts are listed like this:

⌘+D

This instruction means that you should hold down the ⌘ key, press the D key, and then release both keys. Sometimes, you have to press three, or even four, keys together, as in ⌘+Option+Shift+comma (,), which is the keyboard shortcut for decreasing type size by one point.

If all this stuff seems a bit foreign to you, don't panic; these basics and other fundamentals of working with the Mac and PageMaker are spelled out in lively detail in Chapter 2. If, after reading that chapter, you'd like some additional guidance on using your Mac, you may want to pick up a copy of David Pogue's *Macs For Dummies*, also published by IDG Books.

How This Book Is Organized

We've divided *PageMaker 6 For Macs For Dummies*, 2nd Edition, into six parts, not counting this introduction, to make it easy for you to find the material you need right away. Each part has anywhere from three to five chapters, so you don't have to worry about making a lifelong commitment to find something out.

Part I: What Does This Thing Do (and Where Do I Begin)?

If you're brand new to PageMaker or to desktop publishing in general, you'll probably feel a little intimidated when you first start up the program. But never fear — Part I provides the basics you need to know to start conquering the sometimes wild and woolly world of digital layout. Chapter 1 explains when to use PageMaker and when to use your word-processing program to create the text for your documents. Chapter 2 shows you how to start up PageMaker 6 and then takes you on a tour of the various buttons, menus, and windows that you'll work with throughout your PageMaker journeys. And then, when you're primed to use PageMaker, Chapter 3 shows you how to take the first steps in laying out a document.

Part II: Putting Words on Paper

This part contains everything you need to know about putting text in your PageMaker documents. You discover the basics of typography — for example, which fonts can add to the impact of headlines like "Princess Di Gives Birth to Alien Baby!" and which ones can soften the effect of disclaimers such as

"Manufacturer is absolved of any responsibility if user's skin turns green." You also discover how to dump text from your word processor into PageMaker, how to change the size, type style, and spacing of text, how to check your spelling, and how to get PageMaker to automatically format your text for you. On top of all that, you find out how to create some cool text effects, such as drop caps and shadowed text.

Part III: Say It with Pictures

Here's where you explore PageMaker's graphical side. Chapters in this part explain how to bring graphics that you've created in programs like Illustrator or Photoshop into your layout and how to draw your own simple graphics inside PageMaker. You also find out how to add color to your documents and how to manipulate graphics by rotating them, skewing them, applying special-effects filters, and the like.

Part IV: Pumping Up Your Layout Power

This part shows you how to combine text and graphics into layouts that will make your competition sweat with anguish — and envy your layout efficiency. Chapter 12 walks you through the process of laying out an entire publication, while Chapter 13 is loaded with tips for designing effective newsletters, ads, brochures, and other documents. In Chapters 14 and 15, you find out how to get more layout work done in less time by taking advantage of templates, master pages, automatic indexing, and other advanced features. By the end of this part, you'll be a certified PageMaker power user.

Part V: You Mean There's More?

At this point, you've mastered everything you need to know to put together professional-looking documents — now you're ready to find out how to get those documents from your computer screen and into the hands of your readers. This part covers such topics as how to print your documents, how to prepare your document for delivery to a service bureau or commercial printer, and how to exchange documents with colleagues — even those who use the Windows (gasp!) version of PageMaker.

Part VI: The Part of Tens

This is the water-cooler part of the book. It's chock full of tidbits, advice, trivia, and other data about PageMaker that you can share with your colleagues during a work break or tell your friends at Tuesday bowling night. (On second thought, maybe not. But you *can* use these tidbits to help, impress, dazzle, or amuse your co-workers.) Some of this part's contents may seem obvious, some not, but all are based on remembering those little details and lessons that only experience can provide. Save yourself some bumps along the road and check out this part.

Icons Used in This Book

To alert you to special passages of text that you may especially want to read, we've put in a bunch of modern hieroglyphics (proudly known as *icons*) to help guide you.

This icon points out one of those nitty-gritty techno-details or background explanations that you shouldn't have to know but that will come in handy if (a) something goes wrong and you have to ask an expert for advice, or (b) you want to impress your boss.

Here's some information that you should put on a Sticky Note and slap on your monitor. You never know when it will come in handy and save you some effort or time.

Here's something that you should remember but could easily forget because the information may seem unimportant at first. Trust us when we say that you'll need it later.

Not everything works the way it should, or at least the way you expect. These icons let you know when an action (or lack thereof) may cause a problem, such as destroying your data.

Not everything works . . . oops, already said that. Anyhow, this icon is a cross between a tip and a warning; it describes ways in which PageMaker acts in a manner other than what you may expect. You're in no danger of losing data, but you may be unnecessarily perplexed. This information shows you how to get things back to normal or work around the oddity.

This icon points out features that are new or have changed in this latest version of PageMaker.

Where to First?

That's up to you — as mentioned earlier, this book is designed to appeal to a variety of reading styles. If you have a specific question, you can go to the index and track down the answer that way. If you want to know more about one type of feature, use the table of contents to find the appropriate chapter. If you're totally new to layout and desktop publishing, just move on to the next page and begin reading at a comfortable pace. Or, if you're experienced in manual layout and paste-up but you've been forced to switch to a computer by evil forces bent on cyborg domination of the earth, you can skip Chapters 4 and 13 and concentrate on the rest.

Remember, always consult a physician before beginning any new training program. (Jane Fonda taught us that one!) Then again, in this case, you may want to consult with a licensed psychologist.

No, really, we're just kidding. We promise that this book, unlike some others on the subject, won't leave you in a PageMaker panic. So if you have any fears about your ability to use this powerful program, put them aside. With this book by your side — for easier reading, you may want to prop it up against that stack of unpaid bills on your desk — you, too, can turn out sensational documents from your very own computer.

Part I

What Does This Thing Do (and Where Do I Begin)?

The 5th Wave   By Rich Tennant

"WHOA, HOLD THE PHONE! IT SAYS, 'THE ELECTRICITY COMING OUT OF A SURGE PROTECTOR IS GENERALLY CLEANER AND SAFER THAN THAT GOING INTO ONE, UNLESS-UN-LESS- YOU ARE STANDING IN A BUCKET OF WATER.'"

In this part . . .

*I*magine that you're taking a camping trip. You wouldn't just hop in the Miata or on your motor scooter and toddle off. No, first you'd figure out what you need to take with you, and then you'd figure out how to get there — maybe by taking a taxi to the airport or just piling your camping gear into the Westfalia. Likewise, before you launch PageMaker or your word processor, spend a few minutes to figure out exactly what you want to accomplish and then how you want to do it. This part shows how to find the road map to your destination.

In addition to explaining when to use PageMaker and when to rely on your word processor, this part covers the basics of starting up the program, finding your way around the screen, and using your computer's mouse and keyboard to get the program to actually *do* something. After you're feeling comfortable with your new digital surroundings, this part shows you how to create your very first PageMaker document and start setting up your pages.

Chapter 1

Why Can't I Just Use My Word Processor?

*W*hether you use Microsoft Word, WordPerfect, or some other popular word processor, you have all the tools you need to produce your documents, right? After all, most high-end word processors let you import pictures, display multiple columns, go crazy with fonts, and do all sorts of layout tasks. What the heck do you need another program for?

Well, to put it in layman's terms, to keep you from going bonkers. Sure, you can do rudimentary layout with a word processor, but using one to publish a newsletter or catalog is like using a bicycle to go from San Francisco to Boulder. It's slow, it's exasperating, it requires lots of preparation, and you probably won't make it. When it comes to layout, Microsoft Word is a bicycle with a flat tire and WordPerfect is a tricycle with streamers on the handle bars.

By contrast, PageMaker is a corporate jet with all the amenities of home. PageMaker transforms page layout into a relatively painless and sometimes even pleasurable experience. Best of all, you'll find yourself trying things that you'd never dare attempt with a word processor (and would regret if you did).

The Face-to-Face Challenge

Don't misunderstand: There's nothing wrong with word processors. A good word processor does a terrific job at creating many types of documents. So how do you know when to use PageMaker and when to use a word processor? The answer depends on what sort of document you're creating. Here's a quick look at how PageMaker stacks up against word processors when it comes to handling various document-creation tasks.

Formatting text

Both PageMaker and your typical best-selling word processor let you format text with little effort. Switching to italics in a word processing program is as simple as pressing ⌘+I, while going to boldface is as simple as ⌘+B. In PageMaker, you just press ⌘+Shift+I or ⌘+Shift+B. (You can use the same keystrokes to switch italics or boldface off.) You can also use the menus or palette options provided in either program to format text. So if all you're doing is writing letters or memos that use a little text formatting, don't bother with PageMaker — a word processor is fine. Going back to the bicycle/plane analogy, simple formatting tricks amount to no more than a jaunt to the corner store. Taking a plane is hardly the solution, even if one is parked in the driveway.

When you move beyond basic text formatting, the scales quickly tip in PageMaker's favor, however. You can handle drop caps, leading, paragraph spacing, kerning, and a bunch of other formatting options (that are examined in future chapters) much more expediently in PageMaker than in a word processor. Figure 1-1 shows an example of the type of text you can turn out in PageMaker. Yes, you *can* create a similar looking document in a word processor (assuming that you're using one of the major word processing programs, that is). But it requires much more time and effort.

Figure 1-1:
Creating
professional-
looking
text is
much easier
—and
faster — in
PageMaker
than in
a word
processor.

Press Awards
continued from page 1

Overall Works
Best Computer Magazine
(100,000 or more circulation)
■ WINNER: *Macworld.*
□ RUNNER-UP: *NewMedia.*
□ RUNNER-UP: *PC Magazine.*

Best Computer Magazine
(less than 100,000 circulation)
■ WINNER: *Upside.*
□ RUNNER-UP: *Computer Artist.*
□ RUNNER-UP: *VAR Business.*

Best Computer Newspaper
(100,000 or more circulation)
■ WINNER: *Computerworld.*
□ RUNNER-UP: *Communications Week.*
□ RUNNER-UP: *Computer Reseller News.*

Computer Press Awards Judging

To select the best of each year's body of work, the CPA solicits entries in print.

The CPA Awards Committee also formalized some judging practices: First, a

Using multiple columns

Look at a professionally produced magazine or newsletter. Chances are that the text is organized into multiple columns. Even the text in this book — which is laid out in PageMaker, by the way — features a second, much slimmer column on the left side of the page for figure captions and the like.

Now look at a report in your In basket. Chances are it has only one column that's almost as wide as the entire page.

But so what? Who needs columns? You've never understood why anyone uses them in the first place, and you certainly don't need them.

Well, think again. Multiple columns are part and parcel of publishing because they make it easy to integrate multiple elements — both graphics and stories — into a layout. Having multiple columns means that you can change the width of a graphic freely without wreaking havoc on your layout. Multiple articles (an article is known as a *story* in PageMaker) can fit on a page without interfering with each other. Each page is a balancing act, and columns provide the structure needed to keep it from flying apart at the seams. (And here you thought it was just because artists like to do things that the rest of us can't.)

In the early days, the ability to create multiple columns alone was enough reason to invest in PageMaker. Today, you can create multiple columns in a word processor. But the process is awkward, even in a powerful program, such as Word or WordPerfect. You have to do a lot of formatting in dialog boxes. With all the mousing and clicking that's required, you feel like you're in the gym doing power training on your hands.

But PageMaker lets you drag columns around, repositioning and resizing them at will, just as if they were physical objects floating above the surface of your page. PageMaker also makes it much easier to place two stories on a page so that a four-column article, for example, starts above a three-column article, as demonstrated in Figure 1-2. Clearly, PageMaker wins the multiple-column contest.

Importing graphics

Uh-oh, the gap between word processors and PageMaker is about to grow into a chasm. The latest versions of Word, WordPerfect, and some other word processors are certainly capable of importing graphics. But now try working with those graphics. The fact is, just because a program can do something doesn't mean that it can perform the task well enough to make it worth your while.

Say that you want to reposition a graphic at the beginning of a paragraph and have the text wrap around it. In PageMaker, you just drag the graphic to where

Figure 1-2: PageMaker makes it easy to set up and arrange different numbers of columns on the same page.

you want it and turn on the text wrap feature. (Chapter 9 shows you how.) You can even make the wrap follow the shape of the graphic, as shown in Figure 1-3. If you want to do the same in a word processor, get ready for some major work. It will take you so long that you may as well draw each character by hand.

Of course, PageMaker also lets you draw lines, squares, and circles, as well as apply shades of gray to boxes and other elements. You can also accomplish these feats in a well-equipped word processor, but the process is time-consuming and difficult.

Defining colors is another big disappointment in a word processor. And rotating graphics involves a 12-step program that'll leave you wound up tighter than a knot. In PageMaker, you can rotate graphics to any angle with a couple swift clicks of your mouse button. You can just as easily skew, resize, and crop graphics. Figure 1-4 shows how the graphic from Figure 1-3 looks after being rotated and skewed in PageMaker. (Skewing and rotating are covered in Chapter 10; cropping is covered in Chapter 9.)

Although word processors are constantly adding more graphics controls, you clearly need a page-layout program like PageMaker if you really want to use graphics effectively in your document.

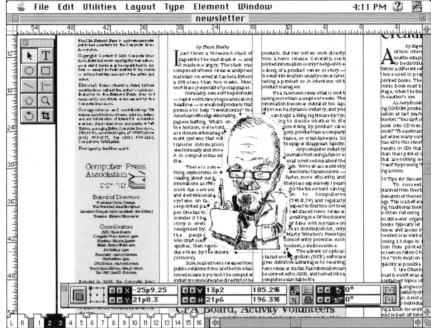

Figure 1-3:
PageMaker
lets you
wrap text
around the
exact
boundaries
of a graphic.

Figure 1-4:
PageMaker
lets you do
all sorts of
things with
a graphic,
such as
rotating and
skewing it.

Combining multiple elements

Word processors are really good at handling a long, single document, whether or not it has headlines and bullets. But word processors are very bad at combining multiple stories that start on one page and continue on other pages. In fact, the only way to create such a document in Word or WordPerfect is to cut and paste the contents of each page. Then, if you need to edit the text, you have to remember which page each story jumps to and cut and paste the text among the pages. In PageMaker, the text for each story is linked from page to page, so if information is added at the beginning, the text is automatically shuffled onto the subsequent pages.

The best way to illustrate this feature is with a newsletter. Figure 1-5 shows the newsletter's opening page, which contains two stories plus a contents box. Figure 1-6 shows an interior set of pages, on which several stories continue from previous pages and some continue on to later pages. Word processors simply don't provide the kind of features you need to produce layouts like these. This is a case in which PageMaker wins by a knockout.

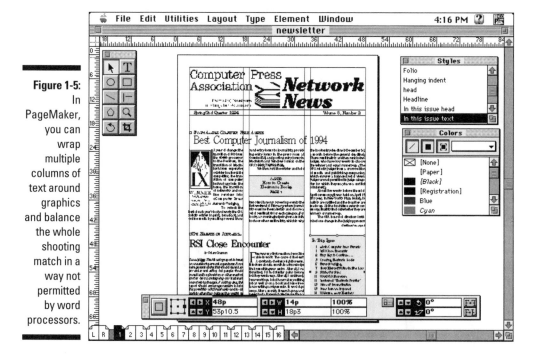

Figure 1-5: In PageMaker, you can wrap multiple columns of text around graphics and balance the whole shooting match in a way not permitted by word processors.

Figure 1-6:
Mixing multiple stories in neighboring columns on a two-page spread is something you just can't do in a word processor.

Generating tables of contents, indexes, and page numbers

You'd expect a word processor to be good at handling business needs, such as generating indexes and tables of contents. But you may not expect a page-layout program to offer similar features. PageMaker does. In fact, Word, WordPerfect, and PageMaker are about evenly matched in this regard.

PageMaker even gives you the ability to combine a series of documents into a *book*. Every chapter in this book is a separate PageMaker document, but the whole thing is part of a larger structure, enabling the designers to renumber pages, add index entries, and generate a table of contents automatically. If you're working on a multiple-chapter report with some colleagues, for example, you can use PageMaker's book functions to renumber all the pages of each chapter after you add a page to Chapter 3. You don't need to open each chapter individually and renumber its pages manually.

Even if you don't use PageMaker's sophisticated typographic and graphics features, you may find it highly useful in creating indexes and tables of contents in business documents. By combining its page-layout skills with its business-document skills, you can go far beyond what a word processor can do. Forget the hype about *document processors* — that's just a fancy name for a word processor that's stuffed with features that still don't match what PageMaker can do. As your grandma used to say, "You can bring a donkey to the racetrack, but you can't make him win." (She never said that? Well, she probably would have if properly coerced.)

A word processor offers some pretty sophisticated controls for footnotes, headers, footers, and endnotes. PageMaker concentrates on headers and footers. If you want to use footnotes, you have to do it the old-fashioned way, adding them by hand. Fortunately, PageMaker can import your word processor's footnotes as endnotes — they all appear at the end of the story, rather than at the bottom of the page where the footnote occurs — so you won't lose any footnoting or endnoting done in your word processor.

When to Use Which Program

PageMaker, Word, and WordPerfect are all good tools. And although in some cases one type of program is clearly better than the other, you don't always have to choose between them. You can do a lot of work in your word processor and then import that work into PageMaker for further refinement, especially for layout. Think of the advantages: Layout artists can keep editors from messing in the PageMaker layouts by restricting them to features in Word or WordPerfect, and editors can make sure that layout artists don't skip over the text formatting to focus on the graphics. (Artists sometimes look at text and consider it to be the stuff that holds the graphics together, sort of like the Wonder Bread that holds the good-tasting peanut butter and jam.)

Which formatting should I do in PageMaker?

If you're working on a text-heavy layout — and most layouts, from newsletters to reports, use a lot of text — use your word processor to create and edit that text. That's what it's for, after all. Save PageMaker's Story Editor, the built-in word processor explained in Chapter 5, for touch-ups, minor edits, and those documents that are mostly graphics with little text, such as advertisements.

Go ahead and apply the following formatting in your word processor:

- **Boldface**
- *Italics*
- <u>Underlines</u>
- Bullets: •

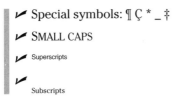

✔ Special symbols: ¶ Ç * _ ‡

✔ SMALL CAPS

✔ Superscripts

✔ Subscripts

You have to do this kind of local formatting work in one place or the other, and it's easier to do it in the place where the editing happens. Why? Because such character formatting is almost always related to the content of the text, and it's the writer or editor who's familiar with that content. Sure, whoever is doing the layout can apply the formatting in PageMaker, but that person probably isn't the writer or editor and thus won't know what points should be stressed through italics or underlines or whatever.

For the same reason, it's good to use style sheets in your word processor if you'll be using styles in your layout. (Styles are explained in depth in Chapter 7.) The styles don't have to look the same in your word processor as they do in PageMaker, but they have to have the same names. For example, if you have a style named *Heads* in your word processor and one called *Headlines* in PageMaker, rename one or the other so you have one common headline style name. That way, a headline that you create in your word processor will be formatted automatically when you import it into PageMaker. You save the layout staff work and reduce the chances that they will incorrectly format a title (or other type of paragraph style). If you follow this technique, the imported text takes on the attributes defined in PageMaker's styles. So you can make the text look one way in your word processor (where, after all, the layout is different) and another in your PageMaker layout without any extra work.

Even if you're the one who will be doing both the writing and layout, do the character formatting in your word processor, which is the place where you're focusing on the meaning of your text. When you get to the layout stage in PageMaker, you'll have more things on your mind than content — you'll be worried about things like how many columns of text you want and whether the headlines fit properly. Even if you have remarkable powers of concentration and coordination — you can walk and chew gum while rubbing your head and patting your tummy — it's still not a good idea to work on layout and meaning and editing and drawing all at once. You'll have more luck if you keep these different elements of the page-production process separate.

Another good reason to concentrate on one operation at a time is that it's usually easier to edit in your word processor. That's what a word processor is designed to do, after all. However, there are some formatting techniques you should not attempt in your word processor. The following document-production techniques have very little to do with the meaning of your text and should be handled in PageMaker:

- **Drop caps:** Don't try to import a drop cap from your word processor into PageMaker. You get the big first character, but the text around it won't wrap as it should, and you'll have to reformat it in PageMaker anyway.

- **Tables:** When you import a table from your word processor, PageMaker strips out the formatting, so don't bother creating fully functioning tables with individual cells and the whole rigmarole. However, you can put tabs between table elements and then do the tab formatting in PageMaker to create a table with your imported text.

- **Font and size formatting:** PageMaker will import these elements. But unless the formatting you're using in your word processor will be used in the final PageMaker layout, you're just making more work for the layout person, who has to undo your formatting and then apply the correct formatting for the layout. So just use whatever combination of font and size is most legible on-screen.

- **Columns:** Don't do layout formatting, such as creating multiple columns, in your word processor, because PageMaker ignores all that formatting when you import your text. (If you want to do the layout in your word processor, why bother having PageMaker at all?)

When do I import graphics?

Another thing not to do in your word processor is import graphics. Don't place a drawing that you created in CorelDRAW!, for example, into your text inside your word processor and then try to bring the whole enchilada into PageMaker.

Yes, PageMaker supports these so-called *embedded graphics* (PageMaker refers to them as *in-line graphics* because they are inside lines of text), which it considers to be special symbols in your text. The problem is that the quality of the embedded graphics may deteriorate. It's sort of like making photocopies. You copy a copy and you get what's politely called a *second-generation* copy — a yucky, blurry, fuzzy copy that you give to someone else only in desperation because you lost the original. Well, a similar thing can happen when using second-generation embedded graphics.

The reason graphics can lose quality when imported into PageMaker as part of a text document is similar to why making photocopies of a photocopy leads to poor image quality: You're not working with the original. Programs like Word don't always copy the original file when you import a graphic; they sometimes copy a lower-resolution placeholder and link it to the original image. When you print, the higher-quality original is sent to the printer. But when you import the text file into PageMaker, the lower-resolution placeholder is imported, not the higher-resolution original. Figure 1-7 shows how an image imported directly into PageMaker compares with the same image imported into Word, edited slightly in Word's Picture Editor, and then imported into PageMaker. This quality problem won't always happen, but it can, so why risk it?

Figure 1-7:
A graphic imported into PageMaker (left) and the same image edited in a word processor and imported with some text (right).

What if I want to combine lots of different elements?

If your PageMaker document will include multiple elements — tables, graphics, sidebars, bulleted lists, columns of text, and so forth — don't try to combine all those elements in your word processor. You'll just have to separate the various components and lay them out again in PageMaker.

That doesn't mean that you can't have multiple segments in your text file — just not elements that you will lay out separately. Here's a rule of thumb: If an element will be positioned independently of another element, it should be in its own file. Thus, your tables should each be in their own files. Your graphics should be in their own files. So should your sidebars (those little stories that are often in a box or have a shaded background). But your bulleted lists can stay in the text because they're part and parcel of the story and will flow with the rest of the text. Your *headlines* (titles) and *bylines* (author credits) should stay with their text, too.

What about the table of contents, index, page numbers, and footnotes?

You can specify in Word or WordPerfect which words, phrases, or styles you want included in your table of contents and index. But don't actually generate the table of contents or index before importing the text into PageMaker — the chances of the page numbers being the same in the PageMaker layout as in your word processor are about the same as a finding a snowball on an Acapulco beach.

As mentioned earlier, PageMaker retains a word processor file's footnotes (notes placed at the bottom of the page) and endnotes (notes that are lumped together at the end of the chapter so that they don't get in the way of the rest of the pages). But PageMaker converts footnotes to endnotes when importing text. Still, it's usually most convenient to do the footnoting in your word processor — which likely has a footnoting feature — and then either cut and paste each footnote into the appropriate location in your PageMaker layout or just accept them as endnotes at the end of your story.

As for headers and footers (elements that you want to place at the beginning and end of each page, respectively), don't bother creating them in your word processor. PageMaker ignores them when you import your document. If you want to use headers and footers in your word processor document for your own organization, fine, but they won't appear in the PageMaker layout unless someone adds them manually.

Page numbering done in a word processor is also ignored in PageMaker. But you can use it anyway — it will help you keep track of the order of pages printed during the editing stage, before you import the text into PageMaker.

What PageMaker Offers You

Don't let this comparison of word processing and page layout obscure the strengths that PageMaker offers — the reasons you bought the program in the first place. Here's a quick recap of what you get for your PageMaker investment:

- You can do more precise text formatting, giving your documents a more sophisticated appearance.

- You can combine multiple stories, images, and tables to present complex information in a way that's easy for the reader to grasp.

- You can combine multiple chapters and create books with a common index, table of contents, and page numbering.

- You can output documents to high-resolution printers in order to create professional-looking publications.

- You can add color to your documents.

- You can use special effects to call attention to key points and to simply make your overall publication more attractive.

- You can use Version 6's new online publishing capabilities to create documents specifically for distribution over the Internet or via your office network, as explained in Chapter 18.

In other words, you get a lot of bang for your buck! The rest of this book tells you how to start taking advantage of your investment.

Chapter 2

Starting, Scrolling, and Other Vital Stuff

. . . .

In This Chapter

▶ Starting PageMaker

▶ Getting acquainted with Version 6

▶ Clicking, dragging, double-clicking, and other mouse tricks

▶ Zooming in and out on your pages

▶ Mucking about in dialog boxes and menus

▶ Saving your work and shutting down PageMaker

. . . .

*T*he good news about PageMaker 6 is that it enables you to create brochures, newsletters, and all sorts of other documents with less effort and
less time than ever before. The bad news is that you have to use a computer to
do it. And that means that you have to fling yourself headlong into the world
of computer geekdom. You have to find out about such terms as *click, drag,
dialog box,* and *submenu.* You even have to shake hands with a *mouse,* for
heaven's sake.

If this is your first encounter with a computer or a desktop publishing program,
you'll no doubt feel a little overwhelmed in the beginning. But after a few days
of working with PageMaker, you'll discover that things really aren't as complicated as they seem. It's all a matter of discovering some basic lingo and becoming familiar with what you see on your monitor's screen. To that end, this
chapter walks you gently through the initial steps of bringing PageMaker to life,
moving around on-screen, and using your mouse and computer keyboard to
make the program actually do something. By the end of the chapter, you, too,
will be confidently tossing about phrases like "navigating the interface" and
"⌘+Option+click with the Zoom tool" — thereby qualifying for a seat at the
computer-geek lunch table. And if that's not something to look forward to,
what is?

If you're already familiar with PageMaker, you may just want to skim through
this chapter and read the sections marked with the Version 6 icon. Then again,

you may want to read the whole chapter carefully — you may discover a few tricks and techniques you didn't know.

Although this chapter explains the basics of working with PageMaker on the Mac, we strongly advise you to pick up a copy of David Pogue's *Macs For Dummies,* also published by IDG Books Worldwide, if you're brand new to Macintosh computing. It provides a ton of Mac basics, tips, and tricks that we simply don't have room to cover in this book.

Powering Up PageMaker

Assuming that you've installed PageMaker on your hard drive (if you haven't, see the appendix at the back of this book for installation instructions), starting PageMaker is a pretty simple process. Just do the following:

1. **Turn on your computer.**

   Unless you believe in Zen computing, this step is essential.

2. **Double-click on your hard drive icon.**

   After your Mac finishes its start-up dance, you should see a little icon that represents your hard drive in the upper-right corner of your screen. Double-click on the icon. (That is, place the mouse *cursor* — that little black arrow that moves when you move your mouse — over the icon and press the mouse button twice in rapid succession.) A window displaying the various programs and other stuff stashed on your hard drive appears.

3. **Double-click on the Adobe PageMaker 6.0 folder.**

   A new window appears, this time containing the various bits and pieces that comprise PageMaker, as shown in Figure 2-1.

4. **Double-click on the Adobe PageMaker 6.0 icon.**

   (It's the one that's highlighted in Figure 2-1.) After a few seconds of whirring and humming noises (from your computer, not the coworker in the next cubicle), you should see the PageMaker *splash screen* — which is the digital equivalent of a billboard announcing PageMaker's arrival. The splash screen disappears after a few seconds, leaving you with a screen that looks pretty much the way it did before you double-clicked on the PageMaker icon.

   Don't panic — PageMaker hasn't disappeared. See that little icon in the upper-right corner of your screen? It should look something like the PageMaker icon you double-clicked on to start the program. The icon is your clue that PageMaker is ready to go, just sitting there waiting to carry out your next command.

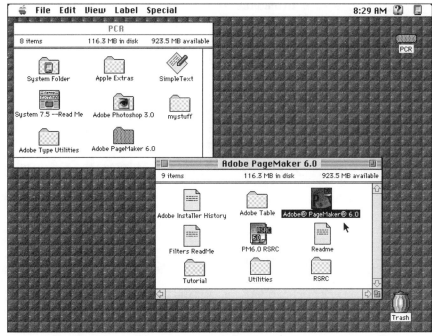

Figure 2-1:
Double-click
on the
Adobe
PageMaker
6.0 icon
to start
PageMaker.

TIP

5. Hide any other open windows.

If you want to hide any windows that aren't part of the actual PageMaker program, press the mouse button while holding the mouse cursor on the PageMaker icon in the upper-right corner of your screen. Don't let up on the mouse button yet! When a list of options appears, move the cursor over the Hide Others option and release the mouse button.

Clicking Your Way to Happiness

You probably didn't notice it, but you've already made great strides on your road to computer geekdom — well, you did if you read the preceding section, which introduced you to *double-clicking.* Right off the bat, you discovered one of the most important mouse-related terms, and except for that slight tic you acquired in your right eye, you didn't suffer any ill effects at all.

Now that you know how painless it is to become one with your computer, here's a rundown of other mouse terms you need to understand, along with a recap of those presented earlier:

✔ To *move* the mouse is to simply move the mouse cursor. No button-pressing required.

✔ To *click* is to press the mouse button once and then release it. For example, if you're advised to "Click on the PageMaker icon," place your mouse cursor over the icon and then press and release the mouse button.

✔ To *double-click* is to click on the mouse button twice in rapid succession without moving the mouse.

✔ To *drag* means to press the mouse button, hold the button down as you move the mouse, and then release the button.

✔ If we ask you to ⌘+*drag* or ⌘+*click,* hold down the ⌘ (command) key while you click or drag. Similarly, when you see the instructions *Option+click* or *Option+drag* — well, we think you're bright enough to figure out what to do. After all, you were smart enough to buy this book, right?

Saying Hello to Version 6

When you first start PageMaker 6, the screen is pretty barren — all you see are a few words across the top of the screen and a few icons representing your hard drive, a floppy drive (if you have a disk in the drive) and the Trash, that handy Mac dumping ground for files that you no longer want. Exciting, it ain't. But don't let appearances fool you — behind this simple interface await all kinds of powerful functions and commands.

Just in case you weren't born into a family of chipheads, the term *interface* refers to the collection of buttons, icons, scroll bars, and other on-screen stuff that enables you to communicate with your computer.

To start uncovering PageMaker's goodies, press ⌘+N to open a new document (also known as a *publication* in PageMaker lingo). You're immediately confronted by a big white box — known as a *dialog box* — that's full of frightening options. For now, ignore them and press Return or click on OK (you find out all about this dialog box in Chapter 3). The dialog box disappears, and you see something that looks a lot like Figure 2-2.

Here's a handy guide to help you navigate the PageMaker interface (the various components are labeled in Figure 2-2):

✔ Across the top of the screen is the *menu bar,* which holds — surprisingly enough — menus. A *menu* is nothing more than a list of related commands. The menu bar offers eight different PageMaker menus plus three menus common to other Macintosh programs: the Apple menu, Help menu, and Application menu. The section "Ordering Commands from the Menus," later in this chapter, explains how to use these different menus.

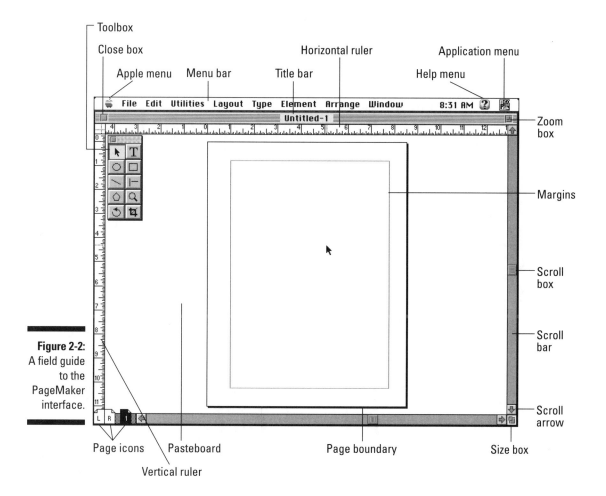

Figure 2-2:
A field guide to the PageMaker interface.

- The *title bar* shows the name of the document — in this case, Untitled-1.

- Click on the *close box,* in the upper-left corner of the screen, to close the current document. If you've done some work in your document and you haven't saved your document yet, PageMaker asks whether you want to do so. (You'll find more information about saving documents at the end of this chapter.)

- The *zoom box,* in the upper-right corner of the screen, and the *size box,* in the lower-right corner, change the size of the current window. Try this: Drag the size box a few inches toward the center of the screen to make the window smaller. Now click on the zoom box. Presto! The window expands to show the whole contents of the window. Now, click on the zoom box again. The window shrinks back to its smaller size. You can enlarge it by either clicking on the zoom box once more or by dragging the size box.

✔ Beneath the title bar is the *horizontal ruler.* Along the left edge of the document window is the *vertical ruler.* You use the rulers to precisely position elements on a page, as discussed in Chapter 3.

✔ Along the right edge of the publication window is a *scroll bar.* Click on the up-pointing *scroll arrow* or the down-pointing scroll arrow to move the on-screen display up or down to reveal more of your document. To move in bigger increments, drag the *scroll box* up or down. You can also click in the scroll bar, on either side of the scroll box, to jump from one spot in your document to another.

✔ Along the bottom of the window is another scroll bar. Use this scroll bar — and its accompanying scroll box and scroll arrows — to shift the view of your document to the right or left.

✔ An even quicker way to move around the screen is to use the hand cursor, known in some regions as the *grabber* cursor. Just press and hold down the Option key while dragging up or down with any tool but the Zoom tool. (The Zoom tool is the one that looks like a magnifying glass.) A little hand appears while you drag. When you release the Option key, the cursor changes back to the cursor for the tool you were using.

✔ That big rectangle in the center of your screen represents your new *page.* The blue and pink lines inside the page represent the left, right, top, and bottom page *margins.*

✔ The area outside the page boundary is called the *pasteboard.* It's sort of like the electronic version of a drafting table — it's a handy holding area for graphics or other elements that you may want to place on your pages at a later time. Stuff on the pasteboard doesn't print when you print the document.

✔ The little icons in the bottom-left corner of the window — called *page icons* — represent the pages of your document. You click on these icons to move from page to page. (The document in the figure is a one-page document, so you see only one page icon. If you create a multipage document, you see an icon for every page.) The L and R icons represent the document's left and right Document Master pages, discussed in Chapter 14.

✔ Last, but not least, is the *toolbox,* located in the upper-left corner of the window. It's essential to creating, placing, and manipulating text and graphics in PageMaker, which is why it's discussed in glorious detail in "Tinkering with the Toolbox" two sections from here.

Ordering Commands from the Menus

You can access all PageMaker's commands and features by making selections from the menus at the top of the screen. Version 6 offers one new menu — the Arrange menu, which contains commands related to positioning elements in your documents, as discussed in Chapter 10.

✔ To choose a command, press and hold the cursor on the menu name, move the cursor over the command you want, and then release the mouse button.

✔ When you choose some menu items, you're presented with a submenu. (The arrow after a command name indicates that the command has a submenu.) The submenu contains commands related to the first menu item you chose. To choose a submenu command, just drag from the main menu command over to the submenu command and then release the mouse button.

✔ For an even quicker way to choose a command, try using the command's *keyboard shortcut.* The available shortcuts are listed to the right of the menu commands. The shortcut for the Print command, for example, is ⌘+P. If you make the effort to memorize the keyboard shortcuts for the most commonly used commands, you'll save yourself a lot of time.

✔ If you click on the question mark icon in the menu bar, you can access PageMaker's online help system. Trouble is, the information in the help system contains basically the same information as the PageMaker manual — only it's less convenient because the Help window covers up part of your document. Better turn to this book for help instead.

✔ If you press and hold on the PageMaker icon in the far-right corner of the menu bar, you display the Application menu, which contains a list of all other programs that are currently running. You can switch to another running program by choosing its name from the menu. Choose Show All to display the windows for all running programs; choose Hide Others to hide all windows but those belonging to the active program.

✔ Press and hold on the Apple icon at the far-left corner of the screen to display the Apple menu. The commands on this menu, except for one, are related to your Mac in general rather than specifically to PageMaker (although some affect how PageMaker performs some actions, such as printing). If you choose About PageMaker, though, you display a screen that shows you the name of the person to whom the program is registered and the program's serial number. This menu option can come in handy if you forget your name.

Tinkering with the Toolbox

The PageMaker toolbox, also referred to as the *Tool palette,* is the digital version of a layout artist's tool chest. The tools are the instruments that you use to do your layout work. In Version 6, you get ten tools, which is two more than in Version 5. To select a tool, click on its icon in the toolbox. The mouse pointer changes to indicate what tool you've selected. Figure 2-3 shows the tools and their respective cursors.

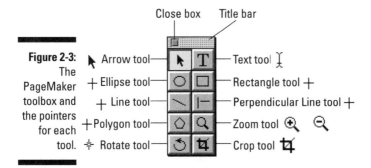

Close box   Title bar

Figure 2-3:
The
PageMaker
toolbox and
the pointers
for each
tool.

Arrow tool — Text tool

Ellipse tool — Rectangle tool

Line tool — Perpendicular Line tool

Polygon tool — Zoom tool

Rotate tool — Crop tool

✔ New to Version 6 are the *Zoom tool* and the *Polygon tool.* You can use the Zoom tool to magnify or reduce your view of your document, as explained in the upcoming section, "Changing Your View." The Polygon tool is useful for drawing basic polygons (gee, there's a surprise), as discussed in Chapter 10.

✔ You can move the toolbox to a new location by dragging its title bar.

✔ If you want to close the toolbox entirely, click on its Close box. Choose Window⇨Toolbox to display the toolbox again.

✔ The *Line, Ellipse, Rectangle, Perpendicular Line,* and *Rotate tools* are covered in Chapter 10. The Perpendicular Line is sometimes called the Constrained Line tool, because lines that you draw with it are constrained to 45 degree angles (or multiples of 45 degrees — 0 degrees, 90 degrees, and so on).

✔ You use the *Crop tool* to cut away unwanted portions of graphics, as described in Chapter 9.

✔ You use the *Text tool* to create and edit text, as described in depth in Part II.

✔ The *Arrow tool* is the workhorse tool in PageMaker. You use it to select, move, and resize text blocks and graphics. Upcoming chapters explain everything you need to know. (PageMaker calls this tool the *Pointer tool.* We think Arrow tool is easier to remember, given the tool icon's shape, so we use that term in this book.)

Sorting through the Other Palettes

In addition to the Tool palette, you can display six other palettes. The palettes give you a convenient way to access some of PageMaker's most commonly used functions and commands. Figure 2-4 shows all the palettes on-screen together.

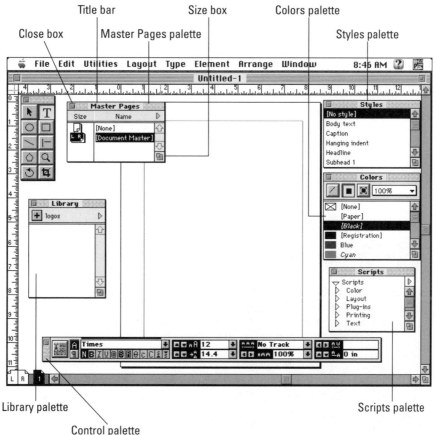

Figure 2-4:
A look at
Version 6's
palettes.

- ✔ The palettes can eat up a lot of screen space, so you'll probably want to keep as many hidden as is convenient.

- ✔ To display a palette, click on its name in the Window menu. A check mark next to the palette name means that it's displayed. Click on a palette's close box to remove it from view. (Note that the first time you click on the Library palette in the Window menu, a dialog box opens. In this dialog box, you create your first library. From then on, the palette itself displays when you choose the Library palette item in the menu. Libraries are discussed in Chapter 14.)

- ✔ Drag a palette's title bar to move it to a new on-screen location. Drag the palette's size box to resize the palette.

- ✔ You can use the buttons and boxes on the Control palette to format text, resize and reposition text and graphics, and do all sorts of other things, as explained in Parts II and III. The palette changes depending on which tool you have selected; Figure 2-4 shows the palette as it appears when the Text tool is selected.

✔ The Styles palette and the Colors palette give you a quick way to apply styles and colors. *Styles* give you a way to automatically apply formatting to your text, as explained in Chapter 7. Chapter 11 discusses adding color to your document via the Colors palette.

✔ The Library palette provides access to *libraries,* where you can store text and graphics that you use frequently. Libraries are explained in Chapter 14.

✔ The new Master Pages palette is covered in Chapter 14. The Scripts palette, also new to Version 6, offers access to *scripts,* which are miniprograms designed to automate certain tasks. (They're similar to the macros used by some word processing programs, if that helps.) Because scripts are an advanced function, we don't cover them in this book. Chapter 14, however, contains ideas on how to use other PageMaker features to automate many of your layout chores.

Talking Back to Dialog Boxes

When you choose a command from one of PageMaker's menus, you're likely to be greeted by a *dialog box.* A dialog box is PageMaker's way of telling you it needs more information before it can carry out your wishes. The following list explains the different elements found in dialog boxes and what to do with them. The various bits and pieces are labeled in Figure 2-5.

✔ A box in which you can enter numbers or text is called an *option box.* Double-click on an option box to highlight its contents. Then enter the correct information from the keyboard. To move from option box to option box without using the mouse, press Tab.

✔ *Pop-up menus* — also called *drop-down lists* by some folks — contain lists of options. Press and hold the mouse button on the menu to display the list of options, move the cursor over the option you want to select, and then release the mouse button.

✔ You turn some options on or off by clicking on the corresponding *radio button.* When the option is turned on, a black dot appears in the center of the radio button. You can turn on only one radio button in a group of radio buttons at a time.

✔ Click on a *check box* to turn the corresponding option on or off. An X in the box indicates that the option is turned on. You can turn on as many check boxes in a group as you want.

✔ *Icons* give you a pictorial representation of what a particular option does. Click on an icon to select that option.

Option box

Pop-up menu · Check box · Button

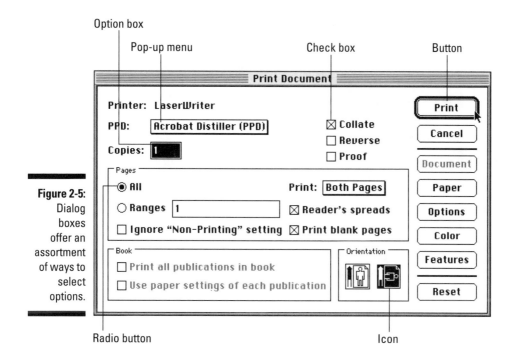

Figure 2-5:
Dialog
boxes
offer an
assortment
of ways to
select
options.

Radio button · Icon

✔ The normal, rectangular *buttons* in a dialog box enable you to initiate a command or open other dialog boxes to access more related options. In the dialog box shown in Figure 2-5, for example, you can click on the Print button to close the dialog box and begin printing or click on the Paper, Options, Color, or Features button to open more dialog boxes full of printing options.

✔ Notice that the Print button is encircled by a heavy black line? That line indicates that you can select the option by pressing the Return key instead of clicking on the button, if you prefer.

✔ Some options are "grayed out" — dimmed — in the dialog box because they're not applicable to what you're attempting to do. For example, the Book options in Figure 2-5 are grayed out because the document being printed isn't part of a booked publication. (Booked documents are explained in Chapter 15.)

Changing Your View

When you first open a new document, PageMaker displays your page in what's known as Fit in Window view. In this display mode, you can see your entire page in the publication window. If you want to take a closer look at your work — or, alternatively, step back even farther for a long-range view — you can either choose commands from the Layout menu or use the new Zoom tool.

- ✔ Choose Layout⇨View to display a submenu of several preset page magnifications.

- ✔ Choose Actual Size to see your text and graphics at the size they will print.

- ✔ Choose Entire Pasteboard to zoom out so that you can see all objects on your pasteboard.

- ✔ You can select some view sizes using keyboard shortcuts. Press ⌘+(zero) to choose Fit in Window view, ⌘+1 to choose Actual Size view, ⌘+5 to choose 50 percent view, and ⌘+2 to choose 200 percent view.

- ✔ An even quicker way to zoom in and out is to use the new Zoom tool, labeled back in Figure 2-4. To zoom in, click on the Zoom tool to select it. Then click on the area you want to magnify. (The plus sign in the magnifying glass cursor indicates that you're zooming in.) The spot you click becomes the center of your screen.

- ✔ To zoom out, press and hold the Option key as you click with the Zoom tool. The cursor changes to a magnifying glass with a minus sign in it to indicate that you're zooming out.

- ✔ Keep clicking with the Zoom tool to further magnify or reduce your view. The center of the magnifying glass cursor appears blank when you're zoomed all the way in or out. You can magnify your view by as much as 800 percent.

- ✔ ⌘+Option+click to switch back and forth between Fit in Window view and Actual Size view. To switch between Actual Size and 200 percent size, ⌘+Option+Shift+click.

- ✔ You can also drag with the Zoom tool to surround a portion of your page with a dotted rectangle, known in desktop publishing circles as a *marquee*. When you release the mouse button, the area you surrounded is magnified so that it fills the screen.

- ✔ To temporarily access the Zoom tool while you're working with another tool, press and hold ⌘+spacebar. When the cursor changes to the zoom in cursor, click to zoom in or drag to marquee the area you want to zoom in on. To temporarily access the zoom out cursor while you're working with tool other than the Zoom tool, press and hold ⌘+Option+spacebar. When the zoom out cursor appears, click or drag to marquee a specific portion of your page.

Dealing with Multiple Documents

You can open as many documents at a time as your computer's memory will allow. To see two or more open documents side by side, choose Window⇨Tile.

To display your open windows so that they're layered on top of each other, with only the title bars sticking out, choose Window⇨Cascade. To switch from one open document to another, click on the inactive document's title bar or choose its name from the Window menu.

To switch from PageMaker to another running program, choose the program's name from the Application menu (press and hold on the PageMaker icon in the far-right corner of the menu bar to display the menu).

Shutting Down and Saving Your Work

When you decide you've had enough of PageMaker for the day, you need to do two things: close your document and close PageMaker.

To close a document and save it for the first time, do as follows:

1. **Click on the Close button in the document window.**

   Or press ⌘+W. PageMaker responds by displaying a dialog box asking whether you want to save any changes you've made to your publication.

2. **To save your changes, click on Yes or press Return to display the Save Publication As dialog box, shown in Figure 2-6.**

   If you don't want to save your changes, click on No to close the document and skip to step 9. Click on Cancel if you decide that you're not ready to close the document after all.

3. **Name your publication.**

   When you first open the Save Publication As dialog box, the filename option box (labeled in Figure 2-6) is highlighted. To enter a new name for your document, just begin typing.

4. **Select a file destination.**

   Tell PageMaker where you want the file to be stored by double-clicking on a folder name in the scrolling list on the left side of the dialog box. Use the Folder pop-up menu, Desktop button, and Disk icon (labeled in Figure 2-6) to locate the folder you want to use, if necessary.

5. **Choose a file type.**

   The Save As radio buttons offer three choices. Select the Publication option to save your document as a PageMaker 6 document. Choose Template to save your publication as a template, as explained in Chapter 14. And if you want to be able to open your publication in PageMaker 5.0, choose the A Copy in 5.0 Format radio button.

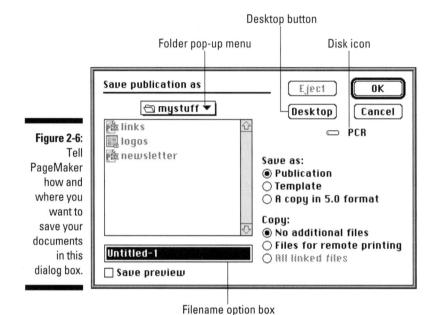

Desktop button

Folder pop-up menu

Disk icon

Figure 2-6:
Tell
PageMaker
how and
where you
want to
save your
documents
in this
dialog box.

Filename option box

If you choose the A Copy in 5.0 Format option, some features of your publication may be modified. You'll lose any master pages other than the Document Masters and any polygons created with the Polygon tool, for example. In addition, locked objects are unlocked, and objects you grouped with the Group command are ungrouped. Some other high-end functions also don't translate well.

6. Choose a Copy radio button.

In most cases, you should choose the No Additional Files option. If you're saving your publication right before sending it to a service bureau or commercial printer for printing, select Files for Remote Printing, as discussed in "Sending Documents to Service Bureaus," in Chapter 18. If you're creating a publication that contains linked text or graphics, as explained in Chapter 16, and you want all the linked files to be stored in the same folder as your publication, choose All Linked Files.

Placing the linked files in the same folder makes it easier to copy all the necessary files to a floppy disk or SyQuest cartridge — which you might need to do if you plan on sharing your document with a colleague, for example.

7. Decide whether you want to save a preview.

A Macintosh program called Adobe Fetch enables you to catalog the images and documents on your hard drive. If you choose the Save Preview check box, PageMaker stores a thumbnail (reduced size) snapshot of the first page of your document for use in the catalog.

8. Click on OK or press Return.

PageMaker saves your file.

9. Choose File⇨Quit or press ⌘+Q to shut down PageMaker.

See, that wasn't so bad, was it?

To ensure that you won't lose hours of work if your computer crashes while you're toiling in PageMaker, save your publication early and often. After you've saved a publication for the first time, you can just press ⌘+S to save it again. PageMaker doesn't even bother you with the Save Publication As dialog box again. To save all open publications in one fell swoop, press ⌘+Option+S. Get in the habit of pressing ⌘+S frequently — you'll save yourself loads of grief when your computer decides to freak out on you (notice that we said *when*, not *if*).

The next time you work on the saved document, PageMaker doesn't display the Save Publication As dialog box after you click on Yes in step 2. It just saves your document using all the settings you used the first time you saved. If you want to save a copy of a document under a new name or make other changes to the save options, choose File⇨Save As to display the Save Publication As dialog box. Then enter a new name in the filename option box.

Every time you switch from one page in your document to another, PageMaker saves the page you switched from, giving you some extra crash protection. For more on this nifty feature, see "Undoing Bad Moves" in Chapter 5.

Now that you've become acquainted with PageMaker's screens, dialog boxes, and so forth, you're ready to actually *do* something with the program. The next chapter shows you how to open a document and do just that.

With all this new computer wisdom under your belt, you'll no doubt receive that invitation to lunch with the chiphead crowd very soon. Remember to have some floppy disks sticking out of your shirt pocket — it's kind of like a status symbol among gangs of computer nerds. Also, be sure to make some sneering wisecracks about that copycat Windows 95 program that all the PC users are bragging about these days.

Chapter 3

It's a Brand New Page! (Now What?)

• •

In This Chapter

▶ Opening new and existing documents

▶ Setting up margins

▶ Dividing your page into columns

▶ Establishing rulers and guides (and figuring out what to do with them)

▶ Using the new Guide Manager

• •

*P*ageMaker 6 is sort of like Arnold ("Ahnüld") Schwarzenegger. No doubt you're thinking, "Oh, sure, and WordPerfect reminds *me* of Benji," but bear with us for a second. If you're like most people, the first time you saw Ahnüld on TV or whatever, you didn't think "actor" or "savvy businessman," you thought, "Get a load of this muscle-bound troglodyte. Is he a dim bulb or what?" And yet, despite the fact that no one over ten years old would select Ahnüld as his or her favorite actor, he remains the biggest box-office draw in this and almost every other country. Furthermore, unlike dozens of other celebrity Neanderthals who made millions and then promptly squandered every cent before they turned 35, Ahnüld invests his money shrewdly. Reputedly, nearly every business deal that the guy makes turns to gold.

So as you may imagine, a school of thought exists that says maybe Ahnüld's not nearly as dumb as he looks. Maybe he just acts dumb so that his audience won't feel threatened by the true Ahnüld, who is a thinker of Brainiac proportions.

The same is true for PageMaker. After you start the program, all you see are a few menus at the top of the screen. Nothing fancy. Nothing at all, in fact, to lead you to believe that you didn't waste some perfectly good money on another hopelessly rinky-dink piece of software. But, as you discovered if you had the good sense to read Chapter 2, PageMaker's simple facade is only that — a facade.

You see, PageMaker knows that it's way smarter than anyone short of Arnold "The Brain" Schwarzenegger, but it *pretends* to be dumb at first so that you won't feel insecure. Then, as you warm up to the program, it reveals more and more of its power, until pretty soon, you're fooled into thinking that you're hot stuff. It's a stealth program just as surely as Ahnüld is a stealth intellectual.

In this chapter, you get a glimpse beyond PageMaker's unassuming exterior and start discovering its inner strengths. You find out how to take the first step in the page layout process — setting up columns and margins — and how to use tools such as ruler guides and the new Guide Manager to make placing text and graphics into your layout easier.

Opening a New (or Used) Document

In the old days, the first step in page layout was to grab a layout board — a thin piece of white cardboard that sported light blue vertical and horizontal gridlines. Layout artists pasted text and graphics on the board, using the gridlines to align elements on the page.

In PageMaker, you start the layout process by grabbing the electronic equivalent of a layout board: a document (referred to as a *publication* in the official PageMaker dictionary). You can either start a new document or open an existing one.

Starting from scratch

To open a new document, choose File⇨New or press ⌘+N. PageMaker responds by showing you the Document Setup dialog box, which enables you to establish certain settings for your publication, such as the page margins. To get a detailed explanation of the options in this dialog box, skip ahead to the "Setting Up Your Pages" section. But if you just want to get to a blank page and leave the setup chores for later, press Return or click on OK to accept the default settings.

Working on an existing document

To open an existing document, choose File⇨Open or press ⌘+O to display the Open Publication dialog box, shown in Figure 3-1. Choose the folder that contains the document you want to open from the folder pop-up menu. Then double-click on the filename in the scrolling list to open the document.

If you choose the Original radio button, you open the original document. If you choose the Copy radio button, PageMaker opens a copy of the document. This option is great if you want to experiment with making changes to a publication. If you don't like the results, the original version of the document is still intact.

If you want to open a publication that you've worked on recently, you don't have to mess with the Open Publication dialog box. Just choose File⇨Recent Publications and then select the document name in the resulting submenu.

Filenames   Folder pop-up menu

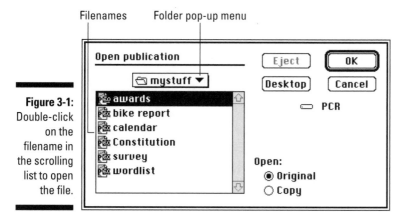

Figure 3-1:
Double-click
on the
filename in
the scrolling
list to open
the file.

Open publication		Eject	OK
mystuff ▼		Desktop	Cancel
awards		⊂⊃ PCR	
bike report			
calendar			
Constitution		Open:	
survey		⦿ Original	
wordlist		○ Copy	

Setting Up Your Pages

When you choose File⇨New or choose ⌘+N to create a new document, you get the Document Setup dialog box shown in Figure 3-2. This dialog box is where you give PageMaker basic instructions on how to set up your document. But nothing's set in stone; after you create your document, you can change these settings at any time by choosing File⇨Document Setup.

Remember that we told you that PageMaker doesn't like to overwhelm you? Well, that's not *always* true. The Document Setup dialog box is a prime example of PageMaker doing its absolute best to frighten you into an apoplectic fit. It's like Ahnüld grabbing one of his investment bankers by the lapels, sticking an Uzi up the guy's nose, and shouting, "I want you to siphon off the equity from my multimillion dollar portfolio of no-load mutual funds and inject it into a development of nonqualifying HUD projects that we'll convert into luxurious high-rise office suites (after we displace the tenants under the guise of urban renovation) *and I want you to do it now!*" Sure, it's an everyday occurrence at the venerable institution of Schwarzenegger and Sycophants, Ltd., but you never quite get used to it.

So, to prevent you from entering some kind of computer-induced seizure, the next few sections examine each of the options in this dialog box one at a time.

```
┌─────────────────────────────────────────────────────────────┐
│  Document Setup ─────────────────────────      ┌──────────┐  │
│                                                │    OK    │  │
│     Page size: │Letter│                        └──────────┘  │
│                                                ┌──────────┐  │
│  Dimensions: │8.5    │  by │11      │ inches   │  Cancel  │  │
│                                                └──────────┘  │
│  Orientation: ◉ Tall  ○ Wide                                 │
│                                                ┌──────────┐  │
│      Options: ⊠ Double-sided                   │Numbers...│  │
│               ⊠ Facing pages                   └──────────┘  │
│               ☐ Restart page numbering                       │
│                                                              │
│  Number of pages: │3  │      Start page #: │1  │             │
│   ┌─ Margins ──────────────────────────────────────────┐    │
│   │  Inside │█      │ inches   Outside │1     │ inches   │    │
│   │    Top  │0.75   │ inches   Bottom  │0.75  │ inches   │    │
│   └────────────────────────────────────────────────────┘    │
│                                                              │
│  Target printer resolution: │600   │ ▷│ dpi                  │
└─────────────────────────────────────────────────────────────┘
```

Figure 3-2:
You define the basic settings for your page in this dialog box.

Before you can tell PageMaker how to set up your pages, you need at least some idea of how you want your finished publication to look. You don't need to have your entire layout planned, and you can always change things around after you've worked on your publication for a while, but it helps to have answers to the basic layout questions. Do you want your newsletter to have three or four columns of text per page, for example? Do you want to print your document on regular size paper or some nonstandard page size? If you don't have the faintest idea how you want your pages to look, browse through Chapter 13, which gives some layout and design tips and examples.

Page-size settings

Select your page size from the Page Size pop-up menu. Chances are, you'll want to select Letter ($8^1/_2 \times 11$ inches), but lots of other sizes, such as Legal ($8^1/_2 \times 14$) and Tabloid (11×17), are also available. When you select a page size, its measurements appear in the Dimensions option boxes.

If you want to lay out a document that has a different size than one of the predefined page sizes (for example, you're creating business cards or a fold-over brochure), activate the Custom option by simply entering the measurements in the Dimensions option boxes. (You don't need to select the Custom option from the Page Size pop-up menu, although you can if you want to waste some time.)

Making changes to your defaults

The simple interface that you get when you first launch PageMaker has an additional purpose (other than allowing you to think that you're smarter than the program). As it turns out, any command that you choose when no document is open becomes a default setting for all future documents. This is PageMaker's handy-dandy way of letting you adjust settings so that all new documents use them.

As you find out how to use the various options in this and other chapters, you may discover that you keep changing certain settings over and over again. To eliminate this utter waste of your time, close all open documents and implement your changes once and for all by choosing the appropriate command from the appropriate menu. Your revised settings become the new defaults.

You may be surprised to discover how many default settings you can change. The following list contains some examples. Don't worry if you don't know what even half of these items mean; they're just presented here to stick a few subliminal flags in your brain. When you come across comprehensive descriptions of one setting or another in a later chapter, the flag will go up, and you'll think, "You know, I can change the default for this option by closing the current document and choosing this here command." That's the idea, anyway. Whether or not it works is a matter for historians to discuss. Those historians who don't have anything better to do with their time, that is.

- ✔ Options in the Preferences and More Preferences dialog boxes, which include ruler measurement units, guide settings, the Story Editor font, and nudge settings

- ✔ Document setup options such as page size, orientation, and numbering

- ✔ Multiple paste repeating values and offset amounts

- ✔ Index and table of contents formatting

- ✔ Number of columns, ruler display, and guide snap

- ✔ Automatic text flow

- ✔ Type style, font, size, tab, indentation, and other text settings

- ✔ Text wrap settings

- ✔ Line weights and fill patterns

- ✔ Style sheets

- ✔ Link settings

- ✔ Color definitions

- ✔ Palette display and location

To establish these defaults, you either choose a command from the menu bar or choose File⇨Preferences and make your selections in the Preferences dialog box. Additional default settings are available by clicking on the More button in the Preferences dialog box to open the More Preferences dialog box. Remember, you need to close any open documents to establish new default settings.

Tall or wide?

For Orientation, select the Tall radio button if you want the long side of the page to go from top to bottom of the document. This option is called *portrait* in some programs, because that's the way portrait paintings are generally oriented. Select Wide if you want the page to have the long dimension go from side to side (called *landscape,* because that's the way paintings of landscapes are generally oriented). Most standard publications — letters and magazines, for example — use the Tall orientation.

All pages in a document must be oriented the same way. Therefore, if you want both tall and wide pages in your layout (maybe there's a chart that you want to print in Wide orientation because its rows are really long), put your landscape (wide) pages in a separate PageMaker document from your portrait (tall) pages. (Of course, you can keep everything in one document and just rotate that really wide chart 90 degrees, as explained in Chapter 10, so that it appears horizontal when it prints, but then you have to twist your head in order to read or edit the text on-screen. And although Ahnüld no doubt would recommend this type of aerobic workout, moving your mouse along one plane while your head is tilted on another requires a degree of hand-eye coordination that most 21st century cyborgs lack.)

Number of pages and page numbers

To tell PageMaker how many pages you want in your document, enter a number in the Number of Pages option box (now *there's* a shocker).

The Start Page # option is set to 1 by default, which makes sense for most documents; the first page in the document is numbered as page 1. If you choose a different number, the first page in the document is assigned that number, and each page thereafter is numbered accordingly. So, if you use 2 as the Start Page # , the first page is numbered page 2, the second page is page 3, and so on. Why would you do this? Perhaps the first page of your document is laid out vertically while the rest of the publication is oriented horizontally. You would create a single-page portrait (tall) document for the cover, and a second landscape (wide) document that begins at page 2 for the rest of the publication.

Among the cluster of Options check boxes is a Restart Page Numbering check box. It's normally deselected. It only comes into play if you use PageMaker's book feature to number pages across a series of documents, as explained in Chapter 15.

If you click on the Numbers button, PageMaker displays the Page Numbering dialog box. Here, you can choose the types of numbers that PageMaker uses to number your pages. Normally, people use Arabic numbers (1, 2, 3, and so on).

But sometimes, Roman numerals (i, ii, iii, or I, II, III, and so on) or letters (a, b, c, or A, B, C, and so on) are more appropriate — such as for prefaces, indexes, and other subsidiary pages. By the way, you don't need to use this dialog box unless you want to change the default setting, which is Arabic numbers.

Keep in mind that whatever numbering scheme you pick for your pages, the numbers that appear in the page icons in the bottom left corner of the document window will always be Arabic numbers. These numbers have no effect on the printing of your document; they're only there to keep you abreast of what's happening on-screen. PageMaker figures that you're probably more used to reading Arabic numbers than Roman numerals.

Margins and side settings

PageMaker assumes that you'll be reproducing your finished documents on two-sided pages. That's what the Double-sided check box means. However, if you'll only be printing on one side, uncheck the option.

What difference does it make whether a document is two-sided or one-sided? Often, none. But there's a good reason to have the option. Think about a report bound in a ring binder — the kind with three holes on the inside of each sheet of paper. When you're setting up such a document, you want to leave enough space on the inside of the sheet to account for the holes. So you'd make the left margin a little wider than the right margin to leave enough room, right? That's great for the right-hand pages. But if you're printing double-sided, the left-hand pages are in trouble. Their right margins aren't wider, yet their right side is the side that's near the holes. Whoops. By having a double-sided option, PageMaker can track pages' *inside* and *outside* margins rather than their left and right. The inside margin for a right-hand page is the left margin, but for a left-hand page, it is the right margin. In this example, you would set a wide inside margin to accommodate those holes. PageMaker figures out which way to shift the text on each page for you.

You can see this feature in action by checking and unchecking the Double-sided box. When the option is selected, the first two Margins options change to Inside and Outside (as in Figure 3-2); when the option is deselected, they become Left and Right.

Whatever margins you set, keep in mind that you can still put text or graphics anywhere on the page — the margins don't prevent that. They merely provide a visual clue for where more text and graphics should go. PageMaker also tries to keep text within the margins when it flows text inside a page.

The Facing Page check box is grayed out (unavailable) unless Double-sided is checked. The Facing Page option lets you position text or graphics to straddle the gap between pages. In other words, a large page element goes to the edge of

The wonderful world of dpi

Resolution is measured in terms of *dpi* — pronounced *dee-pee-eye*, not dippy — which stands for dots per inch. When you print to a laser printer, a dot-matrix printer, an imagesetter, an inkjet printer, or anything more advanced than two cans tied to a string, everything is converted to a series of dots. For a black-and-white document, the pattern of black dots on the white paper simulates the shades of gray that you see. But if you use a magnifying glass, you'll see the dots. (For color printing, there are four sets of dots per page: one cyan, one magenta, one yellow, and one black. The way these colors combine when overprinted creates the range of colors that you see.)

A printer's dpi number tells you the size of the dots. The smaller the dots, the finer the image, because it gets harder and harder for the human eye to see the dots as they decrease in size. Small dots fool your eye into thinking that it's seeing true shades of gray or color hues.

Take a look at the following figure. At left, it shows an image reproduced at 1270 dpi, which is what an imagesetter can achieve and the setting that is used for magazines and books. At right, it shows portions of the same image reproduced at smaller dpi sizes: 600, 300, and 72 dpi.

Suppose that you plan on printing the final document on a 1270-dpi imagesetter but you have a 300-dpi laser printer in your workgroup and you'll be using the laser printer to proof your document on a daily basis. To make sure that you're prepared for the final output device, enter the imagesetter's resolution, 1270, into the Target Printer Resolution option box.

the left-hand page and continues onto the right-hand page, as demonstrated in the first example of Figure 3-3. If you're printing on a laser printer, don't select this option, because all laser printers have a margin around the page on which they can't print. (It's where the printer grabs the page as it moves through the printer mechanism.) So text and graphics printed to the edge of the page get cut off. (Of course, if you're taking your final document to a commercial printer for output on an imagesetter — which can print all the way to the edge of a pager — and will just use your laser printer to print proof copies, go ahead and use facing pages in your document.) The bottom example in Figure 3-3 shows what happens to the text from the top example when the Facing Page option is deselected.

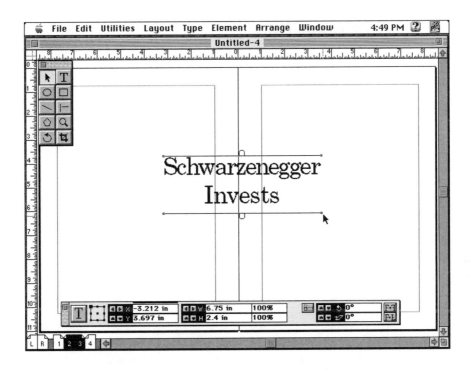

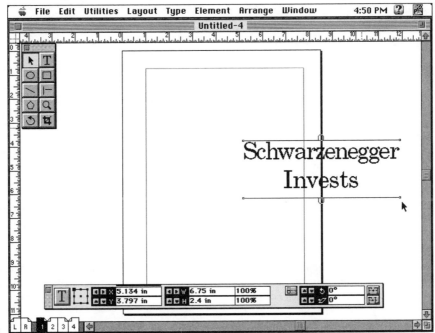

Figure 3-3:
With Facing
Page
checked
(top), you
can place
elements
across
pages.
With it
unchecked
(bottom),
you can't.

Printer settings

In most cases, the Target Printer Resolution setting shown in the Document Setup dialog box corresponds to the resolution of your printer. If you're working on a document that will be sent to an imagesetter or other high-resolution device for final printing but you're using a lower-resolution device like a laser printer for proofing, set the Target Printer Resolution option to match the final printer's settings. (For more on resolution, see the sidebar "The wonderful world of dpi.")

Dividing Your Document into Columns

As mentioned in Chapter 1, one of the advantages of using PageMaker instead of a word processor is that you can easily place text and graphics in columns. Whether you're setting up a new document for the first time or making adjustments to an existing document, you establish column settings by choosing Layout⟷Column Guides. The Column Guides dialog box shown in Figure 3-4 leaps to the screen.

Here, you can set up the number of columns and the amount of space between them (called a *gutter* by publishing types). Figure 3-4 shows the dialog box with sample settings and the effects of those settings on the pages behind the dialog box.

The dialog box you see may be slightly different, depending on the following:

> ✔ If you're working on a multipage document and selected both Double-sided and Facing Page in the Document Setup dialog box, you can establish different column settings for left and right pages. To do so, select the Set Left and Right Pages separately check box at the bottom of the Column Guides dialog box (as shown in Figure 3-4).

> ✔ If you deselected the Double-sided checkbox in the Document Setup dialog box, you won't get separate fields for Left and Right pages.

After you make your selections and press Enter, PageMaker displays dotted lines — called *column guides* — on your page. When you place text into your document (as explained in Part II), it falls within the column guides. Guides don't print when you print your document.

> ✔ By default, PageMaker creates columns of equal size and spaces them evenly across your page. But you can change the width of any column by dragging its column guide. The gutter distance between columns stays the same.

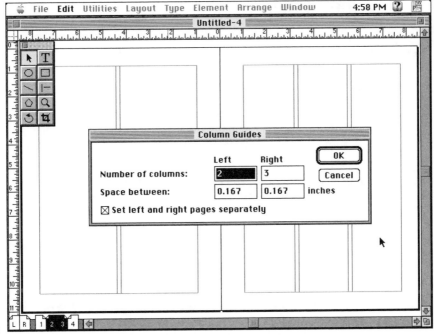

Figure 3-4:
You can establish different column settings for your left- and right-hand pages.

✔ If you want to lock your column guides into place so that you don't inadvertently move them, turn on the Lock Guides command (Layout⇨Guides and Rulers submenu).

✔ Suppose that you have a three-page document, and you set the margins and columns for a *spread* (two facing pages). But if you move to page 3 by clicking on the page icons in the bottom-left corner of the PageMaker window, you discover that no columns are set for that page. What gives? You told PageMaker what you wanted to do, and now it's ignoring you, just like your kids when you tell them to turn off that stupid Barney show and watch something that provides a realistic portrayal of dinosaurs, like "The Flintstones."

The problem is that the Column Guides command only affects the pages you're currently viewing. That may be okay when you're working in a small document, but what if you're creating a 112-page annual report? Choosing Column Guides 56 times may get a little repetitive. Luckily, you can set columns for your entire document by using something called *master pages,* discussed in Chapter 14, or by using Version 6's new Guides Manager feature, explained later in this chapter.

✔ You can create different numbers of columns on the same page — for example, you may want three columns on the top half of a page and two columns on the bottom half. But you can only do so after you place some text in your page or create text blocks to hold the text (placing text is explained in Chapter 5). For how-to's, see Chapter 12.

✔ If you turn on the Snap to Guides function (choose Layout⇨Guides and Rulers⇨Snap to Guides or press ⌘+Shift+G), the column guides take on a magnetic personality. Any text or graphics that you place near a column guide snaps into alignment with the guide. (When you have the command turned on, elements also snap to ruler guides, as explained in the upcoming section, "Making page elements snap to it.")

✔ To make sure that you don't grab a column guide while you're trying to select a neighboring graphic or other element on the page with the Arrow tool, press ⌘ as you select. (Selecting stuff is explained in the next chapter.)

✔ The last thing you should know about column guides is that you can control how PageMaker displays them. The Layout⇨Guides and Rulers submenu gives you two choices. If you select Guides in Front, the guides display on top of every element they pass through. If you select Guides in Back, they display behind elements and so are visible only where there are no graphics or text on the page. In either case, the guides don't print when you print the document — they're only visible on-screen.

In the Preferences dialog box (File⇨Preferences), you can change the default guides setting for all new documents you create. Be sure to close all open documents before choosing File⇨Preferences.

Setting Rulers and Ruler Guides

The rulers you see at the top of each publication window aren't ordinary rulers. Like Ahnüld the Intelligent, the rulers have hidden capabilities, all designed to make it easier for you to correctly position text and graphics on your pages.

If the rulers aren't visible on-screen, press ⌘+R to display them. If you want to hide the rulers and free up some screen space, press ⌘+R again.

Choosing a unit of measurement

By default, the rulers use inches as the unit of measurement. But you can change to another measurement unit by opening the Preferences dialog box (File⇨Preferences), shown in Figure 3-5. This dialog box also enables you to establish other preferences that affect the way PageMaker implements certain options and commands, as discussed earlier in the sidebar "Making changes to your defaults."

To get quick access to the Preferences dialog box, double-click on the Arrow tool icon in the toolbox.

Figure 3-5:
Set your ruler and guide defaults in the Preferences dialog box.

To set ruler preferences, you use two pop-up menus: Measurements In and Vertical Ruler. The Measurements In option determines what unit of measurement will be used throughout your layout — not only in the rulers, but also in dialog boxes, the Control palette, and so on. Chances are, you'll choose Inches or Picas; the inch is the basic measurement unit in the U.S., and the pica is the preferred system of measurement in U.S. publishing. But you can also choose Millimeters (the unit used in Canada and most of the rest of the world) and Ciceros (the unit used in European publishing). If you choose Inches Decimal, you get 10 tick marks per ruler inch rather than the standard 32. Use whatever measurement system you're comfortable with.

The Vertical Ruler setting lets you choose a different measurement system for the vertical ruler. It doesn't affect other parts of the PageMaker interface. Why does PageMaker give you this second measurement option? The answer is based on a publishing tradition that you probably won't ever care about. But here goes anyhow: In traditional publishing, layout artists measured text width in picas and length in inches. The text's column width was usually narrow, so using a finer measurement system made sense. But the text length could be tens or even hundreds of inches for a magazine or newspaper article — maybe thousands of picas. Thus, the two measurements. You still hear the occasional reference to *column inches* at some crusty old newspapers, but you should avoid using the term in polite company.

Another alternative is to use the Custom option and define your own Vertical Ruler measurement units. You may want to use this option to establish a measurement unit that represents lines of text. Of course, the height of a line depends on the text's *leading* (the amount of space between lines), which changes from document to document and even within a single document. So no single measurement unit can accurately reflect all lines of text throughout a publication. But you can set the Vertical Ruler measurement unit to the number of points used for the basic body text's leading. Then you can easily count lines or, if the text in your text blocks aligns to the Vertical Ruler's increments, you can make sure that graphics and other elements line up with the text's baselines.

A pica is roughly equal to $1/6$ inch, and a point is equal to $1/12$ pica (or approximately $1/72$ inch).

You'll rarely use the last ruler setting, the Zero Lock command, which is found in the Layout⇨Guides and Rulers submenu. It's easier to show you this setting than explain it, so look at the ruler in Figure 3-6 and compare it to the ruler in Figure 3-4. Notice that the numbers on the rulers have moved. At the upper-left corner of the rulers is an icon that looks sort of like a cross. This icon is the *ruler origin box.* By dragging the box, you can move the zero points, as demonstrated in Figure 3-6. Choosing Zero Lock prevents you from making this change. If you do somehow move your zero points and want to put them back in their default positions, just double-click on that cross-like part of the ruler.

Why would you want to change the zero point on your ruler? Well, you might do so if you're *tiling* your document. As explained in Chapter 17, tiling is a feature that lets you print small sections of an oversized document, such as a poster, on a proofing printer that can only handle small sheets of paper. After printing, you tape the sections together to create a mock-up of your poster. Each time you create a tile, you reset the zero point to mark the upper-left corner of the area you want to print.

Resetting the zero point also comes in handy when you're trying to measure distances between two elements, especially if you're not a math whiz. For example, if you want to find out how much space you put between graphic A and graphic B, you can drag the zero point to line up with graphic A. Then you can quickly see the exact distance between the two elements, with no messy addition or subtraction involved.

Making page elements snap to it

You can set up PageMaker so that page elements *snap* to ruler positions. When the snapping function is turned on, PageMaker aligns anything that you draw or place on the page along one of the tick marks on the ruler (whether or not the ruler is displayed). If you drag a graphic near a ruler increment, for example, the graphic jumps into alignment with the increment. It's a great way to make sure that elements aren't positioned all cockeyed from one another, creating those slight disparities in alignment that make folks bug-eyed as their brains notice that something is amiss (though they can't quite figure out what it is).

ruler origin box

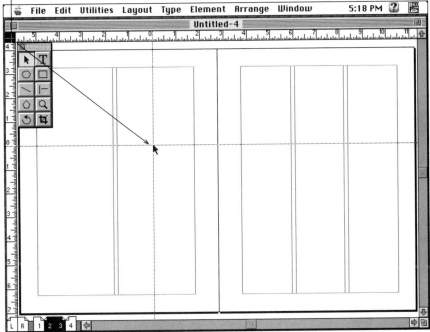

Figure 3-6:
Drag from
the ruler
origin box to
change the
locations of
the zero
points on
the rulers.

✔ To turn on the ruler snap function, choose Layout⇨Guides and
   Rulers⇨Snap to Rulers, as shown in Figure 3-7. A check mark next
   to the option name means that it's turned on.

✔ If you don't want to go to all that work to choose the command, just press
   ⌘+Shift+Y, as in, "Yowsa, what the heck is Y doing here?"

✔ If you select inches as your measurement unit, as explained earlier,
   elements snap to the nearest $1/32$ of an inch; if you select picas, they snap
   to the nearest point.

Creating ruler guides

Rulers are great as general positioning aids. But what if you want to line an
element up to something more specific? That's where *ruler guides* come in
handy. Look at Figure 3-8 and notice the dotted horizontal line that extends
along the bottom of the chart. That line is a ruler guide. Look below the ruler
guide for a similar line and a special double-arrow cursor. That's a ruler guide in
the process of being created. The ruler guides made it easier to properly
position the chart and the label text. Another horizontal ruler guide was used to
line up the footnote text beneath the chart, and a vertical guide was used to line
up the footnote text with the left edge of the chart.

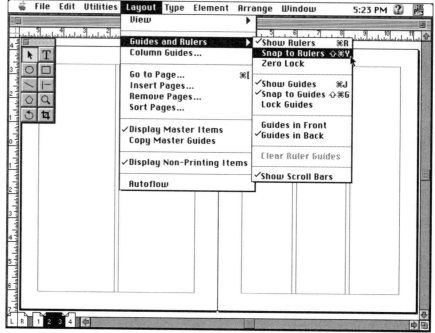

Figure 3-7:
Controls
over rulers
and guides
reside in the
Layout
menu.

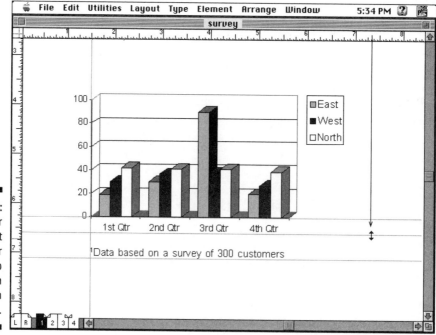

Figure 3-8:
Pull a ruler
guide out
from either
ruler to help
position
elements on
your pages.

To create a ruler guide, move the cursor to a ruler, hold down the mouse button, and drag a ruler guide out to where you want it to be. (You can drag from either ruler: The horizontal ruler at the top of the screen gives you horizontal guides, and the vertical ruler along the left side gives you vertical guides.)

✔ When you're positioning elements with your mouse, you can use guides to ensure alignment, not just as a general target. If you select Snap to Guides from the Layout⇨Guides and Rulers submenu (⌘+Shift+G), any text or graphic you place near a ruler guide jumps into alignment with that guide. You get instant, accurate alignment.

✔ When the Snap to Guides command is turned on, elements snap to column guides as well as ruler guides, as explained earlier, in the section "Dividing Your Document into Columns."

✔ To move a guide, just drag it with the mouse. If you don't want guides — whether column guides or ruler guides — to be movable, select Layout⇨Guides and Rulers and then choose Lock Guides.

✔ To remove a guide, drag it back to the ruler. To remove all guides, choose Layout⇨Guides and Rulers⇨Clear Ruler Guides.

✔ If you're trying to select a graphic or text object with the Arrow tool but you keep selecting a guide instead, press ⌘ as you select the object.

✔ As with column guides, you can specify whether ruler guides appear in front of or behind other page elements. Just choose Guides in Front or Guides in Back from the Layout⇨Guides and Rulers submenu. Or, to change the default setting, close all open documents, double-click on the Arrow tool icon in the toolbox to open the Preferences dialog box, and then choose the appropriate Guides radio button.

Making Your Own Prefab Layout Grids

If you find yourself using the same arrangement of margins, columns, and ruler guides in lots of different documents, you may want to create a custom *layout grid* using PageMaker's new Guide Manager plug-in. When you open a new document, you just tell PageMaker to apply your grid, and voilà — all your guidelines appear on the page. No more of that backbreaking business of dragging lines from rulers and choosing options in dialog boxes.

Creating and saving your grid

You can create a grid by choosing Utilities⇨PageMaker Plug-ins⇨Guide Manager and entering values into the Guide Manager dialog box, shown in Figure 3-9. As you choose the number of columns, ruler guides, and so forth that you want to use, the page preview in the upper-left corner of the dialog box updates to reflect your decisions.

But an easier way to create a grid is to first set up your margins, columns, and guidelines on a blank page and then copy all your settings using the Guide Manager's Copy option, like so:

1. **Open a new publication and set up your columns, margins, and ruler guides.**

   If you need help, read the preceding sections of this chapter.

2. **Choose Utilities⇨PageMaker Plug-ins⇨Guide Manager.**

   The intimidating Guide Manager dialog box (shown in Figure 3-9) appears. Luckily, you can ignore most of the options when you're creating a grid layout in this fashion.

3. **Choose a library to hold your grid.**

   To save your grid for future use, you need to put it in a library. In PageMaker, a *library* is a storage vault where you can place items that you use frequently, such as company logos, mastheads, and in this case, layout grids. You can create different libraries to hold different types of elements — for example, you may want to create a library to hold all the grids you use for the different pages of a newsletter in a library called "Newsletters." (Libraries are covered in more detail in Chapter 14.)

   To open an existing library, click on Open Library, select a library name from the file list box, and then click on Open. To create a new library, click on New Library, enter a name for your library in the Create Guides Library option box, and make sure that the Adobe PageMaker 6 folder is selected in the Folder pop-up menu. Then click on Save. You're returned to the Guide Manager dialog box, where you should see the name of your selected library at the top of the dialog box.

4. **Choose New Grid from the Grid pop-up menu and name your grid.**

   When you choose New Grid from the pop-up menu, PageMaker asks you to name the grid. Enter a name and then click on OK.

5. **Click on Copy Guides.**

   You see the dialog box shown in Figure 3-10.

6. **Choose which guides to include in the grid.**

   Select the Copy checkboxes for the guides you want to copy. For example, if you want to copy all column guides, vertical ruler guides, and horizontal ruler guides, check all three of the Copy check boxes, as shown in Figure 3-10.

   If you create your grid template in a publication that uses facing pages, specify whether you want to use the guides from the left or right page by selecting one of the radio buttons below the Copy check boxes.

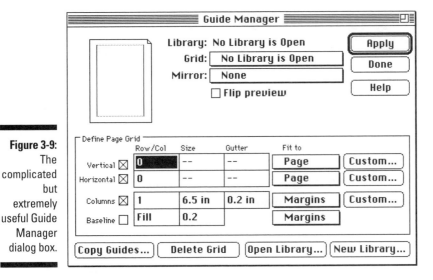

Figure 3-9:
The
complicated
but
extremely
useful Guide
Manager
dialog box.

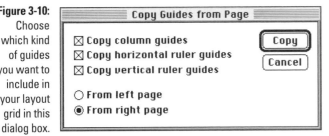

Figure 3-10:
Choose
which kind
of guides
you want to
include in
your layout
grid in this
dialog box.

7. Choose a Mirror option.

The Mirror pop-up menu offers options that enable you to apply a "mirrored" — or horizontally flipped — version of your grid to specified pages. You may use this option if you want the inside margin of a right-hand page to be the inside margin of a left-hand page. If you choose None, the inside margin of a right-hand page becomes the outside margin when applied to the left-hand page.

If you are working in a double-sided document when you open the Guide Manager dialog box, the preview in the upper-left corner of the dialog box shows how the guides will appear on a right-hand page. If you want to preview a left-hand page, check the Flip Preview box.

8. Click on Done.

Applying a grid layout

After you save your grid to a library, you can apply it to any page or pages in an open publication. Here's how:

1. **Choose Utilities⇨PageMaker Plug-ins⇨Guide Manager.**

   Up comes the Guide Manager dialog box, as shown back in Figure 3-9. If the Library field doesn't show the name of the library that holds the grid you want to use, move on to Step 2. If you do see the one you want, skip to Step 4 and consider this your lucky day.

2. **Click on Open Library.**

3. **Select the library that holds the grid and click on Open.**

4. **Choose the grid from the Grid pop-up menu.**

5. **Click on Apply.**

   The Apply Guides to Page dialog box springs into view, as shown in Figure 3-11.

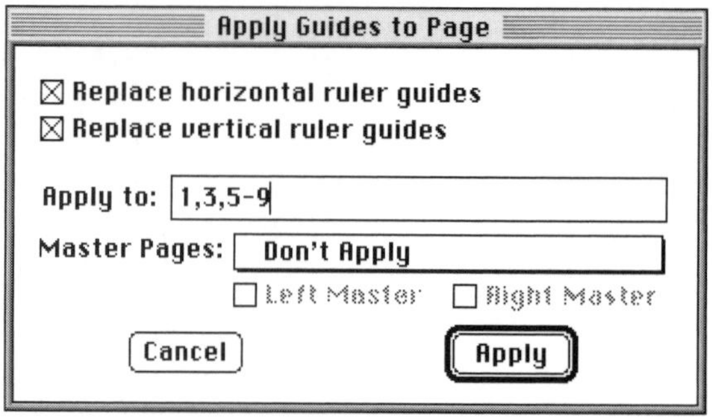

Figure 3-11:
You can specify how you want your grid applied to specific pages by making selections in this dialog box.

Apply Guides to Page

☒ Replace horizontal ruler guides
☒ Replace vertical ruler guides

Apply to: | 1,3,5-9

Master Pages: | Don't Apply

☐ Left Master   ☐ Right Master

[Cancel]   [Apply]

6. **Specify how and where you want PageMaker to apply the grid.**

   If you want to replace any existing horizontal ruler guides in your document with those in the template, check the Replace Horizontal Ruler Guides check box. If you don't want to replace them, uncheck the box. Ditto for the Replace Vertical Ruler Guides check box.

In the Apply To option box, specify on which pages you want to put the grid. You can enter individual page numbers, separating them with a comma, or you can enter a range of pages, separating the start and end pages with a hyphen. Or you can use a combination of the two. If you want to use the grid on pages 1, 3, and 5 through 9, for example, you can enter **1, 3, 5-9** in the option box.

If you want the grid applied to a master page, type the name of the master page in the Master Pages option box. (Master pages are explained in detail in Chapter 14.) If you don't want the grid applied to any master pages, choose Don't Apply from the pop-up menu.

7. Click on Apply.

PageMaker applies your grid and returns you to the Guide Manager dialog box.

8. Click on Done.

PageMaker closes the Guide Manager dialog box.

Your document should now sport a shiny new grid. It's all ready for you to load it up with text and graphics — which just happens to be the subject of the next 12 chapters of this book.

Part II

Putting Words on Paper

The 5th Wave

By Rich Tennant

YEAH, BUT YOU SHOULD SEE HOW NICELY IT CENTERED EVERYTHING.

In this part . . .

To some people, the subject of placing, formatting, and editing text is about as dry as a mouthful of sand. Well, if that's your take on the topic, you're in for a surprise. In PageMaker, text becomes art. For one thing, it's a cinch to change typestyle, size, font, text spacing, and alignment — you know, all the ordinary stuff that folks do when laying out text. And because it's so easy to change basic formatting features, you can experiment with different type treatments until you find the look that's just right for your subject matter and audience. Secondly, PageMaker lets you create all sorts of interesting text effects that enable you to not only add visual interest to your documents, but to hammer home the point of an article or advertisement. In short, the opportunities for creative expression are unlimited.

This part contains the information you need to turn every-day, ordinary lines of text into pages that come alive with such gusto that people won't have any *choice* but to read them.

Chapter 4

All I Need to Know about Fonts and Type

*I*f you've ever prepared a document for a client, a boss, a teacher, or any of life's other authority figures, you know that the appearance of your text can make as big an impression on your prospective reader as the quality of your writing and research. In high school, you were more likely to get a good grade if you typed your report and put it in a plastic binder than if you wrote it with crayon on a greasy paper bag that your mom threw out because it was too disgusting to even use as a trash-can liner. Nowadays, you're more likely to impress folks if you publish your report on a laser printer than if you sketch it on a few sticky notes and stick them on an associate's ink blotter.

But laser printing isn't good enough. Anyone with a Mac whose ⌘ and P keys are working can print a document. The trick is to make your laser-printed text look better than the other guy's laser-printed text.

This book is full of design tips that can help you transform your plain document into something special. But before you can understand these tips, you need to discover a few terms of the typographic trade.

The vocabulary of desktop publishing is based on the language of traditional typesetting, which has its roots in the 15th century. Somewhere near the middle of the century, one Johannes Gutenberg invented movable type, an innovation that was as instrumental in bringing books and literacy to Renaissance Europe as the Model T was in bringing mechanized transportation to folks at the close of the Industrial Revolution. Thanks to its link with history, PageMaker offers the occasional obscure term, such as *font, leading,* and *kerning.* Long-dead geezers such as Aldus Manutius and Claude Garamond may have understood these terms right off the bat, but you may not. Suffice it to say, if you want the lowdown on type, read this chapter.

A Beginner's Guide to Type

If your experience with page design or laser printing is limited or next to nil, you may have problems understanding why so many people devote so much attention to the appearance of a bunch of letters. If you've seen one typeface, you've seen them all, right? What's all the commotion? Why not just enter your text, print your document, and be done?

Right about now, some books on publishing probably would offer a flowery discussion about the rich heritage of typesetting and letterforms and all that other twaddle you so rightly don't care about. Instead, we lay it on the line as simply as possible: The purpose of good type design is to make people *want* to read your pages.

Many folks wrongly construe this statement to mean that you should sweat over your designs until you've rendered elaborate works of art that'll knock your readers' socks off. The truth is that a lot of nit-picking and worrying can result in some hideously ugly designs.

The best designs tend to be the most simple. Although stylish pages may elicit more oohs and aahs, loose, straightforward, unobtrusive type is more likely to be read by a wider variety of people.

So don't go thinking that you need to expand your font library or purchase a $30,000 typesetter. The road from word processing to type design is paved with little more than a few basic terms and concepts.

 If this book had a Don't Freak Out icon, it would appear next to this paragraph. But the Remember icon will have to do in a pinch. Keep in mind that this chapter is only an introduction to the terms of typesetting and desktop publishing. Everything discussed in this chapter is covered in more detail in later chapters. This chapter is your chance to get your feet wet without getting in over your head.

Font terminology

In computer typesetting, the term *font* is frequently used as a synonym for *typeface.* But back in the days of hot metal type, a clear distinction existed. Because characters had to be printed from physical hunks of lead, an entirely separate font of characters was required to express a change in typeface, style, or size.

Things have changed quite a bit since then. Computer users now can access *scalable fonts*, which are mathematical definitions of character outlines. These outlines can be *scaled* (enlarged or reduced) to any size, independent of the resolution of your screen or printer. The scaling may be handled directly by your printer, as is the case for fonts built into PostScript laser printers, such as the Apple LaserWriter. If you rely on a less sophisticated printer, such as the StyleWriter or Personal LaserWriter LS, you can use a font-management utility, such as Adobe Type Manager (ATM), to scale fonts accurately on-screen, thus eliminating jagged edges (see Figure 4-1). Or you can use TrueType fonts, which scale automatically if you're using System 7.0 or later.

Figure 4-1:
Large text shown as it appears on-screen with Adobe Type Manager installed (top) and without (bottom).

Smooth type with ATM

Jagged type without ATM

A single font can satisfy any number of size requirements but can convey only a single *typestyle.* The plain and bold styles of a typeface, in other words, are supplied as two separate fonts. Therefore, in computer typesetting, every font carries with it both unique typeface and typestyle information.

Serif and sans serif typefaces

The most common typefaces available to personal computer users are Helvetica and Times, shown in Figure 4-2. These typefaces were chosen more for their differences than their similarities. For example, although it was created in 1931 for the London *Times* newspaper, Times derives much of its classic appeal from the so-called "transitional" faces of the 1700s. The lines of each character change gradually in thickness, a phenomenon known as *variable stroke weight*, and terminate in tapering — or *bracketed* — wedges called *serifs*. By contrast, Helvetica is a modern font. Influenced by the 20th-century Bauhaus school of design, which fostered a disdain for old-style ornamentation, the strokes of Helvetica characters are rigid and almost entirely uniform in weight. Helvetica also lacks serifs, making it a *sans serif* face. (*Sans* is the French word for "without;" hence, *sans serif* means "without serifs.")

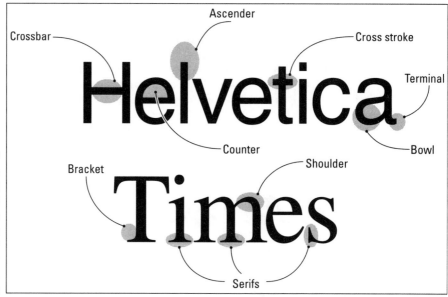

Figure 4-2:
The
anatomy of
type, as
applied to
two popular
laser printer
fonts.

Designer typestyles and families

To enhance the visual interest of a page, you can mix some Helvetica text with some Times text. Unfortunately, Helvetica and Times don't look so hot together. Helvetica is heavy and large; Times is more fragile and tends to appear smaller at similar type sizes. To help you spark up a page without mixing typefaces, type designers create variations on typefaces called *typestyles*. Because these typestyles are designed to be used together, you run no risk of mucking up a page as you diversify its text. For example, you can mix different styles of Helvetica within a document to add some variety to a page without worrying that the styles may clash.

Helvetica and Times can each be displayed in one of four designer typestyles, shown in Figure 4-3. Each typestyle is a separate font. Together, each set of four typestyles makes up a *type family*.

Different typestyles emphasize text in different ways. Plain text — sometimes called *roman*, meaning upright with serifs — is by far the most common variety. Plain text is used to display *body copy*, which comprises the large blocks or columns of text that represent the heart and soul of information contained on a page. The *italic* (cursive) or *oblique* (slanted) style may be used within body copy to highlight a foreign or unfamiliar phrase or simply to stress a word. The *bold* style is relegated to special text, such as captions and headlines. The italic style may also be applied to special text; you can even italicize bold text to create a *bold italic* style.

Helvetica
Helvetica Bold
Helvetica Oblique
Helvetica Bold Oblique

Times Roman
Times Bold
Times Italic
Times Bold Italic

Figure 4-3: Different fonts from the Helvetica family are destined to be used together. The same is true of members of the Times family.

Type size terminology

After you choose a font to govern the fundamental appearance of your text, you can further enhance and distinguish elements of your page by changing the size of individual characters and words. Large type indicates headlines, logos, and the like; moderately small type serves as body copy; very small type indicates incidental information including copyrights and disclaimers. Combined with typestyle, the size of your text directs the attention of your readers and helps them to find the information that is most important to them.

To understand how to size type, you must first understand how type is measured. To begin with, type has four basic kinds of characters. The horizontal guidelines that serve as boundaries for these characters are labeled in Figure 4-4.

- The *baseline* is the imaginary line on which the characters rest. *Leading* is the amount of vertical space between the baselines in a block of text.

- *Capital letters* extend from the *baseline* upward to the *cap height* line. Examples include *A, B,* and *C.* Numerals (*0123456789*) also qualify as capitals.

- *Medials* fit entirely within the space between the *baseline* and the *x-height* line. Examples include *a, c,* and *e.*

- *Ascenders* are lowercase characters that extend above the cap height line. Examples include *b, d,* and *k.*

✔ *Descenders* are lowercase characters that extend below the baseline. Examples include *g, j,* and *p.*

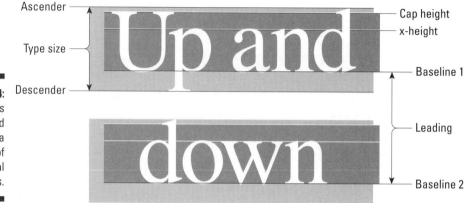

Ascender — Cap height
— x-height
Type size
Baseline 1
Descender
Leading
Baseline 2

Figure 4-4:
Type is
measured
using a
series of
horizontal
guidelines.

Not every character fits snugly into one of these categories. For example, the lowercase characters *i* and *t* violate the x-height line but are nonetheless considered medials; the dot of the *i* isn't considered an integral part of the character, and the *t* doesn't extend even so far as the cap height line. Other times, a letter qualifies as both an ascender and a descender, as is the case for the italic *f* in a serif font. Nonletters, such as %, #, and &, are generally capitals, but several violations exist — among them, $, §, and many forms of punctuation, including parentheses.

Hot stuff, huh? Well, for those of you who are worried that we're delving too deeply into the territory of typo-dweebology, let's get straight to the point: The size of a character — known predictably as its *type size* — is measured from the topmost point of the tallest ascender to the very lowest point of the deepest descender. Type size is calculated in a unit of measure called *points*, where one point equals $1/72$ inch (just over $1/3$ millimeter), which is why you frequently see type size called *point size*. So a character that measures 0.167 inch from tip to tail becomes 12-point type, the equivalent of pica type on a conventional typewriter — remember those?

In addition to changing type size, font, and style, you can improve the appearance of a page by varying the spacing between lines, between paragraphs, and even between individual letters of type, as explained in Chapters 6 and 7.

What kind of fonts should I buy?

In addition to deciding which typestyle and size you want to use, you have to decide at some point which *font format* you want to use. That's right, just as you can get your favorite rock band's songs on either CD or cassette, you can buy computer fonts in different formats.

The two major font formats in desktop publishing are PostScript and TrueType. You can also buy variations on PostScript and TrueType fonts — PostScript GX and TrueType GX. GX fonts work with QuickDraw GX technology, offered in System 7.5. QuickDraw GX offers a variety of cool font features that you can take advantage of if you use GX fonts. Unfortunately, like a lot of programs, PageMaker doesn't support QuickDraw GX — and even has trouble printing some non-GX PostScript fonts correctly if you have QuickDraw GX installed. So, for the purposes of using PageMaker, stay away from GX fonts and QuickDraw GX.

Adobe Systems (the same folks who now bring you PageMaker 6.0) developed the PostScript font format, which is the standard for professional printing. The TrueType format is the result of an unlikely joint venture between Microsoft and Apple Computer, who decided to put aside their differences for a moment to try to break Adobe's lock on the font market.

Today, TrueType and PostScript fonts are priced about the same, and both formats offer pretty much the same selection of typefaces and level of quality. So which one do you buy? It depends on how you plan to print your documents. If you plan to output everything on your home or office printer, you'll probably want to stick with TrueType. TrueType fonts work with just about every model of desktop printer, and Macs running System 7.0 or later offer built-in support for the TrueType format. Low-end laser and inkjet printers usually can't print PostScript fonts, although a font manager called ATM (Adobe Type Manager) lets you print PostScript fonts to non-PostScript printers. Be forewarned, however, that the printer may take eons to print your pages.

Many midrange and high-end laser printers support PostScript fonts as well as TrueType fonts. But if you plan on working with service bureaus or commercial print shops to produce your documents, you need to find out whether their equipment requires PostScript fonts. Because PostScript has been the professional printing standard for so many years, some high-end prepress machines have problems with the TrueType format.

Yes, You Can Have Too Many Fonts

If you're new to electronic publishing, you can easily go overboard with type. After years of being restricted to the pica or elite type on your typewriter, you suddenly find yourself with all kinds of interesting typefaces at your disposal. "Hey," you think, "wouldn't it be cool to put the headline in this font that looks like a ransom note and put the body type in this font that looks like something a 16th-century monk wrote with a quill and ink?"

At the risk of dampening your creative spirit, we feel compelled to remind you that people are more willing — and able — to read type that has a simple, clean look than they are to struggle through type that's set in a very stylistic font. Also, be wary of mixing too many typefaces on the same page. As a rule of thumb, limit yourself to one or two different typefaces — perhaps one serif and one sans serif face — per document and use different typestyles (bold and italic) and type sizes to give your pages some variety.

Every font that you load into your computer eats up memory and storage space. And every font you use in your document consumes memory when you print your pages or save your document to disk. So in addition to the aesthetic considerations, keeping your font collection in check is important to conserving your computer's resources. For our recommendations on what comprises a good font library, see Chapter 21. And if you want more information about installing, using, and removing fonts on your Mac, check out *Macs For Dummies* by David Pogue (IDG Books Worldwide).

Chapter 5
The Joy of Text

● ●

▶ Entering text directly in PageMaker

▶ Importing text from a word-processing program

▶ Fixing mistakes

▶ Working with text blocks

▶ Editing text in the Story Editor

▶ Using the spell checker and word search feature

● ●

*R*emember back in the fourth grade, when the world's most evil teacher, Mrs. Sneets, made you write a letter to a senator in cursive writing? You had to use one of those cartridge pen thingies — the ones that leave big old blobs of ink on your paper if you're not careful. The Evil Mrs. Sneets insisted that each and every word of your letter be *perfect*. One ink blob, one cursive *S* without the appropriate curlicue, and you had to start all over from scratch. On the whole, you spent about a zillion hours (including a few that you should have been able to spend at recess, playing murder ball) creating a document that pleased The Evil. And then the stupid senator didn't even write you a real letter back — he just had his secretary send you some lame form letter that didn't even *mention* your request to have the FBI do some checking up on one Mrs. Harriet M. Sneets.

Happily, those days are behind you forever. Now that you have PageMaker, you'll never again have to worry about ink blobs and making the perfect cursive *S*. You can generate a document full of fabulous looking words with hardly any trouble at all. And if you do make a mistake, correcting it is easy. Why, you're almost certain to get the job done way before recess time.

If you've used a word processor, you already know a lot of what you need to know to create text in PageMaker. The process you use to delete or add a word, for example, is pretty much the same as in Microsoft Word or WordPerfect. But in PageMaker, you put text in text blocks, which are like storage containers for all your well-thought-out words (and your not-so-well-thought-out ones, too). This chapter explains the basics of getting your thoughts down on paper and also gives you the low-down on using PageMaker's built-in spell checker and search-and-replace function.

Importing Text vs. Entering Text Directly

You can put text into your PageMaker document in two ways: You can *import* text (PageMaker calls this *placing* text) or enter text directly.

To *import* text simply means to copy the contents of a word-processor document into PageMaker. As an alternative, you can use PageMaker's own text-editing tools to compose your text in PageMaker. These aren't either/or options — you'll probably import some of your text and enter some directly.

Following are some tips on which kinds of text to create in your word processor and which to create right in PageMaker.

- Compose your *main text* — the stories and the like that make up the bulk of your publication — in a word processor and import the text into PageMaker. Why? Because a word processor is designed for just this kind of work. And almost everyone has a word processor, so a group of people can exchange drafts of stories for editing and approval purposes if necessary. Also, if different people are working on different stories for the publication, it would be pretty hard (not to mention downright chaotic) to have each person enter their text into the main PageMaker document. Instead, the different writers and editors should create and refine the stories in their word processors and then turn the whole batch over to the PageMaker layout person.

- Create the embellishments and adjustments — titles, tables of contents, and corrections — in PageMaker. Typing in a newsletter's issue date or writing a headline in your word processor and then importing it into PageMaker doesn't make a lot of sense. In the first case, importing such a small piece of text is more work than just creating the text in PageMaker in the first place. In the second case, the headline created in the word processor probably doesn't fit in the space allotted by the layout, so you have to rewrite it or at least edit it in PageMaker anyhow.

Entering text directly into your PageMaker document

If you want to create text right in your PageMaker document, just follow these steps:

1. **Click on the Text tool or press Shift+F2.**

   The Text tool is labeled in Figure 5-1. When you choose the tool, the cursor changes from an arrow to the text cursor, also labeled in the figure.

2. Click at the spot where you want to enter the text.

After you click, a blinking insertion marker indicates where the next letter you type will appear. If you click within a set of column guides, PageMaker automatically moves the insertion marker to the left edge of the column. If you don't have any columns set up, the cursor jumps to the left margin of the page. (When you don't specify that you want two or more columns, PageMaker views your document as having one big column that stretches from the left margin to the right margin. So in this case, the margin guides really serve as column guides.)

3. Start typing.

PageMaker places the text you type within the column (or margin) guidelines.

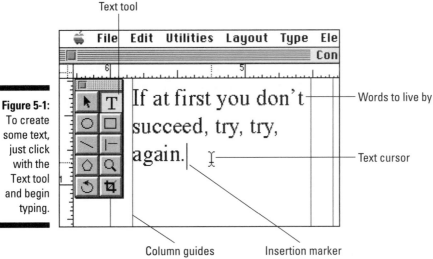

Figure 5-1:
To create
some text,
just click
with the
Text tool
and begin
typing.

 When you zoom out on the page and enter text in a small type size, PageMaker displays your text as a bunch of little Xs — a feature known as *greeking text*. To see the actual characters you typed, zoom in on your document by choosing a larger view size from the Layout⇨View menu or by using the Zoom tool.

To control how PageMaker greeks text, choose File⇨Preferences (or double-click on the Arrow tool icon in the toolbox) to display the Preferences dialog box. Then click on the More button to open the More Preferences dialog box, where you change the value in the Greek Text Below option box. For example, if you set the value at 5 pixels, PageMaker greeks any characters smaller than 5 pixels in size.

If you don't want the text to stretch across an entire column or to stay within the confines of a column — for example, maybe you want to place a headline across three columns — you can create a *text block* before you begin typing:

1. **Select the Text tool.**

2. **Drag to create a text block.**

   Click at the place where you want text to begin. Then drag to create a rectangle big enough to hold your text, as shown in Figure 5-2. Don't worry about drawing the text block perfectly; you can always resize and reshape the block, as explained in the upcoming section "Working with Text Blocks."

   When you release the mouse button to end your drag, the lines that indicate the boundaries of the text block disappear. Don't panic — the text block is still there; you just can't see it.

3. **Start typing.**

   The text stays inside your new text block.

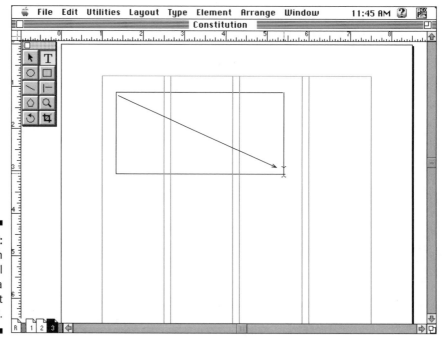

Figure 5-2:
Drag with the Text tool to create a new text block.

Importing text

To place text from a word-processor document (or other program) into a PageMaker document, follow these steps:

1. Choose File⇨Place or press the keyboard shortcut, ⌘+D.

PageMaker gives you the Place Document dialog box, shown in Figure 5-3.

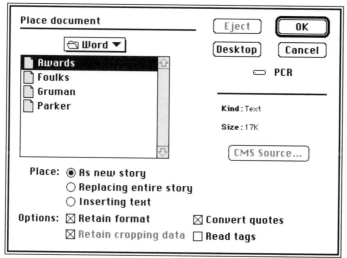

Figure 5-3: The Place Document dialog box lets you import text files into your layout.

2. Select the text file in the scrolling list box.

Navigate through your folders and drives in the normal Mac fashion until you locate the file you want and then click on the file.

3. Choose placement and formatting options.

First, the placement options. The three choices are pretty straightforward: As New Story brings the text in as a new, separate story, in addition to whatever you may have in your publication already. Replacing Entire Story substitutes the text for the text in the story that's currently selected (you select a story by clicking on its text block with the Arrow or Rotate tool or clicking inside the text block with the Text tool). Inserting Text adds the text into the currently selected story, placing the imported text at the location of the text cursor. This option appears only if you have selected a story by clicking in it with the Text tool.

Story is PageMaker's term for an article or other chunk of text. A story comprises all the text in a single text block or in a group of linked text blocks (linked blocks are explained later in this chapter).

Second, the text formatting options: Retain Format, Convert Quotes, and Read Tags. You should be familiar with the text you're importing before selecting any of these options — you can look at the text first in a word processor to see, for example, whether the text uses style sheets or includes character formatting. If the text does use styles or formating, you must decide whether you want to retain the styles and formatting. (This issue is covered in more detail in Chapter 7, in the section "Importing styles.") The Retain Cropping Data option is grayed out (unavailable) because it affects graphics that you import, not text.

4. Click on OK or press Return.

PageMaker redisplays the current page and shows you a status box indicating that it's importing the text as you requested. When PageMaker finishes importing the text file, and you move the cursor onto the page or pasteboard, the cursor changes to a paragraph shape (📝) or a snake shape (🔃).

Note that when you choose File⇨Place to begin the importing process, you don't have to be at the page where you want the text to be placed. You can switch pages after importing the text but before clicking at a location at which it will be placed (as described in the next step). But you'll find it easier if you're at the desired page before you import the text.

5. Click at the spot where you want PageMaker to place the text.

Depending on the setting of the Autoflow option in the Layout menu, the text flows across the page, within the current column, or through several pages (which PageMaker creates if needed), as described in the upcoming sidebar, "The three faces of text insert."

Chapter 12 offers more details and tips on placing imported text into your document — and moving the text around after you put it there.

The three faces of text insert

PageMaker is a big fan of using icons to tell you what it's doing or capable of doing. In the case of placing text, you have three possibilities:

📝 The paragraph icon indicates manual text flow, which lets you place just one column of text. To get this icon, make sure that Autoflow is unchecked in the Layout menu.

🔃 By holding the Shift key when placing text, you get the semiautomatic flow icon, which lets you place one column right after another.

🔃 By selecting the Autoflow icon in the Layout menu before placing text, you tell PageMaker to place all the text in as many columns on as many pages as necessary. If you press ⌘ as you click, you temporarily disable automatic text flow and return to manual text flow.

Working with Text Blocks

After you create a text block, you can move it around the page and change its size and shape by using the Arrow tool. Before you can do any of that, however, you have to first *select* the text block by clicking on it with the Arrow tool. PageMaker displays the boundaries of the text block, shown in Figure 5-4. The official PageMaker manual refers to these boundaries as the *windowshade*.

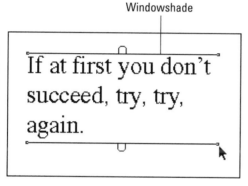

Windowshade

Figure 5-4: Drag on a window-shade handle to resize a text block.

If at first you don't succeed, try, try, again.

✔ To move a text block, place the Arrow tool inside the block and press and hold the mouse button until the cursor changes to a four-way arrow. Then drag the text block to a new position. (You can move the block before you see the four-way arrow, but if you do, PageMaker only displays the text block and not the text during the move.)

✔ You can also move a selected text block by pressing the arrow keys on your keyboard — a great technique for nudging a text block a short distance. Each press of an arrow key moves the text block .01 inch. Hold down the ⌘ key as you press an arrow key to move the text block 0.1 inch. You can change the default nudge distance by entering new nudge values in the Preferences dialog box (File⇨Preferences).

✔ To resize a text block, drag one of its windowshade handles, labeled in Figure 5-5. You can drag vertically, horizontally, or diagonally.

✔ A dashed box extending from the bottom of a text block means that the text block isn't long enough to accommodate the current line of text. If you drag the windowshade handle to the bottom of that dashed box (or past it), the line of text will fit.

✔ The little tabs on the top and bottom of the text block — called *text placement handles* — give you information about the text inside the text block. Figure 5-5 shows the three different text placement handles you may encounter. A red, down-pointing arrow in the bottom tab handle means that the text block doesn't have enough room for all the text. You can either enlarge the text block (by dragging its handles) or click on the red tab. When you click on the tab, PageMaker redisplays the paragraph placement icon. Click at the spot where you want to put the overflow text. An empty bottom tab means that no more text needs to be placed.

✔ After you place overflow text, you see a plus sign in the bottom tab of the initial text block. You also see a plus sign in the top tab of the overflow text block. The plus signs indicate that the two text blocks are linked together — that is, the two text blocks each hold part of the same story. For more information about working with linked text blocks, see Chapter 12.

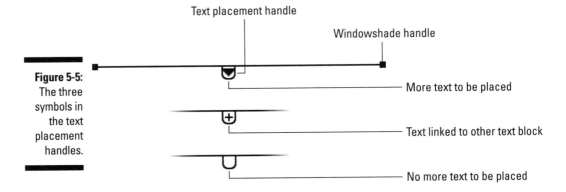

Text placement handle

Windowshade handle

Figure 5-5:
The three
symbols in
the text
placement
handles.

More text to be placed

Text linked to other text block

No more text to be placed

✔ To delete a text block, select it with the Arrow tool and then press the Delete key (called the Backspace key on some keyboards). PageMaker zaps both the text block and the text inside it into electronic oblivion.

✔ Text blocks can work in some unexpected ways, especially when you're laying out a document that has multicolumn pages and lots of linked text blocks. We've presented just the basics in this chapter. For a more in-depth discussion of working with text blocks, read Chapter 12.

Editing Text

Nobody gets everything right the first time. Fortunately, mistakes are pretty easy to fix in PageMaker. If you need to make substantial changes — or if you want to check the spelling of your text — use PageMaker's built-in word processor, the Story Editor, as described later in this chapter. But if you need to make only a few small changes, you can just select the offending text with the Text tool and make your edits as follows:

✔ To insert text, click at the spot where you want to add text. Then start typing. PageMaker shoves all the text that falls after the insertion marker to the right to make room for the new characters.

✔ To delete text, drag over the characters to highlight them. (The highlight means that the characters are selected.) Then press Delete.

✔ Alternatively, you can click with the Text tool to the right of the first character you want to banish from your page. Then press the Delete key until you've wiped off all the text you don't like.

✔ To replace selected text with new text, just begin typing.

✔ To move text from one place to another, select it and then choose Edit⇨Cut or press ⌘+X. PageMaker whisks the selected text out of the text block and into a temporary holding tank, known as the Clipboard. Place your cursor at the spot in your PageMaker layout where you want to place the text and choose Edit⇨Paste or press ⌘+V. PageMaker puts the text into its new home.

✔ You can also use the Clipboard to copy a piece of text and then place the copy in a new location. Select the text, choose Edit⇨Copy or press ⌘+C, place the cursor at the spot where you want to place the copied text, and press Edit⇨Paste or ⌘+V.

Just for good measure, following are a few selection tips to keep in mind:

✔ In addition to dragging over text to select it, you can click at the start of the text you want to select, press Shift, and click at the end of the text.

✔ To quickly select a word, double-click on the word. Triple-click (that is, click the mouse button three times rapidly) to select a paragraph.

✔ To select all the text in a story — which includes all the text in a text block plus the text in any linked text blocks — choose Edit⇨Select All or press ⌘+A.

Editing Text Inside the Story Editor

If you're making a lot of changes to your text, you'll find it easier to work in the Story Editor, PageMaker's built-in word processor, than in the normal layout view. For one thing, PageMaker can process your edits in the Story Editor faster than in layout view. In addition, the Story Editor offers such word-processing features as a search-and-replace function and a spell checker.

To open the Story Editor, select the Text or Arrow tool, click inside the story you want to edit, and then choose Edit⇨Edit Story or press ⌘+E. Another method is to triple-click on the text block with the Arrow tool selected. The Story Editor appears, as shown in Figure 5-6.

Tab

Line break

Style name

Paragraph break

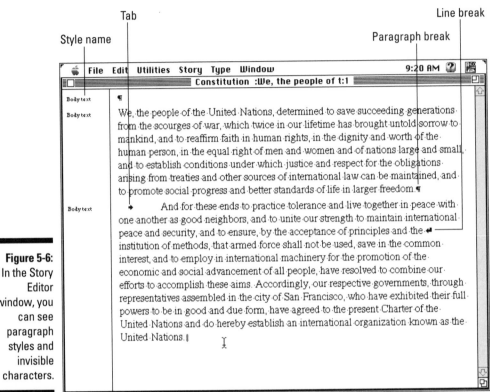

Figure 5-6:
In the Story
Editor
window, you
can see
paragraph
styles and
invisible
characters.

You can also create an entirely new story in the Story Editor and then place it into PageMaker. Make sure that your cursor is outside all text blocks and press ⌘+E. After you enter your text and close the Story Editor, PageMaker shows you a dialog box that asks whether you want to place the text. Click on the Place button to get the text placement cursor. Then place your text as you normally would.

Before we go any further, you should know a few things about the Story Editor window:

✔ The Story Editor displays all text in the selected story. Whether the story continues across 70 pages or is only a single word long, all text in the story is available in the window. Just use the arrow keys and scroll bar to scroll to the portion of the story that you want to edit.

✔ When you open the Story Editor, several menus change. The Layout menu is replaced by the Story menu, the Element and Arrange menus disappear, and a few commands that were previously dimmed in the Utilities menu become available.

- You can't access any of the PageMaker tools inside the Story Editor. It's as if the Text tool is perpetually selected.

- You can apply formatting commands, including fonts, type sizes, style sheets, and all the others, to text inside the Story Editor, but you don't see the results of your changes. (Formatting commands are the subject of Chapters 6 and 7.) The Story Editor shows all text in a single typeface and type size, regardless of its real formatting. You can still see typestyles such as bold and italic, however. This setup may seem weird, but it's actually good news. The Story Editor is designed especially for text editing; showing only one font and type size helps the Story Editor run faster.

- The left column of the Story Editor window shows the style applied to each paragraph (styles are explained in Chapter 7). If no style name appears in the column, no style is applied to the text. If you don't want to see the style name column, deselect the Display Style Names command in the Story menu.

- In the Story Editor, you can view invisible characters, such as tabs, line breaks, and paragraph breaks, as labeled in Figure 5-6. Spaces appear as small dots. Seeing these characters can be very useful; they're normally invisible, so you can easily lose track of these characters. But if you want your invisible characters to stay invisible, uncheck the Display ¶ option in the Story menu.

- You can change the way the text looks on-screen if you don't like its appearance. Choose File⇨Preferences and click on the More button to display the More Preferences dialog box. The options toward the middle of the dialog box, spotlighted in Figure 5-7, allow you to change the appearance of Story Editor elements on-screen. To change the typeface and size, select new options from the Font pop-up menu and enter a value into the Size option box. Keep in mind that your changes have no impact on the font and size of the actual text; the only purpose of these options is to make your text more legible on-screen in the Story Editor.

To change the Story Editor settings for all future documents you create, close any open documents before you open the More Preferences dialog box. Note that you can change the default settings for whether style names and paragraph marks (and other invisible characters) are displayed as well as change the font and type size.

- All selection techniques work the same way in the Story Editor as they do in the standard layout view. Double-click on a word to select it, triple-click to select a paragraph, press ⌘+A to select the entire story, and so on.

- Changes made inside the story window are automatically applied to your document, just as if you had edited the text in the standard layout view.

- To close the Story Editor and return to the layout view, click on the Close box of the Story Editor window, press ⌘+W, or choose Story⇨Close Story.

```
                        More Preferences
  ┌─ Text ─────────────────────────────────────┐   ┌──────────┐
  │ Greek text below: 9      pixels             │   │    OK    │
  │ ☐ Turn pages when autoflowing               │   └──────────┘
  │ ☒ Use typographer's quotes                  │   ┌──────────┐
  │ TrueType display: ◉ Preserve line spacing   │   │  Cancel  │
  │                   ○ Preserve character shape │   └──────────┘
  └─────────────────────────────────────────────┘
  ┌─ Story editor ──────────────────────────────────────────┐
  │ Font:  Geneva              ☒ Display style names         │
  │                            ☐ Display ¶ marks             │
  │ Size:  12     ▷  points                                  │
  └─────────────────────────────────────────────────────────┘
  ┌─ Graphics ──────────────────────────────────────────────┐
  │ Define standard display by ◉ Size:      64    kBytes     │
  │                            ○ Resolution: 100 ▷ %         │
  │       Alert when storing graphics over:  32   kBytes     │
  └─────────────────────────────────────────────────────────┘
  ┌─ PostScript printing ───────────────────────────────────┐
  │ Memory freed for graphics:  Normal                       │
  └─────────────────────────────────────────────────────────┘
```

Figure 5-7:
In the More
Preferences
dialog box,
you can
change how
text is
displayed in
the Story
Editor
window.

✔ You can also return to the layout view without closing the Story Editor, which makes accessing the Story Editor faster the next time around. Either press ⌘+E (Edit➪Edit Layout) or click in the layout window in the background, if visible. Click on the Story Editor's title bar (if visible) or press ⌘+E to make the Story Editor window active again.

Checking Your Spelling

Another benefit to editing your text in the Story Editor is that you gain access to a spell checker and a search-and-replace function.

To spell check your text, choose Utilities➪Spelling or press ⌘+L to display the Spelling dialog box, shown in Figure 5-8. Click on the Start button to instruct PageMaker to begin looking for misspelled words. (The Start button changes to the Ignore button after you start the spell checker.) When PageMaker finds a word that doesn't match any spellings in its dictionary, it displays the word at the top of the dialog box. Provided that the Alternate Spellings check box is checked, PageMaker also offers a list of alternates below the Change To option box.

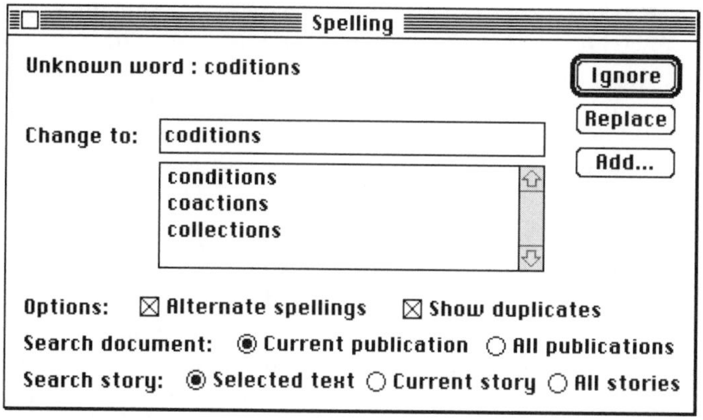

Figure 5-8:
The Spelling
dialog box
lists
misspelled
words and
offers
alternate
spellings.

At this point, you have three options:

- ✔ **Select an alternate:** Click on an alternate spelling to make it appear in the Change To option box. Then click on Replace or press Return to change the word in your document and search for the next misspelling. Or just double-click on the correct word to do the same thing in a single action.

- ✔ **Correct the word manually:** If no correct alternates appear, you have to locate the correct spelling the old-fashioned way: by looking it up in the dictionary. So much for progress, eh? When you find the right spelling, enter it into the Change To option box and click on Replace or press Return.

- ✔ **Ignore the word or add it to the dictionary:** If the word is spelled correctly — not even PageMaker knows every word on the planet — you have two choices. Either continue on to the next misspelling by clicking on the Ignore button or add the word to PageMaker's dictionary, as explained in the next section.

Here's how the remaining options in the Spelling dialog box work:

- ✔ **Show Duplicates:** Selected by default, this check box instructs Page-Maker to search for any repeated words. The makers of the B-movie *Attack of the the Eye People* — that's how the title read on-screen — could have used the Show Duplicates option. Unfortunately, spell checkers didn't exist back then. Leave this option turned on.

- ✔ **Search Document:** If you choose the Current Publication radio button, PageMaker checks text in the current document according to the Search Story settings you choose (discussed next). The All Publications option is useful if you're creating booked publications, as discussed in Chapter 15. If you select this option, PageMaker checks all documents in the current book list. Keep in mind that checking multiple documents at once may take a lot of time.

✔ **Search Story:** These radio buttons let you check only the selected text in the Story Editor; all text in the story, whether selected or not; or all stories throughout the entire PageMaker document. Select the All Stories option at least once before saving the final version of your document, so that no text block is left unchecked. The Selected Text option is grayed out (unavailable) unless you select some text before opening the spell checker.

Teaching PageMaker to spell

PageMaker can be a little irritating in its zeal to find misspelled words. You can't tell the program to ignore words that contain only a single letter, abbreviations composed entirely of capital letters, or words with special punctuation (as in *PageMaker's* vs. *PageMaker*). To get PageMaker to stop bugging you about a specific spelling, you have to add the spelling to the dictionary.

To add lots of new words to the dictionary — for example, if you want to add a list of employee names or technical terms — use the separate Dictionary Editor program, as described later in this chapter. But if you just want to add a word or two, click on the Add button in the Spelling dialog box. The dialog box shown in Figure 5-9 appears.

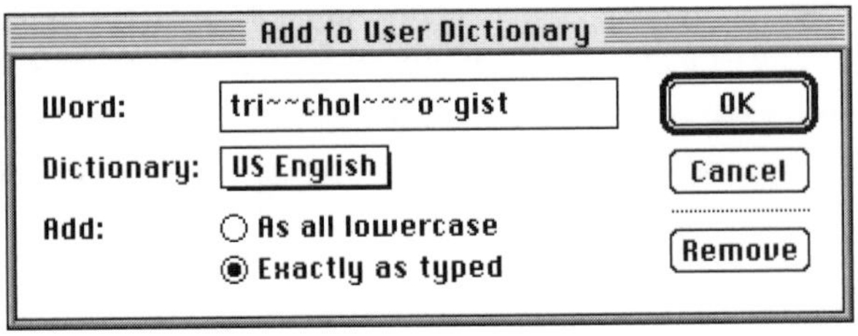

Figure 5-9: Use this dialog box to add a word to PageMaker's spelling dictionary.

Add to User Dictionary	
Word: `tri~~chol~~~o~gist`	[OK]
Dictionary: [US English]	[Cancel]
Add: ○ As all lowercase ● Exactly as typed	[Remove]

✔ The Word option box contains the word as it's spelled in your document. Tilde (~) symbols divide the word into syllables. Each tilde represents the location of a possible hyphen. The number of tildes indicates precedent. In other words, PageMaker is more likely to break the word at a two-tilde point than a one-tilde point.

✔ The original tildes represent PageMaker's best guess. If you don't like the location of a tilde or the precedent applied to a specific hyphenation point, delete a few tildes, add a few more elsewhere, and so on. For example, if you prefer that PageMaker hyphenate *trichologist* as *tri-chologist*, rather than *trichol-ogist*, position more tildes between the *i* and *c*, as in *tri~~~chol~~o~gist*. You can enter up to three tildes in a row to represent a very high level of preference. If you never want the word to hyphenate, delete all tildes from the word.

A trichologist, by the way, is the scientific term for hairdresser. Isn't it amazing how much knowledge you can glean from one $19.99 book?

✔ If the misspelled word begins with an uppercase character because it appears at the beginning of a sentence, but you want PageMaker to save the word using only lowercase characters, select the As All Lowercase radio button near the bottom of the dialog box. If the word is a special term — such as PageMaker — that should always be capitalized exactly as it appears in the Word option box, leave the Exactly As Typed radio button selected.

Click on OK to add the word to PageMaker's dictionary. After the program adds the word, you'll be returned to the Spelling dialog box.

In case you're wondering, the Remove button allows you to remove words from the dictionary. Say you accidentally add the word *tricologist* instead of *trichologist*. To get rid of it, click on the Add button in the Spelling dialog box (the word that appears in the Change To option box doesn't matter). Then enter *tricologist* into the Word option box — with or without tildes, again it doesn't matter — and click on the Remove button. The misspelled word is out of there.

Adding lots of new words to the dictionary

Adding words to your dictionary using the method just described is fine if you want to add a few words as you're spell-checking a document. But if you need to add a long list of words — for example, a list of technical or scientific terms used in your industry or a list of brand names that have odd capitalization (such as *PageMaker*) — give the new Dictionary Editor utility a whirl. The Dictionary Editor, a separate program that comes bundled with PageMaker, enables you to import a list of words that you create in a word processor and add all the words to the dictionary in one fell swoop.

To add a list of words using the Dictionary Editor:

1. **Create a list of the words you want to add to the dictionary.**

   You can type your list in a word processor or any program that can save files in text-only format. Put a carriage return, space, or tab between each word you want to add to the dictionary.

2. **When you've finished typing your list, start the Dictionary Editor program.**

   You'll find the program in the Utilities folder in the Adobe PageMaker 6.0 folder. Double-click on the Dictionary Editor icon to start the program.

If your Mac responds with a dialog box saying that it can't find the Linguists folder, choose the Adobe PageMaker 6.0 folder from the Folder pop-up menu, and then open the RSRC folder. Select the Linguists folder from the scrolling list of folder names and then click on the Select button.

3. **Choose File⇨Open, select the dictionary you want to edit, and click on OK.**

Assuming that you chose U.S. English as your dictionary when you installed PageMaker, the main PageMaker dictionary file is called ALDUSN.UDC. You'll find the file in the US English folder, which is inside the Proximity folder, which is inside the Linguists folder, which the preceding tip told you how to locate. (Whew!) After you click on OK, you see a dialog box that contains a list of words, a Word option box, and buttons that enable you to add, replace, and remove words from the dictionary. But you're going to import your list, not add words one at a time, so you can ignore the dialog box.

4. **Choose File⇨Import.**

The Import Text Document dialog box, shown in Figure 5-10, appears. In the scrolling file list, select the file containing the list you want to import. The dialog box offers two other options: Hyphenate On Import Using Algorithm (say *that* three times fast) and Import Words Already In Dictionary. If you choose the former option, the Dictionary Editor hyphenates your words according to how it thinks they should be hyphenated. If you don't, the Dictionary Editor doesn't hyphenate your words at all (you can add hyphenation information later if you want).

If you choose the second option, the Dictionary Editor replaces any word that has the same spelling as a word you import with the new word. For example, you can overwrite *Pagemaker* with *PageMaker*.

5. **Click on OK.**

Your new words appear in the Dictionary Editor's word list.

Figure 5-10:
Use the
Dictionary
Editor to
import a list
of words
into your
PageMaker
spell-
checking
dictionary.

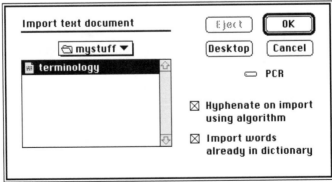

6. **Adjust the hyphenation of your new words.**

   If you chose the Hyphenate On Import Using Algorithm radio button in step 4, the hyphenation marks for your new words display in the scrolling list. If you want to change the hyphenation for a word, double-click on the word to place it in the Word option box and add or delete tildes, as explained earlier in the section "Teaching PageMaker to spell."

   If you didn't choose the Hyphenate On Import Using Algorithm button (really, that name is entirely *too* long), double-click on the word to place it in the Word option box. Then choose Edit⇨Hyphenate to see the Dictionary Editor's suggested hyphenation. Add or delete tildes as necessary.

7. **Click on Replace to make the Dictionary Editor accept any changes you make to a word.**

8. **Choose File⇨Save to save your amended dictionary and choose File⇨Quit to shut down the Dictionary Editor program.**

Finding that Special Word

The Spelling command searches your text for spelling errors. But what if you have something more specific in mind? Suppose, for example, that you're pretty sure that you mentioned Vice President Muckimuck of Company X in your document, but you're not totally sure. No one wants to anger a VP — particularly the Muckmeister — so you decide that you'd better double-check. The question is, how?

The answer is Utilities⇨Change. When you choose this command (or press ⌘+H) when working in the Story Editor, PageMaker displays the Change dialog box, found at the bottom of Figure 5-11.

PageMaker actually offers two commands for finding text, Utilities⇨Change and Utilities⇨Find. The Find command is specifically designed for finding text that you don't want to change. But what's the point? As Figure 5-11 demonstrates, the Find dialog box merely offers fewer options than the Change dialog box; you'll find nothing unique about the Find dialog box, so you have no reason to use it. Furthermore, by sticking with Utilities⇨Change for all your searching needs, you have to memorize only one keyboard equivalent, ⌘+H.

Hunting down some text

After you display the Change dialog box, enter the characters that you want to find in the Find What option box. Then press Return or click on the Find button, which turns into the Find Next button after you click it. If the first instance of the text isn't the one you were looking for, press Return again (or click on the Find Next button). PageMaker notifies you when it reaches the end of the text. That's all there is to it.

Figure 5-11:
The Find dialog box (top) is merely a stripped down version of the more functional Change dialog box (bottom).

```
┌──────────────────────── Find ────────────────────────┐
│ Find what: │United Nations              │   [   Find   ]│
│ Options: ☐ Match case  ☐ Whole word      [Type attributes...]│
│ Search document:       Search story:     [Para attributes...]│
│ ◉ Current publication  ◉ Selected text                │
│ ○ All publications     ○ Current story                │
│                        ○ All stories                  │
└───────────────────────────────────────────────────────┘

┌────────────────────── Change ────────────────────────┐
│ Find what:  │United Nations            │  [  Find next  ]│
│ Change to:  │Endangered Species        │  [   Change    ]│
│ Options: ☐ Match case  ☐ Whole word     [ Change & find ]│
│ Search document:       Search story:    [  Change all   ]│
│ ◉ Current publication  ◉ Selected text  [Type attributes...]│
│ ○ All publications     ○ Current story  [Para attributes...]│
│                        ○ All stories                  │
└───────────────────────────────────────────────────────┘
```

You can modify your search by selecting either (or both) of the Options check boxes:

- ✔ **Match Case:** If you select this option, PageMaker finds only those instances of a word that match the capitalization of the text entered into the Find What option box. For example, when searching for *Muckimuck*, PageMaker ignores the colloquial use of *muckimuck* and searches for the word exclusively in its proper noun form.

- ✔ **Whole Word:** When selected, this option searches for whole words and not just partial words. For example, if you search for *hang*, you may also find *hang*er, *chang*e, and *shang*hai. To eliminate all words but *hang* from your search, select the Whole Word option.

You also have access to the same Search Document and Search Story options that are present in the Spelling dialog box. To find out how these work, back up a few pages to the section "Checking Your Spelling" and read the earlier descriptions.

Searching by format

You can also search for text that's formatted in a certain way. For example, you may want to find only boldface references to Muckimuck. To search your text in this fashion, click on either the Type Attributes or Para Attributes button. If you choose Type Attributes, you get the Change Type Attributes dialog box, shown in Figure 5-12, which enables you to search for certain formatting characteristics, such as font, type size, and typestyle. The settings shown in the figure, for example, tell PageMaker to search for 12-point bold Helvetica text. If you choose the Para Attributes button instead, you can search for three different paragraph formatting characteristics: style, alignment, or leading.

Change Type Attributes

Find what:

Font: Helvetica   OK

Size: 12   ▷ points   Leading: Any   ▷ points   Cancel

Set width: Any   ▷ % Size   Track: Any

Color: Any   Tint: Any   ▷ %

Type style: Bold

Change to:

Font: Any

Size: Any   ▷ points   Leading: Any   ▷ points

Set width: Any   ▷ % Size   Track: Any

Color: Any   Tint: Any   ▷ %

Type style: Italic

In either dialog box, select the formatting you want to locate from the options in the top half of the dialog box — those in the Find What section. (The options in the bottom half of the dialog box controls the formatting of replacement text, a subject discussed later in this chapter.)

Press Return or click on OK to exit the Change Type Attributes dialog box and return to the Change dialog box.

Searching for special characters

In addition to checking for plain old everyday text, you can search for invisible characters (paragraph breaks and tabs), em spaces, discretionary hyphens, and other special PageMaker characters (explained in Chapter 8). You search for these characters by entering special codes into the Find What option box. All codes include the caret (^) character, which you create by pressing Shift+6. Table 5-1 lists the most common codes (most are the same codes you use in Microsoft Word).

Table 5-1	Character Search Codes	
Character	*Search Code*	*Note*
Tab	^t	*t* for tab
Carriage return	^p	*p* for paragraph
Line break (Shift+Return)	^n	*n* as in line, possibly
Discretionary hyphen	^-	
Automatic hyphen	^c	
Nonbreaking hyphen	^~	
En dash	^=	
Em dash	^_	
Standard space	^w	*w* for white space
Nonbreaking space	^s	
Thin space	^<	< because it's so thin
En space	^>	> because it's thicker
Em space	^m	
Nonbreaking slash	^/	

Capitalization of code characters doesn't matter. For example, both ^t and ^T find tabs.

PageMaker provides one other special character code, ^?. This so-called *wildcard character* searches for absolutely any character of text. So if you enter *spr^?ng,* you'll find *spring, sprang,* and *sprung.* You can even use more than one wildcard character in a row. If you enter *spr^?^?^?,* you'll also find *sprint, sprite, sprout,* and *spruce.*

But wait. With all these caret codes, how do you manage to find a regular old caret? The answer is to enter two carets in a row (^^).

Replacing found text with new text

Now suppose that VP Muckimuck got the ax and that former mail-room worker Upstart has risen to the job. The company newsletter is going to press tomorrow, and you need to replace every instance of *Muckimuck* with *Upstart.*

Again, the Change dialog box is your key to success. Enter *Muckimuck* in the Find What dialog box and *Upstart* in the Change To option box. Then use one of the following combinations of buttons:

✔ To change every instance of *Muckimuck* to *Upstart*, click on the Change All button. PageMaker automatically changes every occurrence of the text.

✔ To check each occurrence of *Muckimuck* before changing it — perhaps a couple of Muckimuck's duties are being transferred to Department L's VP Rapier — click on the Find button. When PageMaker finds an occurrence of *Muckimuck*, you have the option of changing it to *Upstart* by clicking on the Change & Find button, which changes the text and searches for the next occurrence. Alternatively, you can enter *Rapier* into the Change To option box and then click on Change & Find. Or finally, you can click on the Find Next button to leave this occurrence of *Muckimuck* intact and search for the next one.

✔ The Change button just changes the selected text without searching for the next occurrence. Most likely, the only time you'll want to use this button is when searching for a single occurrence of a word.

✔ The character codes listed in Table 5-1 work in the Change To box as well as in the Find What box — with one exception. You can't enter the code for automatic hyphenation into the Change To box.

✔ To control the formatting of the replacement text, click on the Para Attributes or Type Attributes buttons and make selections from the Change To sections of the respective dialog boxes. (These dialog boxes are discussed in more detail earlier, in the section "Searching by format.")

To this day, PageMaker doesn't offer an option to undo changes made from the Change dialog box, as do Microsoft Word and other word processors. So make sure that you really want to change your text — and that you've entered the correct characters in the Find What and Change To option boxes — before you initiate this command. (You can try pressing Shift and choosing File⇨Revert to revert to the last mini-saved version of your document, as explained in the next section, but the odds aren't great that it will work.)

Undoing Bad Moves

PageMaker offers a couple of other ways to correct your mistakes: the Undo command and the Revert command. Memorize these two commands — you'll probably use them a lot.

✔ Edit⇨Undo (⌘+Z) reverses your last action. For example, if you delete a paragraph of text and then think better of it, you can choose Undo to get your paragraph back. Whew, that was a close one!

✔ PageMaker only remembers the last action you took, so you have to choose Undo immediately after you goof up. If you click the mouse button or do anything else — and we mean *anything* else — before choosing Undo, the command won't work.

✔ If you change your mind about undoing something, you can choose Edit➪Redo to undo your undo. But you have to choose Redo before you do anything else, including clicking the mouse. How's that for a fine how-do-you-do?

✔ If you choose Undo after typing text, PageMaker erases everything you've typed since the last time you clicked the mouse, not just the last word or character you entered.

✔ File➪Revert gets rid of all the edits you made since the last time you saved your document. It's like getting a fresh start on the day's work.

✔ PageMaker automatically performs what it calls "mini-saves" when you take certain actions, such as moving to a new page, switching between layout and Story Editor view, and printing a document. You can revert to the last mini-saved version of your document by holding down the Shift key as you choose File➪Revert.

✔ Undo can't undo everything. It won't undo most File menu commands (Print, Save, and so on); Type menu commands (font and typestyle settings, for example); or changes you make using the Style and Color palettes. Which is yet another good reason for remembering the cardinal rule of computerdom: *Save early and save often.* That way, if you really mess things up and need to use the Revert command to get rid of the evidence, you don't lose a whole day's work.

You now know the basics of placing text into your PageMaker document — but the fun's only just beginning. In the next three chapters, you find out how to do all sorts of things with text, from making minute adjustments to spacing (an absolute joy for perfectionists) to creating shadowed text and drop caps. Be sure to also check out Chapter 12 for more information on working with text blocks. In that chapter, we discuss how to lay out text in a document that contains multiple stories on each page.

Chapter 6

Making a Bold (or Italic) Statement

● ●

● ●

*E*ver notice how different categories of magazines at your local newsstand use different kinds of type on their covers and in their headlines? What's that — you say you're always so busy trying to sneak a peek at the *Enquirer* without anyone seeing you that you don't have time to pay attention to such things? Well, take our word for it: Magazines rely heavily on type size, font, and typestyle to distinguish themselves. *Fortune* magazine, for example, uses a bold, no-nonsense serif font in its logo — a style that reflects the publication's all-business, power-suits-and-briefcases attitude. *People* magazine's logo, on the other hand, uses a casual, colorful outline type that says, "Hey, it would be a lot more fun to read *our* magazine than that stodgy old financial rag, wouldn't it?"

Magazines pay high-priced consultants an embarrassing amount of money to help them choose the right type treatment for their logos, headlines, and body text. Publishers are willing to lay out all that cash because they know that type is a critical ingredient in creating the magazine's image. And in a world where way too many publications are vying for our limited reading time, creating an image that readers respond to is essential to survival.

Choosing the right font, type size, and typestyle is critical to the success of your publications, too. Your text can either make people want to put down their *People* magazines and read what you've got to say or convince them that your document is perfect for lining the hamster cage.

Fortunately, PageMaker makes experimenting with different type treatments easy, as you find out in this chapter and the next. You can change 12-point bold Helvetica type to 14-point Times italic with just a few clicks of the mouse. You can apply other formatting attributes, such as character spacing, paragraph spacing, and paragraph alignment, just as quickly.

If you're new to publication design and you want some pointers on what kind of text to use where, browse through Chapter 13, which provides some examples of good type treatments. (Who needs a high-priced design consultant when you've got us, right?)

Making Friends with the Control Palette

To change the way your text is formatted, you first have to select the text with the Text tool, as explained in Chapter 5. After you select the text, you can apply formatting attributes by choosing commands from the Type menu or by using the buttons and pop-up menus in the Control palette. You can also apply some formatting by pressing keyboard shortcuts. (The upcoming Table 6-1 offers a list of some of the available shortcuts and indicates the Type submenu under which you'll find the formatting command.)

Using the Control palette, shown in Figure 6-1, is by far the quickest way to apply basic formatting. To display the palette, choose Window⇨Control Palette or press ⌘+apostrophe. When the Text tool is active, the Control palette offers two modes: text mode (which PageMaker calls *character mode)* and paragraph mode. You switch between the two by clicking on the mode icons in the Control palette (labeled in Figure 6-1). Text mode is the default setting when the Text tool is active, but if you switch to paragraph mode, the palette retains paragraph mode the next time you select text. When the Arrow tool is selected, the palette offers controls for positioning, rotating, and otherwise manipulating graphics and text blocks, as discussed in Chapter 10.

In text mode, the palette offers buttons for changing font, type size, typestyle, character width, leading, kerning, and tracking. (*Leading* refers to the amount of space between lines of text; *kerning* and *tracking* are methods of adjusting the spacing between individual characters.) You can also shift a character so that it rests a little above or below the text baseline. In paragraph mode, the palette provides buttons for setting paragraph formatting options, such as paragraph alignment, spacing, tabs, and indents. The paragraph side of the palette is discussed in Chapter 7.

To apply formatting using the Control palette, just select the text you want to format and then click on the palette formatting buttons, enter values into the palette option boxes, or choose options from the palette pop-up menus. To make a word boldface, for example, double-click on the word to select it and then click on the B typestyle button. To unbold the word, select it and click on the B button again.

Close box

Text mode   Font   Size   Tracking   Kerning

Figure 6-1:
The Control
palette as it
appears in
text mode.

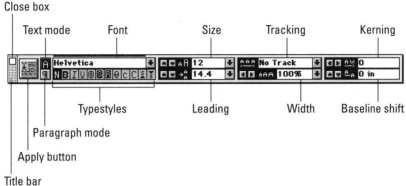

Typestyles   Leading   Width   Baseline shift

Paragraph mode

Apply button

Title bar

Keep in mind these tips when using the Control palette:

✔ The triangle symbols next to some options are *nudge icons*: Clicking on the
up and right triangles nudges the value to the next highest increment;
clicking on the down and left triangles nudges the value to the next lowest
increment. If you hold down the ⌘ key when clicking a nudge icon,
PageMaker multiplies the nudge increment by ten. For example, clicking on
the Size nudge arrow nudges the type size in .10-point increments;
⌘+clicking nudges it in 1-point increments.

✔ If you click on an option in the palette, your formatting changes are
automatically applied to the selected text. But if you type a new value into
an option box, you have to click on the Apply button or press Return to
apply the new formatting. Alternatively, you can press Tab to apply the
formatting and move to the next option in the palette.

✔ The value for the Baseline Shift nudge controls is based on the value set
for the Vertical Nudge settings in the Preferences dialog box's Control
Palette section. (Use File⇨Preferences or double-click on the Arrow tool in
the toolbox to open the dialog box.) Baseline Shift is explained in more
detail later in this chapter.

✔ You can't change the nudge settings for the other formatting options on
the Control palette; the amount of "nudging" that occurs with each click of
a nudge arrow is fixed.

✔ To hide the Control palette, click on its close box. To move it around on-
screen, drag its title bar.

Table 6-1	Text Formatting Options	
Formatting	*Keyboard Shortcut*	*Menu Path*
All caps	⌘+Shift+K	Type⇨Type Specs
Baseline shift	None	Type⇨Type Specs⇨Options
Boldface	⌘+Shift+B	Type⇨Type Style⇨Bold
Font	None	Type⇨Font
Italics	⌘+Shift+I	Type⇨Type Style⇨Italic
Kerning	⌘=Delete[1]	Type⇨Paragraph⇨Spacing
Leading	None[2]	Type⇨Leading
Normal	⌘+Shift+spacebar	Type⇨Type Style⇨Normal
Outline	⌘+Shift+D	Type⇨Type Style⇨Normal
Reverse	⌘+Shift+V	Type⇨Type Style⇨Reverse
Shadow	⌘+Shift+W	Type⇨Type Style⇨Shadow
Size	None[3]	Type⇨Size
Small caps	⌘+Shift+H	Type⇨Type Specs
Strikethrough	⌘+Shift+slash (/)	Type⇨Type Style⇨Strikethru
Subscript	⌘+Shift+hyphen	Type⇨Type Specs
Superscript	⌘+Shift+plus	Type⇨Type Specs
Tracking	None[4]	Type⇨Expert Tracking
Underline	⌘+Shift+U	Type⇨Type Style⇨Underline
Width	None[5]	Type⇨Set Width

[1]When cursor is placed between two characters, ⌘+Delete kerns characters together $\frac{1}{25}$ em space; ⌘+Shift+Delete kerns them apart by the same amount.

[2]⌘+Shift+A sets leading to Auto.

[3]⌘+Shift+period increases size to next largest size in menu; ⌘+Shift+comma reduces to next smallest size; ⌘+Option+Shift+period increases one point size; ⌘+Option+Shift+comma reduces one point size.

[4]⌘+Shift+Q sets tracking to No Track.

[5]⌘+Shift+X sets width to 100 percent (normal).

To change the default character formatting settings for all future documents you create, make selections from the Type menu when no document is open. To set the default settings for the current publication, select the Arrow tool and then make your selections.

Choosing a Font and Typestyle

Figure 6-2 shows the Control palette's Font pop-up menu and Type Style buttons. You can also find all these options by choosing Type⇨Font, Type⇨Type Style, or Type⇨Type Specs; but unless you really like clicking your way through menus (you masochist, you), you're better off using the palette.

Figure 6-2:
These Control palette buttons provide a quick way to choose a font and typestyle.

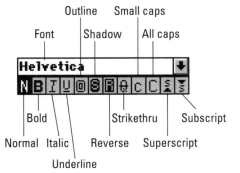

To change the font for selected text, just choose a new font from the Font pop-up menu. If no text is selected, the next text you type will appear in the new font.

The Typestyle buttons offer 12 choices, as follows (keyboard shortcuts are included just for good measure):

✔ **Normal (⌘+Shift+Spacebar):** This setting, curiously enough, uses the typeface's normal style. Go figure.

✔ **Bold (⌘+Shift+B):** Bold text is great for headlines, subheads, and other text that you want to emphasize on a page.

✔ **Italic (⌘+Shift+I):** Italic type is typically harder to read than normal or bold type, so use it sparingly. Short quotes and picture captions are two potential applications.

✔ **Underline (⌘+Shift+U):** You may never want to use this button. Generally speaking, text that you underline on a typewriter, such as a book title, is italicized in typesetting. The sentence, "After again reading <u>Gone with the Wind</u> by Margaret Mitchell, I had to lay off sugar substitutes for a week," for example, becomes "After again reading *Gone with the Wind*. . . . "

✔ **Reverse (⌘+Shift+V):** Choose this style to make your text the same color as the paper. If the text appears in front of a colored background, the effect is *reversed type* (just as the name suggests). If no object is in back of the text, the text is *invisible*. This latter technique is useful for creating custom spaces.

✔ **Strikethru (⌘+Shift+backslash (\)):** The strikethru style — nice spelling, huh? — gives you a way to mark text that is scheduled to be deleted from the final version of a document. The strikethru style is a useful editing tool when two or more people are working on the same document. Both on-screen and when printed, strikethru text is adorned by a horizontal line that runs midway through each character.

✔ **Outline (⌘+Shift+D):** This style traces the outline of each character with a thin line. Throughout its history, PageMaker has occasionally had problems printing outline text, sometimes making the outlines so thin that they would not reproduce. Though that problem has been remedied — or so we're told — you may want to lay off this style just to be safe.

✔ **Shadow (⌘+Shift+W):** This effect places a shadow behind your text. Reserve this effect for logos and other display type. You can see some examples of shadow type being used in a logo in Chapter 13, in Figure 13-12.

✔ **Small Caps (⌘+Shift+H):** This option replaces all lowercase letters with miniature capitals, sized to the approximate height of a lowercase x. Small caps are generally used to represent familiar initials that sometimes pop up in body copy, such as 900 BC or 10:30 AM. The small caps don't interrupt the natural flow of the text as they might at full size (900 BC or 10:30 AM).

To change the size of your small caps, choose Type⇨Type Specs (⌘+T) and click on Options to display the Type Options dialog box, shown in Figure 6-3. Then raise or lower the Small Caps Size value. (You typically don't need to change the small caps size unless you're using small caps on type that's larger than about 24 points.)

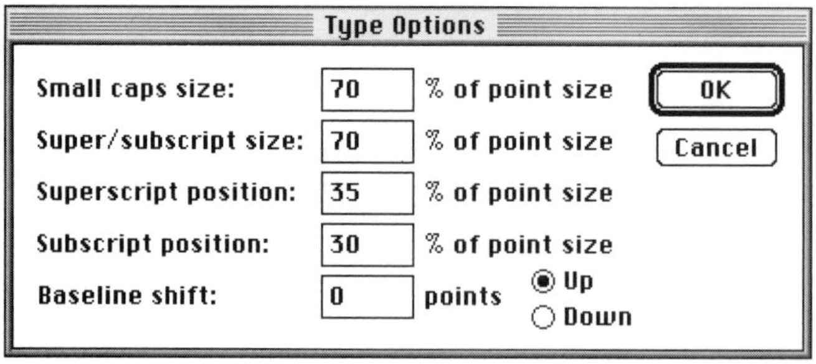

Figure 6-3:
You can specify how you want PageMaker to size and position small caps, superscript, and subscript characters.

Type Options		
Small caps size:	70	% of point size
Super/subscript size:	70	% of point size
Superscript position:	35	% of point size
Subscript position:	30	% of point size
Baseline shift:	0	points ● Up ○ Down

OK Cancel

✔ **All Caps (⌘+Shift+K):** Selecting this option changes all selected characters, whether capital or lowercase, to capitals. This option does not affect numbers and other symbols.

The All Caps function doesn't work on characters typed with the Caps Lock key down.

✔ **Superscript (⌘+Shift+plus):** Selecting this option raises selected text slightly and makes it smaller, like the 3 in $6^3 = 216$. Superscripts are useful for creating mathematical equations, footnotes, and fractions. As with small caps, you can adjust the way your superscript text appears by changing the values in the Type Options dialog box. You can change both the superscript size and its position relative to the normal text.

✔ **Subscript (⌘+Shift+hyphen):** This option lowers text slightly and makes it smaller, like the 1 in the equation $x_1 + y_1 = a$. Subscripts are used almost exclusively in equations.

Change the Super/Subscript Size value to 65 or 70 percent for most text under 14 points. PageMaker's default of 58.3 percent is definitely too small. Also, change the Superscript Position to 35 percent and the Subscript Position to 30 percent for typical text — where the point size is 8 to 12 points and the leading is 1 to 2 points more than the text size. These settings keep your superscript and subscript characters readable while minimizing the chances that they'll bump into your normal text. For example, a subscript doesn't bump into the ascender (the part that sticks up) of an *h* or *l*.

In all cases, you click on the Control palette button once to turn on the typestyle for the selected text and click on it again to turn the style off. The keyboard shortcuts work the same way; pressing the shortcut when the style is turned off activates the style and vice versa.

Note that when printing to PostScript printers, you cannot apply a style over a font that already includes that style. For example, if you choose the Helvetica Bold typeface and then choose Type⇨Type Style⇨Bold, PageMaker doesn't make the Helvetica Bold type any bolder. Instead, PageMaker ignores the Bold command. You can, however, apply styles on top of styles with many non-PostScript printers.

If the first press of a shortcut or formatting button doesn't work, try it again. If the first few characters you've selected are already formatted in the style you're selecting, you may have to choose the option twice to affect all the text.

Enlarging and Reducing Type

As with font and typestyle, you can choose a type size by using the Control palette. Select the text you want to enlarge or reduce, choose a new type size from the Size pop-up menu (labeled back in Figure 6-1), and then click on the Apply button or press Return. Or, if you prefer, choose Type⇨Size and click on one of the available type sizes.

✔ The options on the Control palette and the Size menu represent the most commonly used type sizes — based on sizes used back in the old hot-lead days. But they're no more acceptable than thousands of other possible type sizes you can use. To specify your own custom size, double-click on the Size option box, enter the size you want, and click on the Apply button or press Return. Or choose Type⇨Size⇨Other, enter a value in the option box, and press Return. You can even enter decimal values, such as 11.3 and 21.5.

✔ Press ⌘+Shift+period to enlarge the selected type to the next option in the pop-up menu. Press ⌘+Shift+comma to reduce the type. For example, press ⌘+period to enlarge 24-point type to 30-point type; press ⌘+Shift+comma to reduce 12-point type to 11-point type. If you want to be even more exact, you can enlarge or reduce text in 1-point increments by pressing ⌘+Option+Shift+period or ⌘+Option+Shift+comma.

✔ By changing the type size, you scale text proportionally; that is, you enlarge or reduce text the same amount horizontally and vertically. But you can also scale the width of selected characters independently of their height by changing the Width value in the Control palette (labeled back in Figure 6-1) or by choosing options from the Type⇨Set Width submenu.

Choose a value larger than 100 percent to expand type; choose a value lower than 100 percent to condense it. To enter a custom percentage value, double-click on the Width option box in the Control palette, enter the value, and click on the Apply button. Or choose Type⇨Set Width⇨Other and enter a new value.

✔ If you don't like the way your expanded or condensed text looks, select 100% from the pop-up menu, choose Type⇨Set Width⇨Normal or press ⌘+Shift+X to restore the type to its proportional type size.

Spacing Out

Another way to change the appearance of your text is to adjust the amount of vertical and horizontal space between characters. Spacing is one of the most important aspects of page design, because it determines the visual relationship between individual characters and entire lines of type.

Figure 6-4, for example, shows two paragraphs of text, identical in content, font, typestyle, and size. Only the spacing is different. The left paragraph uses tight vertical spacing and loose horizontal spacing between words. The paragraph isn't entirely illegible, but it's difficult to read because your eye is tempted to read downward, in the direction of least resistance: "We United mined . . ." and so on. In the right-hand paragraph, the vertical spacing is increased and the space between words is decreased, eliminating any question as to the direction in which words should be read.

Figure 6-4:
Two identical columns of text subjected to different vertical and horizontal spacing.

> We, the people of the United Nations, determined to save succeeding generations from the scourge of war, which twice in our lifetime has brought untold sorrow to mankind, and to reaffirm faith in fundamental human rights, in the dignity and worth of the human person, in the equal right of men and women and of nations large and small, and to establish conditions under which justice and respect for

> We, the people of the United Nations, determined to save succeeding generations from the scourge of war, which twice in our lifetime has brought untold sorrow to mankind, and to reaffirm faith in fundamental human rights, in the dignity and worth of the human person, in the equal right of men and women and of nations large and small, and to establish conditions under which justice and re-

The concept of character spacing is pretty straightforward, but the actual process is more involved. You can specify the amount of space between lines of type, the amount of space between one word and the next, the amount of space between individual letters within a single word, the amount of space between paragraphs and columns — well, you get the idea. Spacing is a lot of work.

Leading is the space between the lines

As explained in Chapter 4, *leading* (pronounced *ledding*) refers to the distance from the baseline of one line of type to the baseline of the next line of type. (For a refresher course on baselines, leading, and other text-measurement terms, flip back to the "Type size terminology" section of Chapter 4.) Leading is measured in points, just like type size.

Back in the old days, printers used to space out lines of type by inserting horizontal strips of lead between them. More lead strips meant more space between lines. Hence, the space between lines came to be known as *leading*.

Now lead is dead, but its legacy lives on. In an effort to make the idea a little more straightforward to new users, some programs call the space between lines of type *line spacing*. But PageMaker, possibly in reverence to Aldus Manutius and all those other dusty old gaffers, sticks with *leading*. Long live tradition, even if it does require two paragraphs of explanation.

- ✔ To change the leading between selected lines of text, choose a new value from the Control palette's Leading pop-up menu. (It's the first one to the right of the typestyle buttons.) Or choose an option from the Type⇨Leading submenu.

- ✔ To space body text, you generally should stick with the Auto setting, which is 120 percent of the type size. This amount of leading gives the text more room to breathe and makes it easier to read. For headlines and other large type, match the leading size to the type size — an arrangement known as *solid leading*.

- ✔ Using the Auto setting can create a problem if a line of type contains differently sized characters — for example, a drop cap mixed with regular body text. PageMaker bases the Auto leading amount on the largest character, which can result in unevenly spaced lines of text. If you're working with this sort of text, turn off Auto leading and choose a leading setting from the Leading pop-up menu.

- ✔ If you want to double-space the text — say, for a copy-editing draft or a preliminary report — choose the second-to-last option in the pop-up menu or Type⇨Leading submenu. Choose the last option in either menu to triple-space the text.

- ✔ Remember reading that the Auto leading setting is equal to 120 percent of the type size? Well, that's the Auto leading setting when you first use PageMaker, but it doesn't have to remain that way. If you decide that you prefer some other automatic leading amount, choose Type⇨Paragraph and click on the Spacing button to display the Paragraph Spacing Attributes dialog box (it's shown in Figure 6-5 if you want to take a peek ahead). Then enter a new value into the Autoleading option box. All text formatted with the Auto leading setting changes to your new specification. If you make changes with no documents open, the setting becomes the default for all future documents.

- ✔ While you're in the Paragraph Spacing Attributes dialog box, change the Leading Method option from Proportional to Baseline. Doing so doesn't noticeably affect your document; it just requires the document to use the leading method that's used by typographers, which helps ensure good output when you send files to a service bureau or professional printer for printing.

The leading options control the space between individual lines of text in a paragraph. To change the amount of space between paragraphs, you need to switch the Control palette to paragraph mode and change the values in the Space Above and Space Below pop-up menus, as explained in Chapter 7.

Word and letter spacing

Word spacing determines the width of the space between each word and its neighbor; *letter spacing* determines the horizontal space between individual characters (whether they're letters, numbers, punctuation, or some other kind of symbol).

To access PageMaker's word and letter spacing options, you have to leave the comfort and safety of the Control palette. Choose Type⬦Paragraph or press ⌘+M (as in, "*My*, that's a curious shortcut."). Then click on the Spacing button to display the Paragraph Spacing Attributes dialog box, shown in Figure 6-5.

Figure 6-5:
You can
change
word and
letter
spacing
options in
this dialog
box.

Paragraph Spacing Attributes

Word space:			Letter space:			
Minimum	75	%	Minimum	-5	%	OK
Desired	100	%	Desired	0	%	Cancel
Maximum	125	%	Maximum	25	%	Reset

Pair kerning: ☒ Auto above 4 points

Leading method: Autoleading:
○ Proportional   120 % of point size
○ Top of caps
◉ Baseline

Looks confusing, huh? Well, in fact, this dialog box *is* pretty confusing. What with all those Minimum and Maximum values to set, you can get mired down in this dialog box pretty quickly. So instead of giving you the long, drawn-out facts, here's the short story: Each value represents a percentage of a normal, every-day, space character. A value of 100 percent is a standard space, a value of 200 percent is the width of two spaces, and so on. The default letter spacing is 0 percent, because characters in the same word don't usually have any spaces between them.

PageMaker likes to have room to wiggle, so rather than setting the word and letter spacing to exact values, it asks you to specify a range. Tell PageMaker the Minimum space it can use when space is tight, the Maximum space it can use when there's plenty of room to maneuver, and the Desired space to hit when conditions are ideal. Consider *justified* text — text that lines up exactly on the left and right margins, as in a paperback novel. (You discover how to create justified type in Chapter 7.) To justify type, PageMaker needs to change the space between words and letters on the fly to accommodate each line of type. The Minimum and Maximum values represent the range PageMaker can work in.

Figure 6-6 shows text subject to different word and letter spacing values. Notice that the word spacing changes from one row to the next but remains constant throughout each row. Meanwhile, the letter spacing changes from one column to the next but remains constant throughout each column. Cool, huh? The values in the figure represent the values entered into the Desired option boxes.

When text is not justified — like the paragraphs in Figure 6-6 — PageMaker spaces text according to the Desired value alone. This fact brings up one more rule: The Desired value must be smaller than the Maximum value and larger than the Minimum value. So to lower the Desired word spacing to 50 percent in Figure 6-6, for example, the Minimum value has to be 50 percent or lower.

So now you know how to change word and letter spacing. But the real question is *why,* isn't it? Well, to be perfectly honest, letter and word spacing don't rate very high on the list of controls you may use frequently. In a pinch, when you need to cram lots of type into a small area or spread out sparse type to fill an empty page, word spacing and letter spacing can provide a quick solution.

But spacing changes are a forced solution at best. As you can see from Figure 6-6, most spacing alterations — especially changes in letter spacing — yield some pretty unreadable results. The more attractive *and* more convenient solution is to adjust type size and leading. If making adjustments is not practical — for example, you generally wouldn't want to apply a size and leading to one paragraph that is different from the size and leading of another paragraph in the same story — use letter spacing and word spacing as a last resort.

Figure 6-6:
Three varieties of word spacing meet with three varieties of letter spacing. The center example shows unaltered text.

W: 50%, L: 75%	W: 50%, L: 100%	W: 50%, L: 125%
We, the people of the United Nations, determined to save succeeding generations from the scourge of war, which twice in our lifetime has brought untold sorrow to mankind, and to reaffirm faith in fundamental human rights, in the dignity and worth of the human person, in the equal right of men and women	We, the people of the United Nations, determined to save succeeding generations from the scourge of war, which twice in our lifetime has brought untold sorrow to mankind, and to reaffirm faith in fundamental human rights, in the dignity and worth of the human person, in the equal	We, the people of the United Nations, determined to save succeeding generations from the scourge of war, which twice in our lifetime has brought untold sorrow to mankind, and to reaffirm faith in fundamental human rights, in the dignity and worth of the
W: 100%, L: 75%	**W: 100%, L: 100%**	**W: 100%, L: 125%**
We, the people of the United Nations, determined to save succeeding generations from the scourge of war, which twice in our lifetime has brought untold sorrow to mankind, and to reaffirm faith in fundamental human rights, in the dignity and worth of the human person, in the equal right of men and women	We, the people of the United Nations, determined to save succeeding generations from the scourge of war, which twice in our lifetime has brought untold sorrow to mankind, and to reaffirm faith in fundamental human rights, in the dignity and worth of the human person, in the equal right of men and	We, the people of the United Nations, determined to save succeeding generations from the scourge of war, which twice in our lifetime has brought untold sorrow to mankind, and to reaffirm faith in fundamental human rights, in the dignity and worth of the
W: 150%, L: 75%	**W: 150%, L: 100%**	**W: 150%, L: 125%**
We, the people of the United Nations, determined to save succeeding generations from the scourge of war, which twice in our lifetime has brought untold sorrow to mankind, and to reaffirm faith in fundamental human rights, in the dignity and worth of the human person, in the equal right of men and	We, the people of the United Nations, determined to save succeeding generations from the scourge of war, which twice in our lifetime has brought untold sorrow to mankind, and to reaffirm faith in fundamental human rights, in the dignity and worth of the human person, in the equal	We, the people of the United Nations, determined to save succeeding generations from the scourge of war, which twice in our lifetime has brought untold sorrow to mankind, and to reaffirm faith in fundamental human rights, in the dignity and worth of the

However, changing the Maximum setting for Word Space to 125 to reduce the normal space between words is a good idea. PageMaker's default setting of 150 often results in a gap-toothed appearance.

Letter spacing's more sophisticated cousin: kerning

Kerning means to change the amount of space between a single pair of characters. In PageMaker, you can kern characters in two ways — automatically and manually.

Here's the lowdown on automatic kerning. Font designers specify that certain pairs of letters, called *kerning pairs*, should automatically be positioned more closely together than the standard letter spacing allows. The letters *T* and *o* are an example of a kerning pair. When placed next to each other, their normal side-by-side spacing results in an incongruously loose appearance, as demonstrated in the first example in Figure 6-7. By turning on the Pair Kerning check box in the Spacing Attributes dialog box (choose Type⇨Paragraph and click on the Spacing button), you instruct PageMaker to automatically kern all kerning pairs so they fit more snugly together, as shown in the second example in Figure 6-7.

Figure 6-7:
The *T* and *o*
kerning pair
when the
Pair Kerning
option is
turned off
(top) and on
(bottom).

Tomato
Tomato

If you're not satisfied with the amount of letter spacing between any two characters — whether or not the characters are defined as a kerning pair — you can adjust the kerning manually. Click between the two characters in question to position the insertion marker and then adjust the value in the Control palette's Kerning option box (the top option on the far right of the palette). Or press one of the following key combinations:

✔ Press ⌘+Delete or ⌘+Left arrow to kern the characters together $^1/_{25}$ of an em space. (An em space is roughly equivalent to the width of the letter *M* in the current type size.)

✔ Press ⌘+Shift+Delete or ⌘+Right arrow to kern the characters apart $^1/_{25}$ em space.

✔ For more precise work, press Option+Delete or ⌘+Shift+Left arrow to kern characters together $^1/_{100}$ em space.

✔ Press Option+Shift+Delete or ⌘+Shift+Right arrow to kern the characters apart $^1/_{100}$ em space.

For example, if you have 10-point type, pressing ⌘+Delete moves the characters 0.4 point closer ($^1/_{25}$ of 10 points = 0.4).

What the heck is tracking?

You can apply kerning across multiple characters at a time by using PageMaker's *tracking* options. *Tracking* is the smartest kind of letter spacing because it varies the spacing of entire selected stories in general increments and according to the type size of the text.

You can select a tracking option from the Tracking pop-up menu in the Control palette (it's the one with the three little *A*s above a horizontal arrow, shown back in Figure 6-1) or by making a selection from the Type⇨Expert Tracking submenu.

The Normal option loosens spacing by 1 percent when applied to 12-point type but tightens spacing when applied to 48-point type and larger. Tight loosens small text by half a percent but begins tightening spacing at 36-point and larger. Very Tight kerns text together regardless of size. Both Loose and Very Loose always loosen text to some degree. If you choose No Track, PageMaker doesn't apply any tracking at all.

The tracking setting should usually be set to Loose. If you think Loose is too spacey, choose Normal or Tight but definitely stay away from No Track, which is the default setting.

The Edit Tracks option in the Expert Tracking submenu enables you to permanently alter the way PageMaker tracks certain fonts. Stay away from this option until you get that PhD in typography.

Making characters jump off the baseline

The option box at the bottom right of the Control palette lets you shift characters up or down so that they rest above or below the baseline. Moving characters off the baseline can be helpful for creating special effects, such as the one shown in Figure 6-8.

Select the characters you want to shift and then click on the up or down arrows next to the option box to move them in .01 increments. Alternatively, you can change the Baseline Shift value in the Type Options dialog box, but you have to make your way through two levels of dialog boxes, so this method is reserved only for people with too much time on their hands.

If you want to change how far the characters shift with each click of an arrow, enter a new value into the Vertical Nudge option box in the Preferences dialog box (File➪Preferences).

Figure 6-8:
Using the baseline shift controls, you can make text leap off the baseline.

By now, your head's probably bursting with text formatting information — you probably never imagined that you could wreak such havoc on the alphabet. "But wait! There's more — much more!" Yes, for only $19.99, you get not only all this titillating information but also all the fascinating details provided in the next chapter, which provides even more ways to space, align, and otherwise manipulate your text. And you were wondering whether you paid too much for this book.

The 5th Wave By Rich Tennant

MY GOD! IT'S WORKING! I'M GETTING ITALICS!

Chapter 7
Making Your Text Feel Comfortable

• •

• •

*Y*ou know how you feel when you're jammed up against 20 strangers in an elevator that's designed to hold 15 people? Crowded, that's how. You can't move, you can't breathe, and you're pretty sure that surly-looking guy behind you didn't poke you in the back with his briefcase by accident.

Well, sometimes text feels just like that. Without enough white space to separate them, lines of text very quickly become uncomfortable and unpleasant. Pretty soon, the *T*s in one line are swiping at the tails of the *Y*s in the line above them, and the *g*s are grabbing the hats of the *F*s below them. You can have an all-out text shoving match going in no time. Not only do you wind up with cranky text, you create documents that look so text-heavy that no one wants to read them.

On the flip side of the coin, text can sometimes get so spread out that the characters become isolated and lonely. Although this scenario is decidedly an unhappy one for your text, it's doubly difficult for your readers, whose eyes have difficulty deciding what word they're supposed to read next.

As the master of your document, you need to give your text enough room to breathe without shoving words and letters so far apart that no one can tell what's what. Luckily, PageMaker's features give you precise control over text spacing.

Chapter 6 explains how to adjust the space between words, letters, and individual lines of text. But you can also fiddle with the spacing between paragraphs and the spacing between text and the surrounding margins or columns — all of which you discover how to do in this very chapter.

After you get the formatting for a paragraph of text just so, use PageMaker's *styles* to save your choices, as explained at the end of this chapter. Then, when you want to use the same formatting on another paragraph, you just choose the style from the Style palette or Control menu, and PageMaker applies all the formatting automatically. In addition to the spacing controls, you can record character formatting, such as font and type size, in a style.

Adjusting Paragraph Spacing

When you enter text into a document, a *paragraph break* — created by pressing Return — indicates the end of one paragraph and the beginning of the next. You can adjust the amount of space that comes before a paragraph and after a paragraph by choosing Type⇨Paragraph (⌘+M) and changing the Before and After values in the Paragraph Specifications dialog box. Or just enter new values into the Space Before and Space After option boxes on the Control palette.

To display the Control palette, choose Window⇨Control Palette (or press ⌘+apostrophe). Then select the Text tool and click on the paragraph mode icon on the left end of the palette to change from text mode (discussed in Chapter 6) to paragraph mode. Figure 7-1 shows the paragraph formatting that you can handle via the Control palette.

After you enter a value in one of the Control palette option boxes, click on the Apply button (labeled in Figure 7-1) or press Return to apply your changes. Or press Tab to apply your formatting and move to the next option box in the palette.

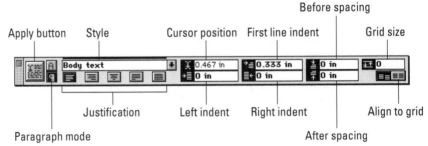

Figure 7-1: The Control palette as it appears in paragraph mode.

Before spacing
Apply button   Style   Cursor position   First line indent   Grid size
Justification   Left indent   Right indent   Align to grid
Paragraph mode   After spacing

Why does PageMaker offer you separate controls for the space before and after a paragraph? After all, if you insert space after one paragraph, PageMaker automatically adds space before the paragraph that follows. The reason is to gain greater control.

Suppose that you're creating styles to apply a set of custom formatting attributes to different kinds of paragraphs (as covered later in this chapter). You may want the heading style to include Before spacing, so that a big gap always appears before the headline. But you may want the caption style to include After spacing, so that a gap follows every caption. If PageMaker offered only Before spacing or After spacing, you wouldn't have this kind of flexibility.

Following are some tips to keep in mind when you're adjusting paragraph spacing:

✔ Unlike type size and leading, the Before and After values are not measured in points. Instead, they're measured in the current unit of measurement, which may be inches, picas, or millimeters, as discussed in the "Setting Rulers and Ruler Guides" section of Chapter 3. The unit in force is listed to the right of each option box.

✔ Don't just insert extra paragraph breaks to add space between paragraphs. Doing so can screw up your layout — if one of those extra paragraph breaks ends up at the top of a column, for example, you'll be left with unwanted space. So always use the Before and After spacing options to put space between paragraphs.

✔ If you *want* an extra space at the top of a column or page, though, you have to create that space using a paragraph break (press Return) because you can't apply Before spacing to a paragraph that's placed at the top of a column or page. Likewise, you can't add After spacing to a paragraph that's at the bottom of a column or page.

✔ You can break a line at any point without inserting a paragraph break by pressing Shift+Return. This is known as inserting a *line break.* Lines separated by line breaks remain part of the same paragraph.

The Paragraph Specifications dialog box, shown in Figure 7-2, offers a bunch of other options to help you control how your paragraphs are placed within a column or page:

✔ Column Break Before and Page Break Before enable you to insert a column or page break before a selected paragraph. Use these options when you want to be sure that a paragraph appears at the top of a column or page.

✔ It's considered a publishing faux pas when the last line of a paragraph appears in a different column or page than the rest of its paragraph. It's considered equally gauche to let a page break or column break separate the first line of a paragraph from the rest of the paragraph. When the solo line is the last line of the paragraph, it's called a *widow*; when it's the first line, it's an *orphan.* The Widow and Orphan Control settings keep you from making such gaffes.

Paragraph Specifications

Indents: Paragraph space:

Left [0] inches   Before [0] inches

First [0] inches   After [0] inches

Right [0] inches

[OK]

[Cancel]

[Rules...]

[Spacing...]

Alignment: [Left]   Dictionary: [US English]

Options:

☐ Keep lines together   ☐ Keep with next [0] lines

☐ Column break before   ☐ Widow control [0] lines

☐ Page break before   ☐ Orphan control [0] lines

☐ Include in table of contents

Figure 7-2:
You can set paragraph indents, spacing, and alignment controls in this dialog box.

You can tell PageMaker that if it needs to put a page or column break in the middle of a paragraph, it must place the break a certain number of lines away from the first or last line. You specify the number of lines in the Widow and Orphan Control option boxes. Most of the time, though, you can just leave these options unchecked and say to heck with elitist publishing snobs. If it really bothers you to have a single line of a paragraph at the bottom or top of a column, set both values to 1 or 2.

✔ If you don't want a paragraph to break at the end of a page or column, select the paragraph and then select the Keep Lines Together option. Often, though, you end up with uneven columns at the bottom of your page when you use this option.

✔ To make sure that the last line of a paragraph is placed directly above the first line of the following paragraph, select the Keep With Next option. In the option box, specify how many lines in the second paragraph need to be kept together with the last line of the first paragraph. This option is very useful for keeping subheads or heads with the first paragraph in the section. Without this option, subheads and heads can sometimes wind up isolated at the bottom of a page or column.

✔ To further separate your paragraphs from each other — or to separate a group of paragraphs from the surrounding text — you can add a thin line (called a *rule* in publishing jargon). Click on the Rules button to tell PageMaker where to put the rule and how big to make it. You can also draw rules with the Line tool, as explained in Chapter 10.

If you want to adjust the space between the individual lines in a paragraph, switch the Control palette to text mode and change the value in the Leading option box, as explained in Chapter 6.

Indenting Paragraphs

To indent a selected paragraph, enter new values into the Indents option boxes in the Control palette (labeled in Figure 7-1) or in the Paragraph Specifications dialog box (choose Type➪Paragraph or press ⌘+M). The options work as follows:

- **Left:** Enter a value into this option box to indent the entire left side of a paragraph.

- **First:** This option is the most useful. Use it to indent only the first line of text in a paragraph, rather than using a tab. Note that PageMaker indents the first line relative to the left indent setting; if you set the left indent at 1 inch and first indent at 1 inch, for example, the first line of the text is indented 2 inches from the margin. To create a *hanging indent* — that is, an indent in which the first line is shoved to the left of the rest of the paragraph, enter a negative first-line indent value. Chapter 8 shows how to use hanging indents to create numbered and bulleted lists.

- **Right:** Enter a value into this option box to indent the entire right side of a paragraph. By creating both a left indent and a right indent, you can reduce the width of the paragraph, as you may want to do to indicate a long quote in a document.

The option box directly above the Left Indent option on the Control palette shows the horizontal position of your cursor. (You can't change this value; it's just a reference guide.) Knowing the cursor position can come in handy when you're setting indents. You can click at the spot where you want to position your indent, note the cursor position, and enter that same value in the appropriate Indent option box.

You get an error message if your left indent, or the combination of your first-line indent and your left indent, is a negative number. PageMaker simply won't let you have the text extend to the left of the column margin.

If you're like most new users, you're probably thinking, "Why not just enter a tab to indent the paragraphs? It's not like it takes a lot of time. It may even be easier than dealing with these weird option boxes." The answer is, indents are more flexible. Say that you set up first-line indents throughout your document. You show the finished result to your boss, who says, "Dang, that's good! Just one thing: I don't like the indents. Get rid of them."

If you use tabs, you have to delete every one of them manually. If you use indents, no problem. Just select all the text, change the first-line indent value, and you're finished.

Either way, be sure to exclaim, "Wow, that was certainly a lot of work deleting all those tabs!" so that your boss thinks you're working hard.

Aligning Lines of Type

PageMaker gives you two ways to align the line of type in your paragraphs. First, you can change the *justification,* which refers to the way the lines of text align respective to the left and right edges of a margin or column. Second, you can adjust the vertical position of lines of text in one column to align them with lines of text in a neighboring column.

Choosing a justification option

You have five different justification choices, which you can select by clicking on the alignment icons on the Control palette (see Figure 7-3) or by choosing commands from the Type⇨Alignment submenu.

Figure 7-3: The Control palette's justification buttons.

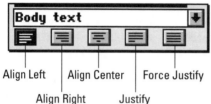

Align Left | Align Center | Force Justify

Align Right | Justify

Figure 7-4 shows examples of all but one of the alignment options, Force Justify. The only difference between the Justify alignment option and the Force Justify option is that Force Justify justifies every line of type without exception, while Justify justifies all but the last line of type (as in the figure).

Now, just because you have five alignment options doesn't mean that you have to use them all in the same document. Copy that's aligned left — more commonly known as *flush left* or *ragged right* copy — generally looks best when combined with a flush left headline, for example. In fact, the only alignment option that's guaranteed to look great in any kind of document is flush left. Some designers even go so far as to argue that a flush left paragraph's ragged appearance lends visual interest to the text and helps to compensate for much of the back-and-forth monotony of reading.

Justified text is also very popular but is applicable almost exclusively to body copy. And because of its rigidly formal appearance, justified text can be limited in its appeal; it looks great in the *Wall Street Journal* but can look square, stodgy, and downright uninteresting when used in a flier or advertisement. In the case of body copy, the general rule of thumb is this: Align short blocks of text flush left; reserve justification (called *full justification* by some folks) for very long documents.

Align Left (ragged right)

We, the people of the United Nations, determined to save succeeding generations from the scourge of war, which twice in our lifetime has brought untold sorrow to mankind, and to reaffirm faith in fundamental human rights, in the dignity and worth of the human person,
in the equal right of men and women and of nations large and small, and to establish conditions under which justice and respect for the obligations arising from treaties and other sources of law can be maintained.

Align Center

We, the people of the United Nations, determined to save succeeding generations from the scourge of war, which twice in our lifetime has brought untold sorrow to mankind, and to reaffirm faith in fundamental human rights, in the dignity and worth of the human person,
in the equal right of men and women and of nations large and small, and to establish conditions under which justice and respect for the obligations
arising from treaties and other sources of law can be maintained.

Align Right (ragged left)

We, the people of the United Nations, determined to save succeeding generations from the scourge of war, which twice in our lifetime has brought untold sorrow to mankind, and to reaffirm faith in fundamental human rights, in the dignity and worth of the human person,
in the equal right of men and women and of nations large and small, and to establish conditions under which justice and respect for the obligations arising from treaties and other sources of law can be maintained.

Justify

We, the people of the United Nations, determined to save succeeding generations from the scourge of war, which twice in our lifetime has brought untold sorrow to mankind, and to reaffirm faith in fundamental human rights, in the dignity and worth of the human person, in the equal right of men and women and of nations large and small, and to establish conditions under which justice and respect for the obligations arising from treaties and other sources of international law can be maintained.

Figure 7-4:
Four of PageMaker's alignment options. The gray lines represent the axis to which the text block is aligned.

To align text from the keyboard, select your text and the press ⌘+Shift with the first letter of the alignment option. For example, ⌘+Shift+L aligns selected text left, ⌘+Shift+R aligns it right, and ⌘+Shift+J justifies it. Press ⌘+Shift+F (as in *Force* Justify) to justify every line of text, including the last, and press ⌘+Shift+C to center it.

Aligning text in neighboring columns

Figure 7-5 illustrates a problem you may encounter when your columns of text include large headlines or graphic elements. The headline or graphic may shove subsequent lines of text out of vertical alignment with the text in the neighboring column. The result is an unprofessional, sloppy look.

To bring the wayward text into alignment, first note the leading value used for the text. Then enter that value into the Grid Size option box in the Control palette (it's the top option at the right end of the palette). Then select the paragraph *before* the one that contains the misaligned text and click on Align to Grid icon in the Control palette (it's labeled in Figure 7-1).

Alternatively, you can choose Type⇨Paragraph, click on the Rules button, click on the Options button, and then choose the Align Next Paragraph to Grid check box in the Paragraph Rule Options dialog box. What a lot of work! (But this extra effort is sometimes necessary, such as when you're creating styles, as explained at the end of this chapter.)

You can't use this method to align text in paragraphs that use different leading amounts. Also, you may need to adjust the size of your text blocks slightly to make up for the shift in text.

Figure 7-5:
Use the
Align to Grid
feature to fix
this kind of
misaligned
type across
columns.

Text doesn't line up; causes fits of hysteria

Doctors are reporting seeing an increasing number of patients who become distraught after reading documents in which the baselines of text in neigborhing columns don't align.

The problem is easily avoided, says researcher P. H. Michael, a respected scientist who specializes in the field of type-alignment anxiety. "If people would just learn to use the Align to Grid option," says Michael, "we wouldn't have so many stressed out people coming into our offices for help."

Setting Tabs

Tabs can be useful when you want to align columns of data, such as in the tables used in this book. To set tabs for a particular paragraph, select the paragraph and then choose Type⇨Indents/Tabs or press ⌘+I to open the Indents/Tabs dialog box, shown in Figure 7-6.

To set tabs for an entire story, click with the Text tool inside the text block, press ⌘+A (or choose Edit⇨Select All) to select all the text, and then choose the Indents/Tabs command. To establish default tab settings, choose the command when no document is open.

Although you can set paragraph indents in the Indents/Tabs dialog box, using the Control palette or the Paragraph Specifications dialog box, as explained earlier in this chapter, is much easier. Using the ruler in the Indents/Tabs dialog box can be tricky, even if it is a more visual approach. Of course, if you feel more comfortable setting indents here, go for it. But all those little tab and indent thingamabobs floating around can get pretty confusing.

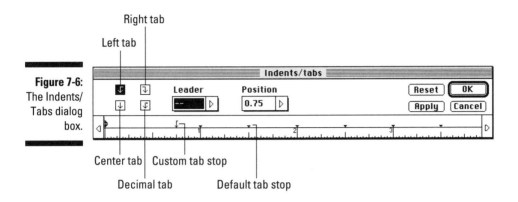

Figure 7-6:
The Indents/
Tabs dialog
box.

Setting tabs can be dicey because no matter how carefully you map out where
you think tab stops should be for particular text, things often don't work out
right the first time. That's why an Apply button is in this dialog box: If you click
on the Apply button after setting tab stops, PageMaker displays the currently
selected text with these tab settings applied (the text has to have tab characters in it, of course). If the tabs aren't right, just change them or click on Cancel
to get out of the dialog box. (The Reset button puts back the default tab
settings: a left-aligned tab every half inch.)

To create tabs, follow these steps after opening the Indents/Tabs dialog box:

1. Click anywhere on the ruler to create a tab stop.

You can select the tab and drag it to change its location. When you add a
tab, PageMaker automatically gets rid of all the default tab stops to the left
of the new tab. If you set another tab stop, any default tabs between that
tab and the first one you created are deleted.

**2. Click on the icon representing the alignment you want the tab stop
to have.**

The top two icons represent left alignment and right alignment, respectively; the bottom two icons are for center and decimal alignment. In a left-
aligned tab, text after the tab character begins at the tab location and
continues to the right. In a right-aligned tab, text typed after the tab
character ends at the tab and begins to the left. In a center tab, the tab
becomes the center point for text entered after the tab. In a decimal tab,
text (usually numbers) aligns on the first period (decimal point) found
after the tab character. Or, if no decimal point is present, the text is aligned
on the rightmost number or character.

3. If you want a tab leader, select a leader type.

A *leader* is a repeating sequence of characters, usually periods, that fills
the space between the text before the tab and the text after the tab. The
Leader pop-up menu offers four leader options: periods, dashes, underlines, and Custom. If you choose Custom, you can enter up to two custom

characters into the Leader option box. (If you enter two, the characters alternate, such as *+*+*+*+*+.) Actually, you don't have to go to the trouble of choosing Custom to enter custom leader characters; just enter them into the Leader option box, and PageMaker understands that you want to use the Custom option.

4. Repeat Steps 1 through 3 for each tab you want to create.

You should know a few other things about using tabs:

- ✔ The Position pop-up menu offers these choices: Add Tab, Delete Tab, Move Tab, and Repeat Tab.

- ✔ Don't bother using the Position pop-up menu for its first two options (Add Tab, Delete Tab). Just click on the ruler to insert a tab stop and drag a tab marker away from the ruler to delete it.

- ✔ The Move Tab option is good for precisely positioning a tab stop. Just click on the tab to select it, enter a new value in the Position option box, and then select the Move Tab option. The tab moves to the numerical location you indicated.

- ✔ The Repeat Tab option also comes in handy and works as follows: Suppose that you have a five-inch column. If you define a tab stop at the one-inch mark and select Repeat Tab from the Position pop-up menu, you get a tab every inch across the column.

- ✔ If you have very wide columns, the entire column may not display in the Indents/Tabs dialog box. Use the arrow icons at the far left and right of the dialog box to scroll through the column.

- ✔ When creating a style to automate paragraph formatting (as explained later in this chapter, in the section "Letting Style Sheets Do the Formatting"), set only those tab stops that you'll use frequently. You can always use the Indents/Tabs dialog box to set individual tab stops for specific paragraphs.

- ✔ Don't use tab stops to indent the first line of a paragraph. Instead, use the first-line indent control, as explained earlier, in the section, "Indenting Paragraphs."

Controlling Hyphenation

Hyphenation is a mark of professionalism in publishing. It has nothing to do with proving that you remember how to properly hyphenate words, such as *hy-phen-at-ed*. It has to do with the more mundane fact that hyphenation gives typesetters more opportunities to create even spacing, because they have more chances of having a similar number of characters on each line.

The narrower your columns, the more you'll want hyphenation, because the narrower the columns, the more chances that you'll get awkward spacing if you turn hyphenation off. Fortunately, PageMaker does the hyphenation for you.

In Version 5, you pressed the shortcut ⌘+H to access the hyphenation controls. That shortcut now displays the Master Pages palette (covered in Chapter 14). Sadly, PageMaker no longer offers a shortcut for the Hyphenation function.

To tell PageMaker how you want to hyphenate your text, choose Type⇨Hyphenation. The Hyphenation dialog box, shown in Figure 7-7, appears. The options are simple:

✔ Keep Hyphenation set to On for most text. Exceptions are headlines and other large text.

✔ Select the radio button for Manual Plus Dictionary as the hyphenation method. PageMaker looks at a dictionary of words for your current language rather than figure out where the hyphens go on its own. (That's what Manual Plus Algorithm does — and it's no match for using a dictionary, even if it is a little faster.) The Manual Only setting requires you to insert hyphens yourself using ⌘+hyphen, which defeats the purpose of automatic hyphenation in the first place.

Figure 7-7:
Choose your hyphenation settings here.

```
╔══════════════ Hyphenation ══════════════╗
║                                          ║
║ Hyphenation: ● On  ○ Off    ┌────────┐  ║
║                             │   OK   │  ║
║  ○ Manual only              └────────┘  ║
║  ● Manual plus dictionary   ┌────────┐  ║
║  ○ Manual plus algorithm    │ Cancel │  ║
║                             └────────┘  ║
║                             ┌────────┐  ║
║ Limit consecutive hyphens to: │ Add... │ ║
║                      ┌───┐   └────────┘  ║
║                      │ 3 │               ║
║ Hyphenation zone: [0.5    ] inches       ║
╚══════════════════════════════════════════╝
```

✔ You can have a serious argument with a professional typographer over the best setting for Limit Consecutive Hyphens To. Choose a number between 2 and 4, and you'll be all right. The higher the number, the more consecutive lines can end with a hyphen. The more such lines, the harder it is for your eye to track which line to jump to next. Conservative typographers say to set this value to 2, although moderates say 3. The more adventurous among us say set this value at 4. After all, if you have four hyphenated lines in a row and they're making the text hard to read, you can always manually override the hyphenation.

✔ To override hyphenation, enter ⌘+hyphen — called a *discretionary hyphen* or a *soft hyphen* — at your preferred hyphenation spot. Doing so doesn't guarantee that the word will be hyphenated, only that *if* PageMaker needs to hyphenate the word, it will put the hyphen at the spot you indicated. (Entering ⌘+hyphen right before a word tells PageMaker not to hyphenate it.) *Never* hyphenate by using the keyboard hyphen character — if the text wraps, the hyphen moves with it, and you have stray hyphens in your text.

✔ Set the Hyphenation Zone between 0.2 and 0.6 inches — the default 0.5 is fine for most text, although for narrow columns (3 inches or less), a smaller value gives PageMaker more flexibility. PageMaker does not hyphenate a word that begins within the hyphenation zone. Hence, the rule is this: The larger the zone, the fewer hyphenations and the rougher the rag of the text; the smaller the zone, the more hyphenated words and the smoother the rag.

✔ To establish new default settings that will be applied to all new documents, choose Type⇨Hyphenation when no document is open.

Sometimes, PageMaker doesn't know how to hyphenate a word — maybe it's a company name or a rarely used word, or maybe it's a word like *project* that is hyphenated different ways depending on whether it is a verb or a noun. You can add such words to PageMaker's dictionary by clicking on the Add button in the Hyphenation dialog box. The process is the same as adding words in the Spelling dialog box, as described in Chapter 5, in the section "Teaching PageMaker to spell."

If you highlight the word in your document before opening the Hyphenation dialog box, the word appears in the Word option box, all ready for your edits, after you click on the Add button.

Letting Style Sheets Do the Formatting

Styles — also called *style sheets* — enable you to apply a bunch of different formatting options (type size, style, paragraph indents, leading, and so forth) with just a mouse click or two. Although you may take a while to get into the habit of using styles, once you do, you'll find it well worth the effort.

For example, if you decide that you want all your headlines to appear in a particular typestyle and size, with a certain amount of before and after paragraph spacing, and with the Align Next Paragraph to Grid feature turned on, you can create a style called *Headlines.* Then, instead of formatting each headline one by one, first setting the style, then the size, and then the paragraph spacing, and so on, you just apply the Headline style to the appropriate heads. PageMaker automatically does all your formatting for you.

You might create one style for your first-level headlines, one for second-level heads, one for body text, and one for your picture captions. Styles not only give you more time to work on more important matters than formatting, they ensure consistency. You don't have to remember from one day to the next what formatting you're supposed to use for a particular text element.

Creating and editing styles

Here's how to define a new style:

1. Choose Type⇨Define Styles or use the shortcut, ⌘+3.

PageMaker displays the Define Styles dialog box, shown in Figure 7-8. If you selected text before opening up the dialog box, the [Selection] option is highlighted, which means that PageMaker has collected all formatting information for the selected text and will base the new style's characteristics on it. If no text is selected, the new style is based on the characteristics of a style called No Style, which all PageMaker documents have.

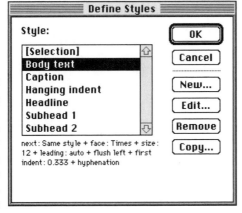

Figure 7-8:
You can create new styles or edit existing styles in this dialog box.

2. Click on the New button.

You get the Edit Style dialog box, shown in Figure 7-9. Enter the name of the new style in the Name field. Notice that the Based On and Next Style fields are already filled in, either with No Style or whatever style was applied to the text that was selected when you entered the Define Styles dialog box. If you want to base the new style on a different style, select that style from the Based On pop-up menu.

Microsoft Word defines a default style called Normal, and chances are that the text you create in Word has this style applied (it is, after all, the default). If you create a style in PageMaker called Normal, Word text using the Normal is redefined to use the PageMaker Normal style.

Using styles saves you from having to apply your basic body style — the style used for the bulk of your text — in PageMaker. It's especially handy because you can't edit the settings for No Style, so you can't really use that as your body style. (The chances that the No Style formatting will match your body style's settings are close to zero.)

Figure 7-9:
You can define the settings for a new style or change settings for an existing style in this dialog box.

Edit Style

Name: `Body lead`

Based on: `Body text`

Next style: `Same style`

Body text + next: Same style

[OK]
[Cancel]
[Type...]
[Para...]
[Tabs...]
[Hyph...]

3. Choose a Next Style option.

Some text elements are always followed by text that has a different style. For example, a byline may always be followed by text that uses the Normal style. In cases such as this, you should set the Next Style option box to that other style (use the pop-up menu to select any existing style). Otherwise, select Same Style.

4. Use the Type, Para, Tabs, and Hyph buttons to access the Type Specifications, Paragraph Specifications, Indents/Tabs, and Hyphenation dialog boxes.

This is the point at which you specify how you want to format any text to which you apply the style. Set the options in the various dialog boxes just as you do to format text normally.

If you check the Include in Table of Contents check box in the Paragraph Specifications dialog box, the style that you're creating or editing is included in any table of contents generated by PageMaker for the document. Chapter 15 explains how to create a table of contents.

5. Click on OK in each dialog box until all dialog boxes are gone.

Congratulations! You have a new style.

And now for a few final thoughts on styles:

✔ To modify an existing style, use the Define Styles dialog box just as if you were creating a new style, but click on the Edit button instead of the New button. You can delete a style by clicking on the Remove button.

✔ If you want to use styles defined in another PageMaker document, click on the Copy button and find the document through the dialog box. After you select the document, click on OK. You may get a prompt asking whether it's okay to copy over existing styles. If you give PageMaker the go-ahead, any style in your current document whose name is the same as in the other document is replaced by the other document's style. Be careful when using this feature.

✔ You can define styles based on the formatting of existing text. One way is to select some formatted text and go to the Define Styles dialog box as described earlier; the formatting of the selected text becomes part of the new style. Or you can use the Control palette instead. To use this method, click with the Text tool inside the paragraph that contains the formatting you want to turn into a style. Make sure that the Control palette is in paragraph mode, highlight the style name, enter a new name, and press Return. The result is a new style.

A similar technique is to highlight the text, hold down the ⌘ key, and click on No Style in the Styles palette, shown in Figure 7-10. (To display the palette, press ⌘+Y or choose Window⇨Styles.) Doing so takes you to the Edit Style dialog box, in which you can enter the new style name and make changes. This method isn't as fast as the Control palette method, but it does let you make further changes to the style more easily. You can also ⌘+click on an existing style name in the Styles palette to edit the style.

✔ You may notice that a paragraph's style name sometimes has a plus sign after it. The plus sign means that the selected paragraph's formatting has been modified from the style's settings. Perhaps, for example, you italicized some text or changed the margin for that paragraph. Note that the text cursor has to be on the modified portion of the paragraph; the plus sign appears only if the currently selected text in the paragraph is different from the style settings.

✔ To make the styles you define available to all future documents, close all open documents and then define or edit your styles. To be safe, quit PageMaker after you finish defining your default styles. PageMaker saves the default settings to disk when you quit the program. Doing so ensures that, if your machine crashes or you encounter a system error, you don't lose all your work.

Figure 7-10:
The Styles palette offers a quick way to create, edit, and apply styles.

Importing styles

When you import text from a word processor and check the Retain Format check box (in the Place dialog box), PageMaker loads any styles and text formatting defined in the word processor document. PageMaker adds many default formatting settings for options that the word processor doesn't offer, such as tracking. But the basics — such as font, size, indents, and alignment — are all brought into PageMaker along with the text.

The Place dialog box offers an option called Read Tags. You may think that you need to check this box in order to import your styles — especially if you're familiar with programs that use the term "style tags" instead of "styles." But if you select the Read Tags option, you actually are turning off the automatic style-import feature. You use the Read Tags option to import text that was formatted to work with earlier versions of PageMaker, in which you placed the style name, enclosed in angle brackets, at the beginning of a paragraph to indicate what style you wanted PageMaker to apply to the text. (If you want PageMaker to give a paragraph the Body Text style, for example, you place the code <Body Text> at the beginning of the paragraph.) You can still use this method if you're importing text from a word-processing program that doesn't offer styles. It's time-consuming, and you may find it easier to simply format the text in PageMaker, but if you want to take a crack at using tags, the PageMaker manual gives you the lowdown on all the codes and formatting requirements.)

Sometimes, the text you're importing has a style name not defined in PageMaker. When this happens, PageMaker creates a new style (based on No Style). PageMaker adds an asterisk (*) to the style name so that you can tell that the style is undefined in PageMaker. If you don't have a Credit style in PageMaker but a Credit style is in an imported Word document, for example, PageMaker applies a style called *Credit** to the paragraphs coded with Credit. Simply edit the style settings the normal way and change the name back to *Credit*.

Applying styles to paragraphs

To apply a style to a paragraph, just click inside the paragraph with the Text tool, click on a style name in the Control palette, and then click on the Apply button or press Return. To apply styles to a range of paragraphs, click with the Text tool in the first paragraph, press Shift, click inside the last paragraph in the range, and then choose a style name in the Contol palette. You can apply styles in Story Editor view (explained in Chapter 5) and in Layout view.

For another way to choose styles, display the Styles palette by choosing Window⇨Styles or pressing ⌘+Y. Then click on a style name to apply the style to the selected text. If your document uses lots of styles, using the Styles palette instead of the Control palette to choose styles may be easier because you can resize the palette as needed to display all your style names at once.

To view all styles applied to your document, switch to Story Editor view and choose Story⇨Display Style Names. (For more information about the Story Editor, see Chapter 5.)

Styles are but one of the features that PageMaker offers to automate the formatting of your text. PageMaker also provides commands that add page numbers to your document, create drop caps and bulleted lists, and insert all kinds of special typographic symbols. Intrigued? Well, we wrote the next chapter just to satisfy your curiosity.

Chapter 8

Fancy Type Tricks

Chapters 5 through 7 cover all the practical-but-boring stuff you can do with text. Now it's time to discover a few fancy text tricks. This chapter explains how to create and use drop caps, reverse text, special symbols, and a bunch of other neat stuff. You also find out how to create professional-looking bulleted and numbered lists.

But before we begin, a little cautionary note is in order: Use these effects sparingly. Why? Well, a document filled with fancy text tricks is kind of like a barking dog. A few tricks, like a few barks, attract attention and get people to read your document, which is always job number one. But if you throw in too many tricks, the document starts barking so loudly and so frequently that your reader is unable to focus on your message. An overly fancy document can appear pathetic and even irritating in its desire to attract attention. As any dog learns after it chews up your favorite pair of slippers, there's good attention and there's bad attention, and the quality of the attention generally works inversely to the quantity. In other words, a little goes a long way.

Begin with a Big Cap

One of the easiest ways to make your document look a little more lively is to start each story off with a bang. A big capital letter at the beginning of an article can help set it apart from neighboring articles. It also serves as a visual guide-post, clearly showing where the article begins.

There are two kinds of big caps: the *initial cap,* which is basically just a big capital letter at the beginning of a story, and the *drop cap,* which is lowered into the article. Examples of both appear in Figure 8-1.

Initial cap ——— **W**e, the people of the United Nations, determined to save succeeding generations from the scourge of war, which twice in our lifetime has brought untold sorrow to mankind, and to reaffirm faith

Drop cap ——— **W**e, the people of the United Nations, determined to save succeeding generations from the scourge of war, which twice in our lifetime has brought untold sorrow to mankind, and to reaffirm

Figure 8-1: The initial cap rests on the baseline with the rest of the text on the first line (top); the drop cap drops below the baseline (bottom).

Big cap maintains high profile

Making an initial cap is only slightly harder than it looks. When you make the first character of text larger than the others, PageMaker has a habit of messing things up a bit, which requires a little fixing up on your part. Here's how it works.

1. **Select the first character in your story.**

   Drag over it with the Text tool. Presumably, you start your sentences with a capital letter, so this letter will serve well as an initial cap.

2. **Select a larger type size.**

   Either select it from the Type⇨Size submenu or from the Control palette. You can also press ⌘+Shift+period or ⌘+Option+Shift+period a few times to enlarge the cap incrementally.

3. **Change the font.**

   This step is optional, but sometimes initial caps look a little more distinctive if you select a different font. In Figure 8-2, for example, the initial cap is set in 60-point bold New Century Schoolbook, which contrasts nicely with the Helvetica text.

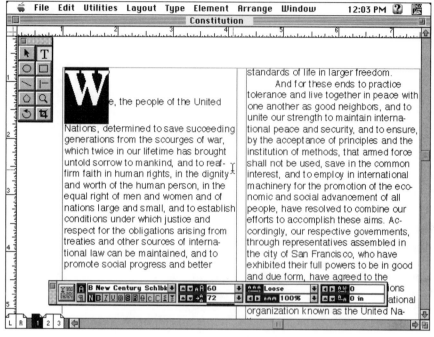

Figure 8-2:
The result of
changing
the first
letter to 60-
point bold
New
Century
Schoolbook.

4. Adjust the leading if necessary.

Take another look at Figure 8-2. Notice that big gap between the first line of type and the ones that follow? This happens if the leading for your story was set to Auto, which changes the leading to 120 percent of the type size. Because the size of the first character grew, the leading grew, too. To fix things, first select some text in the paragraph — make sure that the initial cap is not selected — and make note of the value in the leading field of the Control palette. For example, if you have 12-point type, you will have 14.4-point leading (if Auto leading is selected).

Next, press ⌘+A to select all the text in the story. Then change the leading value in the Control palette to the one you noted in the preceding paragraph and click on the Apply button or press Return.

5. Add some carriage returns.

As shown in Figure 8-3, the top of the initial cap looks cut off. This bit of weirdness doesn't affect the printing of the character, but it does shove the top of the initial cap outside the boundaries of the text block — possibly interfering with other elements on the page or violating your margin setting.

Chapter 7 warns against inserting extra paragraph breaks between paragraphs of text. Well, here's an exception to the rule. To bring the initial cap back into the text block, move the insertion point to the beginning of

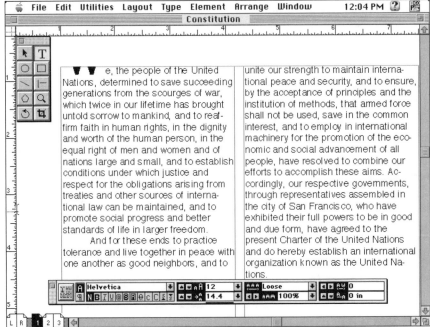

Figure 8-3:
The top of
the initial
cap appears
to be cut off.

the text block by pressing the left-arrow key. Then press Return a couple of times. To complete the effect, force the screen to redraw. You can do this by pressing ⌘+Shift+F12, pressing the keyboard shortcut for the current view size (⌘+5 for 50 percent view, ⌘+2 for 200 percent view, and so on), or scrolling the cap off and then back onto the screen. In Figure 8-4, for example, the view size is magnified to 200 percent.

6. **Kern the cap closer to the rest of the text.**

   Finally, you need to eliminate that awful gap between the initial cap and the other letters in the word. Click just to the right of the initial cap with the Text tool, as shown in Figure 8-4. Then press ⌘+Delete a few times to kern the letters closer together. If you kern too far, press ⌘+Shift+Delete to spread the letters.

See, we told you that this was more complicated than you thought it would be. Who'd have thought that increasing the size of a single letter could entail so much wiping of the old brow?

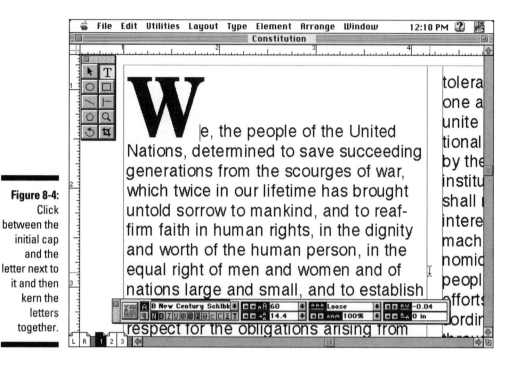

Figure 8-4:
Click
between the
initial cap
and the
letter next to
it and then
kern the
letters
together.

Big cap gets down with the little letters

Drop caps are about a zillion times — give or take a few million — easier to
create because PageMaker automates the process. The program includes a
feature that automatically creates drop caps to your specifications. All is not
perfect in the world of drop caps — they're difficult to edit, PageMaker doesn't
always size your text correctly, and the drop cap feature won't work if your text
is already kerned — but as long as you prepare your text correctly, the process
is swift and straightforward.

1. **Change the font and type style of the first letter in the paragraph if
   desired.**

   This step is optional. In Figure 8-5, the _W_ was changed to bold New
   Century Schoolbook.

2. **Apply the Drop Cap plug-in.**

   With the first letter selected, choose Utilities⇨PageMaker Plug-ins⇨Drop
   Cap to display the Drop Cap dialog box shown in the middle of Figure 8-5.

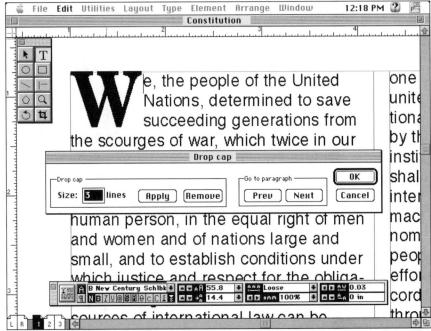

Figure 8-5:
The Drop
Cap plug-in
automatically
converts a
selected
character
into a
drop cap.

3. Specify the size of the cap.

In the Drop Cap dialog box, specify the size of a character in terms of lines
of type. Enter the number of lines you want to fill into the Size option box
and then click on the Apply button. In Figure 8-5, the Size value is 3, so the
drop cap is three lines of type tall. PageMaker automatically sizes the
character, moves it down, and tabs the surrounding text so that the
characters don't overlap.

4. Create any other drop caps in your document.

The Drop Cap dialog box in Version 6 sports two new buttons: Prev and
Next. Using these two buttons, you can move the cursor to paragraphs
before or after the current paragraph. You can then apply drop caps to
those paragraphs without having to close and re-open the dialog box.
Granted, you may not have much use for this feature — after all, how many
drop caps will you want in the same document? — but it's nice to know
that it's there if you need it.

5. Click on OK to close the dialog box.

That's all there is to it.

One unfortunate aspect of the Drop Cap feature is that it eliminates hyphens in the lines that contain the drop cap. Hyphenated words remain split in two, but the hyphens themselves disappear. Frankly, you can't do a whole lot other than manually insert the hyphens. Also, if you edit the lines that surround the drop cap, the drop cap may not wrap properly around the new text. For that reason, create your drop caps only after you've done the final edits on your text.

If you ever want to get rid of the drop cap, select the character, choose Utilities⇔PageMaker Plug-ins⇔Drop Cap, click on the Remove button, and then click on OK. Note that if you want to change the size of the drop cap — to make it two lines tall instead of three, for example — you have to remove the current drop cap and then apply the new size. PageMaker won't let you simply change the value in the Size box and click on the Apply button.

Be careful, though, if you have modified any lines of text affected by the drop cap. Any kerning, line breaks, tabs, and so on, other than those put in by the Drop Cap plug-in, won't be removed when you remove the drop cap. Also, if you made modifications to your text after creating the drop cap, the addition may screw up the text spacing in the process of removing the cap. Similarly, any hyphens you manually added will remain, but as the text reflows, they'll most likely end up in the middle of a line instead of at the end.

Reverse Text Tricks

Chapter 6 mentions how the Reverse command (Type⇔Type Style⇔Reverse) works. But it doesn't go into much detail about how and when you should use it.

The Reverse command is most useful for setting white text against a colored background. The following steps describe how to use the command to create a logo that is half black against a white background and half white against a black background, as shown in Figure 8-6. This is a simple effect, but it's guaranteed to add some visual interest to just about any page.

Here's how to create this effect:

1. **Enter some text.**

   Create a new text block and enter two words.

2. **Set the font and type size.**

   Press ⌘+A to select the entire text block. Then change the font and type size as desired. In the example in Figure 8-6, the text is 60-point Helvetica Bold. As is always the case when creating special text effects, big text is best.

Figure 8-6:
Draw a
rectangle
around a
piece of text
(top), fill it
with black,
reverse the
text, and
send the
rectangle to
the back to
create white
text against
a black
background
(bottom).

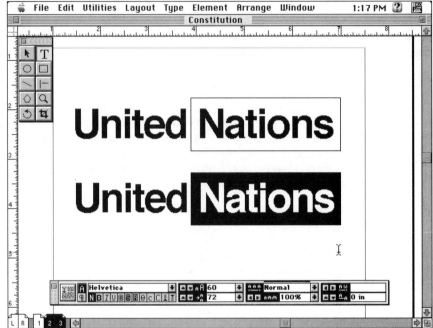

3. Draw a rectangle around the second word.

Select the Rectangle tool (it's the one right beneath the Text tool). Then drag from the spot where you want one corner of your rectangle to the opposite corner to create a box around the word, as shown in the top example in Figure 8-6. If you don't draw the rectangle exactly right the first time, don't worry. You can edit the shape by selecting it with the Arrow tool and then dragging one of its handles.

To create this effect, you need to make sure that text wrap is turned off for the rectangle. To do so, select the rectangle with the Arrow tool, choose Element⇨Text Wrap, and click on the far left Wrap Option icon in the Text Wrap dialog box.

4. Make the rectangle black.

With the rectangle selected, choose Element⇨Fill⇨Solid. This step changes the rectangle from transparent to black. You can no longer see the second word.

5. Reverse the second word.

Select the Text tool and then double-click on the second word to select it. Even though the rectangle is in the way, the word becomes selected. Then click on the Reverse (R) button in the Control palette, choose Type⇨Type Style⇨Reverse, or press ⌘+Shift+V. Now click outside the text to deselect it. Your text now should look something like the bottom example of Figure 8-6.

You may think that you're finished creating this reverse text effect, but you're not quite there. If you scroll your document so that the text goes off the screen and then scroll the text back into view, you'll find that the black rectangle is now covering up your white text again. Dang!

6. **Send the rectangle behind the text.**

To glue the black rectangle permanently behind the text, select the Arrow tool, select the rectangle by clicking on it, and then choose Arrange⇨Send to Back (⌘+B). Now that white text is planted firmly on top of its black background.

You more adventurous types may be wondering, "Can I do the same thing to a single letter? Can I make a letter half black and half white?" Nope, you sure can't. Sorry. You have to use a drawing program like CorelDRAW! to pull that off. And then you have to read *CorelDRAW! 6 For Dummies*, published by this same publisher. It's the perfect companion book for the perfect companion product. (The fact that one of the authors of the book you're now reading wrote *CorelDRAW! 6 For Dummies* is purely coincidental.)

However, you *can* do something almost as cool. If you set a reverse version of a text block in front of a standard version of it, you get an engraved effect like the one shown in Figure 8-7. The effect is subtle, but it's worth learning.

Figure 8-7: Engraved text created by setting reverse text in front of a black version of itself, against a white background (top) and a gray background (bottom).

The following steps make the process crystal clear:

1. **Create some new text.**

   Make it big.

2. **Copy the text.**

   Switch to the Arrow tool and click on the text block to select it. Then choose Edit⇨Copy or press ⌘+C to copy it to the Clipboard. Doing so saves the text for later use.

3. **Press ⌘+Option+V.**

   This wonderful and little-known keyboard equivalent pastes what you just copied to the Clipboard at the exact location where it was when you copied it. So what you get is one text block positioned directly in front of another.

4. **Nudge the text block down and to the right a little.**

   Or down and to the left, or up and to the left, or whatever. The point is, nudge it. You can nudge a selection by pressing the arrow keys. Each press of the arrow key moves the selection 1 point in the direction indicated on the key. The effect shown in Figure 8-7 required pressing the right-arrow key twice and the down-arrow key twice. (If 1-point nudges are too large, you can change the nudge settings by choosing File⇨Preferences.)

5. **Reverse the text.**

   Select the Text tool (Shift+F2), click inside the text, and press ⌘+A to select all the text. Then click on the Reverse button in the Control palette or press ⌘+Shift+V to change the text from black to white. Because the copied word is still selected, it looks like things are backward — you see black type in front of white type — but when you deselect the text block (by clicking outside of it), you get the first effect shown in Figure 8-7.

If that effect is too subtle for you, draw a rectangle around the text and fill it with light gray by choosing Element⇨Fill and Line and choosing the solid fill option and the 20 percent fill tint option. Then send the rectangle to the back of the document (⌘+B). The second example in Figure 8-7 shows the outcome.

Bulleted and Numbered Lists

Point by point — that's a great way to make your message clear. Nothing grabs a reader's attention like a good, old-fashioned bulleted or numbered list.

Typically, bulleted and numbered lists use one of two formats:

✔ **Lead-in:** In this case, the bullet or number is simply the first character in the paragraph, followed by a space. The paragraph usually has the first line indented.

✔ **Hanging indent:** The bullet or number hangs out to the left of the text's left margin. Usually, the bullet aligns with the leftmost point of the column, and all text in the paragraph is indented to a point a little to the right of the bullet.

Figure 8-8 shows the two styles in action. Usually, it makes no difference which style you use — both look good and are easy to read. However, the longer the bulleted paragraphs are, the more awkward the hanging-indent technique can look.

You can create bulleted and numbered lists in three ways. You can use PageMaker's Bullets and Numbering plug-in, which applies bullets and numbers to selected paragraphs automatically; you can just type in your bullets and numbers manually in PageMaker; or you can create your bullets and numbers in your word processor, before importing your text into PageMaker. Because the plug-in has some limitations, you'll probably find yourself using the latter two methods more often than not.

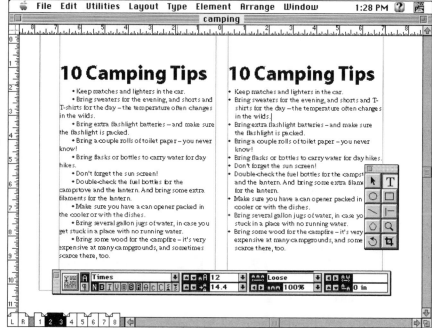

Figure 8-8:
Good-looking bulleted text is usually one of two types: lead-in (left) or hanging indent (right).

If you're creating a lead-in list, not much special formatting is required. Just type the number or enter the code for a standard bullet character, Option+8 (in word processors, you sometimes use Option+spacebar or ⌘+spacebar instead). Then enter a space before the paragraph text. Using an em space or en space, described later in this chapter, ensures consistent spacing between the bullets or numbers and the text that follows them.

If you want to create a hanging-indent list, you need to establish special tab and indent settings to correctly position your bullets or numbers, as explained next.

Formatting your text for a hanging-indent list

To format your text as a hanging-indent list, first set the indents, as follows:

1. **With the Text tool, select the paragraph(s) you want to format.**

2. **Set the first-line indent to a negative number.**

   Enter the value in the Control palette or Paragraph Specifications dialog box (Type⇨Paragraph). Entering a negative number moves the bullet (or, in a numbered list, the number) out past the text's left margin.

3. **Set the left indent to the same number, only make it a positive number.**

   For example, if you set the first-line indent to –0.1, set the left indent to 0.1. This setting moves the entire paragraph back to the right so that the bullet or number stays inside the column and the text remains indented to the right of it.

If you want, you can simply put a space between a bullet or number and the text that follows it. But using tabs instead gives you more control over the spacing.

You have two options: You can put a tab after the bullet or put a tab both before and after the bullet. In the first case, you're just trying to control the distance between the bullet and the text that follows it. In the second case, you're trying to position the bullet relative to the column's left margin as well as determine the space between the bullet and the following text. You use the second approach more often if you're using nonstandard bullet shapes (described later in this chapter). The second approach also comes in handy if you have long bulleted or numbered items that could be buried in a sea of text and you want to create some break in the left margin to compensate. Figure 8-9 shows examples of bulleted lists that illustrate the difference in the two techniques.

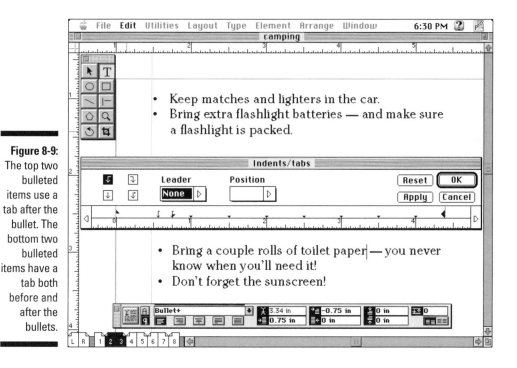

Figure 8-9:
The top two
bulleted
items use a
tab after the
bullet. The
bottom two
bulleted
items have a
tab both
before and
after the
bullets.

Here are some issues to keep in mind when you're formatting text for hanging-indent lists:

✔ To set up your tab stops, press ⌘+I or choose Type⇨Indents/Tabs to display the tab ruler (it's shown in Figure 8-9). Try different settings and click on the Apply button to preview them. When you like what you have, click on OK.

✔ The tab stop that separates the bullet (or number) and the text should match the left indent for the paragraph. If you set the left indent to 0.188 inches, for example, create a tab at 0.188.

✔ If you're setting tabs for a numbered list, make the first tab a right-aligned tab and the second tab a left-aligned tab. Setting a right-aligned tab aligns numbers to the right — in other words, the *0* in *20* aligns with the *5* in *15*. If you're going to use a separator (period, bracket, and so on) after each number, be sure that your tab stop leaves room for that character. Or use a decimal tab, which aligns numbers by the separator.

✔ Because getting the indent and tab settings just right can be a lot of work, create styles for your numbered lists and your bulleted lists, as explained in Chapter 7. You can then quickly apply the proper formatting to all paragraphs in your list. PageMaker has a prefab Hanging Indent style, which may or may not suit your needs.

✔ If you'll be using the styles for multiple documents, such as each issue of a newsletter, create styles with the same names in your word processor and apply them to your bulleted or numbered lists there. That'll save you the time of going through your layout looking for text that needs to have the bullet or number style applied.

Don't forget to enter a tab before and after your bullet character or number when you're creating your list text, whether you're creating the text in your word processor or in PageMaker. Otherwise, your tab settings won't do diddly to align your list.

PageMaker has a counter-intuitive response in setting tab stops that affects how your bulleted and numbered lists look. When using inches as your unit of measurement, you're restricted to certain settings if you position tab markers with the mouse. You can set tabs to 0.156, for example, but not at 0.15. What's happening is that PageMaker is moving the tab markers to the nearest tick mark on the ruler, overriding your ostensibly WYSIWYG (What You See Is What You Get) placement. The solution is to select each tab stop one by one and enter the value you want in the Position field. Or you can switch your measurement system to picas and points, the more exact system used by professional layout artists. A pica is $1/6$ inch and is made of 12 points (so there are 72 points in an inch).

Using the Bullets and Numbering plug-in

The Bullets and Numbering plug-in can provide a quick way to add bullets or numbers to your list text. But this plug-in does have some disappointing drawbacks, too. You may want to flip to the end of this section to read about them before deciding whether you want to use the plug-in.

The plug-in won't work unless the paragraphs that will get the bullets or numbers are first formatted as hanging indents (as just described).

Here's how to use the plug-in to create a bulleted list:

1. **With the Text tool, select the paragraph(s) you want to format with bullets.**

   Or, if you want to format a series of sequential paragraphs, click inside the first paragraph in the batch. If you want to apply bullets to all paragraphs in the story or all paragraphs that have a certain style applied, click inside the story.

2. **Choose Utilities⇨PageMaker Plug-ins⇨Bullets and Numbering.**

   The Bullets and Numbering dialog box, shown in Figure 8-10, appears.

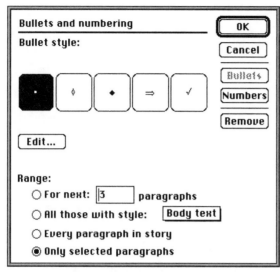

3. Choose a Bullet Style option.

PageMaker offers you five default bullet choices. If you don't care for any of these choices, move on to step 4 to choose a different style. If one of the predefined bullet choices suits your needs, click on it and skip to step 6.

4. Click on a Bullet Style button and then click on Edit.

The Bullet Style button you click will be replaced by the bullet you're about to define. After you click on Edit, you see the Edit Bullet dialog box (shown in Figure 8-11), where you can pick a font, size, and character for your bullet. It's best to use a size that's close to the size of your text, for reasons that we'll explain shortly.

If you're having trouble seeing what the bullet will look like, increase the font size to enlarge your view. When you're satisfied with the bullet character, change the setting back to the size you want to use in your document.

Keep in mind that filled circles aren't the only kind of bullets, although they're the most common. You can use all sorts of characters and symbols as bullets, including arrows, triangles, logos, stylized letters, and — as in this book — check marks. Figure 8-12 shows a sampling of bullet characters created using the ornamental font Zapf Dingbats.

5. Click on OK.

You should see your bullet on the Bullet Style button you clicked before entering the Edit Bullet dialog box.

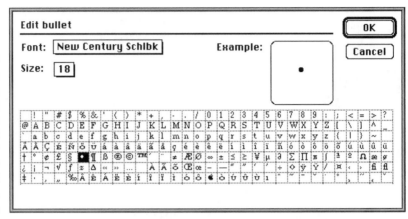

Figure 8-11:
You can
choose a
custom
bullet
character or
change the
size and font
of a bullet.

6. Choose a Range radio button.

You specify which paragraphs should get the bullets with the Range options. For example, if you want to apply bullets to paragraphs that have a certain style applied, choose the All Those With Style radio button and choose the style name from the pop-up menu.

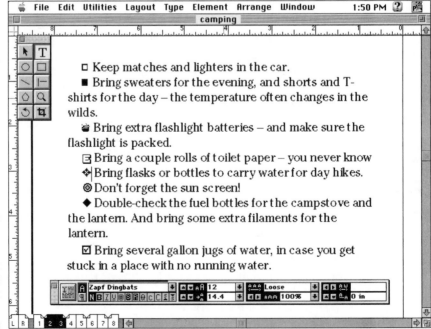

Figure 8-12:
An
assortment
of distinct
bullet
characters.

7. Click on OK.

PageMaker applies the bullets as you specified. If necessary, you can adjust the indent and tab settings by making changes to the individual paragraphs or by editing the style you're using for your bulleted paragraphs.

To create a numbered list, do as follows:

1. With the Text tool, select the paragraph(s) you want to number.

Or, if you want to number a series of sequential paragraphs, just click inside the first paragraph in the batch. If you want to number all paragraphs in the story or all paragraphs that have a certain style applied, just click inside the story.

2. Choose Utilities⇨PageMaker Plug-ins⇨Bullets and Numbering.

3. Click on Numbers.

The dialog box shown in Figure 8-13 appears. In the dialog box, specify what style of numbers you want, whether you want a separator such as a period or bracket after the number, and the starting number for the list. Then select a radio button to tell PageMaker which paragraphs you want to number by choosing a Range radio button.

4. Click on OK.

PageMaker applies the numbers to your paragraphs.

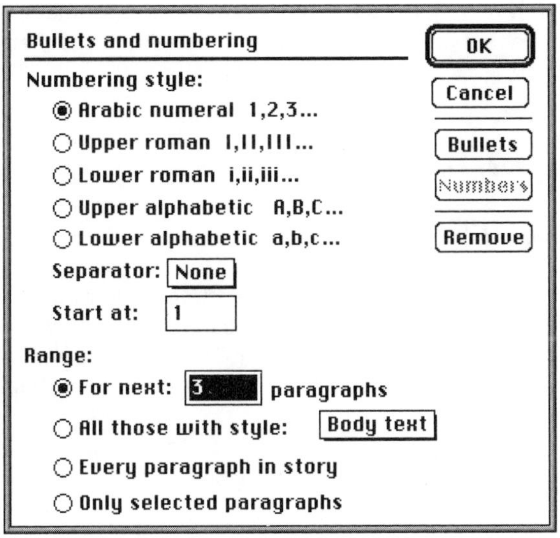

Figure 8-13:
Choose a numbering style and the range of paragraphs to be formatted in this dialog box.

Bullets and numbering

Numbering style:
- ⦿ Arabic numeral 1,2,3...
- ○ Upper roman I,II,III...
- ○ Lower roman i,ii,iii...
- ○ Upper alphabetic A,B,C...
- ○ Lower alphabetic a,b,c...

Separator: [None]

Start at: [1]

Range:
- ⦿ For next: [3] paragraphs
- ○ All those with style: [Body text]
- ○ Every paragraph in story
- ○ Only selected paragraphs

[OK]
[Cancel]
[Bullets]
[Numbers]
[Remove]

To remove the numbers or bullets from a list, select the affected paragraphs, choose the Bullets and Numbering plug-in, and click on the Remove button.

As mentioned earlier, the plug-in does have some drawbacks to keep in mind:

✔ If you choose a bullet size that's larger than your text size, you may get mispositioned bullets. Also, the tab and indent settings for your hanging indent may require adjustment. Unfortunately, you can't change the settings in the Bullets and Numbering dialog box; you have to change the tab and indent settings through the Indents/Tabs dialog box.

✔ If you insert or delete a numbered item in a list, PageMaker doesn't update the numbers in the list automatically. You have to make the changes manually or re-apply the plug-in to the list.

✔ The plug-in doesn't offer any Apply or Preview button, so you can't see how your bullets will look before you place them on your paragraphs. If you don't like the results, you have to choose the plug-in again and use the Remove button to get rid of your existing bullets. Then you have to choose the plug-in again to re-apply different bullets.

✔ The Bullets and Numbering dialog box remembers the last bullet you used. That's great if you want to use the same bullet as you did before. If not, you have to go through the process of defining a bullet again through the Edit Bullet dialog box.

All in all, if you want to apply bullets or numbers to a list, you'll probably find it easier to do the job either manually in PageMaker or in your word processor before importing your text. Many word processors have automatic numbering and bulleting features that are more flexible and expedient than PageMaker's.

Typographic Symbols and Special Characters

The preceding section explained how to create numbered or bulleted lists using indents. The bullet (Option+8) is only one of the many special characters and symbols that you can access inside PageMaker. The following sections describe these special characters and provide a little background about them.

TIP

Making lists more effective

Now that you know how to create bulleted and numbered lists, here are a few tips on making them more effective — and attractive:

- As mentioned earlier, it's a good idea to put at least an en space (⌘+Shift+N) after a number to set the number apart from the text. Using en spaces or other fixed width spaces ensures consistent spacing. (En spaces and fixed width spaces are described in the section "Typographic Symbols and Other Special Characters," in this chapter.)

- For simple lists, ordinary round bullet characters and standard numbers are fine. But if you have lots of text or long items in a list, you can do more. For example, put the numbers in boldface and follow them with a two- or three-word summary (maybe in boldface, too) of the paragraph's contents. That's a great way to drive home the points, especially in a list of steps or rules. You can do the same with bullets.

- You may also use different bullet characters or styles. For example, if you're listing winners in a contest, you may make the winner's bullets solid and the finalist's bullets hollow. Or you may use lead-in bullets for short items in one list and use hanging-indent bullets for a series of multiple-line explanations in another list.

- No matter how you do it, the thing to consider is whether it's important to differentiate types of lists and then figure out how to do so in a way that is pleasing and not confusing or distracting. The differences should be obviously tied in to differences in the types or contents of text.

Curly quotes and apostrophes

"Trevor, get back in the house this instant!" screamed Mary, ready to throttle the child.

"Trevor, honey, time to come in," Mary called casually.

See the difference? The straight quote (") is wooden and severe, while the curly quotes (" and ") are expressive and frankly more interesting to look at. It's also worth noting that the straight quote looks the same regardless of which side of the quotation it appears on; the curly quotes provide visual clues as to whether you're starting a quotation or finishing one.

But most folks use the straight quote because it's readily accessible from the keyboard — it's right there next to the Return key. The curly quotes are hidden.

✔ To access the open curly quote ("), press Option+left bracket ([).

✔ To access the close curly quote ("), press Option+Shift+left bracket ([).

✔ To access the open single curly quote ('), press Option+right bracket (]). Single quotes are frequently used to indicate quotes inside quotes, as in, "So Henry said to me, 'Darla, don't you ever wear that perfume again.' I mean, who does he think he is? Calvin Klein?"

✔ To access the close single quote ('), press Option+Shift+right bracket (]). This is also the preferable symbol for an apostrophe — *don't* is better than *don't*.

If you can get in the habit of using these keyboard shortcuts, you'll be able to use curly quotes and apostrophes at your own discretion. In other words, you can use curly quotes when you want quotes and straight quotes when you want feet and inch (or minute and second) symbols. But you can also tell PageMaker to automatically substitute a curly quote when you hit the straight quote key.

Choose File⇨Preferences (or double-click on the Arrow tool icon in the toolbox) and click on the More button inside the Preferences dialog box. After the More Preferences dialog box appears, select the Use Typographer's Quotes check box. From now on, PageMaker creates the correct curly quote symbol when you press the straight quote key. The same goes for apostrophes.

PageMaker does not, however, change the straight quotes that you have already entered into your document. To change existing quotes, you have to re-enter them or replace them by using the Find and Change feature in the Story Editor (explained in Chapter 5). To type a straight quote mark — the symbol for inches — press ⌘+Shift+left bracket ([). To type a straight single quote mark (a.k.a. the foot symbol), press ⌘+Shift+right bracket (]).

If you want PageMaker to substitute typographer's quotes for regular quotes in a story that you're importing into your layout, check the Convert Quotes box in the Place dialog box.

Nonbreaking spaces and hyphens

We're all familiar with the space character. You're no doubt also familiar with the hyphen, also known as the small dash. But you may not know that you can access four additional kinds of spaces and four additional kinds of dashes inside PageMaker:

✔ Nonbreaking spaces, fixed width spaces, em spaces, and en spaces

✔ Nonbreaking hyphens, discretionary hyphens, em dashes, and en dashes (minus signs)

The first variation on the space and dash is the *nonbreaking* character. Standard spaces and hyphens allow words to "break" from one line to the next. If you bind the two with a nonbreaking space or hyphen, however, PageMaker treats the two words as a single word and breaks them down to a second line together, as demonstrated in Figure 8-14. Both characters are useful for improving the appearance of ragged right (flush left) text by cutting down on the raggedness a little. In the figure, for example, the word *was* in the second-to-last line in the top paragraph sticks out way past the end of the preceding line. Joining it to the word *the* with a nonbreaking space evens things out a bit.

To access a nonbreaking space, also called a *hard space,* press Option+spacebar. To access the nonbreaking hyphen, press ⌘+Option+hyphen.

Avoid using nonbreaking spaces in a justified paragraph. PageMaker can't vary the width of a nonbreaking space the way it can a standard space character, so nonbreaking spaces may look too thin or too fat compared with their standard space neighbors.

At the end of the day, Eugene
always took time to say good- —— Standard hyphen
bye to his aging mother. She
didn't seem to much care if he
said good-bye or good
riddance, but he figured it was —— Standard space
the right thing to do.

Figure 8-14:
Standard
hyphens
and spaces
can break
across lines
(top), but
nonbreaking
characters
do not
(bottom).

At the end of the day, Eugene
always took time to say
good-bye to his aging mother. —— Nonbreaking hyphen
She didn't seem to much care if
he said good-bye or good
riddance, but he figured it
was the right thing to do. —— Nonbreaking space

If you want to keep more than two words together on the same line, you may find it easier to use this alternative route: Select the text that you want to keep together, choose Type⇨Type Specs (⌘+T), and choose No Break from the Line End pop-up menu.

Fixed-width spaces

Another kind of space is the fixed-width space, introduced in the "Creating Bulleted and Numbered Lists" section earlier in this chapter. PageMaker provides three kinds of fixed-width spaces, all of which are nonbreaking:

✔ Press ⌘+Shift+M to access the *em space*, which is as wide as the type size is tall — so a 12-point em space is 12 points wide, roughly the width of a capital letter *M*.

✔ Press ⌘+Shift+N to access the *en space*, which is half the width of an em space (about the width of a small letter *n*).

✔ Press ⌘+Shift+T to access a *thin space*, which is one quarter the width of an em space, or about the width of a lowercase *t*.

Use fixed spaces when tabs just won't work. In Figure 8-15, tabs separate the days from the text in the left-hand paragraphs. Because the tabs line up, as shown by the dotted line, the result is a huge gap after *Tuesday* and a smaller gap after the longer word *Wednesday*. Using em spaces instead of tabs equalizes the gaps, as shown on the right side of the figure.

Minus signs, em dashes, and discretionary hyphens

As mentioned earlier, you will find four kinds of special dashes (above and beyond the standard hyphen). In addition to the nonbreaking hyphen, there's the discretionary hyphen (⌘+hyphen), discussed in the "Hyphenation" section of Chapter 7. This hyphen only appears when PageMaker needs it to break a word across two lines.

The remaining dashes are the *en dash* and *em dash*, which are the same widths as their en and em space counterparts. Use the en dash (Option+hyphen) to represent a minus sign in mathematical equations. Use the em dash (Option+Shift+hyphen) to separate thoughts, as in, "So, anyway, I was hiking with Mark — you know, the guy with the mousy brown dreadlocks — when this giant badger attacked us and started gnawing on Mark's ankle."

Tuesday   I don't know how to tell Ted the engagement is off. He was so sweet today that I almost regretted falling in love with Bob.

Wednesday   What a jerk Ted is! He was so full of himself this morning, I just had to let him have it. "I love Bob!" I shouted so all

Tuesday   I don't know how to tell Ted the engagement is off. He was so sweet today that I almost regretted falling in love with Bob.

Wednesday   What a jerk Ted is! He was so full of himself this morning, I just had to let him have it. "I love Bob!" I shouted so all

Figure 8-15: Text separated with tabs (left) and em spaces (right).

Automatic page numbers

You can add page numbers to your document the hard way, by typing them in on every page, or the easy way, by inserting PageMaker's automatic page numbering code. By using the code, you don't have to go in and renumber all your pages if you add or delete a page for your document; PageMaker does the job for you. And if you place the page number code on your master pages, as explained in Chapter 14, you only have to enter the code once for your left-hand pages and once for your right-hand pages (assuming that you're creating a double-sided document).

To add the code for automatic page numbering, just click with the Text tool at the spot where you want the page number to appear and then press ⌘+Option+P. Bingo — PageMaker puts in the correct page number. You can select the number and format as you would any other text. If you're adding page numbers to master pages, you see the code LM or RM instead of the actual page number (LM for a left master page and RM for a right master page). But your publication pages carry the correct page numbers.

PageMaker numbers your documents according to the settings you make in the Document Setup dialog box (File⇨Document Setup), as explained in Chapter 3.

Fractions

Never use a slash (/) to create a fraction. A special fraction character, which you access by pressing Option+Shift+1, is available to all Macintosh applications. This character is specially kerned to accommodate numbers on either side of it. Here's how to create a perfect fraction in PageMaker:

1. **Type your fraction.**

   For example, to create the fraction $^3/_4$, press 3, Option+Shift+1, 4.

2. **Superscript the numerator.**

   The numerator is the number before the fraction symbol — in this case, 3. Select the numerator with the Text tool and press ⌘+Shift+plus to superscript it.

3. **Subscript the denominator.**

   The denominator follows the fraction sign. Select it and press ⌘+Shift+hyphen to subscript the character.

   Yuck, the numerator is too small, and the denominator falls below the baseline. No good! The problem is that PageMaker's default superscript and subscript settings aren't set up to accommodate fractions. Luckily, you can change them.

4. **Select the fraction and press ⌘+T or choose Type⇨Type Specs.**

   The Type Specifications dialog box appears. Click on the Options button to open the Type Options dialog box.

5. **Adjust the superscript and subscript settings.**

   To make your fractions picture perfect, change the Super/subscript size value to 55, change the Superscript position value to 35, and change the Subscript position value to 0 so the denominator rests on the baseline. Then Click on OK twice to exit out of all the dialog boxes.

Other unusual characters

So far, we've explained a lot of characters that you didn't even know you needed. But what about all those characters that you *are* searching for? Like the degree symbol, the cent sign, the copyright symbol, and so on? Table 8-1 shows how to access these characters inside PageMaker.

Table 8-1	Accessing Special Symbols	
Symbol	*What It Looks Like*	*How to Create It*
Degree	°	Option+Shift+8
Cent	¢	Option+4
Pound	£	Option+3
Yen	¥	Option+Y
Florin	ƒ	Option+F
Copyright	©	Option+G
Trademark	™	Option+2
Registered trademark	®	Option+R
Paragraph	¶	Option+7
Section	§	Option+6
Dagger	†	Option+T
Double dagger	‡	Option+Shift+7
Plus or minus	±	Option+Shift+plus
Divide	÷	Option+slash(/)
Accent grave	`	Option+grave key (`)+letter that gets the accent[1]
Acute accent	´	Option+E+letter that gets the accent[1]
Dieresis	¨	Option+U+letter that gets the accent[1]
Tilde	~	Option+N+letter that gets the accent[1]
C cedilla	ç	Option+C (Option+Shift+C for capital)
Down question	¿	Option+Shift+question mark (?)
Down exclamation	¡	Option+1
Ellipsis	…	Option+semicolon

[1] Press and release the Option+key combination before you type the letter that gets the accent.

Although these are the most important symbols, many others are available. To find any other symbols, open the Key Caps desk accessory by choosing Apple⇨Key Caps. Then choose a font from the Key Caps menu and press the Shift and/or Option keys to view the various symbols in the on-screen keyboard. Be sure to check out the Symbol and Zapf Dingbats fonts, which offer special math and ornamental symbols.

Part III
Say It with Pictures

The 5th Wave   By Rich Tennant

"FRANKLY, I'M NOT SURE THIS IS THE WAY TO ENHANCE OUR COLOR GRAPHICS."

In this part . . .

You may not have realized it, but in addition to being a powerful page layout program, PageMaker is also a mini-graphics studio. It doesn't offer the kind of image editing or drawing capabilities that you'll find in a full-fledged graphics program, such as Photoshop or Illustrator, but it provides the basic tools you need to create simple graphics and also to manipulate photographs, scanned images, and drawings that you import from other programs.

This part shows you how to work with imported graphics and how to use PageMaker's drawing tools to create basic graphic elements right inside your PageMaker layout. It also explains how to turn your black-and-white pages into Technicolor masterpieces. By the time you're finished with these three chapters, you'll be so full of the artistic spirit that you'll probably feel the urge to cut off an ear.

Chapter 9
Adding Pretty Pictures

. . . .

. . . .

This chapter is about graphics, the one thing you can't create in PageMaker. Oh, sure, you can draw lines, rectangles, polygons, and ellipses, but unless you intend to limit yourself to crude drawings of smiley faces and Mr. Potato Head, you need more sophisticated tools.

That's why PageMaker lets you import graphics. You can create a picture in just about any graphics program you choose, save the artwork to disk using one of several different file formats, and insert it into your PageMaker publication. Inside PageMaker, you can crop and resize the graphic, label it with text, or wrap text around it to create irregular columns and other fancy effects.

Wrapping text around a graphic is a particularly great option. Why? Well, back in the days before PageMaker and desktop publishing, it cost serious money to wrap text around graphics because each line of text had to be individually measured and typeset — sometimes even placed on the page by hand, one line at a time. If the text changed, the whole expensive and time-consuming process had to begin again. Even rectangular wraps were expensive because they required fairly complex typesetting codes. So only big, glossy, state-of-the-art magazines with big staffs did text wrap with any frequency. Even then, you could expect the art director and production staff to spend about 6,000 meetings discussing how to make sure there was enough time to do text wrap.

Today, even a lowly word processor can do rectangular text wrap, and any desktop publishing program worth its weight in rubber cement can do nonrectangular wraps, the kind that follow the contours and shape of an image.

But before you get to have fun with text wrap, you have to understand how to place the graphics you're wrapping around — which happens to be the subject of the first part of this chapter. The second part of the chapter explains how to crop and resize imported graphics and how to use the different text wrap options that PageMaker offers.

Preparing Graphics for PageMaker

Just as you need to prepare text in your word processor for use in PageMaker, you need to prepare your graphics for importing. And naturally, the preparation you need to do depends on the program you used to create the graphic and the type of graphic you created.

Graphics come in two basic types: *bitmap* and *vector*. Bitmap graphics are made up of square dots called *pixels,* and vector graphics are made up of lines. For example, everything printed by your laser printer becomes a bitmap graphic on the page because the entire page is composed of a series of black dots on the white paper — take a magnifying glass and check!

Some programs create their images the same way, using a pattern of colored or black dots to render an image. Paint programs, scanners, and photo editors generally create bitmaps. Adobe Photoshop, Claris MacPaint, and Fractal Design Painter are probably the most popular paint and photo-editing programs, but another dozen or so programs exist.

Bitmap images are good for representing continuous ranges of colors with soft edges, such as impressionist paintings and photographs. But because they are made up of patterns of dots, enlarging or reducing them too much can make the dots ungainly or too fine to reproduce well.

Vector drawings, on the other hand, are great for high-contrast art, such as weather maps, architectural plans, logos, charts, informational graphics, and all kinds of other bright, colorful artwork you might see in *USA Today*. A vector drawing is composed of lines, circles, and other shapes that can be stretched, combined, and otherwise manipulated, all without appearing the least bit jagged. Adobe Illustrator and Macromedia FreeHand are the best-known drawing programs for the Mac, but, again, other programs provide similar capabilities.

When you print a vector drawing, it's converted to a bitmap graphic by the printer. So why doesn't an enlarged or reduced drawing reproduce poorly, like an enlarged or reduced bitmap image? Because with a drawing, the computer sends the graphic to the printer as a series of mathematical equations that define the lines, circles, and other components of the graphic. The printer solves those equations and renders the graphic using as many printer dots as it can, to create the smoothest possible look. But with a bitmap, the number of dots used to represent the graphic is fixed in stone when you first create the graphic in your painting program. Your printer can't add or delete dots — and neither can PageMaker. So if you change the size of a bitmap graphic in PageMaker, you're actually making the dots bigger or smaller — that's the way the dots print.

Keep in mind that most vector programs can export a bitmap version of their drawings, and that some programs let you combine bitmap and vector images in one file. The words *bitmap* and *vector* are techie terms, and many people are now using the terms *image* and *drawing* to refer to these types of formats. This book calls them *image* and *drawing* as well, and uses the term *graphic* to mean both. (Figure 9-1 shows examples of bitmap and vector art.)

Figure 9-1:
The two types of graphics: bitmap (left) and vector (right). The top center graphic is also a vector drawing, illustrating that this type of graphic appears smooth when printed small or large.

What formats can PageMaker import?

PageMaker can import many formats of graphics — as long as you installed the filter for that format when you installed PageMaker. The following list explains the major formats that PageMaker supports; if you try to load a file in one of these formats and get a message saying that PageMaker doesn't know how to place it, get your install disks or CD, run the installer program, and perform a Custom install to add the missing filter (for more information, see the appendix, "How to (Re)Install PageMaker").

PageMaker can import any of the following major formats, plus a few other more obscure formats. (All the formats listed here support color and grayscale graphics, unless noted.)

Image formats

- **TIFF:** TIFF, the Tagged Image File Format, can be produced by most graphics programs. TIFF is the standard image format on the Mac and on most PCs.

- **PCX:** PCX, the PC Paintbrush format, is a PC standard similar to TIFF.

- **BMP:** BMP, the Windows bitmap format, is the format used by Windows' built-in screen shot program. Most programs support it, but because the TIFF and PCX formats came along earlier and are more standardized, BMP is rarely used by professionals.

- **MacPaint:** The first image format for the Macintosh computer, MacPaint remains a black-and-white-only format to this day. In fact, it's highly unlikely that you'll run into MacPaint images unless they're very old and come from the Mac.

- **PICT:** The Macintosh Picture format, PICT is very common. PICT has a variant called PICT2, which PageMaker also supports. Note that PICT can be a drawing format as well as an image format.

- **PCD:** PageMaker can import images stored in Kodak's Photo CD format. But it can't store Photo CD images in your PageMaker file, as it can images stored in other graphics formats, because Photo CD files are simply too large. (This issue of storing graphics inside your documents is discussed in detail in Chapter 16.) Because of this limitation, PageMaker must be able to access the original image each time you open your document — which means that if you share your file with other people or take it to a service bureau, you'll have to give them the image CD as well.

  To get around this problem, you have two options. You can either open the image in an image editor such as Photoshop and save it as a TIFF file (or other acceptable image format) before bringing it into PageMaker. Or you can take advantage of an option that PageMaker offers when you try to import a Photo CD image directly, which is to save the file in the CIE Lab TIFF format (a special variety of TIFF). Both options result in smaller file sizes, enabling you to either store the image file in your PageMaker document or save to a floppy disk or other removable storage media (such as a SyQuest cartridge).

Drawing formats

- **EPS:** The Encapsulated PostScript format is the standard drawing format for professionals. Almost every program that supports PostScript printers can create it, and it's incredibly reliable. The problem is that only PostScript printers can print EPS graphics. If you're going to print your document on a non-PostScript printer, don't use EPS.

✔ **DCS:** DCS, the Desktop Color Separation format, is another variant of EPS in which each of the four colors used in professional printing — cyan, magenta, yellow, and black — has its own file. These four files are then coordinated by a fifth file (the DCS file), which is what is actually imported into PageMaker. Don't worry about this format unless you want to print professional-quality, full-color graphics.

✔ **WMF:** The Windows Metafile Format was the first Windows drawing format and is still common for low-end and mid-range graphics programs. Note that WMF also supports images.

✔ **PICT:** The first Mac drawing format, PICT is the Macintosh equivalent of WMF and is very common. PICT can also be an image format.

✔ **DXF:** The Digital Exchange Format is used by CAD (computer-aided design) programs on PCs and Macs.

If PageMaker doesn't support your graphics program's native file format (the one that's used by default), chances are that the graphics program allows you to save files in a format that PageMaker does support. For example, PageMaker cannot import the MacDraw format, but MacDraw can export (save) files in PICT format. Similarly, Photoshop has its own format (PSD) but can save images in TIFF, PCX, EPS, and several other formats that PageMaker supports.

Previous versions of PageMaker imported the native Adobe Illustrator format (AI), but Version 6 does not. However, you can save Illustrator documents in the EPS format to bring them into PageMaker.

What to do before you import

In most cases, you can just import a graphic file as is, with no preparation. But in some cases, you need to do something special.

If you want to place files that were created on a PC into your PageMaker document, you may need to rename the file first. For more information, see Chapter 18.

Preparing images

For images, the most important thing to do is to get rid of any extraneous information. For example, if the image area is 3×5 inches, and the bottom 2 inches are blank, crop out those bottom inches in your image-editing program before saving the file. Similarly, if you want only a portion of the image used in the PageMaker layout, crop out the parts you don't want (save the cropped file to a new name if you want to have a copy of the original file for use elsewhere).

Cropping is selecting the part of an image that you want to keep and getting rid of the rest — like clipping a photo from a magazine and throwing the rest of the page away. Most image-editing programs have cropping tools.

Cropping in PageMaker is easy, so you may be tempted to do the cropping there instead of in your image editor. But there's a good reason to crop the image in the original program: That 2 inches of blank space is actually a series of white dots. Those dots take up disk space and space inside the PageMaker file. When you crop in PageMaker, you're not changing the actual image file, just hiding part of it, and the hidden portion continues to consume disk space. Another advantage to cropping in the source program is that you are ensured that whoever does the layout has only the part of the image you want them to use.

Here are a few additional image preparation issues to keep in mind:

- **Color type:** If your source image is color and you will be printing your document in grayscale or black and white, convert the graphic to a grayscale or black-and-white image before importing it into PageMaker. (Again, save the altered file with a new name if you want to preserve the original.)

  You should convert the graphic before importing it for two reasons. First, the file will be smaller, which saves disk space and decreases print time. Second, although PageMaker can convert color images to grayscale or black-and-white images on its own, your image editor is likely to do a better job.

- **Size and resolution:** For color and grayscale images, make sure that the image size is the same as it will be in your PageMaker layout. Enlarging or reducing an image can make it hard to read or just downright ugly. Enlarging more than 25 percent can result in very blocky images. Reducing more than 25 percent can cause distortions called *moirés*.

  Reducing more than 25 percent can also increase print time because the dots that make up the image get smaller as you reduce the image. Often, the dots are smaller than the printer can reproduce, which means that PageMaker has to combine some dots to make them printable, a process that can take some time.

- **PC TIFFs:** PC versions of TIFF are different from Mac versions of TIFF. Usually, PageMaker can detect whether the file was saved in PC or Mac TIFF, and everything works fine. When PageMaker can't make this determination, the symptoms are obvious: The image looks like a photographic negative. You can fix this problem by resaving the TIFF file in Mac TIFF format (Photoshop has this feature, for example) or by loading the TIFF file into a Mac image-editing program and using its invert feature to make a negative of the negative, which changes the image back to normal. Then use that version of the file in PageMaker.

What's this new color management thing?

Computer monitors, printers, scanners, and other pieces of electronic publishing equipment all perceive and reproduce colors a little differently. Certain types of equipment can reproduce a broader range of colors than others — a color printer, for example, can produce fewer colors than a color monitor. Because of this, the colors you see on your monitor may not match the colors you get when you print your document.

A *color management system* — CMS, for short — compensates for the color discrepancies between the different pieces of equipment involved in publishing your document. A CMS keeps track of the range of colors that each piece can reproduce and makes sure that your on-screen image reflects the colors that your printer can actually produce. If your image contains any colors that your printer can't handle, the CMS replaces them with the nearest equivalent available from your printer.

PageMaker 6 is equipped with the Kodak Precision Color Management System, which is just one of many color-management programs available. If you choose File➪Preferences and click on the CMS Setup button, you can specify whether you want PageMaker to use the Kodak CMS, a CMS that you've bought from a different vendor, or no CMS. You can also specify what types of devices you'll be using to produce your documents, so the CMS knows how to adjust colors.

However, unless you're experienced with using color-management software, it's best to stick with the default CMS settings. Generally, you need to worry about color management only if you're producing very high-end color graphics. If you encounter lots of problems because your on-screen colors and your printed colors don't jive, ask a PageMaker guru or your service bureau representative for help in making adjustments to the CMS settings.

When you import a Photo CD image, PageMaker displays a dialog box that enables you to crop the image, change the image dimensions or resolution, sharpen the image, and rotate and flip the image. PageMaker also offers controls (via Element➪Image➪Image Control) that enable you to adjust the contrast and brightness of 1-bit and grayscale images. But if you have access to an image-editing program such as Photoshop, you're better off making such changes in that program. You'll have a greater degree of control and flexibility than in PageMaker.

Preparing drawings

The following information applies to drawings saved as EPS files, because those are the most complex. For other types of drawings, you really don't have anything to prepare ahead of time for import into PageMaker.

✓ **Colors:** If you defined colors in an EPS file created in, say, Illustrator or FreeHand, PageMaker imports those color definitions along with the file and adds them to the list of colors in the Colors palette (see Chapter 11 for more details).

If a color already defined in your PageMaker file has the same name as a color in the imported EPS graphic, you'll see a dialog box asking whether you want to preserve the existing PageMaker color definitions or use the EPS file's definitions. Sometimes, neither answer is right — you want both. So make sure that you use unique names in PageMaker and your drawing program. (For non-EPS drawings, this is not a problem because all colors in imported files are immediately translated to a mix of red, blue, and green and no longer have names.)

✔ **Fonts:** EPS drawings that include text formatted with typefaces that are not built into your printer or installed and active on your Mac may not print correctly. The fix is to convert the text to curves in your drawing program before importing the file into PageMaker.

✔ **Previews:** EPS drawings from PCs may display as gray boxes. This happens because an EPS file is actually a program that tells the printer how to draw the image. What you see on-screen is actually a bitmap preview, and the preview format created by a PC program may not be Mac-compatible. Also, some older EPS files may not include a preview file at all. But not to worry, the file will print correctly.

Bringing Graphics into Your Layout

After you've prepared your image as described in the first part of this chapter, you're ready to import it.

PageMaker refers to the process of bringing a file into your layout and then positioning it on your page as *placing*. This book tends to use the word *import* to refer to the process of bringing a graphic into your file and the word *place* when referring to the PageMaker commands or when the focus is on the positioning of the graphic.

To import a graphic

1. **Go to the page in your layout where you want to place the graphic.**

   (Note that any graphic placed in a master page, described in Chapter 14, will appear on all pages in the document that use that master page.)

2. **Change your view so that you can see the whole page, or at least the area in which you want to place your graphic.**

3. **Select a text block or existing graphic if desired.**

   If you want the new graphic to replace an existing graphic, click on the existing graphic with the Arrow tool to select it. If you want the new graphic to be an *in-line graphic* — one that moves with a particular piece of text — select the Text tool and click on the location in the text where you want the graphic to be inserted. (Think of an in-line graphic as a special text character that happens to be a graphic.)

4. Choose File⇨Place (Ctrl+D) to open the Place dialog box.

Figure 9-2 shows the dialog box. Sort through your drives and folders to find the file you want to place and then click on the filename. Note that PageMaker displays only the files for which it recognizes the format *and* has the appropriate import filter.

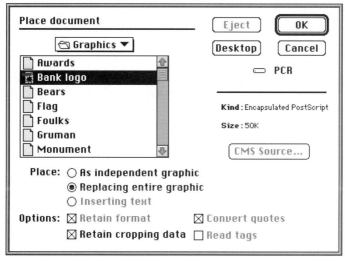

Figure 9-2:
The Place
dialog box
lets you
import
graphics
into
PageMaker.

5. Choose a Place option.

The Place options in the lower-left corner of the dialog box change depending on whether you clicked inside a text block or selected a graphic in your layout in step 3. If you selected a graphic with the Arrow tool, you can choose Replacing Entire Graphic to replace the selected graphic with the new one. If you don't want to replace the selected graphic, choose As Independent Graphic.

When you replace a graphic, any text wrap, sizing, or effects (such as rotation) that you applied to the old graphic are automatically applied to the replacement as well. Select the Retain Cropping Data check box if you want to apply any cropping you did to the current graphic to the replacement graphic. (Cropping is explained in more detail later in this chapter, in the section "Cropping.")

If you clicked inside a text block with the Text tool before choosing File⇨Place, you can make the imported graphic an in-line graphic by choosing As Inline Graphic (like you needed us to tell you that). Or you can choose As Independent Graphic to place the graphic amid the text but keep it as a separate entity from the text block.

If you didn't select anything or you selected a text block with the Arrow tool before choosing the Place command, you get only one option, As Independent Graphic.

Note that all the Place options don't appear until after you click on the name of the file you want to import.

6. Click on the OK button.

If PageMaker has trouble importing the graphic, it displays a dialog box telling you that the filter does not support the file format. Open the graphic in the program that created it to make sure that it's OK and resave it before trying to import it again.

You may also get a dialog box that says the file is very large and asks you to confirm whether to copy the graphic into PageMaker. Whether you answer yes or no, PageMaker places the graphic; by *copy*, it means bring a copy of the graphic file into the PageMaker file. Chapter 16 provides more information about this option.

7. Place the graphic if necessary.

If you chose the As Independent Graphic option, you see a small square icon that changes depending on the type of graphic you're importing. Figure 9-3 shows the various icons and the types of graphics they represent. The upper-left corner of the icon represents the upper-left corner of the graphic. Move the cursor to where you want to place the graphic and click the mouse button. Your graphic appears.

If you chose As Inline Graphic or Replacing Entire Graphic, your graphic appears at the spot you clicked with the Text tool or in the position of the graphic being replaced.

What's a color model, anyway?

RGB (red, green, blue) and CMYK (cyan, magenta, yellow, black) are the two main *color models* (methods of creating colors) in most programs. RGB is the color model used in computer monitors and in slide makers. CMYK is the color model used by printers.

When you're creating colors, most programs ask you to choose the color model you want to base the colors on. If you're creating slides or documents for electronic distribution — which means that your audience will be viewing your document on their computer monitors — pick RGB. If you're printing your document on paper — any kind of paper — pick CMYK. However, be aware that colors you see on your monitor and those you get on your printed piece may vary. This happens because the monitor displays colors according to the RGB model, while a printer uses the CMYK model.

Figure 9-3:
The place
icons for
imported
graphics.

🖼 TIFF	
🖼 Bitmap image	
📐 Vector graphic (drawings)	
📄 Encapsulated PostScript (EPS)	

Fine-Tuning a Graphic

When placed, a graphic is the same size as in the originating program. You may not like that size. Fortunately, you can change it. Notice the little black rectangles around the edges of the graphic. These rectangles are called *handles*, and you can use them to resize or crop a graphic. Figure 9-4 shows a graphic's handles, as well as the cursor you see when you select a handle (the two-headed arrow cursor).

Figure 9-4:
Select an
imported
graphic to
display eight
tiny square
handles
(left). Drag
one of the
handles to
resize the
graphic
(right).

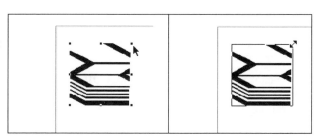

Resizing

To resize a graphic, select the Arrow tool, click on the graphic to select it, and then drag one of the graphic's handles. Dragging away from the graphic makes it bigger; dragging toward the graphic makes it smaller. Note that the handle you choose is significant. Choosing a center handle resizes the graphic in one dimension (the handles on the side change its width, while those on the top and bottom change its height). Choosing a corner handle resizes both dimensions.

Don't resize bitmap images more than 25 percent, or you may end up with moirés or blocky images when you print your document. Instead, resize your graphic in the program you used to create it or in an image-editing program.

You can easily distort a graphic by resizing it along one dimension or by dragging a corner handle at any angle but 45 degrees. Most mere mortals don't have the kind of coordination that's required to precisely calculate the angle that they're moving the mouse. Fortunately, you can resize a graphic proportionally, so that it does not become distorted: Hold down the Shift key while dragging. Be sure to release the mouse button *before* you release the Shift key.

Resizing by mouse makes a lot of sense when you're experimenting. But you can resize graphics more precisely by using the Control palette, as Figure 9-5 shows. If you know the degree of enlargement or reduction, you can specify it in the palette and have PageMaker apply it for you. Or you can enter the new dimensions or click on the Nudge arrows to change the values gradually, until the size looks right to you. A good technique is to use the mouse to do a rough resizing and then use the Control palette for fine-tuning.

Before entering resize values into the Control palette, you need to select a *reference point* by clicking on one of the handles (the little black squares) on the Proxy button (labeled in Figure 9-5). The handles around the edge of the Proxy button correspond to the handles around the edge of your graphic. The center square corresponds to the center of your graphic. The selected Proxy button handle appears larger than the other handles.

- ✔ If you click on a handle in the Proxy button, the corresponding point on the graphic stays put as you resize the graphic.
- ✔ If you double-click on a handle in the Proxy button, it changes into a two-headed arrow, and the corresponding point on the graphic moves as you resize the graphic.

Try resizing an object using both methods to get a feel for the way each works.

To the right of the Resize icon is an icon that indicates proportional resize, which means that if you change one of the resize percentages (to the left of the Resize icon), both the horizontal and vertical percentages are changed to the same value. If you click on the Proportional Resize icon, you get a different icon, one that represents independent resizing along the horizontal and vertical axes. When this icon is active, you can specify different horizontal and vertical percentages. For some graphics — black-and-white (1-bit) bitmaps — PageMaker displays a third icon that resizes the graphic to a resolution that is compatible with the selected printer (if the image does not match, the printer icon has an *X* in it). Figure 9-6 shows the three icons.

Figure 9-5:
The Control palette lets you resize a graphic by entering the percentage of enlargement or reduction.

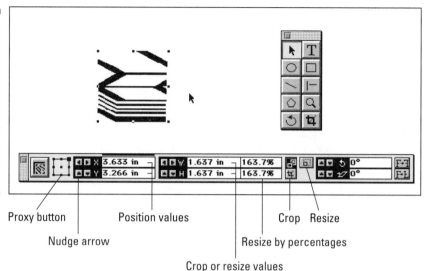

Proxy button   Position values   Crop   Resize

Nudge arrow   Resize by percentages

Crop or resize values

Independent resize ⌐

Proportional resize

Figure 9-6:
Three icons that control how you resize graphics in PageMaker.

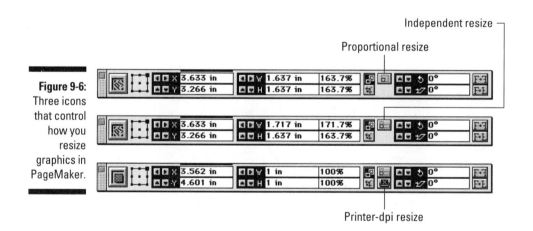

Printer-dpi resize

Cropping

To crop a graphic, select the Crop tool (⌐⌐), click on the graphic to select it, and drag one of the graphic's handles. Drag toward the center of the graphic to crop out part of the graphic; move away from the center to uncrop a previously cropped graphic.

If you don't crop the graphic exactly right the first time, don't panic. Remember, you're not actually deleting any of your graphic when you crop it in PageMaker; you're just hiding it from view.

Just as with resizing, the handle you pick determines whether the crop is along one dimension or two. Also, holding the Shift key while cropping ensures a proportional crop (although most crops are not proportional because you usually want to get rid of a particular portion of the graphic).

If you like the size of your cropped image but want to show a different portion of the graphic, place the Crop tool cursor in the center of the graphic and press and hold the mouse button. When the hand cursor appears, drag to scroll around your image. When the portion you want to show is within the boundaries of the cropped graphic, release the mouse button.

If you prefer, you can use the Control palette to crop a graphic. Click on the Crop icon in the palette (identified in Figure 9-5) and then click or double-click one of the handles on the Proxy button (also labeled in Figure 9-5) to set a reference point for your crop.

✔ As with resizing, if you click on a Proxy button handle, the corresponding point in your graphic remains stationary during the crop. If you double-click on a Proxy button handle, the corresponding point in the graphic moves during the crop.

✔ Click on the center reference point in the Proxy button to crop a graphic evenly from all sides. (In-line graphics can be cropped only from the center when you use the palette.)

✔ Note that when you use the palette for cropping, the percentage fields disappear — you can crop only by using the nudge arrows or entering the crop values in the W and H (width and height) option boxes.

Wrapping Text around Graphics

When you place a graphic over some text, one of two things happens: The graphic overprints (covers) the text, or the text *wraps* — moves out of the way of the graphic. You rarely want to obscure text with a graphic, so it'd be nice if PageMaker could automatically wrap text around graphics you place. Lucky for you, PageMaker can.

By default, text wrap is turned off — which is a setting that you'll definitely want to change because you'll almost always want your text to wrap around graphics. (You can turn off text wrap for a selected graphic if needed.)

To establish automatic text wrap as the default setting, follow these steps:

1. **Open PageMaker but don't open any documents.**

2. **Choose Element⇨Text Wrap to display the Text Wrap dialog box.**

   Figure 9-7 shows the default settings.

Rectangular Wrap

No Wrap   Irregular Wrap

Figure 9-7:
By default,
the No
Wrap option
is selected;
it's a good
idea to
change the
default so
that the
Rectangular
Wrap option
is turned on
instead.

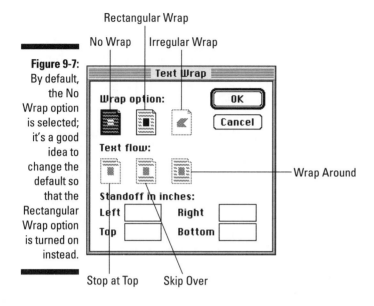

Wrap Around

Stop at Top   Skip Over

3. Select the wrap icons you want.

The icons in the dialog box represent different text wrap options, which
are described in more detail later in this section. Select the ones that
match your needs. Most people select the top, middle icon (Rectangular
Wrap) and the bottom, right one (Wrap Around), as shown in Figure 9-8.

Figure 9-8:
Common
settings in
the Text
Wrap dialog
box:
Rectangular
text wrap is
turned on,
and text is
set to wrap
around both
sides of the
graphic.

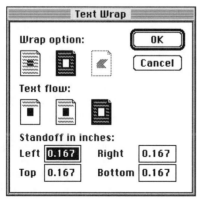

4. Enter the standoff settings.

The *standoff* is the margin between the graphic and the text. A dotted box appears around the graphic to represent the standoff area. The diamonds in the corners are the standoff box's handles. (Flip ahead to Figure 9-11 for a look at a standoff box with its handles displayed.) The default settings — 0.167 inches, or 1 pica — are fine for most uses.

You rarely would have a standoff of 0, which would eliminate any space between the graphic and the text. In multicolumn text, a pica is the standard margin between related elements, such as graphics and text, or between columns. But in some cases, you'll want more space — for example, if you have a single, page-wide column and large graphics and you need to put a fairly large space, perhaps 0.3 to 0.5 inches, between elements so that they don't seem too crowded. Note that you can set the standoff separately for all four sides of the graphic — left, right, top, and bottom. Do so when it makes sense, such as when it looks better to have, say, more space along the sides than at the top and bottom of the graphic.

The icons in the top row of the Text Wrap dialog box, from left to right, represent No Wrap, Rectangular Wrap, and Irregular Wrap. No Wrap is self-explanatory, and Rectangular Wrap means to wrap around the invisible box that contains the imported graphic. No matter the actual shape of the graphic, PageMaker places it in an invisible box, which is what the handles are attached to. The last option, Irregular Wrap, is grayed out until you manipulate a standoff box, which is explained a little later. Figure 9-9 shows the various results for these options.

So much for the top row of icons in the Text Wrap dialog box. Now for the Text Flow icons. From left to right, the icons represent these options: Stop at Top, Skip Over, and Wrap Around. If you choose the Stop at Top icon, the text box stops above the graphic and continues at the top of the next column or page.

The Skip Over option stops the text block at the top of the graphic and resumes the text block below. Use this option if your graphic is not as wide as your text column *and* if it is not aligned against one side of the column. Otherwise, you'll get text that's split vertically by the graphic, not just horizontally. This option is typically used in documentation and simple business reports.

The last option — the one you'll likely use most often for newsletters and fancier documents — is Wrap Around, which makes sure that the text flows any place in the text block where the graphic isn't. Thus, it can be used to make a graphic the equivalent of a drop cap or to have two columns wrap around a graphic placed between them. Figure 9-10 shows the various results, good and bad, for these text-wrap options.

Figure 9-9:
Samples of
the three
kinds of text
wrap: No
Wrap (top),
Rectangular
Wrap (left),
and
Irregular
Wrap (right,
around the
whale's tail).

That's all there is to it, at least for setting the defaults.

When you move a graphic, the text that wraps around it reflows as needed based on the graphic's new position. If you move the graphic into a new area of text, that text wraps around the graphic. Similarly, if you place, modify, or resize text where a graphic is located, that text wraps as well. The whole point of desktop publishing is to automate the layout process — and here's proof that PageMaker does.

You can select multiple graphics and apply text-wrap settings to all simultaneously. To select multiple graphics, Shift+click on each graphic or drag around all the graphics with the Arrow tool.

Figure 9-10:
Samples of three types of text flow: Wrap Around (left page), Stop at Top (first column, right page), and Skip Over (middle column of right page).

Special Effects with Text Wrap

The one setting you can't set as a default is irregular text wrap. You must select a graphic before you can apply this option, which is great for creating special effects, such as the one shown in Figure 9-11.

The following steps walk you through the process of using irregular text wrap on a graphic-by-graphic basis:

1. **Select the graphic with the Arrow tool.**

2. **If the default text flow setting is not Wrap Around, use Element⇨Text Wrap to open the Text Wrap dialog box.**

   Make sure that the lower-right icon (Wrap Around) is selected and set the standoff values.

But wait! What about that icon in the Text Wrap dialog box for Irregular Wrap? The truth is, you don't need it. In fact, you can't ever select this icon — it's not selectable. Its only real purpose is to indicate when you have an irregular wrap, although that's obvious just from looking at the graphic.

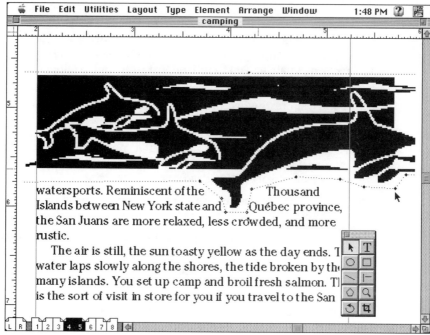

File Edit Utilities Layout Type Element Arrange Window   1:48 PM

watersports. Reminiscent of the Thousand Islands between New York state and Québec province, the San Juans are more relaxed, less crowded, and more rustic.

The air is still, the sun toasty yellow as the day ends. water laps slowly along the shores, the tide broken by the many islands. You set up camp and broil fresh salmon. is the sort of visit in store for you if you travel to the San

Figure 9-11:
The handles
created for
an irregular
wrap around
one image.

3. Click on OK.

The dashed box that indicates the standoff margin appears around your graphic.

4. Drag a diamond-shaped handle to a new location.

Notice how the text wrap follows the new shape of the standoff box.

5. Click to add more handles if needed.

So far, your standoff box has just four handles, limiting you to creating a trapezoid-shaped text wrap. What if you want the wrap to be something else, perhaps circular, or star-shaped? Just click on the standoff box to create a new handle. By adding and moving handles, you can create any sort of polygon shape, and by having enough points, you can simulate a circle or rectangle. To delete a handle, simply drag it onto a neighboring handle.

Just for good measure, here are a few more tips for creating text wraps:

✔ You can manipulate the shape of a standoff by dragging a line segment between two handles.

✔ If you create a truly horrible irregular text wrap and want to cancel it, choose Element⇨Text Wrap and select the Rectangular Wrap icon (top middle). Your standoff box and its handles revert to the rectangular settings.

- ✔ The new Group command in PageMaker 6 makes it easier to wrap a text block around another text block than in earlier versions. Select the text block around which you want to wrap other text and choose Arrange⇨Group. PageMaker then perceives your text block as a graphic element, enabling you to turn on text wrap and manipulate the standoff just as you would for a regular graphic.

- ✔ If you want text to overprint a graphic, turn off text wrap for the graphic. Then make sure that the text block is in front of the graphic — use Arrange⇨Send to Back (⌘+B) if the graphic is selected or Arrange⇨Bring to Front (⌘+F) if the text block is selected. You can use this technique in reverse if you want to obscure text with a graphic, perhaps when creating a piece of artwork within PageMaker.

- ✔ You can wrap text around graphics created in PageMaker, such as lines and circles. Chapter 10 covers PageMaker's graphics tools.

- ✔ Finally, screen redraw can be a pain while you're editing a custom text-wrap boundary. Every time you release the mouse button, the screen redraws. To keep that from happening, press the spacebar while you alter custom text-wrap boundaries.

Chapter 10
Even Prettier Pretty Pictures

Graphics really can add life to a publication. It's a cliché that a picture is worth a thousand words (although it's true in many cases). Well, a picture can also make you want to read a thousand words — that's at least as important as conveying a message visually.

In Chapter 9, we discussed importing graphics and text wrap. In this chapter, you jump into PageMaker's graphics-creation tools, take a peek at PageMaker's image controls, and finally, see how you can merge graphics into text. It's a fun ride. Hang on!

Creating Your Own Graphics

Most of the tools in PageMaker's toolbox work with graphics — only the Text tool doesn't. You can use the middle four tools in the toolbox — the Line, Perpendicular Line, Rectangle, and Ellipse tools — plus a fifth tool, the new Polygon tool, to create graphics.

Perpendicular is techno-speak for lines that go only straight across or only straight up and down. In PageMaker-speak, it also means lines that go at a 45-degree angle (0, 45, or 90 degrees).

When you create a graphic, PageMaker uses the default text-wrap settings (see Chapter 9). This feature can be a pain at times because your defaults for imported graphics may not be appropriate for lines and rectangles that you draw. For example, you may set a standoff margin of 0.2 inches around imported images so that the text doesn't get too close. But if you want to put lines between columns, you may want the lines closer than 0.2 inches to the text. There's really no way around this: You can have only one set of defaults for text wrap, so you should use the settings for the elements that you use most often and just change the settings for the other types of graphics as needed.

When talking about graphics, people use the term *points* to refer to the thickness of a line in a graphic. Whether it's a straight line, a line in a rectangle, or the line in a circle, you measure it in points. So what is a point? A point is equal to $^1/_{72}$ inch, or $^1/_{12}$ pica. (Imagine entering line sizes as inches: You'd have thicknesses like 0.175 and 0.050. No, thank you!)

Working with lines

Chances are, you'll draw lines more than any other type of graphic element in PageMaker. Lines — also called *rules* by publishing folks — are best used as separators. For example, you may put lines above your page numbers and newsletter name (traditionally placed at the bottom of the page) to make it clear where the article text ends. Lines also make great separators between stories on a page. And thin rules can be used to separate columns of text — many newspapers use this effect, especially those like the *New York Times* that seek that old-fashioned look.

In the early days of print, typesetters tried to cram as many letters as possible on a page because paper and printing were so expensive. The font Times was developed for the *Times* of London to be readable at small sizes and with compact spacing, and it soon became a standard. (However, the Times font on most printers is based on a version developed for the *New York Times* to improve readability.) To crowd even more type on a page, newspaper layout artists pushed the columns very close together — to less than 1 pica, or 0.167 inches, apart — making it necessary to add a thin line between the columns so that readers wouldn't get mixed up. These lines were so thin that they were called *hairlines;* today, the term refers to a line that's $^1/_4$ point wide.

Rules of thumb

When drawing lines, follow these *rules* of thumb (pun intended):

- Choose a thinner line over a thicker one. Thick lines can be overkill; if you're not sure how thick something should be, tone it down. Generally, use a hairline or $1/2$-point rule to separate small elements or to act as a boundary between a shaded area and a nonshaded area. Use a 1- or 1.5-point rule to separate larger elements, such as stories, or to create a box around a story. Use 2- or 3-point lines rarely; one possible use is to separate very different elements.

- Put at least 3 points of space between the rule and the nearest text or graphic — 6 to 9 points is best.

- Don't use too many different sizes of lines on the same page or too many lines together.

- Consider putting a thin and thick line next to each other (perhaps 0.5-point and 1.5-points, separated by 1 or 1.5 points of space). PageMaker has some predefined line styles that do this automatically.

Drawing regular lines

To draw a line, click on the Line or Perpendicular Line tool and start dragging at the point where you want the line to begin. Release the mouse button at the point where you want the line to end.

- You don't actually have to switch to the Perpendicular Line tool to get perpendicular lines. If you hold down the Shift key while drawing with the regular Line tool, PageMaker ensures that your line is a perpendicular line. You can even press Shift midway through a drag with the Line tool; PageMaker immediately snaps your line to perpendicular.

- You can modify the size or position of lines by dragging their end points or by selecting the line and changing the Control palette's X and Y values (for position) and L value (for size). The palette is shown in Figure 10-1. In either case, use the Arrow tool to select the line.

- As it does when you're resizing or cropping graphics, the Proxy button in the Control palette indicates the point of the line from which any resizing or positioning will occur. If you click once to select a handle on the Proxy button, the corresponding point in your line remains stationary when you enter new size or position values. If you click twice, the handle turns into a double-headed arrow, and the corresponding point on your line moves when you enter new values. Click on the center point to resize or reposition a line equally from all sides.

✔ If you want to change a perpendicular line into a nonperpendicular line, just change to the Arrow tool, select one end of the line, and drag it to a new location. Because you can drag the end to any location, you can create a nonperpendicular line. (You can also rotate the line by using the Rotate tool in the toolbox or the rotation settings in the Control palette.)

Drawing special lines

Not all lines are solid, and not all are 1-point thick. PageMaker offers several types of lines, and it lets you create your own custom lines, too. Figure 10-2 shows the menu of line types (accessed by choosing Element⇨Line). As you can see, PageMaker gives you a choice of dotted lines, double lines, even dashed lines, all available in several predefined sizes. If you want something else, select the Custom option to open the Custom Line dialog box, shown in Figure 10-3. Here, you pick the thickness, style (such as dotted or dashed), and printing attributes.

✔ You can also select the printing attributes — Transparent Background and Reverse Line — from the Element⇨Line menu; if the features are checked in the menu or in the Custom Line dialog box, they are active.

✔ The Transparent Background option, turned on by default, creates a line that looks like it's printed directly on top of anything beneath it. If you choose a dashed line, for example, anything between the dashes prints.

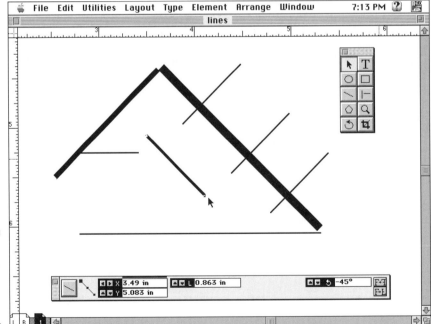

Figure 10-1:
The Control palette when a line is selected.

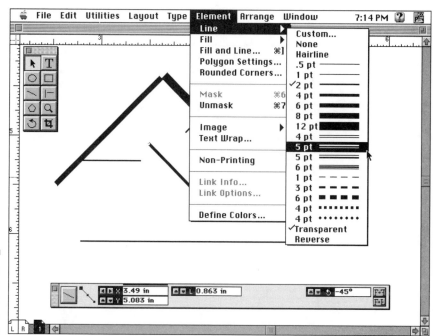

Figure 10-2:
The menu options for lines.

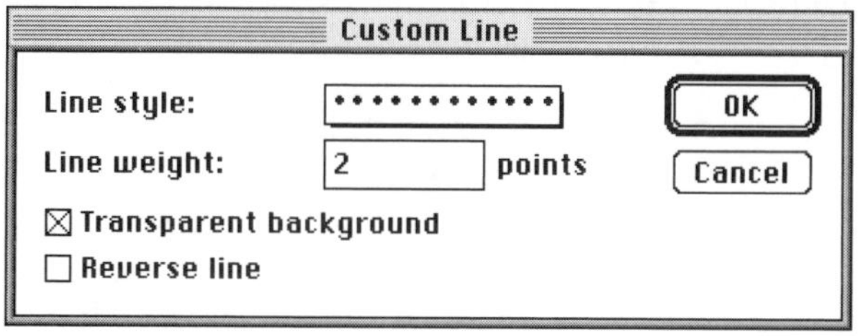

Figure 10-3:
The Custom Line dialog box lets you create any line weight you want.

But if you uncheck the Transparent option, anything between the dashes appears in the paper color (usually white). Figure 10-4 shows the difference between having this option checked and not having this option checked.

✔ The Reverse Line option inverts the color — a black line becomes white, or vice versa. This option is usually unchecked, which leaves the line at its normal color (black, unless you apply a color via the Colors palette).

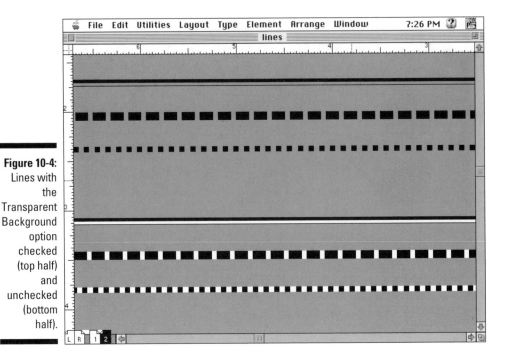

Figure 10-4:
Lines with the Transparent Background option checked (top half) and unchecked (bottom half).

✔ When would you uncheck the Transparent Background option? Here's an example: Say that you're using one of the lines composed of two rules with a space between them. If this line rests on top of a gray box (or perhaps forms its border), it looks more dramatic if it has a paper-colored background. Figure 10-5 shows an example.

✔ If you're working with several lines and you want them to be joined, change to a larger view so that you can ensure that they really do align. (Double-size is a good setting; choose Layout⇨View⇨200% or press ⌘+2.)

One way to help force the lines into alignment is to use PageMaker's snap-to feature. This feature is no panacea, mind you, but it can help. For example, if your lines fall within the column boundaries, turning on Snap to Guides (Layout⇨Guides and Rulers⇨Snap to Guides or ⌘+Shift+G) ensures that the lines end at the column boundaries (where the column guides are located).

✔ To access additional line settings, choose Element⇨Fill and Line to open the Fill and Line dialog box. In the dialog box, you can choose a color and shade for your line and specify whether you want the line to overprint other elements. (The dialog box is discussed in more detail in the section, "Dressing up your shapes.")

Figure 10-5:
Unchecking
the
Transparent
Background
option (top,
in the
border) can
result in a
more
dynamic
look for
certain
types of
lines.

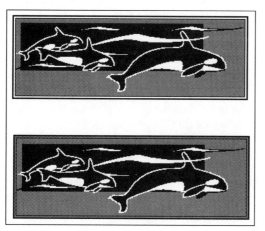

Look again at Figure 10-5. Those four lines actually form a rectangle. For solid lines, it doesn't matter whether you draw a rectangle with the Rectangle tool or draw four lines with the Line tool — you have access to the same line options with either tool. But for other types of lines — for example, lines created with the double-line option — it can make a big difference.

In Figure 10-6, for example, the lines in the bottom image are the same lines drawn for Figure 10-5, except that this time the double-line option was used, making it obvious that these are four lines instead of a rectangle. See how the corners aren't beveled? You'd get similar mismatches if you chose dashed or dotted lines. Plus, when you use the Rectangle tool, you get the option of simultaneously filling in the rectangle with a shade or pattern as discussed in the section "Dressing up your shapes."

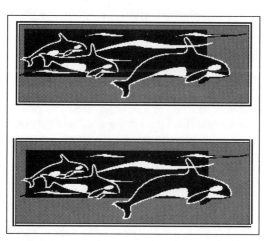

Figure 10-6:
Using the
line options
with a
rectangle
(top, in the
border),
versus
drawing the
four lines
independently
(bottom).

The moral of the story: If you want to draw a box — or any other straight-sided shape, for that matter — use the Rectangle or Polygon tool, discussed in the next section.

Creating rectangles, ellipses, and polygons

PageMaker offers three tools for creating simple shapes: the Rectangle tool, the Ellipse tool, and the Polygon tool (new in Version 6).

- ✔ To create a rectangle, select the Rectangle tool and just drag as you would to create a text block. The point where you start your drag becomes one corner of the rectangle; the point where you release the mouse button becomes the opposite corner. To create a square, press Shift as you drag.

- ✔ To round off the corners of a rectangle, choose Element⇨Rounded Corners and choose the style of corner you want from the resulting dialog box.

- ✔ The Ellipse tool works the same way as the Rectangle tool, except, of course, that it creates ovals instead of rectangles. To draw a perfect circle, press Shift as you drag.

- ✔ The Polygon tool initially draws a five-sided shape. But you can change the number of sides by selecting the polygon and choosing Element⇨Polygon Settings. The dialog box shown in Figure 10-7 appears. The Preview box in the dialog box shows how your polygon will look with the current settings.

- ✔ To create a polygon that has five sides of equal length, press Shift as you drag.

- ✔ To create a star, raise the Star Inset value (a value of 0 represents no star). The number of points in your star matches the Number of Sides value. If you set the Number of Sides value to five, for example, you get a five-pointed star. Figure 10-7 shows the results of three different Star Inset values on the same five-pointed polygon.

- ✔ If you save your publication as a PageMaker 5 document — for example, if you're giving the file to someone who hasn't upgraded to Version 6 — any shape you create with the Polygon tool disappears.

Dressing up your shapes

Whether you're putting a box, a circle, or a polygon around a piece of text (such as for a sidebar) or around a graphic, you'll likely want to apply both line and fill attributes to the shape. Refer back to Figures 10-5 and 10-6 to see a typical combination of a shade of gray and a double-line border.

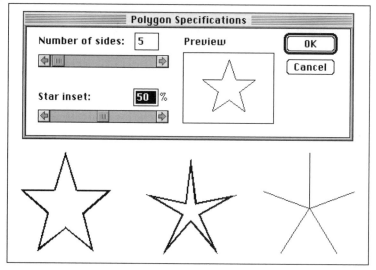

Figure 10-7:
The Polygon Specifications dialog box and the results of three different Star Inset settings: 50 percent (bottom left), 75 percent (middle), and 100 percent (far right).

Fill is a techie term for the color or shading you apply to the interior of an element; this book often uses the word *background* to mean the same thing.

Filling and outlining shapes

To outline a shape, select the shape and then choose Element⇨Line. You have access to the same line settings as you do when creating a simple line, as described earlier in this chapter in the section "Drawing special lines."

To fill an object with a solid color or pattern, select the object with the Arrow tool, choose Element⇨Fill, and select a color or pattern option from the submenu. You can choose either a solid color or a pattern, but not both.

In earlier versions of PageMaker, you could access shades of gray from the Element⇨Fill submenu. In Version 6, you need to choose Element⇨Fill and Line to open the Fill and Line dialog box. Here, you can establish both your fill and line settings at the same time. The dialog box also offers some line settings that aren't available from the Line menu. Figure 10-8 shows the Fill and Line dialog box; Figure 10-9 shows the Fill submenu. (In case you forgot, Figure 10-2 showed the Line submenu.)

  ✔ For fills, you can choose a color, pattern, or tint (shade); for lines, you can choose size and style, color, and tint and specify whether you want a transparent background or reverse line. In addition, you can decide whether the lines and/or fills overprint elements of a different color beneath them.

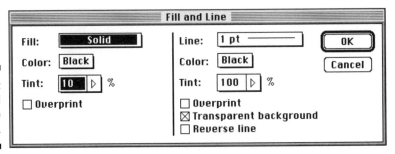

Figure 10-8:
The Fill
and Line
dialog box.

Figure 10-9:
If you just
want to fill
an object
with black
or white or
with one of
PageMaker's
predefined
patterns,
you can
use the
Fill menu.

✔ To *overprint* means to print over anything behind the element instead of obscuring (or *knocking out*) whatever is behind. In most cases, you won't notice a difference. But if you overprint yellow on top of blue, for example, you get green where the two elements intersect. If you don't overprint the yellow, you get yellow where the two elements intersect. Note that you may not see the color mixing on-screen.

✔ You may think that you can create patterns by overlapping several rectangles, each filled with a different color, shade, or pattern, and then checking the Overprint option in the Fill and Line dialog box. Unfortunately, this method works only if you are printing *color separations* (a process used when reproducing color images commercially, as explained in Chapters 11 and 17) and overprint shades of different colors. It does not work for multiple overlapping elements of the same color, nor does it work for patterns (they all have white backgrounds and block out anything under them).

✔ If you want to establish default fill and line settings, make your choices in the Fill and Line dialog box when no graphics are selected. Any subsequent objects that you draw in PageMaker take on the default fill and line attributes.

✔ If you want a drop shadow effect for your rectangle (see Figure 10-10), create a new rectangle of the same size as the current one. (You can just use copy and paste to do this: Select the rectangle, press ⌘+C to copy, and then press ⌘+V to paste.) Then move the new rectangle slightly to the left and down from the original rectangle and choose Arrange⇨Send to Back (⌘+B) to position it behind the original rectangle.

Make sure that the color or shade of the two rectangles is different enough so that the shadow is obvious. Also, if your original rectangle had a border, remove the border from the shadow rectangle (select the rectangle and then choose None from the Line submenu). If you want the original rectangle to be white, you may have to set its fill to Paper so that the rectangle beneath does not show through it.

Figure 10-10:
Creating a
drop
shadow.

✔ The gray shades available in PageMaker — 10, 20, 40, 60, and 80 percent — appear coarser on-screen than they do when printed. On-screen, type looks best over a 20 percent fill, but when printed, it looks best over a 10 percent fill, despite its hard-to-read appearance on-screen.

✔ Don't use a gray level greater than 10 percent behind text. If you're using a light color such as yellow as a background, you can increase the value, depending on the richness of the color. A too-dark background can obscure text.

✔ You can use white or light-colored type on a dark background to highlight an element. Generally, the background should be at least 80 percent gray or a dark, rich color, and the type should be white or a very light color. Typically, the type should be in a bold face because it's harder for the human eye to read light on dark than it is to read dark on light.

✔ For really interesting backgrounds, create patterns or shapes in an illustration or photo-editing program and import the graphic into PageMaker. Crop the graphic to the size of a background rectangle, add rules around it if desired, and place your text or graphic on top. (The effect is sort of like the desktop pattern displayed behind the various icons and open windows at the Finder level on your Mac.) Note that if you're using text, the background graphic should be muted (at least where the text appears) so that the text remains readable. For large text, such as in titles, using a bold typeface, perhaps with an outline or drop shadow, usually removes the need for a muted background.

Creating good-looking borders

Borders around shapes deserve special attention. Following are some tips to creating effective borders:

✔ Borders usually should be no thicker than 2 points. For multiline lines, such as the thick-and-thin line used in Figure 10-6, lines should usually be between 4 and 7 points thick. If they're much thicker, they'll probably overwhelm the other elements.

✔ It's a good idea to put a hairline or 0.5-point rule around grayscale photographic or scanned images — the rule provides a clear demarcation of where the photo ends and the paper begins. Doing so is not a requirement, but it often helps. However, such a rule is rarely needed for color images, because the color stands out by itself from the rest of the black and gray elements on a page.

✔ Borders start at the edge of a shape and proceed inward. Thus, if you have a rectangle with a gray background and a thick-and-thin rule, the space between the two lines making up the rule will be white because that space is outside the rectangle's gray background.

What if you want that space to be gray? Create a new rectangle that is as big as the outside of the first rectangle's border, fill it with the same background as the first rectangle, and then use Arrange➪Send to Back (⌘+B) to position it behind the first rectangle. That puts your gray behind the space inside the rules (in fact, that's what happened in Figure 10-5).

✔ A classy effect is to put rules on the top and bottom (sometimes of different thicknesses) of a background. You have to draw the two rules and make sure that they align with the top and bottom of the background — so that you don't get an awkward gap between the line and the background or see the background seeping past the lines. And if you move the rectangle that serves as the background, be sure to select the two lines, too, so that the elements move together. (Select the Arrow tool, click on the rectangle, and then Shift+click on each of the lines.) You may want to use the Group command, as explained in the section "Grouping objects," later in this chapter, to weld the lines to the rectangle.

You may think that you can save a step by using the Line submenu to add a rule around a photograph or illustration. Sorry, it won't work. But you can do the following: Select the object with the Arrow tool and choose Utilities⟡PageMaker Plug-ins⟡Keyline. Then click on the Attributes button to access the Fill and Line dialog box, select the line that you want to use, and press Return. Enter a value into the Extends option box to specify the distance between the border and the object. For example, if you want to draw the border right on the object, enter 0. Then press Return. You can also apply this command to text blocks, but if you do, use an Extends value of 2 to 6 points.

Creating simple drawings

You can create simple drawings by combining rectangles, ellipses, and lines. We're talking basic stuff here, like a yellow circle in a blue rectangle to represent the sun in the sky, a rounded-corner rectangle in a regular rectangle to represent a TV or computer monitor, or a pattern of lines to represent a mountain range. If you want to do more challenging graphics, use a drawing program or invest in some *clip art* (collections of simple illustrations and photos available on disk and CD-ROM).

Figure 10-11 shows an example of do-it-yourself PageMaker art: a TV with a picture in it. The secret to creating this graphic is to place a transparent rectangle with a thick border line (5 points here) and rounded corners in front of the TV. The border line is a thick-and-thin combination, and Transparent Background is unchecked so that the TV image does not appear between the two lines (instead, a white band appears). Using the rounded rectangle to hide the TV means that the TV image has to be larger than it would appear because there had to be enough to place that rounded-rectangle over.

Moving, Deleting, and Duplicating Graphics

You can move and duplicate graphic elements in the same way that you move and duplicate text blocks:

- ✔ To move a graphic, select the Arrow tool, press and hold the mouse on the graphic, and drag when the move cursor (the four-headed arrow) appears.

- ✔ To nudge a graphic a short distance, select it and then press the arrow keys on the keyboard.

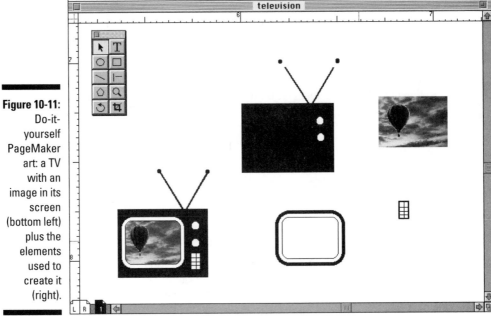

Figure 10-11:
Do-it-
yourself
PageMaker
art: a TV
with an
image in its
screen
(bottom left)
plus the
elements
used to
create it
(right).

✔ To copy a graphic, select it with the Arrow tool and then press ⌘+C or choose Edit➪Copy. Then press ⌘+V or choose Edit➪Paste. PageMaker places the duplicate on top of the original but offsets it a little so that you can see both the duplicate and original. You can then drag the copy to any place in your document.

✔ For precise movements, you can use the Control palette. Select the object and then enter new coordinates for the graphic into the X and Y option boxes. PageMaker places the graphic relative to the handle you've selected in the Proxy button, as it does when you crop and resize graphics. (For more information on the Proxy button, see Chapter 9.)

✔ If you want to banish a graphic from your layout, just select it and press Delete.

But these methods are just the basic techniques for duplicating and positioning graphic elements. PageMaker offers you several more sophisticated ways to copy and place graphics, as outlined in the next sections.

Grouping objects

Suppose that you've created a graphic similar to the one in Figure 10-11 — a graphic composed of more than one element. After getting all the objects just so, you decide that you'd rather place the graphic at the bottom of your page, instead of the top.

You can select all the components of the graphic, by clicking on the first one and then Shift+clicking on all the other elements — or by dragging around them with the Arrow tool — and then dragging the whole kit and caboodle down the page. But what if you change your mind later on in the day and decide that the thing looked better up at the top of the page instead? You'd have to go through the process of selecting all the individual elements again — and there's always the chance that you could miss an element or two or accidentally shift an element out of place.

A better solution is to use the Group command. After you group all the elements in the graphic together, PageMaker treats them as a single entity. You can then easily move, copy, or apply special effects to a graphic without having to worry whether you've selected all of its components. One click on your graphic selects everything. You can group text blocks as well as graphics.

To group elements, first select them by Shift+clicking on them with the Arrow tool or by dragging a marquee around them with the Arrow tool. Then choose Arrange⇨Group or press ⌘+G. If you later want to ungroup the objects, select the graphic and choose Arrange⇨Ungroup or press ⌘+U.

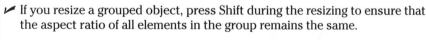

✔ Just because your objects are grouped doesn't mean that you can no longer make changes to the individual components. You can select and edit an element in a grouped object by ⌘+clicking on it. Use the Arrow tool if you want to edit a graphic element and the Text tool if you want to edit text.

✔ If you resize a grouped object, press Shift during the resizing to ensure that the aspect ratio of all elements in the group remains the same.

✔ If you save a publication that has grouped objects in the PageMaker 5 format, the objects are ungrouped because Version 5 does not support the grouping feature.

Aligning and distributing objects

Take a look at Figure 10-12. The document is an announcement trumpeting awards won by IDG Books Worldwide and Macworld (these are real awards). What's so special about this document? Well, notice how the award logos align, as do the text blocks below them. To position elements like this, you can use the mouse and eyeball it — except that takes a lot of work and is usually not accurate. Or you can use the Control palette and calculate the positions for each element — except that takes a lot of work, and few of us are that great at math anyhow. So what's left? The Multiple Paste command, that's what, which you get via Edit⇨Multiple Paste.

Here's a look at how this command works:

1. **Select and copy something.**

   To copy, just press ⌘+C. PageMaker sends the copy to the Clipboard.

2. **Choose Edit⇨Multiple Paste and specify how many copies you want pasted as well as the horizontal and vertical offsets.**

   The offset values tell PageMaker how far apart to space each copy. In the figure, the spacing is 1.2 inches horizontally but 0 inches vertically, which places the copies from left to right in a straight row.

3. **Click on OK, and the copies appear.**

Notice that, in Figure 10-12, not all the elements are the same. The text has been edited, of course, but the logos at the end of the top row are different than the original — they say Finalist, not Winner. How do you do that? Here's how. Copy the Winner logo via the Multiple Paste dialog box and then select one of the

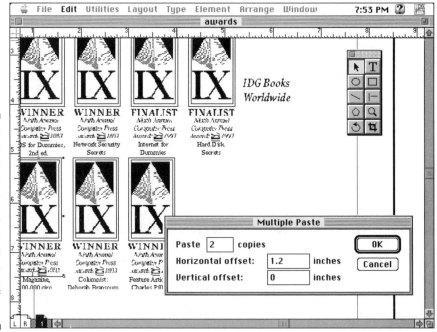

Figure 10-12: By using the Multiple Paste command, you can precisely position duplicates of a graphic, text block, or group of objects.

logos you want to replace with the Finalist logo. Use the Place dialog box
(File⇨Place or ⌘+D) to select the replacement graphic and turn on the Replacing Entire Graphic option. PageMaker places the new graphic precisely where
the old one was. Cool, huh? You can use this technique any time you have a
regular series of similar objects, even if they're different. One example is a stack
of cards, where you can offset each card by, say, a quarter inch horizontally and
vertically and then replace each of the copies with a different card — Queen,
Jack, Ace, and so on.

To align objects that are already placed in your document, use the Align Objects
command. This command not only can align objects either horizontally or
vertically, it can place a specified amount of space between each object —
otherwise known as *distributing* objects. To align and distribute objects, select
them with the Arrow tool and choose Arrange⇨Align Objects (or press ⌘+4).
PageMaker displays the dialog box shown in Figure 10-13.

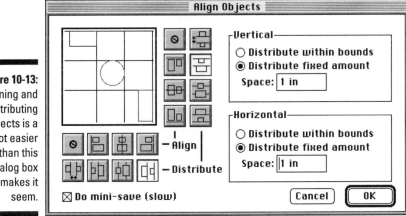

Figure 10-13:
Aligning and
distributing
objects is a
lot easier
than this
dialog box
makes it
seem.

At first glance, the dialog box looks pretty complex, but it's not that bad.
Basically, you get two sets of alignment and distribution options — one set for
vertical alignment and distribution, and one set for horizontal alignment and
distribution. When you click on the various alignment and distribution buttons,
PageMaker gives you a preview to show you what each of the options does; just
keep playing around with the icons until you get the look you're after and then
click on OK to apply your changes. You can choose *either* a horizontal alignment or distribution option for the selected objects, but not both. The same
goes for the vertical alignment and distribution options. You can, however,
choose both a horizontal alignment option and a vertical distribution option (or
vice versa) for the selected objects.

If you choose a distribution icon, some additional options appear. If you choose the Distribute Fixed Amount radio button, you can specify how much space you want to place between each object. Just enter the value in the Space option box. If you choose Distribute Within Bounds, PageMaker places the objects an equal distance apart within the bounds of the selection. For example, if you're distributing objects horizontally, the leftmost and rightmost objects stay put, and the other objects are spaced out evenly between them.

At the bottom of the Align Objects dialog box, you see an option called Do Mini-Save (Slow). Check this option if you want to be able to undo the distribution or alignment changes you're about to make. (PageMaker's normal Undo command can't undo these changes.) If you don't like what you see after you align or distribute objects, immediately press Shift while choosing File⇨Revert to restore your document to the way it looked before you opened the Arrange Objects dialog box.

Don't forget to press and hold the Shift key as you choose File⇨Revert! If you do, you choose the standard Revert command, which undoes everything you've done since the last time you saved your document.

Locking objects in place

It happens to the best of us: You spend an hour getting the various elements lined up on your page just so, and then you accidentally drag something out of place. Or worse, some editor or art director comes in, monkeys with your layout, and wrecks the whole thing.

Version 6 has a feature to help prevent these ugly scenarios. After you get a graphic or text block positioned just so, select it and choose Arrange⇨Lock Position or press ⌘+L. Your object is now stuck firmly to the page, just as surely as if you'd welded it there with Krazy Glue.

- ✔ To unlock an object, choose Arrange⇨Unlock.
- ✔ When you select a locked object, its handles are gray instead of black.
- ✔ You can't delete a locked object; you have to unlock it first.
- ✔ You can edit a locked object as long as your edits don't change the size or position of the object.

- ✔ To make sure that your locked objects stay locked, don't tell your editor or art director about the locking feature. Otherwise, they'll figure out that all they need to do to move your objects around is to choose the Unlock command.

Changing the stacking order

You saw, back in Figure 10-11, how to stack a series of graphics to create a layered picture. When you create elements, they are naturally stacked so that the first one created is at the back, the next one created is on top of that, and so on, until the most recently created element is at the front. But if you were to select an element and move it, it would be put at the front of the stack. (Resizing, rotating, or skewing don't have this effect.)

PageMaker 6 offers four commands that let you vary the stacking order of selected elements. They're all found under the Arrange menu. Figure 10-14 illustrates the process of changing the stacking order. The black circle was moved forward one layer (middle example) and then brought to the front of the group (far right example).

Figure 10-14:
Changing
the stacking
order.

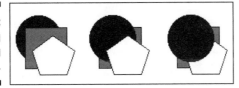

✔ Bring to Front (⌘+F) moves the selected object to the top of the stack.

✔ Send to Back (⌘+B) sends the selected object to the bottom of the pile.

✔ Bring Forward (⌘+8) shifts the object one layer up in the stacking order.

✔ Send Backward (⌘+9) moves the object back one layer in the stack.

✔ If you have trouble selecting an object that's behind another object, ⌘+click on the top object with the Arrow tool. Each time you ⌘+click, PageMaker selects the next object down in the stacking order. Keep ⌘+clicking until you get the one you want.

Applying Special Effects

Up to this point, everything we've covered about graphics has been pretty basic stuff. Oh sure, you've discovered how to create a jazzy border around your graphics and layer objects together to create simple drawings, but that's nothing compared to what's coming in the next few sections. Here's where you find out how to create special effects that will leave those jazzy borders in the dust and those simple drawings wide-eyed with envy.

Rotating, skewing, and flipping

PageMaker lets you flip, rotate, or skew (slant) any text block or graphic. You can apply all these effects — known collectively as *transformations* — from the Control palette. These controls appear on the Control palette when you select an object or text block with the Arrow tool.

- ✔ The flip controls are the ones at the far right that show the letter *F* being changed, as labeled in Figure 10-15. The top one is flip horizontally, or mirror; the bottom one is flip vertically, or upside-down.

- ✔ To rotate or skew a rectangle, just enter the angle of rotation or skew into the option boxes on top right end of the Control palette or click on the nudge arrows. A positive number rotates or skews the object counter-clockwise (in the direction of the arrow in the rotation symbol), while a negative number rotates or skews it clockwise.

- ✔ You can also rotate an object by selecting the Rotate tool and holding the mouse button down while you move the mouse in the direction of the rotation you want. A line connects the Rotate cursor to the object being rotated; this line is the "lever" by which you are rotating the element.

- ✔ All transformations are applied relative to the selected handle on the Control palette's Proxy button, as explained back in Chapter 9.

The selected Proxy button handle is especially important when you're rotating an object. The handle represents the point around which the object is rotated. Figure 10-15 shows the effects of selecting different Proxy button handles. The three rotated rectangles at the bottom all used to line up when they were horizontal; but now that the rectangles are rotated, they don't line up. (The black box in each rectangle was added to show which handle was active; the box will not appear on your objects.) The figure also shows the Rotate tool in action. One last thing to notice: When you rotate an object, the Proxy button in the Control palette changes to a diamond shape.

You can use multiple rotations, sometimes combined with skews, to create a sense of movement. Look at Figure 10-16 for an example. But be careful when you do something like this — the effect can be dizzying! The how-to's are simple: Select a rectangle, skew it slightly to make it look like it was drawn in perspective, and make a series of copies. Rotate each copy by a small amount — say 5 or 10 degrees. Enlarge each copy by about 10 percent and reposition them so they seem to flow along a curve. You can enhance the flow by using different shades for each rectangle. Notice in the figure that the same rotation and skew were applied to the text as to the top rectangle (the settings are shown in the Control palette). By combining text and graphics and applying these effects to them, you can do some pretty amazing stuff.

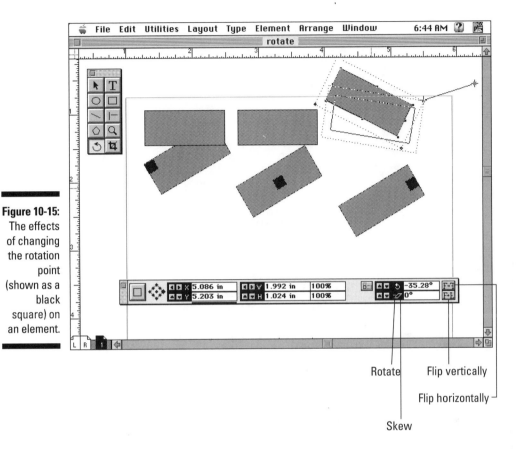

Rotate   Flip vertically

Flip horizontally

Skew

Hate a rotation or skew that you created? You can get rid of it by selecting the object and changing the angle back to 0 degrees. Or, for a faster method if you have more than one effect applied, select the object and use the Arrange⇨Remove Transformation command. Presto! Everything's back to normal.

Distorting a graphic

Take a look at Figure 10-17. The top image is a modified version of the bottom image. Resizing the graphic along the horizontal axis so that it is squeezed together to 53 percent (see the Control palette) changes the killer whales from sleek to fat. The new whales take up a lot less room, leaving space for the logo type. Fat whales are friendly whales (nice and cuddly), and even if making room for the logo type wasn't essential, squeezing the whales to make them look cuddlier may have been nice.

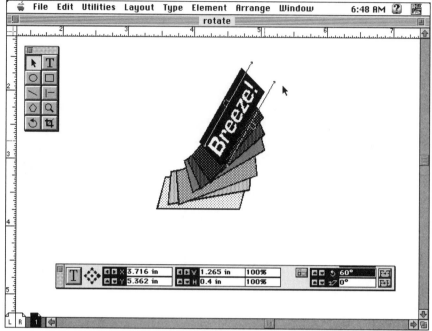

Figure 10-16:
One sample graphic that you can create by skewing and rotating the same image several times.

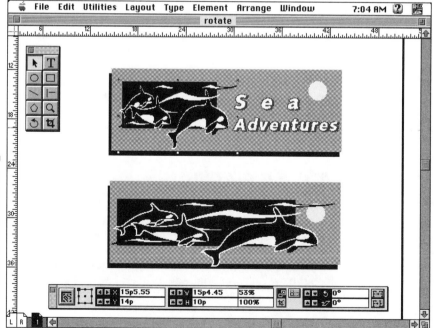

Figure 10-17:
Squeezing the illustration horizontally makes the killer whales cuddly and leaves room for a logo.

Now take a look at Figure 10-18. Once again, the bottom image is the original. The top image is the same as the bottom image except that it's been skewed 30 degrees. The skew makes the killer whales look like they're swimming fast, giving them a sense of motion — don't get seasick! This slight change to an image produces noticeable results.

The killer whales seem to have lost their white in the image at the top of Figure 10-18. They haven't, at least not in the printed version. The reason that the white is missing is that PageMaker sometimes incorrectly displays a skewed or rotated image's colors. But the printout is unaffected.

Embellishing a graphic

Sometimes a very simple embellishment can alter a graphic considerably. Figure 10-19, for example, shows a picture of the government center in Victoria, British Columbia, a picturesque provincial capital in Canada. But by circling the parliament building (by using a circle with no fill, a thick line, and the Reverse option checked) and adding a line of text, the postcardlike photo now screams "political flier!" This technique calls the reader's attention to a detail, loud and clear.

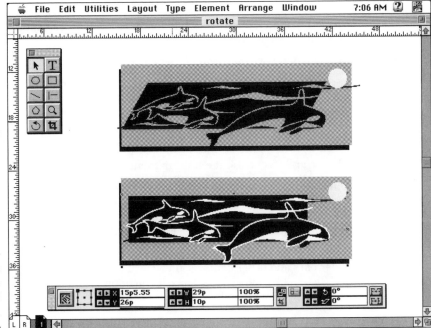

Figure 10-18: When the killer whales are skewed, they seem to be swimming a lot faster — they're no longer so cute and cuddly.

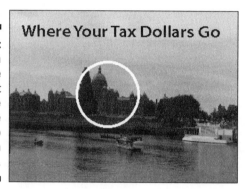

Figure 10-19:
Adding a circle around part of an image tells the reader to focus on that portion.

In PageMaker 6, however, you can go way beyond adding a simple shape to your images. If you're working with RGB, grayscale, or CMYK TIFF image, you can apply some of the same special effects that you can apply in Photoshop, Adobe's popular image-editing program.

PageMaker comes with several special effects built in. To explore them, just do the following:

1. **Select your TIFF image and then choose Element⇨Image⇨Photoshop Effects.**

   The Photoshop Effects dialog box appears. (If you look ahead to Figure 10-21, you can take a peek at it.)

2. **Create a copy of your original image.**

   You can't undo these special image effects. So it's a good idea to apply the effect to a copy of your image rather than the original. To do so, just enter a new name in the Save New File As option box. To store the image in a file other than where the original is stored, click on the Save As button, choose a folder, and click on OK.

3. **Choose an effect from the pop-up menu.**

   You'll want to experiment with the different filters and see what each one can do. But for now, just choose any old effect. Then click on OK. PageMaker buzzes and whirs for a few seconds and then displays a dialog box similar to the one shown in Figure 10-20.

   Here, you can vary the scope of the effects by playing with the various slider bars and other controls. If you select the Preview button, you can see what your image will look like if you apply the effect.

4. **Click on Apply.**

   PageMaker makes some more gurgling noises and then displays your altered image. Figure 10-21 shows the effect of one of the built-in effects, GE Accented Edges, on a grayscale TIFF image.

Figure 10-20:
You can wreak all kinds of havoc on an image by playing with the image-editing effects available by choosing Element⇨ Image⇨ Photoshop Effects.

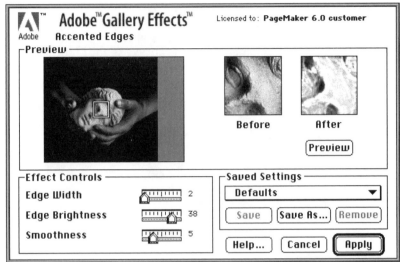

Figure 10-21:
The Photoshop Effects dialog box (bottom) enables you to apply special effects to TIFF images. At top left is an original grayscale TIFF image; at top right is same image after the GE Accented Edges effect was applied.

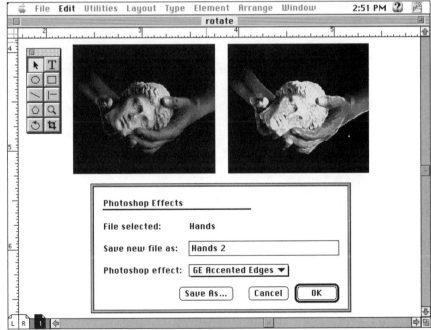

To install additional effect plug-ins, you can add the plug-in to the Effects folder, which is inside the Plugins folder, which is inside the PageMaker RSRC folder. Or, if you own Photoshop Version 3.0.4, you can create an alias — to Photoshop's Plugins folder. You then can access any of the filters in Photoshop's Filter's folder. If you need help creating an alias, ask a Macintosh guru for help.

Using Graphics in Text

The last thing you should know about graphics is how to work with them as if they were text. Although a lot of symbols are available in various typefaces, there's no guarantee that you have the one you want — or that it even exists. For example, you may want to use your corporate logo or icon as a bullet (Or, if you're doing PageMaker books, you may want to include the various cursor icons in the text.) You can create your own font with this character using a program like Fontographer or Ares Software's FontMonger — these work best if you use the character a lot and you have several such characters. But for occasional or per-job use, why not just use PageMaker's embedded-graphics feature? (The PageMaker manual calls this an in-line graphic.) Figure 10-22 shows two examples. Here's how to add an inline graphic:

1. **Place the text cursor where you want the graphic inserted.**

   Do not highlight a piece of text — embedding will not work if text is highlighted.

2. **Use the Place dialog box (File⇨Place or ⌘+D) to select the graphic you want to embed.**

3. **Turn on the As Inline Graphic option (it should be on if you inserted the text cursor).**

4. **Click on OK.**

5. **The graphic is placed at the text cursor's location, and chances are that it is too big.**

   You'll have to resize it. Switch to the Arrow tool and resize the graphic using the control handles — just like any other graphic. (Remember to hold the Shift key if you want to resize the graphic proportionally.)

Figure 10-22:
An
embedded
graphic can
be used as
a bullet
character.

You should know a few things about embedded graphics:

- ✔ The graphic is centered vertically on the line. So if the graphic is taller than the line it is placed in, space will be added above and below the line to make room for the graphic.

- ✔ If an embedded graphic is wider than the current column, it overprints text in any adjacent column.

- ✔ Text wrap controls are grayed out for embedded graphics — not that you'd need them for any reason. (Well, you may want to insert a graphic in a line and have text wrap around it as it reflows with the text. Sorry, but no can do.)

- ✔ You can rotate, skew, or apply image controls (for supported image formats) to embedded graphics. And you can use fills, patterns, and colors — just like any other graphic.

- ✔ Graphics embedded in your word processor are imported as embedded graphics into PageMaker. Note, however, that a graphic embedded in a word processor may not look as good as one embedded in PageMaker — Word, for example, sometimes substitutes a lower-resolution version, especially for formats like EPS.

✔ If you are editing text in the Story Editor, embedded graphics are represented by a black box. Don't worry — they look normal when you're back in Layout view.

✔ You can embed graphics created in PageMaker. For example, say you want a box character. Draw it in PageMaker with the Rectangle tool. Then press ⌘+X to cut (move) the graphic to the Clipboard. Now switch to the Text tool and place the text cursor where you want the box character to be. Paste the character via ⌘+V. Instant embedded graphic!

The 5th Wave   By Rich Tennant

AFTER SPENDING 9 DAYS WITH 12 DIFFERENT VENDORS AND READING 26 BROCHURES, DAVE HAD AN ACUTE ATTACK OF TOXIC OPTION SYNDROME.

Chapter 11

Better Than Crayons

● ●

In This Chapter

▶ Introducing the printing process and spot colors

▶ Applying colors to text and graphics from the Colors palette

▶ Defining your own custom process colors

▶ Accessing libraries of commercial spot colors

▶ Editing and deleting existing colors

● ●

*H*ave you ever commercially reproduced a document in color? If not, you may be in for a shock. Although the process is better than using crayons, it's more expensive and more complicated. You don't just present your printer with a color printout and say, "There you go, my good man. Let me know when you've printed 100 copies of that."

If you did, the printer might respond, "You want me to print this in color?" And he'd ask the question as if it were the most unlikely situation he could imagine.

"Of course I want it in color!" you'd answer, showing him that you mean business. You're not to be toyed with.

"You realize," he'd say slowly, so as not to set you off, "that it'll cost you about $9 million to have this color-separated."

No doubt, you'd inspect this charlatan for a moment and come back with, "Did I miss a few days, or is the inflation in this city a little worse than I had imagined? I suppose that the next time I go to Burger King, a Whopper will set me back a cool billion plus change!"

If the printer happened to be a good-natured sort, he'd probably smile at your amusing joke, sit down with you in a quiet corner, and explain to you the realities of printing. On the other hand, if you happened across him on a particularly trying day, you may find yourself subjected to severe scorn and ridicule, if not actual physical threats. Just to be safe, this chapter gives you the lowdown on color printing so that you won't risk embarrassment or bodily harm when you take your PageMaker documents to the printer. The chapter also explains how to access colors in PageMaker so that you can turn your black-and-white document into a Technicolor masterpiece.

How Inks and Plates Work

The next section of this chapter provides the specifics for applying color to graphics and text. But before we get into the how-to's for creating colored elements, you need a basic understanding of the commercial color printing process. (Even if you're just going to output your document on a color laser or inkjet printer, this information will help give you a better handle on working with colors in PageMaker.)

There are all kinds of wacky printing techniques in the world, but the most common and least expensive commercial solution is *offset printing.* Copies are made by running paper against an inked *plate* that's wrapped around a cylinder. Each plate can handle only one color — called an *ink*. If you want to use more than one ink, you have to add plates, and each plate costs money.

In order to reproduce your color printout, the printer has to separate the colors into their *primary components.* Now, you may recall that in grade school, you learned that you can make any color by mixing blue, red, and yellow — the so-called *primary colors.* But for commercial printing, mixing blue, red, and yellow doesn't work very well. For one thing, blue and red are too dark. Instead of mixing to form a bright purple, like you heard they would, blue and red make a blackish mud that isn't suitable for much of anything.

So, instead of using pure red, blue, and yellow, commercial printers rely on the following primary inks:

- **Cyan:** Pale blue with a hint of green
- **Magenta:** A deep pink with a hint of purple
- **Yellow:** The only color your teacher got right
- **Black:** Because all these light colors need some help when it comes to creating shadows and outlines

The *color separation* process separates your artwork into its cyan, magenta, yellow, and black components. The good news about this process is that you can print a rainbow of colors using only four inks. The bad news is that traditional color separations cost a lot of money — not $9 million, but easily a few hundred.

A less expensive solution is to print color separations directly from PageMaker. As described in more detail in Chapter 17, PageMaker separates colors when you select the Separations option in the Print Color dialog box.

You can print two kinds of separations in PageMaker:

- ✔ **Process colors:** Process colors are the cyan, magenta, yellow, and black separations previously discussed. Process inks are also known by the acronym CMYK. Why not CMY*B*? In the print world, *B* stands for blue, so *K* was adopted for black. Process colors offer the advantage of producing lots of colors using few inks.

  Another reason that *K* designates black is that, as the darkest color, black serves as what printing experts call the *key* registration color in process-color printing. Isn't that interesting? Now you have something you can throw out at bridge parties and chess club meetings.

- ✔ **Spot colors:** Spot colors are separations created using inks *other than* cyan, magenta, and yellow. For example, maybe you want to print a two-color newsletter made up of black and brick red. Rather than using four inks to emulate the brick red, you can just pick a premixed brick red ink to use instead. You don't have a wide range of colors this way, but you only have to pay for two inks.

Professionals with money coming out their ears sometimes mix process and spot colors together. Suppose that you're creating a very colorful piece that requires process colors. But the client's logo — which normally appears in a vibrant orange — looks a little lackluster when printed using CMYK separations. To make sure that the logo looks as vibrant as possible (absolutely nothing is more sacred to a company than its logo), you throw in a spot color orange. It means five inks, but the client is willing to pay.

What you see isn't what you get

Pantone is probably the best known and most prolific vendor of premixed spot colors. PageMaker provides access to the enormous Pantone color library. But because the screen isn't particularly well-suited to displaying spot colors, a particular shade of blue, for example, may appear purple on-screen.

The screen can be equally bad at representing process colors. A color that looks orange on-screen may turn red when printed. What's the solution? Well, you have two options. One is to use a Color Management System, as explained in the sidebar "What's this new color management thing?" in Chapter 9. You'll need a desktop publishing guru to help you set up and use a Color Management System correctly.

An easier — and sometimes more reliable — answer is to buy swatch books. A swatch book

shows how different colors appear when printed. For spot colors, buy the Pantone swatch book. For process colors, buy a swatch book from a company called Trumatch: This excellent book shows just about every color you can create by mixing cyan, magenta, yellow, and black inks. Better yet, Trumatch is the only swatch book created using a personal computer, ensuring the highest degree of accuracy possible.

You should be able to purchase both Pantone and Trumatch swatch books from your commercial printer or at an art supply store.

Remember, though, that even when using a swatch book, you should print a sample of all your colors to make sure that your printed piece looks the way you intended.

Using Color in PageMaker

PageMaker provides access to a few colors right off the bat. If you choose Window⇨Colors (or press ⌘+K), you display the Colors palette, shown in Figure 11-1.

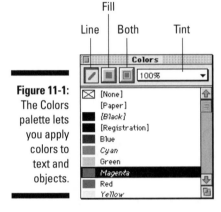

Fill

Line | Both | Tint

Figure 11-1:
The Colors
palette lets
you apply
colors to
text and
objects.

The palette initially offers ten color options, which work as follows:

- ✔ **None:** The first option removes any color that you've applied to an object in PageMaker. You can't use None as the setting for text; if you want to get rid of the color of text, you have to choose Black or Paper. If you apply None to an imported EPS graphic, the graphic's original colors are restored.

- ✔ **Paper:** This option represents the color of the paper. If you'll be printing on a colored paper stock, change this color as described in the upcoming "Changing a named color" and "Changing the paper color" sections.

- ✔ **Black:** Black is the default ink. Use this color when creating black-and-white documents, spot-color documents, and process-color documents. In other words, you always need black. Black is italicized in the palette because it's a process color.

- ✔ **Registration:** Text and graphics colored with Registration appear on all separations printed from PageMaker. For example, suppose you are creating a process-color document. If you type your name and assign the Registration color to it, your name appears on the cyan separation, the magenta separation, the yellow separation, and the black separation. You wouldn't want to actually print this information; it's just a label that tells the printer who the separations belong to.

> ✔ **Blue, Cyan, Green, Magenta, Red, Yellow:** These colors are provided as samples of the kinds of colors you can create. Again, the italicized colors are process colors.

Incidentally, you may have noticed that some colors — None, Paper, Black, and Registration — appear in brackets and others don't. The brackets indicate that the color is permanent and cannot be removed from the Colors palette. You can remove nonbracketed colors at whim, as explained in the section "Other stuff you should know," later in this chapter.

Applying colors

To assign a color to a selected object, follow these simple steps:

1. **Select the element that you want to color.**

   Select text with the Text tool and objects with the Arrow tool.

2. **Specify how you want the color applied.**

   If you're coloring a shape that you drew in PageMaker, you can specify whether you want to color the fill, the line, or both. Click on the Fill icon in the Colors palette to apply a color to the fill; click on the Line icon to color the outline (see Figure 11-1). Click on the Both button to change both fill and line to the same color. If you're coloring an imported graphic or text, you can apply a fill color only.

   You can also apply fill and line colors to shapes that you draw in PageMaker by choosing Element➪Fill and Line and changing the settings in the Fill and Line dialog box, as explained in Chapter 10.

   If you want to apply a tint of color — for example, 20 percent red — to your selected text or object, select a tint percentage from the Tint pop-up menu.

3. **Select the desired color.**

   Click on a color in the scrolling portion of the Colors palette. If you want to see more colors at a time, enlarge the palette by dragging its size box. Of course, you won't have many colors to choose from until you add them, as described in the next section.

Adding process colors to the palette

To add process colors to your palette, choose Element➪Define Colors, which displays the dialog box shown in Figure 11-2. Then click on the New button.

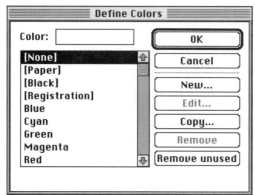

Figure 11-2:
You create,
edit, copy,
and remove
colors from
the palette
in this
dialog box.

PageMaker next displays the Edit Color dialog box, shown in Figure 11-3. To define a color, you have to select a color model from the Model pop-up menu and then define the color by adding and subtracting primary colors. The *color model* determines the primary colors. You can select from three options:

- **RGB:** In the world of printed pigments, cyan, magenta, yellow, and black rule the day. But in the world of light, the primary colors are red, green, and blue. All colors mix to form lighter colors. Red and green, for example, mix to form yellow. Believe it or not! But who cares? In most cases, you're printing to paper, not lighting a stage. The only time to choose the RGB model is when you're creating slides for output on a slide printer or creating documents that you plan to distribute over the Internet or an office network system, where people will be viewing them on a color monitor.

- **HLS:** Here's another model you don't have to worry about. You can call HLS the television color model. You know those knobs on a TV that control tint, brightness, and color? Well, those knobs work just like this model. HLS stands for hue, lightness, and saturation. Hue changes the color, just like the tint knob on a TV. Lightness makes the color lighter or darker, just like the brightness knob. And saturation controls whether a color is vibrant or a little diffused, just like the color knob. If you want to get to know these options, experiment with your TV set. But don't use HLS in PageMaker.

- **CMYK:** Ah, finally, the color model of choice! CMYK stands for our old friends cyan, magenta, yellow, and black — the process colors. Any time you're printing to paper, choose the CMYK option.

When CMYK is selected, the Edit Color dialog box displays four option boxes, one each for cyan, magenta, yellow, and black. To the right of each option box is a scroll bar. Move the scroll box to the right to add a primary color; move the scroll box to the left to delete a primary color. You can also enter values between 0 and 100 percent in the option boxes. As you may expect, 100 percent is full intensity color, 0 percent is no intensity, and other percentages are somewhere in between.

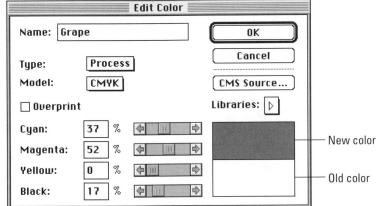

Figure 11-3:
Use the options in this dialog box to define and edit colors.

If you create colors in the RGB model — as you do to create slides that are output on a slide printer, for example — you get three slider bars, one for the red, green, and blue primary colors. But remember that RGB colors mix differently than CMYK colors. If you max out all three sliders — that is, use a value of 255 for each — you get white. A value of 0 for all three slides produces black.

The preview box in the lower-right corner of the dialog box updates to reflect your changes. The top half of the preview box shows the new color you're creating. The bottom half shows the color that was selected in the scrolling colors list in the Define Colors dialog box. Unless you selected a different color from the scrolling list, this color is the same one that's currently selected in the Colors palette. If no document was open when you chose Element⇨Define Colors, the None color appears in the bottom half of the preview box. (Note that any colors you create with no document open become defaults for all future documents.)

After you mix the desired amounts of primary colors together, enter a name for your color in the Name option box. Make sure that the Process option is selected from the Type pop-up menu. Then click on the OK button or press Return.

PageMaker returns you to the Define Colors dialog box. You can now create more colors, edit existing colors, and so on. Or you can press Return to exit the dialog box. Your new colors appear in the Colors palette. Because these colors are process colors, their names appear italicized.

Adding spot colors

Adding a spot color to the Colors palette is very much like adding a process color. You choose Element⇨Define Colors and click on the New button to display the Edit Color dialog box. But instead of mucking about with the CMYK option boxes, you select an option from the Libraries pop-up menu.

Now, it would be natural if you got a little overwhelmed at this point. If your pop-up menu is like most, you'll see enough options to give you the cold sweats. Luckily, the menu is not nearly as difficult as it looks. Assuming that you're working in the United States or with a Pantone-supplied printer, you can stick to *Pantone Coated* or *Pantone Uncoated.*

- ✔ **PANTONE Coated:** Select this option if you'll be printing your final piece to coated paper like the stuff you see in magazines.

- ✔ **PANTONE Uncoated:** Select this option when printing to newsprint, bond paper, or other uncoated stock. If you're in doubt, you're probably using uncoated stock, so go ahead and select this option. What you select really doesn't matter, though. Your printer is probably smart enough to use the correct ink when the actual time comes to reproduce the pages.

You can also use the color libraries to import process colors. Although it's not necessary, importing several colors *en masse* is easier than creating one color at a time. Our personal favorite among the process color libraries is the Trumatch 4-Color Selector. Use it in good health!

After you select a color library, the Color Picker dialog box appears, as shown in Figure 11-4. Most libraries contain hundreds of colors, so don't expect to see all the colors at the same time. To locate a color, use the scroll bar at the bottom of the palette or enter a number into the option box. For example, if you enter 3 when viewing the Pantone collection, the color list scrolls to show the first of the 300-series colors; enter 4 to display colors 340 and up, and so on.

To select a color that you want to add to the Colors palette, just click on it. To add two or more colors at once, Shift+click on each color. To select the colors shown in the Figure 11-4, for example, you click on color 369 and then Shift+Click on 373, 374, and 377. To deselect a color, simply Shift+click on it again. After you select the colors you want to import, click on the OK button to return to the Edit Color dialog box and click on OK again to return to the layout window.

All your selected colors now appear in the Colors palette. Assuming that you used one of the Pantone libraries, the color names are upright — not italic — to show that they're spot colors.

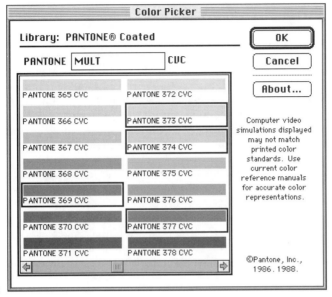

Figure 11-4:
Importing colors from a predefined library is as simple as clicking and Shift+ clicking on a few colors.

Changing a named color

A color that you create is by no means set in stone. You can edit a color long after you create it and, in doing so, change the color of all text and graphics to which the color has been applied. In this sense, colors are a lot like style sheets, enabling you to edit elements globally.

Suppose that you created a two-color document using black and Pantone 3385 Teal. After you've hassled with the document for several days, your boss takes a look and says, "Gee whiz, this is great. But I don't like this pasty green color. I want something brighter, you know, something you might find in Oz. Yeah, that's it, I want Oz Green!"

In the old days, you would have had to hire a hit man to knock off your boss and just hope that the next one was more open to teal. Nowadays, you can change the color of your teal items with almost no effort. Just choose Element⇨Define Colors, select the color from the scrolling colors list, and click on the Edit button. Or better yet, save time and effort by ⌘+clicking on the color you want to edit in the Colors palette. ⌘+clicking bypasses the Define Colors dialog box and opens the Edit Color dialog box directly.

If you want to change a process color, just muck about with the CMYK option boxes and press Return when you're finished. If you want to edit a spot color, select the appropriate collection from the Libraries pop-up menu, select one — and only one — color from the scrolling list, and then click on OK twice to close all the dialog boxes. PageMaker changes your color and all elements colored with that color in less time than it takes to read this sentence.

Changing the paper color

Before moving on, you need to know a little bit about one technical color-editing issue related to paper color. Generally speaking, white paper is the best solution when you're printing full-color artwork from PageMaker because white paper doesn't adversely affect the colors of the inks and permits a wider color range. However, if you're working on a black-and-white document, or one with only one or two spot colors, you may want to reproduce the document on colored paper stock. To get a general feeling for how your elements will look on paper, edit the Paper color in the Colors palette to match the paper stock.

To edit the Paper color, ⌘+click on the word Paper in the palette. Then manipulate the CMYK values until the color matches the paper stock as closely as possible and press Return. PageMaker changes the on-screen page to match the color you specified. All transparent and paper-colored shapes, as well as any reversed text, also update to the new color. Note that PageMaker doesn't show how the color of the paper will mix with the colors of the inks applied to the objects on the page. You just have to imagine the colors as best you can.

Other stuff you should know

You now have been introduced to most of what you need to know about color in PageMaker. But you may want to file away the following additional tidbits for future recall. Some of these items you probably could have figured out on your own, and others are incredibly useful tips. Here goes:

- To add a new color to the Colors palette, you don't have to go through all the rigmarole of entering the Define Colors dialog box. You can enter the Edit Color dialog box directly by ⌘+clicking on either the Black, Registration, or None color in the Colors palette. Because these colors aren't editable, PageMaker lets you add a new color instead.

- To delete a color from the Colors palette, choose Element⇨Define Colors, select the color from the scrolling list, and then click on the Remove button. If the color is applied to some text or a graphic, PageMaker displays a message at the bottom of the dialog box to warn you that these elements will be changed to black. If that's okay with you, press Return.

- All colors that you create are saved with the current document, which means that colors created in one document are not necessarily available to another. To transfer colors from Document A to Document B, begin by opening Document B. Then choose Element⇨Define Colors and click on the Copy button. Locate Document A on the disk and double-click on it. Then click on OK to return to the Layout view. The colors from Document A are now available in the Colors palette.

✔ In addition to editing the appearance of a color, you can change it from process to spot or vice versa. To convert a color on the fly — without bothering with the Edit Color dialog box — just ⌘+Option+Shift+click on it. A process color changes to spot; a spot color changes to process. But you really shouldn't convert a process color to a spot color unless you're going from a Pantone process color to a Pantone spot color. Otherwise, your spot color won't correspond to any ink available at your printer.

✔ If no document is open when you define colors, the colors you define become the default colors for all new documents.

Part IV
Pumping Up Your Layout Power

"This new page layout is really going to give our presentation style!"

In this part . . .

Now that you've acquired the basic PageMaker skills, it's time to really work those layout muscles. In this part, we walk you through the process of laying out an entire PageMaker document. You find out how to place several multicolumn stories on the same page, jump text from one page to the next, and make the available text and graphics fit into the allotted page space. And, in case you need some creative inspiration, we provide an entire chapter of examples of well-designed publications, from ads to product manuals.

In the last two chapters of this part, you build your layout power even further by using some of the PageMaker features that automate many layout chores. After you've got these techniques under your belt, all those pumped-up, steroid-popping designers who used to sneer at you and snap you with wet towels in the locker room will look at you with a new-found respect. They'll probably even ask if they can carry your laptop computer for you.

Chapter 12
The Layout Shuffle

· ·

In This Chapter

▶ Constructing a layout

▶ Placing text across multiple pages

▶ Adding cross-references to jumped text

▶ Changing the number and positions of columns

▶ Rearranging pages

· ·

*L*ayout is not something that happens right the first time. After all, you're working with a whole bunch of pieces, and you're trying to make them fit together as well as look nice. It's like doing a jigsaw puzzle while also figuring out what you want the end result to look like. Even if you have a basic design in mind — like a three-column format — you'll end up placing text and graphics, moving them, moving them again, and modifying some of their settings as you work with other elements and begin to see how the various pieces interact.

Chapter 9 shows how to place graphics into PageMaker, and Chapter 5 shows how to place text. But simply placing text and graphics into your document doesn't lay everything out for you. Why not? PageMaker is not a mind reader, and it has no idea what layout you're visualizing. You wouldn't want PageMaker to automate your job out of existence, would you? You would? Well, give it time. Machines will take over all of our jobs one day, and then they'll round us up and put us in zoos, and our pain and suffering will be over. But in the meantime, you still have to tell PageMaker what to do with your text and graphics.

Starting a Layout

The best way to explain the layout process is to provide you with an example. So this chapter walks you through the steps of creating a simple, three-column, black-and-white newsletter.

Planning your pages

The first thing you should do is make a list of all your stories and all your graphics. Prioritize those elements — which should get prominent attention and appear on the front page or early in the document? Which can be cut or shortened if space is a problem? Which stories include graphics — a chart, a scanned photo, or maybe an illustration?

Sketching out your layout placement ideas before you start the layout is a good idea. Drawing a rough sketch via paper and pencil is really easy — less work than doing it on a computer, even with PageMaker. Figure 12-1 shows such a sketch for the front page of the newsletter we'll use as an example in this chapter. (By the way, the # symbol is a layout convention for "end of story," while the down arrow is a convention for "text continues.")

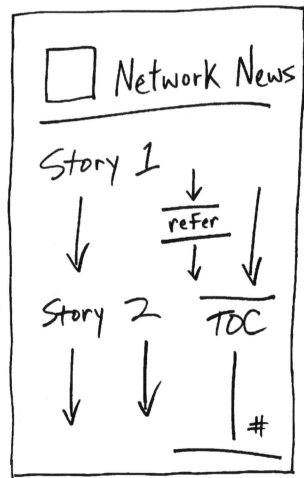

Figure 12-1:
Sketching a
layout
before
implementing
it in
PageMaker
can be a
real time-
saver.

Page 1: Placing stories

Assume that, prior to laying out the newsletter, you created a framework for the newsletter (called a *template*) that has all the stuff that you'll use in every issue of your newsletter — the title and logo, contents box, styles, and so on. (Chapter 14 explains how to create a template.) Figure 12-2 shows page 1 of the template. The template also uses master pages, as covered in Chapter 14, to place elements that appear regularly throughout the newsletter — page numbers, decorative rules at the top and bottom of the pages, and so forth.

Don't panic if you don't know about master pages and templates yet. If you're curious, you can skip ahead to Chapter 14 to find out all about them. But for now, all you need to know is that templates and master pages enable you to automate the placement of the various elements on your pages. The point of this chapter is to explain how to approach the layout process, not to show you how to create the specific newsletter used as an example in this chapter. If some of the information being presented seems a little fuzzy to you, rest assured that everything will fall into place later.

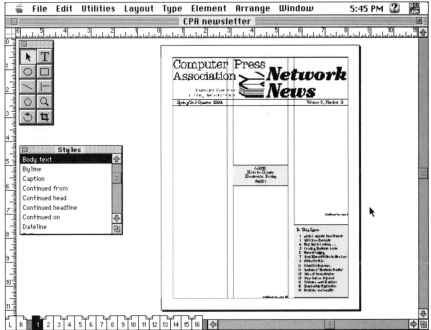

Figure 12-2:
Page 1 of a template for a newsletter.

Anyway, assume that you have your list of stories and graphics and have decided which ones should appear where. The next thing to do is place the lead story, as in Figure 12-3. Notice a few things:

✔ The story (which was created in a word processor and imported into PageMaker) starts about a half inch below the issue date and volume number text. That's no accident. A rectangle with no fill and no line but with text wrap turned on (see Chapter 9) was placed beneath the volume number text. The rectangle ensures proper placement of the imported story. No matter where you click the paragraph icon underneath the volume number text, the story always appears the correct distance away from the text. (Normally, when you're placing text, the text block begins wherever you click the paragraph icon.) Without such a device, you'd have to place the text accurately by eye or place it and then modify its location, either by hand or by using the Control palette's X and Y fields to specify its starting points.

You can also accurately place text and graphics by dragging a ruler guide to the point at which you would like your text blocks to originate. If you turn on Snap to Guides, the loaded text placement icon snaps to the guides you have set up.

✔ The story falls within the column and margin guides established for the page.

✔ By turning on Snap to Guides in the Layout⇨Guides and Rulers submenu (⌘+Shift+G), you can be assured that even if you don't position your story's paragraph cursor precisely on a column's left boundary, it will be positioned there. Otherwise, the text's left boundary will be wherever you click, even though PageMaker still makes the right boundary the nearest column guide.

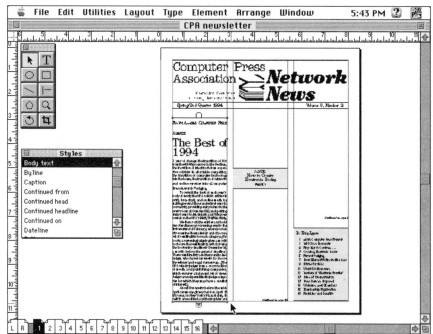

Figure 12-3:
Placing the
first story on
page 1.

✔ PageMaker doesn't always place text inside your column guides. If you click too far away from the column boundary, it doesn't realize that you want the text to be in the column, and it makes the text as wide as it can — either to the page's right margin or to the boundary of a graphic with text wrap turned on. This PageMaker habit can be a real nuisance because you then have to resize the column by hand. The only real way to reduce the chance of this problem is to work in a close-up view so that you can make sure that your cursor is near or on the correct column location to begin with.

✔ The story does not continue on the next column because the Autoflow option in the Layout menu is turned off. (If the option is turned on, PageMaker places the entire story, column after column, page by page, automatically.) Why turn off the option? Because at this point, you probably don't know where you want your text to flow throughout the newsletter, and why have PageMaker do a lot of work that you'll likely undo later? So when would you use Autoflow? Any time your layout is less modular, as when laying out a report or book that flows one story at a time. For more about this option, see Chapter 5.

Holding the ⌘ key when placing text temporarily disables Autoflow.

✔ The headline and *kicker* (the text above the headline) break awkwardly — they clearly should be wider than the column.

✔ As discussed in Chapter 5, that down-pointing triangle at the bottom of the text block (it's red if you have a color monitor) means that there's more text in the story that hasn't been placed.

Now you have to decide what to do next. You can place another story on the first page, or you can fine-tune this story. Neither option is wrong — it just depends on how certain you are of what you want to do.

For this example, suppose that you know that you want the first story to consume the top half of the page, as in the upcoming Figure 12-6 (go ahead, take a peek now). You decide to tackle that text placement before worrying about the second story. The first thing to do is make the headline go across the three columns. This story is the lead story, after all, and its headline should be really hard to miss. To make the change, you just select the bottom right handle on the text block and resize the block (by dragging the windowshade handles up) so that only the kicker and the headline appear, as shown in Figure 12-4.

Now, to lay out the rest of the story within the right column sizes, you need to create a new text block. Pay attention — you need to repeat this process time and time again. Click just once on the red down-pointing triangle in the text block containing the headline. You get the paragraph placement cursor. Click near the left margin of the first column, just below the headline. That places the text back below the headline, as Figure 12-5 shows.

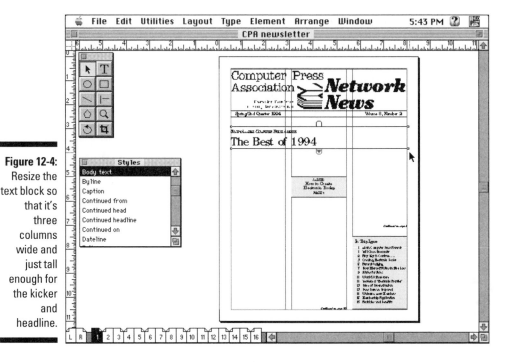

Figure 12-4:
Resize the text block so that it's three columns wide and just tall enough for the kicker and headline.

Because you don't want the text in the first column to go all the way down the column, you have to resize its text block. Select the text block with the Arrow tool and drag up on the text-placement handle or the resize handle.

Now we're going to make another assumption about this layout: You decide that you want the second story's headline to align with the top of the contents box at the lower right of the page. (Take another peek at Figure 12-6 for a preview.) So you have to roll the first story's text up to just above that location. (You need to raise it slightly higher to put some space between the two stories — so that people can easily recognize that there *are* two stories.)

A better way to approach this is to create the right size text block in the first place. For example, after creating the headline text block, you can click on the red down-pointing triangle and then drag to create a new text block that is as wide as the first one but only half as tall. PageMaker reflows the text into your text block.

If you see a dashed box below a windowshade, it means that the depth of the windowshade is not deep enough to accommodate the current line of text. The bottom of the dashed box indicates the text's depth. If you make the window-shade as deep as that dashed box, the line of text fits.

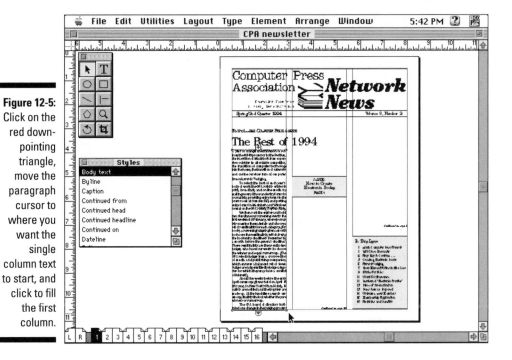

Figure 12-5:
Click on the
red down-
pointing
triangle,
move the
paragraph
cursor to
where you
want the
single
column text
to start, and
click to fill
the first
column.

Continue placing each column the same way: Click on the red down-pointing triangle, move the paragraph cursor to the location where you want to put the text, and click. You can move to other pages — click on the page icons at the bottom of the screen — and continue the placement of the story, if you know where you want the text to go. For now, assume that you've placed the rest of this story's text on page 1 and have also placed the second story. Figure 12-6 shows the result.

Clicking on that down-pointing red triangle, moving the paragraph icon to the new column, going back to the down-pointing red triangle, and so on, and so on, is a real pain. PageMaker's creators aren't sadists, so they added a little something to ease the work. If you are going to place text into several columns, hold the Shift key when you click the paragraph cursor. PageMaker flows the text into the column and then displays another paragraph cursor — no need to click on that down-pointing red triangle. (The difference between this and Autoflow is that *you* get to decide which columns the text is placed in, and at what locations in those columns. With Autoflow, PageMaker places the text in every subsequent column, and it always places text at the top of each column.)

What if you selected that triangle accidentally? You really don't want to create a new column. Just click on any other tool in the Tool palette and then click on the Arrow tool again. The paragraph icon is gone.

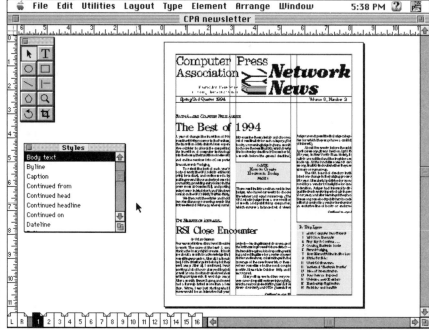

Figure 12-6:
The
completed
placement
of the first
page's two
stories.

That red down-pointing triangle is called, officially, the *down arrow in the windowshade handle,* which is worse than *that down-pointing red triangle.* So, from here on out, it shall be christened the *more-text handle.*

Page 1: Fine-tuning placement

Take a look at Figure 12-7: Notice how the columns don't align? That's an inevitable problem when you're creating a PageMaker layout. Fortunately, you can use the Control palette to fix these off-balance columns by giving them the same vertical coordinates. Here's how.

1. **Select the text block in the first column.**

2. **Select an upper handle on the Control palette's Proxy button.**

   The Proxy button is that little square on the left of the palette; the handle that is thicker than the others is the selected one.

3. **Jot down the Y value.**

   The Y value in the Control palette reflects the vertical position of the text block. In the text block selected in Figure 12-7, it's 23p4 (23 picas, 4 points). The measurement system doesn't matter, by the way — you can use inches if you prefer. Just write the Y coordinate down.

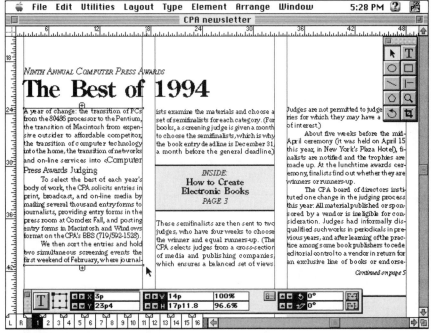

Continued on page 5

Figure 12-7:
The problem
with these
text blocks
is that they
aren't
aligned
correctly.

4. Select the next text block and look at its Y coordinate.

If you want the second text block's Y coordinate to match the first text block's, enter the first text block's Y coordinate (23p4, in this case) in the Control palette and press Return or click on the Apply button (at the far left of the Control palette).

5. Repeat step 4 for every column you want to align.

Another way to align text blocks is by using the Balance Columns plug-in. It's a lot faster to use this addition than to change each column's coordinates in the Control palette. To use this plug-in, select all the columns you want aligned (click on the first text block and Shift+click on the others). Then choose Utilities⇨PageMaker Plug-ins⇨Balance Columns to get the Balance Columns dialog box (shown in Figure 12-8). Choose the left Alignment icon to have all selected columns begin at the Y position of the highest text block; click the right Alignment icon to align the bottoms of all the columns with the bottom of the lowest text block. The bottom two icons in the dialog box let you choose where you want PageMaker to place any leftover lines; choose the left icon if you want them added to the left column, and choose the right icon if you want them added to the right column. Click on OK to close the dialog box and balance the columns.

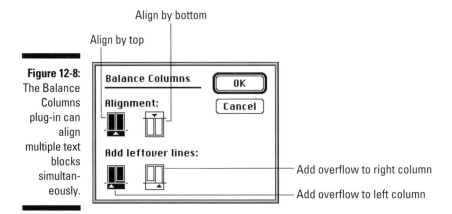

Align by bottom

Align by top

Figure 12-8:
The Balance
Columns
plug-in can
align
multiple text
blocks
simultan-
eously.

Balance Columns

OK

Alignment:

Cancel

Add leftover lines:

Add overflow to right column

Add overflow to left column

So why would you ever align columns the long way described earlier? Because Balance Columns makes an assumption that may not be true: It aligns the columns based on the position of the highest text block (or the lowest, if you're aligning the bottoms). Of course, you can still use this addition and then use the Control palette to change the Y coordinate for all of the text blocks simultaneously. If multiple elements are selected, any changes made to coordinates or other palette values are applied to all the selected elements. Any options that can't be applied to multiple elements don't appear in the Control palette.

By the way, while you're using the Control palette to align columns, you can also change the column width, height, and horizontal coordinate (via the settings in the W, H, and X option boxes, respectively).

With the text blocks aligned, creating the rest of the sample newsletter's first page, shown in Figure 12-9, is just a matter of making a few embellishments:

- ✔ Add a drop cap to the second story. (See Chapter 8 for details on drop caps.)

- ✔ Add a graphic to the first story (instead of a drop cap, the example uses a logo related to that story's contents). (See Chapter 9 for details on wrapping text around graphics.)

- ✔ Add a square box in front of the kicker text. (The square box is just a symbol from a symbols font. You can also use embedded graphics, which are covered in Chapter 10.)

- ✔ Rewrite the lead headline so that it fills up the three-column space. The original headline was too short for the space it occupied — generally, every column should have some headline text above it, although the last column doesn't need to have the headline extend all the way to its right margin.

Figure 12-9:
The final
page 1, with
drop caps,
graphics,
and other
typographic
embellish-
ments
added.

Headlines often have to be rewritten to better fit the layout — they may be too long or too short. If you're just doing layout, have an editor rewrite the headline for you — simply mark on the printout that the headline is too short or too long. If you're doing both the layout and the editing, be prepared to change the headlines as you lay out stories.

Except for putting in the correct page numbers for the cross-references, the contents box, and that "In This Issue" box, you're now done with page 1.

You can use Arrange⇨Group (Ctrl+G) to weld several elements together, enabling you to move them around the page without worrying about changing their position relative to each other. When you get elements in your layout positioned properly, you can use the Lock command (Arrange⇨Lock Position or Ctrl+L) to prevent them from being moved accidentally. For more information about the Group and Lock commands, see Chapter 10.

Pages 2 and 3

At this point, you have a choice: Move on to page 2 or move to the page(s) that will contain the rest of the text from the stories on page 1. Again, the order of creating the pages and placing the stories is not important from a technical view — *you* decide what you want to work on when.

Let's assume though — we're making a lot of assumptions here, aren't we? — that you decide to move on to page 2. In many cases, such as when working on a newsletter, it makes sense to place the start of each story first and then deal with the remainder of each story later. However, that may not be a good approach for other documents. You certainly wouldn't lay out a book that way — you'd place all the text and graphics for one chapter before moving on to the next.

At any rate, take a look now at the blank page 2 (and page 3, because they're on facing pages) in Figure 12-10. The text block with the gray box in the first column is the *masthead* — the text that contains the names of the staff, the mailing address of the newsletter, and other such information. Most newsletters and magazines have something like this, and it's traditionally on the second page. (It can, of course, go anywhere.) Because the masthead appears in every issue, it's an element that you normally place in your template. (Again, creating and using templates is explained fully in Chapter 14.) Imagine that you did so and that the masthead — along with a few other elements, including page numbers and the newsletter title — are already present and accounted for when you turn to page 2 in your PageMaker layout.

That masthead leaves just two columns on page 2 for new material. It's a good idea to use such a regular space to hold regular elements, such as letters to the editor, or the president's message, or a column by a particular contributor to your publication. In this newsletter, a columnist's work gets this position. You place the column as you place any story.

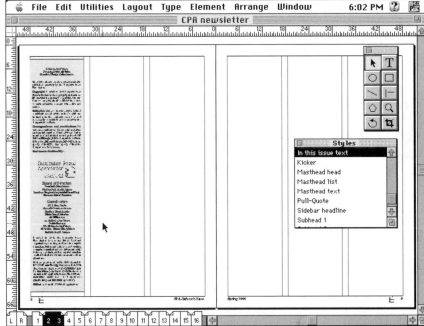

Figure 12-10:
The template for pages 2 and 3.

But let's make this column a fancy one. Suppose that a caricature of the columnist is to appear within the story, with the text wrapping around the graphic. (See Chapter 9 for details on text wrap.) And suppose also that, when you try to place the story and graphic, you don't have enough text from the columnist to fit the available space, as in Figure 12-11.

No matter what you're laying out, you'll run into this kind of situation — text and space almost never match. Usually, you have too much text, but sometimes you have too little. (It's a conspiracy!) If you're dealing with reports and books, you can always add another page (or at least almost always) or go a page short — the length of the document is flexible. That's usually not true for newsletters. Most are printed on 11 x 17-inch sheets and folded — so a sheet contains four pages. If you run short, you have blank pages. If you run over, you have to add blank pages. Even if your elements fit in the number of pages required for printing, you may have some pages with gaps in them, as in Figure 12-11.

If you're responsible for producing newsletters, you'll deal with such gaps frequently. You can do several things to fix the problem. But first, here are some things you should *never* do:

> ✔ Never change the size of the text, the space between lines, or the width of the columns to "stretch" the text. Your text will look awful — amateurish. You get a ransom-note effect, with different-size text throughout. Embarrassing!

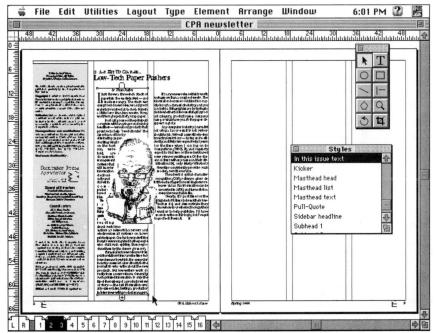

Figure 12-11: Whoops! Even with the graphic, the columnist's material is too short for the space.

✔ Never leave the gaps. They look unprofessional — like you forgot something or were too lazy to handle the problem.

So what can you do? Try the following:

✔ Have extra elements available. Maybe a selection of small cartoons. Or some short stories (such as notes to your reader about upcoming events, "For more information" announcements, "Help wanted" notices, or "Did you know" trivia). This option is the best, because it lets you add information for the reader while giving you layout flexibility. Figure 12-12 shows how to close a gap with such an element. It's a good bet that if you didn't know that the columnist's text was short and this element was added as filler, you would think that the designer planned the page to look this way.

✔ Use *pull-quotes*. Pull-quotes are short excerpts from the text that are printed in larger type and set apart from the story — they may be in a box, between lines, or on a background. (The right page in Figure 12-13 includes a pull-quote.) However, a pull-quote won't solve the problem in Figure 12-11 because the page doesn't have room for one — the graphic is too large and leaves insufficient space for another element in the story. It works in Figure 12-13 because the page has plenty of space — in fact, adding a second pull-quote at the bottom left section of the page may make it look more attractive; now it's pretty dull and gray. Figure 12-14

Figure 12-12: Adding a filler story takes care of the gap — and adds information for the reader. A two-for-one deal!

Figure 12-13: A pull-quote (right side of right page) can fill out a short story and add visual interest to an otherwise dull page.

shows examples of different pull-quotes. Remember, the idea is to call attention to the story's content (so pick interesting excerpts) *and* to offer a visual element on the page that makes it more attractive (so make sure that the pull-quote design isn't altogether ugly).

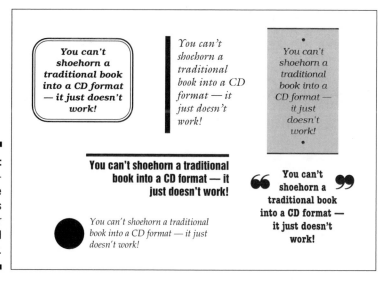

Figure 12-14: A few pull-quote examples presented for your general amusement.

✔ Use a longer headline. Rewrite the headline so it takes two lines rather than one. This method only works occasionally; a two-line headline can be overwhelming if the headline is wide or if its typeface is bold and/or size is large. That's the case in this example newsletter — two-line heads are just too intense.

Look more closely at the filler element on page 2 (refer to Figure 12-13). Notice a couple of things about it:

✔ It's on a gray background, which helps differentiate it from the columnist's text. Notice the lines above and below the background — this design is just a variation on putting a box around a sidebar or small text element. (Why doesn't the text placed on top of the gray background wrap around the background, like the columnist's text does? Glad you asked. If you place a text block so that it falls wholly within a graphic's boundaries, it won't wrap — after all, there's no place for it to wrap to.)

✔ The text runs across the two columns, which also helps differentiate it from the other text. And because of the gray box, the text doesn't quite go all the way to the edge of the columns. To create this element, the text block was resized to leave about 0.2 inches of space on either side. But the work is worth it — the margin of gray around the text makes the text more readable. The first example in Figure 12-15 shows how the text looks without any gray margin. If you use a box instead of a gray background to separate the filler text from the columnist's text, you would have a similar margin.

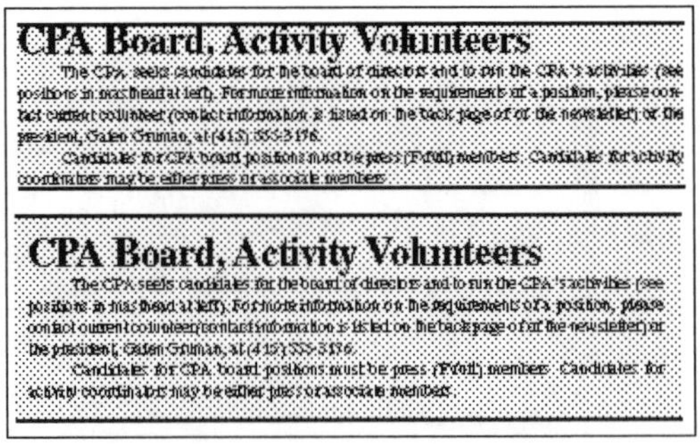

Figure 12-15:
Without any margin between text and graphic elements (top) your design looks cramped. A looser alternative appears at bottom.

The use of a symbol, called a *dingbat*, to indicate the end of a story is a common technique in newsletters, magazines, and other multistory documents. The symbol lets the reader know definitively that a particular story is done. To create a dingbat, pick a character from a symbols font or use an embedded graphic (see Chapter 10). To position it at the end of the line, precede the dingbat character with a tab. In the style for your text, define a right-aligned tab that stops just shy of the column width. For example, if your column is 2 inches wide, place the tab at 1.9 inches. (You need to do so because PageMaker will position the dingbat at the beginning of the next line if it aligns completely against the right margin. Clearly, it *should* work if you make the tab stop the same as the margin location, but *should* doesn't mean *does*.) Chapters 6 through 8 cover special type techniques in more detail.

By continuing the placement of stories on subsequent pages, using the same techniques, you'll soon have the main elements arranged. But you still have to deal with that extra text that will go on other pages. How does it get there, and how does the reader know where it is? Read on.

Handling Jumped Text

Text that starts on one page and continues on another is called *jumped text* among layout *cognoscenti* (that's Latin for *know-it-alls*). You've probably figured out that placing the text on other pages is easy: You click on the more-text icon, move to the page you want to put the text on, click the paragraph icon at the desired location, and continue the layout.

But you need to do one other thing to properly jump text: add continued lines.

What's a *continued line*? It's a line of text that tells the reader where the rest of the story is — what page it came from or what page it continues on to. Figure 12-16 shows both kinds:

- ✔ At the bottom of the first column is a *continued-on line*. It's very simple — just a line in italics that aligns to the right of the column. No frills.

- ✔ The third column contains a *continued-from line,* which is more elaborate. It includes a headline (so that people can find the topic when they flip over to the new page) and a line saying what page the story continues from (for people who may be intrigued by the topic and want to find the beginning of the story). Because unrelated text appears above the continued story, placing a line between the two stories is a good idea to help the reader distinguish the continued head from a subhead in the other story.

Continued on next page

Electronic Books
Continued from page 4

Figure 12-16: Two kinds of continued lines (both highlighted).

When using devices such as headlines, continued lines, and the like, be consistent. Yes, walking on the wild side has its benefits — but not for bread-and-butter elements. Use common techniques for the common elements. For example, notice that both the continued-on and continued-from text in Figure 12-16 are in italics — it helps tie them together and reinforce to the reader that they serve the same function (identifying cross-references). And as before, the line above the continued story helps separate unrelated elements.

In constructing a continued line, don't just type it into the text block containing the story; put the continued line in its own text block, as in Figure 12-16. Otherwise, if you add a line to the story, your continued line will get bumped to a new page.

You should know one more thing about creating continued lines: PageMaker can't manage the cross-referenced page numbers for you. You have to keep track of the page numbers yourself and then update the numbers when the layout is truly complete. (You may want to use an *X* as a placeholder instead of an actual page number; that way, you know which page numbers need to be checked and updated.)

PageMaker also has a plug-in to create continued lines for you. The plug-in's not great, but it's serviceable for many people. One advantage the plug-in offers is that it figures out the right page number — but it doesn't update that page number if the story's page order is changed later. The plug-in, which is called Add Cont'd Line and is available via Utilities⇨PageMaker Plug-ins, automatically adds a *Continued from page x* or *Continued on page x* line above or below the current text block. It also creates a style called *Cont. On* if you choose the Bottom of Textblock option and a style called *Cont. From* if you choose the Top of Textblock column. (Defining these styles first with the settings you want rather than letting the plug-in create them is a good idea. You'll likely want to change the settings of the styles it creates anyhow.) The plug-in rolls down the top of the text block by one line — or rolls up the bottom of the text block by one line — to make room for the continued line.

Because this plug-in shortens the text block for which you are adding a continued line, you may have text missing at the end of your document. The number of lines that end up being pushed into the final text block may not fit in that final text block. To avoid this problem, shorten text boxes that will have continued lines by one line *before* using the plug-in — in other words, make room for the continued line in advance. The plug-in still shortens the text block by a line, but you can lengthen it when the addition is done.

Altering Columns and Text Blocks

After you've laid out text in columns, you may decide that you want to change the number of columns or maybe move a column somewhere else. Be careful. This part of doing a PageMaker layout can really get you in trouble. It's not your fault — the blame is in how PageMaker handles text blocks. If you're not careful, you can delete text accidentally and perhaps permanently. Here's an example of how it works.

Changing the number of columns

Take a look at Figure 12-17. It shows a three-column sidebar in a three-column page. After looking at it, you decide that you want the sidebar to be a two-column sidebar to make it more visually distinct from the rest of the text on the page and its facing page. So all you have to do is select the three columns and change the number of columns to two, right? Wrong — just try to find a command or option to do this. None exists. No, what PageMaker makes you do is delete one column and resize the remaining ones. The deletion of a column is where you can lose text. (If you want to *add* a column, all you have to do is resize the existing ones, click on the more-text icon on the last column's windowshade handle, and place the new column.)

Say that you delete the middle column (using Edit➪Cut or ⌘+X) and resize the other two columns so that they're wider. That deleted text block is removed from the chain, or thread, of text blocks making up the story. Even if you paste the deleted text block back in, it remains apart from the original story — when you select the block, you'll notice that the linked-text icon is replaced by the no-text icon on its windowshade handles. To reinstate the text from that cut block back into the story, you have to switch to the Text tool, select all text in that block (via Edit➪Select All or ⌘+A), place your text cursor at the end of the previous block or the beginning of the next block, and paste that text into the block. A royal pain. (And if you used Edit➪Clear or pressed the Delete key to delete the text block, you can't paste it back in — it's gone for good.)

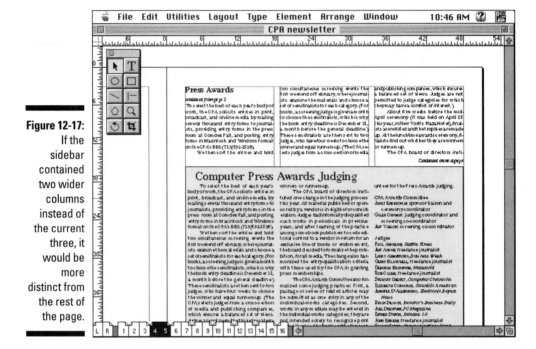

Figure 12-17:
If the sidebar contained two wider columns instead of the current three, it would be more distinct from the rest of the page.

You can recover deleted text and relink it to the rest of the story in another way: reimport the text via File➪Place or ⌘+D. When doing so, you click on a text block containing the story, open the Place Document dialog box, select the text file, and — this is crucial — click on the Replacing Entire Story button before clicking on OK. However, this approach has several potential problems:

✔ If the text was created in PageMaker, there is no text file to reimport.

✔ If the text was changed in PageMaker, those changes will be lost. Even if you exported the changed text from PageMaker to the text file (via File➪Export), much of the formatting done in PageMaker can be lost because this information is not compatible with the text file's word-processor format.

✔ If the source text file was modified in the word processor after you imported it the first time, you'll import the new version, and it may have changed significantly.

What to do? Instead of deleting the unwanted column, select one of the windowshade handles and roll it up (or down) until it touches the other handle. Figure 12-18 shows what this looks like. You don't even have to delete the empty windowshade — if you select any other element and then try to reselect it, you'll find that it's gone — kaput, dead. The text automatically reflows into the remaining columns, but you have to resize the text blocks to fit the new column arrangement.

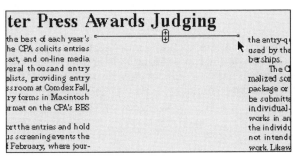

Moving columns or text blocks

The same potential problems exist if you decide you want to move a column of text from one page to another. *Don't cut and paste linked text blocks.*

Instead, use the empty windowshade technique just described to remove the text block from one page. Then click on the linked-text or more-text icon on the bottom of the last remaining text block on the page to get the paragraph icon, move to the new desired page, and click where you want the column to continue. (You get the linked-text icon if the text block you're deleting and adding somewhere else falls within a series of linked text blocks; you get the more-text icon if the text block to be deleted and added elsewhere is the last text block in the series.)

If you want to move a text block within the current page or within the current facing pages, just drag it to its new location.

Inserting columns or text blocks

Say that you have a story on page 6 that continues on page 29, and you discover there's enough free space on page 15 for some of that story. How do you add a text block between two linked text boxes so that the text flows through the new, middle block? You click on the linked-text icon on the bottom windowshade handle of the text block on page 6 or click on the linked-text icon on the top windowshade handle of the text block on page 29. Either way, you get the paragraph icon. Move to page 15, position the paragraph icon where you want to place the new text block linked to those on pages 6 and 29, and click the mouse button. A text block appears, and if you check, you'll see that the text is flowing properly through it from the previous text block and to the next one.

You can use this same technique to start a story earlier in the layout — just click on the no-text icon on the top windowshade handle for the first text block in the story. You can also use it to add columns or other text blocks on the same page, not just on different pages.

Sorting Pages

PageMaker offers one other tool that comes in handy when you're arranging and rearranging a multipage document: the Sort Pages command that you access by choosing Layout⇨Sort Pages. This command lets you move pages around in your layout, which can be very helpful if you want to change the fundamental order of your pages.

When you choose the command, the dialog box shown in Figure 12-19 appears. To move a page to a new location, just click on it and drag it. PageMaker even displays old and new page numbers (the old page numbers are surrounded by dotted page icons, not solid icons), in case you want to undo a move. Of course, you can click Cancel to undo all changes made in the Sort Pages dialog box, too. To get a closer look at your pages, click on the icon that shows a magnifying glass with a plus sign in it (at the bottom of the dialog box). To zoom out so that you can see more of your layout, click on the icon that shows a magnifying glass with a minus sign in it.

To select one page from a two-page spread, ⌘+click on the page. If you want to place a page between a pair of facing pages, press ⌘ while you drag the page over the spread. A black bar appears to show you where the page will be inserted when you release the mouse button.

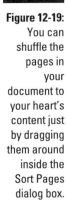

Figure 12-19:
You can shuffle the pages in your document to your heart's content just by dragging them around inside the Sort Pages dialog box.

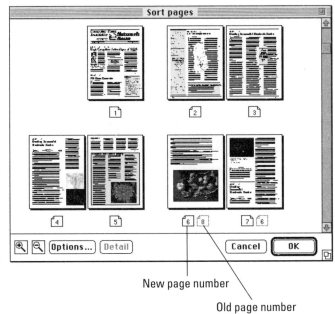

New page number

Old page number

If you click on the Options button, you gain access to several convenient options:

- ✔ Normally, when you have facing pages with different margins and you drag a right-hand page to a left-hand page position, PageMaker rearranges the elements on the page to fit the left-hand page's margins. You can disallow that by checking the Don't Move Elements check box.

- ✔ If you want to move individual pages in a layout that was created as a spread, just uncheck the Facing Pages check box (or to make a single-page document a facing-page document, check that option). Likewise, if you want to stop the document from being double-sided, uncheck that option (or check it to make a single-sided document double-sided).

- ✔ If you want a thumbnail view of the pages (as in Figure 12-19), check Show Detailed Thumbnails, but be aware that this option greatly slows down screen display. If this option is unchecked, you can still get details on a particular page by selecting the page and clicking the Detail button.

When you have the pages rearranged to your liking, click on OK to make your changes final — final, that is, until you change your mind again.

To insert new pages or remove existing pages from the interior of your publication, choose Layout➪Insert Pages or Layout➪Remove Pages, respectively. If you want to add or delete pages from the end of the publication, you can simply change the Number of Pages value in the Document Setup dialog box (File➪Document Setup).

If you've read all the chapters up to this point, you should have a pretty good grasp on the technical aspects of laying out a document in PageMaker. But if you're new to designing publications, you may be a little unsure about just what elements to put where and how to pull everything together into an eye-catching, professional-looking document. Never fear. The next chapter provides some examples and ideas to get you started on the road to design excellence.

Chapter 13

How to Design Stuff They'll Actually Read

• •

In This Chapter

▶ Examples of how you can combine various layout techniques to create good-looking documents

▶ Ads and price sheets that sell

▶ A classy proposal

▶ An anything-but-boring manual

▶ Tips for effective newsletter and annual report design

▶ A collection of cool design ideas

• •

*B*eauty is in the eye of the beholder, and by combining PageMaker's strengths and some basic design know-how, you can put a lot of beauty in the eyes of lots of beholders. But if you're a novice at page design, you can easily feel a little lost when it comes to choosing a font, determining which elements go where, and coming up with an overall design scheme.

To help get you started on the road to good design, this chapter offers some examples of effective newsletters, ads, annual reports, and other business documents. You won't find many specific how-to's on using PageMaker commands and functions — just ideas that will help you develop a sense for how to create professional-looking layouts.

As with any good design ideas, the following ones are based on years of experience and, of course, honest-to-goodness pilfering of other people's good work. Imitation is the sincerest form of flattery, and as long you as don't cross the line into blatant copying, go ahead and flatter as many people as you can. Go to the newsstand and thumb through a bunch of magazines. (But buy just the ones you really like.) Get a couple of colleagues and look through those magazines together. Talk about what you like, what you don't like, and — most important — *why* you react the way you do. You can call this flower-power consciousness-raising or being a copycat, but looking at examples is the best way to learn design.

One last point: Don't confuse the following examples with recipes. We don't pretend to be Picassos or even Harings. Even if we were Big Artists, our designs may not make sense for your documents. After all, the designs you produce must meet several needs: your sense of aesthetics, the requirements of the content being presented, the image you and your organization want to convey, and the financial limitations you are working under (we'd all love to do everything in full, glorious color, but until money comes out of laser printers without resulting in jail terms, we do have some teensy-weensy concerns about the cost).

Look at the following examples as starting points, and don't worry if you come up with designs for your work that look nothing like these.

Price Sheets

A price sheet is fairly functional — at least, it should be. Unfortunately, a price sheet is also the kind of document that's often formatted in type so tiny, so difficult to read, that it's a wonder anybody manages to order anything. Imagine: A company goes out of business because of a poorly designed price sheet. Well, things may not get that bad, but bad enough.

The key to a successful price sheet is making its various elements easy to find and easy to read. Look at Figure 13-1 for an example of such a price list. The thinking that went behind the price sheet is as follows (the numbers in the list correspond to the numbered labels in the figure):

1. Because of the degree of detail provided for each item, the format of the price list calls for horizontal (landscape) pages. Horizontal pages leave room for fuller descriptions of the products.

2. At the top of each page, you see the effective date of the prices, the name of the price list, and a table key (the boldface italics text that lists the stock code, description, and so on). A ruling line separates the price sheet title and the table key, adding visual interest and separating the general information from the specific information — the table key is directly related to the tabbed text below it, while the title and effective date are not.

3. A rule (line) above the page numbers separates them from the product information.

4. The effective date of the prices is in boldface, making the date hard for the reader to miss. Because prices change regularly, the effective date is one piece of information you want to make easy to find.

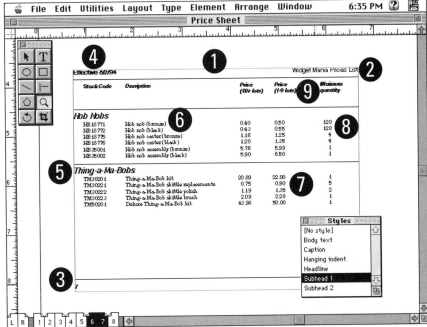

Figure 13-1:
An example
price list
layout.

5. The titles for each product category are in large, sans serif type. They happen to be in the same font (Helvetica) as the title and table key information. This type treatment keeps the number of fonts to a minimum (to avoid the ransom-note effect) and reinforces that different fonts have different meanings: The Helvetica text is the title information, while the New Century Schoolbook text is the basic content. A ruling line above each product category title helps the reader keep product categories separate. Such a rule is particularly useful when the text is so wide, as it is here, because the category titles aren't long enough to be really noticeable on the right side of the page if someone is scanning prices quickly.

6. The text is formatted in a serif typeface, New Century Schoolbook, known for its easy readability. The text is also fairly large for a price sheet — 12 points. A lot of price tables are in tiny (8-point or smaller) text, and they're a pain to read. (Yes, smaller type means more products per page and thus fewer pages to print, which means lower cost. But who cares how much money you save if the end result is that you lose business because customers can't read your price sheet?) The indentation of the text helps the reader quickly find each product category; the category titles hang to the left of the text, acting as a visual speed bump.

7. Prices are aligned using decimal tabs — see how easily you can differentiate expensive items from cheap ones just by looking at the number of digits to the left of the decimal?

8. Numbers in the *Minimum quantity* column are right-aligned for the same reason prices are aligned with decimal tabs.

9. Although the alignment of the table key appears to be the same as for the text, it's not. The tab stops for the two *Price* titles and the *Minimum quantity* title are modified. Why? Decimal alignment for straight text aligns the beginning of the text to the right of the decimal, which means that the *Price* titles appear slightly to the right of the prices. The answer is to change the tab to a left-aligned tab and move the tab stop to the left so that the titles appear to align with the dollar digits of the text's prices.

Similarly, keeping a right-aligned tab for the *Minimum quantity* title would look weird — it would be the only item in the table key that is right-aligned — so a left-aligned tab is used. The tab stop is moved to the left so that the title aligns better with the quantity numbers.

Ads and Circulars

The design of ads, circulars (fliers), and other such sales- and marketing-oriented materials is critical because such publications must work the first time. Readers may be willing to put up with a newsletter design they don't like if the newsletter contains information they find valuable. But an ad needs to attract attention, to hold the reader long enough to deliver its message, and leave that reader with a favorable impression. We've included three ads to show the techniques used to accomplish these goals. Remember, whether you're working on an ad, a report cover, a prospectus, a pamphlet, or other such publication, these techniques apply.

Figure 13-2 shows an ad for a fictitious airline. Notice the following about its design:

1. The large type is kerned so that the spacing between each pair of characters is the same — the letters are just at the point of touching.

2. The small type forces the eye to take a look because of the contrast with the big type above and all the space on either side. This use of contrast is a good way to get attention. Never underestimate the power of type — it is as important as graphics in garnering attention and conveying both the substance and the nuances of the message.

3. The airline logo uses reverse-type and shadow effects on a fairly common font (Bauhaus). Notice the sun symbol to the left of the logo: That's a symbol in the Zapf Dingbats font. The use of symbols really helps establish a logo as a logo, rather than just a bunch of letters. Also notice the use of a catch phrase in the same font as the logo. You would use such a treatment

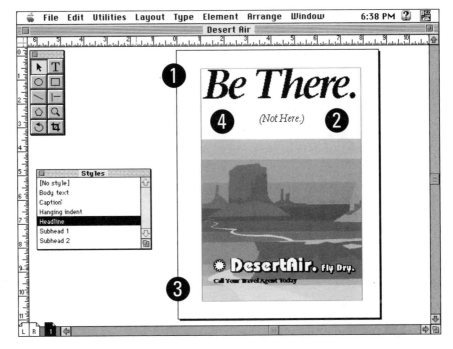

Figure 13-2:
A simple ad
with a
simple
message
deserves a
simple
treatment to
attract
attention.

for a catch phrase that you plan on using in several places — the catch phrase becomes an extension of the logo. (The desert tableau is a color image, and in color, the text is very striking against the colors; in black and white, the text loses a little of that zing.)

4. Notice the use of blank areas — what designers call *white space*. White space provides a visually calm port in a storm of images and text. Be sure to provide these resting spots in all your work.

The ad for a seafood restaurant in Figure 13-3 shows a tighter interplay of text and graphics. The ad also shows, although not at first glance, the power of PageMaker's graphics manipulation tools.

1. Look at the schools of fish (they're in glorious color, although you can't see that in black and white). Three fish were copied and pasted to create the schools. To make sure that your copies don't look like copies, you can use the Rotate and Skew commands to make each fish slightly different from the others. A very slight skew — less than 5 percent — was used in Figure 13-3. The rotation accounts for most of the differences in the appearance of the fish. The lesson: Don't forget to use basic techniques, such as rotating and copying.

2. The text describing all the sumptuous seafood options is wrapped around the pictures of fish, using PageMaker's text wrap feature, explained in Chapter 9.

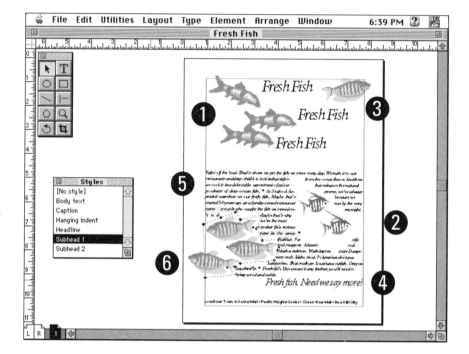

Figure 13-3:
An ad
that has
interplay
between the
text and
graphics.

3. Can you tell what this ad is selling? Why, fresh fish, of course! The repetitive use of the text reinforces the message. Placing the repeating text in different positions among the fish makes sure that the text doesn't look repetitive. (Predictability is a major reason that repetition is boring, and this design finds a way to repeat without being boring.)

4. More repetition. Again different. This tag line reinforces the primary message. In the case of this ad, the restaurant isn't identified by any large text (it is identified in the body text), but this tag line is one the restaurant uses a lot, so the ad can get away with the low-key play of the restaurant's name — for example, if an ad just said, "Have it your way," you'd probably think of Burger King, while "Just do it" would probably evoke images of Nike shoes.

5. All the text here, except the list of locations at the bottom, is in italics, which is unusual. But the fluidity of italics works well with the fish theme (under water — get it?); and because the text is large enough and the layout uncluttered, the italics work.

6. The fish swim past the margins on the page, which makes the page look less boxed-in. Breaking the strict margins to provide a feeling of flexibility and give the eye something unusual to flag on is often a good idea.

Let's take a look at one more ad. This one, shown in Figure 13-4, is not a full page. The ad is one that you'd probably run in an in-house publication: what the big magazines call a PSA (public service announcement). This ad is the kind of thing that you can easily put together using clip art and basic typefaces when you have a hole to fill or need to make an announcement or advertisement for your organization.

Figure 13-4:
A public service announcement for black-and-white reproduction.

1. This simple graphic works well in black and white. Photos can be very effective attention-getters because they scream, "Real!" The simple composition is also pleasing. You'll find many such images in clip art libraries.

2. Simple text with a simple message that ties into the image — that's the ticket. A loud, bold title would have competed with the photo. This one's easy to read, but it doesn't fight for attention. If you see the photo and stop, you see the headline, and that's all that's required. The centering makes sure that you know that the headline goes with the text below. The centered text also follows the centered shape of the chair — when you use many different alignments, your layout can become distracting, so try to stick with one or two. A left alignment may work here, but then the symmetry of the chair is not picked up in the rest of the ad — and such reuse of basic visual themes is a hallmark of pleasing design. People just get all warm and fuzzy with such continuity.

3. The text is short, readable, and justified. Although having justified text seems to violate the minimal-alignment rule, the fact is that centered text is rarely easy to read if you have more than a few lines of it. Justifying the text keeps the symmetry of the centered text because the right and left margins in justified text are symmetrical.

4. We all know what a dashed line means — the page fairly yells, "Cut me out!" To create a dashed box, use PageMaker's Rectangle tool and change the line to a dashed one. (Here, the line is a 1.5-point rule.) To reinforce the "Cut me!" message, you can add a pair of scissors (from a symbols font or from clip art) along a top corner of the dashed box.

5. The box contains the coupon the advertiser wants people to complete. The font here is different (a condensed sans serif, compared to the text's normal serif). This difference reinforces the idea that the coupon is a separate element. You want the reader to think of the coupon as separate so that people know it's okay to remove it from the rest of the ad. The use of a condensed font also leaves more room for people to fill in the information you want. The underlines are right-aligned tabs using an underline tab leader — that's the simplest way to create fill-in-the-blank lines.

Proposals

When you interview for a job, you put on a nice suit to help create a positive first impression. When you put together a proposal — for a potential customer or for your boss — you likewise should make a good impression by paying special attention to the presentation.

Figures 13-5 and 13-6 show the cover and interior pages of a financial brochure. Note that a proposal may have other elements, such as a table of contents or index, depending on its complexity. They're not shown here, but Chapter 15 shows you how to add such components.

Ready to dissect this proposal? Here goes:

1. The first thing to notice is that the proposal cover is in its own PageMaker document. That's because the proposal is divided into multiple sections, each of which starts with a new page 1. The cover has to be in its own document so that each section can start with a new page number. Even if you have only a cover and one section, putting the cover in the document with the rest of the proposal confuses the page numbering because the cover is page 1, not the first real page in the document. PageMaker is unlike your word processor in that you can't have multiple sections and have each section's page numbering independent of the others.

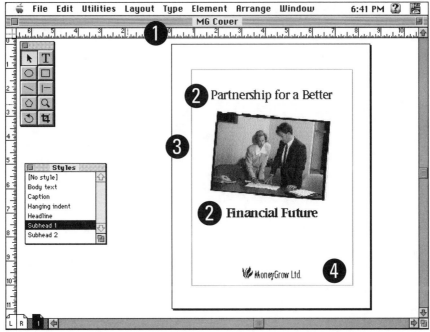

Figure 13-5:
A cover for
a financial
proposal.

2. The font is a conservative serif. Serifs in general have a feeling of substance and tradition behind them, while sans serifs have a modern, more
   artsy feel. This proposal is asking people to part with their money, so the
   ad needs to appear conservative. Notice how the title breaks around the
   image. The first line stresses partnership, which is what the image below it
   conveys. The second line (it's even bolder than the first line) stresses the
   financial aspect. Separating the two lines makes the message of each line
   more obvious.

3. The image is admittedly gratuitous. But imagine what the cover would look
   like without it — boring, that's what. Be sure that the images you use
   reinforce the message you're trying to convey. Here, the picture of two
   people working together reinforces the message of partnership, while the
   fact that they both look like yuppies reinforces the idea of making money.
   (You can really push this concept by having multiple images, each tar-
   geted to a different potential audience. Doing so can be effective, if some-
   what cynical.)

4. The company's logo appears at the bottom of the proposal. Logos bespeak
   corporate. Just using the name is not enough — if you can afford to have a
   logo, you must be a "real" company. Chances are that your company has a
   logo — use it.

5. Interior pages (see Figure 13-6) include the overall title (at left) and the
   chapter title (at right). The rule underneath this header separates it from
   the main text.

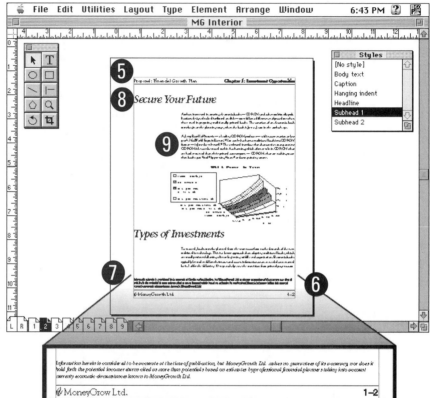

Figure 13-6:
An interior
page from
the financial
proposal.

6. As mentioned, each section has its own numbering, which you can see in the footer. Notice several techniques here: First, a prefix in front of the page number indicates the section. Second, notice the use of conservative fonts throughout (you can see the fonts better in the close-up). Most of the document uses Goudy, which just oozes traditionalism (Goudy is also a very nice-looking font). The page number is in Helvetica, though, which is easy to see as you flip through the pages. This kind of slight departure from the main style can really call attention to something without being annoying. Finally, notice the use of the corporate logo in the footer, even though the company name is not in its logo font. The logo's in Goudy here, to blend with the rest of the text, although the logo could just have easily been in its standard font. Again, here's a subtle embellishment that bespeaks attention to detail.

7. The footer contains some boilerplate disclaimer text that satisfies legal concerns. (The disclaimer text is the fine print in all financial proposals that basically says, "Sure, we say we're the experts. But if we screw up and lose all your money, you take full responsibility for not having seen the risk.") The disclaimer appears in the obligatory small print. The disclaimer

also is in italics, which serves several purposes: It makes the text look nicer, makes the disclaimer more noticeably distinct from the standard text, and makes the text less likely to be read (long blocks of italics do that), taking some of the sting out of the warning. (Cynical, yes, but we are talking about what people really do, not what they *should* do.)

8. The headings within the proposal are large but classy. The use of italics helps, as does the use of a slightly different font. The font is Stone Serif, one with fewer embellishments than Goudy. At larger sizes, some font embellishments that look nice in body copy start calling too much attention to themselves.

9. The body text is indented quite a bit from the left margin, which calls attention to both the headlines and the text. The indentation also keeps the text width from being too overwhelming (the wider the paragraph, the more intimidating it looks). The use of slightly generous leading (12.5 points for this 10-point text rather than a more typical 12 or 11.5 points) also makes the text look less intimidating. (Remember, the proposal is asking people to risk their money, so it must be inviting and soothing.) Last, instead of using indented paragraphs, the proposal uses extra space between paragraphs.

Take a look at some variants of this layout in Figure 13-7. The pages have been resized to booklet form, so the large indents of the original layout didn't work. Figure 13-7 shows two possible solutions: running the text at the full column width and using a large indent for each paragraph to break up some of the boxiness (left) and reducing the indent amount but keeping the same basic style as the original layout (right).

Manuals

Why bother worrying about making a manual look good? No one reads manuals anyway, right? Well, that attitude toward manual design has a lot to do with why no one reads them. The manual almost seems like an afterthought. A good manual is a real treasure. You should consider a manual to be a book and take the same care in writing, editing, and design that you'd expect from a best-selling book.

You can develop straightforward manuals that don't take a lot of time to format but offer more than a mind-numbing sea of gray. Take a look at Figure 13-8 for an example. As you can see, the manual is not very adventurous, but it offers several visual niceties.

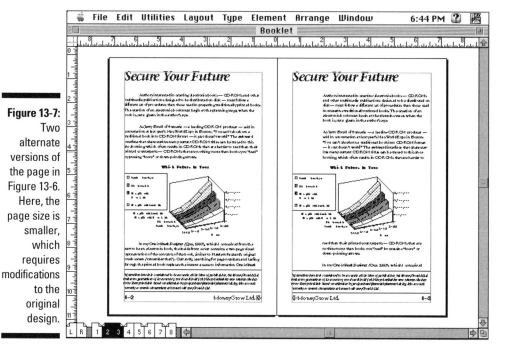

Figure 13-7:
Two
alternate
versions of
the page in
Figure 13-6.
Here, the
page size is
smaller,
which
requires
modifications
to the
original
design.

1. Notice the odd margins — the text takes only about three quarters of the width of the page. That setup does two things: First, the margins keep the text from becoming too wide and off-putting. Second, the margins leave some space for small graphics and *white space* (the designer term for empty page space used to provide visual relief).

2. Guides pulled out from the rulers help position the small graphics and their captions.

3. A thick line spans the full width of the page, tying in the text with the small graphics at the sides. Without such a unifying element, the graphics can appear to be unrelated to the text.

4. The page numbering and manual name at the bottom of the page follow the text margins. The elements could have matched the margins of the ruling line at the top, but by being different yet aligned with a major element, the elements reinforce the text's margins and add some visual interest.

5. With so many elements aligning against different margins, using justified text can make the manual appear too precise or machined. Left-aligned text creates a natural undulation along the right margin. To keep the text from getting too dense in a one-text-column format, new paragraphs are distinguished by extra Before spacing instead of first-line indents.

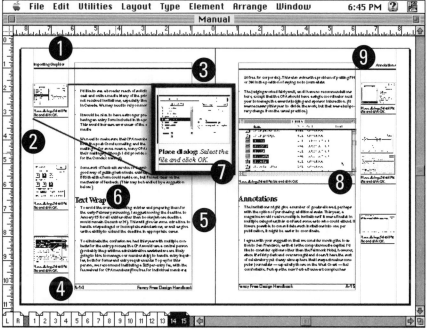

Figure 13-8:
A well-designed manual.

The text font is Cheltenham, which is a very solid-looking font. It's easy to read, even at small sizes, but Cheltenham does tend to be a bit wide. Condensing the text to 95 percent is enough to turn the basic rectangular shape into a squarer shape. The effect is subtle enough that readers don't feel like the type is squished.

6. The titles are simple, using a clean, simple font called Minion Semibold. Notice that the short text helps the reader recognize the topics immediately.

7. Captions are a good place to use typographic effects. Here, the lead-in text is bold, while the rest of the caption is italic. This treatment clearly separates the caption's "headline" from the caption's "text" while also providing some visual contrast. Another bonus: Readers can easily find captions cross-referenced from the main text. Notice, too, the ruling line below the caption. The rule clearly delineates the end of a caption and picks up on the use of ruling lines in the header and footer. Having such mini-themes in your design has the same effect as repeating certain themes in music: It adds continuity, which is reassuring to readers.

8. Although space is set aside for small graphics, some graphics require more space because they are complex. So in this design, the graphics can also fall in the main text's space. The caption is formatted the same as for the smaller graphics, which provides more of that ever-important continuity.

9. The name of the current topic appears at the top of each page to give readers an easy way to find a particular topic as they're browsing through the manual.

You should take note of two other examples of well-designed manuals before moving on: this book, designed by the talented folks at IDG Books Worldwide, and the PageMaker manual, designed by the talented folks at Adobe. Both manuals use a combination of margins, text formats, ruling lines, and small graphics to help you manage your way through the text.

Newsletters

Several chapters of this book use a newsletter as an example. The newsletter is the source of identity for the nonprofit group that publishes it, so even though the newsletter is done very inexpensively, it has to look professional, not cheap.

Well, that example newsletter has changed several times in the years it's been produced. Figure 13-9 shows the first three pages from three different issues — one from 1990, one from 1991, and one from 1994.

Newsletters generally are redesigned every few years. The redesign may be subtle or extreme. But it happens. Why? Because the new art director or publisher wants to put his or her own personal creative stamp on the publication? Well, that's partially true, but the real reason is more basic: Just like clothing styles, design styles change over the years. For example, designs that were "in" ten years ago are considered passé today. If you don't revisit your look every once in a while, you look stale, and people think you're lazy or don't care about them.

Changing needs

The different versions of the newsletter use different fonts and embellishments, yet they all share a basic design:

- ✔ All are based on a three-column format, although the 1991 version uses a staggered three-column grid (notice how the pull-quotes and other elements hang out from the sides).
- ✔ All use the same basic elements on each page: pull-quotes, a short table of contents on the cover, a large masthead on page 2, kickers over the headlines, and bylines.

Figure 13-9:
The evolution of a newsletter's design: 1988-90 (top), 1991 (middle), and 1992-1994 (bottom). Notice that the basic elements are un-changed, but the way they are presented does change, as does the overall feel.

Yet the newsletters differ significantly in other areas:

- ✔ The 1988-90 design is the most basic: sans serif headlines and serif body copy. Both fonts (Helvetica Bold and New Century Schoolbook) are clean and easy to read. The use of condensed, underlined type for the kickers adds the only visual counterpoint to the open, solid look of the type, and even the kickers are clean-looking. The look is solid and respectable, because the organization was making an effort at the time to look clean and fresh.

- ✔ The 1991 design was a radical departure. The design is bolder, busier. The newsletter has a lot of contrast: bold headlines (Helvetica Black and Helvetica Black Condensed) with clean, light text (News Gothic). Both fonts are sans serif fonts — highly unusual because an unspoken rule says that you should never put headlines and text in the same type of font (serif or sans serif) and particularly that you should never use a sans serif font for both. Nonsense! Also, more symbols are used, and the layout is staggered. Things can line up to the three columns, or to the halfway points between columns (or past the first and last column). The look is animated and energetic, suggesting an organization on the move. It was more work to do this layout, and the layout relied on having sidebars and photos to break out (as on pages 2 and 3) from the body text. Unfortu- nately, the design was difficult to pull off every issue, so it was abandoned a year later. The layout was adventurous, but maybe too much for its subject.

- ✔ The 1992-1994 look is hyper-traditional — the "cardigan sweater and fireplace" look. The layout uses two serif fonts — Century Oldstyle for the heads and ITC Cheltenham Book for the body text. Cheltenham is very easy to read because the font is wide and contrasts nicely with the Century Oldstyle, which is bold and angular. Some symbols are used, but they're more subdued than in the previous design. The new design also incorporates drop caps, which add more contrast to the page, and grays, which mellow out the page. This design was meant to reinforce solid traditionalism (it was designed for the organization's 10th anniversary in 1993, although it came out a year earlier). But it's actually a mix of the two previous designs, borrowing the simple structure of the first with the high contrast of the second, the conservatism of the first with some of the flair of the second. The use of nonrectangular text wrap adds interest to the graphic — an extension of the flair in the second generation without the hard edge.

As you can see, the newsletter was designed with a set of goals in mind. The goals changed over time, even though the basic content did not. The opposite can also happen: The content may change over time, although the design and "image" goals do not. That scenario presents a trickier design problem, because you need to update the design to accommodate the new content (such as increased use of profiles, short stories, gossip and rumors, question-and-answer interviews, and so on), while reflecting the feel of the old. For examples, take a look at current issues of *The New York Times, Wall Street Journal, Business Week,*

Time, or *Newsweek*. Then compare their issues from five years ago. Different look and mix of content, but the same feel.

Newsletter basics

A newsletter's main goal is to provide information. So the focus should be on text: how to make it readable, how to call attention to it, how to make sure that the reader can locate all relevant content. Take a look at the newsletter in Figure 13-10. It's the same newsletter as in Figure 13-9 (and elsewhere in this book), but the pages chosen are typical interior pages. These pages show the basic components of the newsletter, around which you add embellishments, such as graphics.

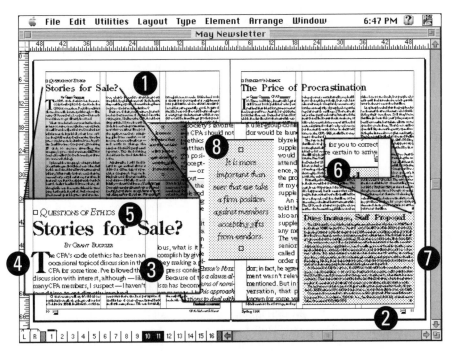

Figure 13-10: The basic elements in a newsletter.

1. Most newsletters are two or three columns wide. A three-column format gives you more flexibility because you can make graphics, sidebars, and separate stories three different sizes (one, two, and three columns wide), making it fairly easy to add such elements to a page. A two-column format is more straightforward but gives you fewer options. It's best for newsletters that are essentially sequential — without multiple stories and sidebars on a page or spread.

2. Make sure that you include page numbers and an identifier of the publication (called a *folio* in magazine-speak). Here, a corporate symbol is placed after the page number to add visual interest and reinforce the identity.

3. The body text uses a very readable, straightforward font: ITC Cheltenham Book. The text is a typical size for newsletters and magazines: 9 points with 11 points of leading. Generally speaking, point size should range from 9 to 10 points (you can use half-point sizes), and leading from 10.5 to 13 points, with the most typical leading being 2 points more than the text size. The text is justified here simply because that makes it look typeset and thus more authoritative. But a flush-left style is fine, too. The paragraph indents are fairly small (0.15 inches) because in justified text, a small indent is enough to give the reader's eye the visual clue it needs to see the new paragraph.

4. The use of a drop cap is an effective way to alert the reader to the beginning of a new story (you can also use a drop cap for the beginning of the story's conclusion). A drop cap also adds visual contrast to the page. Note in this example that the drop cap is a different font than the body text: Century Oldstyle Bold, which is the same font as the headline. Generally, you should boldface the drop cap because that makes the letter more readable — and otherwise, the drop cap looks wimpy, which is not how you want such a big element to look.

5. The headline, the kicker (the type above it, also called a *slug line* for reasons that have nothing to do with gardening), and the byline are all related. Both the kicker and the byline use small caps (a classy look when done in moderation) and italics. They're also in a different font (Goudy Oldstyle) than the headline (Century Oldstyle Bold) and the body text (ITC Cheltenham Book). That gives them continuity with each other while providing a subtle difference from the rest of the text. But be careful when combining multiple fonts like this: If the fonts don't work together, it can be a disaster. A rule of thumb is to restrict the number of fonts (not including variants like boldface and small caps) to two per page. You can break this rule occasionally by using a font that has similarities to one of the other two. In this case, Goudy Oldstyle has the feel of a cross between the other two fonts, so it works well.

6. Ending a story with a *dingbat* — publishing-speak for a symbol — is a nice touch. Here, the dingbat is the corporate logo, which adds another identity reinforcement. Making a dingbat is easy: just add the symbol after the last paragraph, either by putting a tab before it (and defining the tab in your text style to be flush right against the right margin) or an em space (⌘+Shift+M). Either way is fine for justified text — pick one based on your preferences. But use only the em space if your text is not justified.

7. You can make a sidebar or separate, minor story distinct by putting a shaded background behind it (draw a rectangle, change its fill pattern, and send the rectangle behind the text). Make sure that you have a margin between the edge of the background and the text. You can also box a sidebar, with or without the background. Or you can just put a line above and below the background, as done here. Notice, too, that the text is two columns wide, so it really looks different from the surrounding text.

8. A pull-quote attracts readers' attention by calling out some interesting material in a story. In this example, the style follows that of the sidebar: a

shaded background and lines above and below. A square character was placed above and below the quote (it's an embedded graphic in the text, so if the text grows or shrinks, the squares move with it). The characters are just an embellishment — something that adds that little extra touch. The font is the same as that in the byline and kicker (again, to create continuity with other elements on the page while distinguishing the pull-quote from the text immediately around it).

Annual Reports

An annual report is a weird combination of a magazine and a report. An annual report is where you showcase the company to its investors or stockholders, and you want to impress them with your financial performance — or hide the dismal truth, if your earnings were less than stellar. You want to look good in an annual report; it's like having dinner with the boss the week before your annual review. You also have to include a lot of information.

Figure 13-11 shows an example of an interior spread for a bicycle manufacturer's annual report, which manages to combine information and an inviting graphical look. Whatever image you want to convey — hip, traditional, solid, adventurous, irreverent, slick — make sure that your design and graphics reinforce the point throughout.

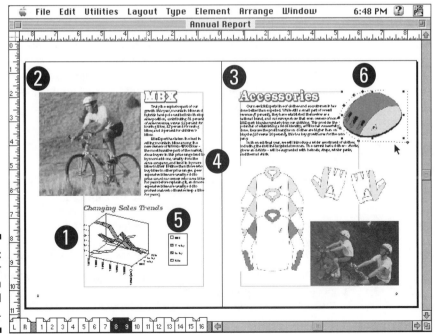

Figure 13-11: Interior pages from an annual report.

1. The margins are a bit lopsided, with plenty of room on the outside to let graphics hang off from the text. Because this annual report is for a sports company, an active, dynamic look makes sense. One way to develop that look is to create a lot of visual motion, which is what you get when elements break outside the basic margins. Note that the text always stays in the margins, but the graphics do only if they show financial information (as on the left page). This design reinforces that the basic content is within the margins, although the illustrations can be anywhere. By ensuring that information is treated consistently, the rushed reader who just wants the facts knows where to look — and where not to look.

2. Color photos are a great way to enhance an annual report, especially if the photos show something active. A picture of the assembly plant workers probably is boring, but a picture of, say, a group of workers from the same shift racing in a velodrome adds excitement and action while at the same time reinforcing the image that the workers trust the products they build. Look for pictures that convey a basic message — "fun," "trust," "hip attitude," "young," "distinguished," "creative" — and you'll make a real impression on your readers.

3. The headlines are in shadow and a color. This treatment makes the headlines hard to miss and visually distinct.

4. The text is basic, with only left alignment so that there is no hard-and-fast boundary. Because this annual report is supposed to be active and fluid, using justified text looks too precise.

5. The financial chart, first produced in Excel, uses a headline entered in PageMaker to match the font of the main headlines. The 3-D chart follows the theme of dynamism and motion.

6. Text wrapping around the helmet introduces more movement in the page and connects the graphic to the text more closely. Because this page has so many graphics, something was needed to connect at least one of the graphics to the text so that the page didn't have a choppy, disjointed look.

Cool Stuff

By combining various techniques, you can create some cool-looking stuff for a variety of documents. Figure 13-12 shows some examples:

- ✔ You can create various embossed-text effects by duplicating a text box and making one text box slightly overlap the other. Then make the text box on top white (or the paper color). Chapter 8 shows you how to create similar effects.

- ✔ By duplicating a text box several times, rotating each copy at a different angle, and then applying different shades of gray to each, you can create a textual graphic. In Figure 13-12, each subsequent copy of the word *Curves!* is rotated 10 degrees more and is 10 percent darker than the preceding copy. Chapter 10 offers some how-to's on rotating and applying shading to graphics.

Figure 13-12:
Combining techniques can produce interesting text and graphics effects.

✔ Each letter in the word *STRETCH!* is 10 percent wider than the previous letter, which gives the text the effect of being stretched. Chapter 6 provides information on how to expand and condense text.

✔ Increasing the space between letters is a popular design effect. You can put spaces (regular spaces, en spaces, or em spaces) between the letters, but using the tracking control ensures that the text is treated as one word. This method also makes changing your spacing settings easier (it's easier to adjust the tracking than to, say, replace em spaces with en spaces between every character). Tracking is covered in Chapter 6.

✔ By combining the skew feature with the shadow feature for text (as in the Action News example), you can alter how a font looks. You might want such an effect when creating a logo, for example. In this logo, the designer went a step further and mirrored the text block and changed its color to a shade of gray (by defining a tint of 40 percent black). For help in creating this sort of effect, see Chapters 6 and 10.

✔ For grayscale images, you can apply a color or tint to make the images ghostly or subtle. A grayscale image is a great way to mute a photo enough so that you can place text over it. See Chapter 11 for information on applying colors and tints.

✔ You can create a cameo effect, such as the one at the bottom center of Figure 13-2 by using the new Mask command. To create an effect like the one shown, use the Ellipse tool to draw an oval that has no fill and just a thin line. The oval should be smaller than the image you want to frame. Place the oval over the image, select both the oval and the image, and choose Element⇨Mask (⌘+6). Your image now is framed by the oval. You can also use the Rectangle and Polygon tools to create masks. (If you don't want a line around your frame, choose Element⇨Line⇨None immediately after you choose the Mask command. You need the line initially so that you can see where you're placing the mask on the image.)

✔ In some publications, the text on the opening page has a radically different style from the rest of the pages. Often, the opening page contains little text because the title and graphics usually take up much of the space. The text that is on the opening page is also treated graphically. One method is to have no paragraph breaks but to use a symbol instead to indicate paragraph breaks, as in the top right example in Figure 13-12.

✔ Although drop caps are popular, you can also use an embedded graphic to accomplish the same purpose. If you want the graphic to be dropped down into the text, you can place the graphic at the appropriate location and turn text wrap on. Chapters 9 and 10 discuss text wrap and embedded graphics, respectively.

✔ The bottom right example in Figure 13-12 was created by making a copy of the original dolphin image, flipping the image horizontally, copying the two resulting images, and flipping them vertically. For information on copying and flipping images, see Chapter 10.

Common Threads

Creative design means taking risks, trying out new ideas. Because it's easy to use PageMaker to try out new ideas — and to abandon those ideas that don't work — set aside some time in every project to play around with your design. Save a copy of your original and then see if you can discover some new approach that adds that special edge. While you're doing that, keep some basic principles in mind:

✔ **Use enough white space.** People need a visual resting place as they thumb through a publication. Give it to them. If you don't, they'll stop reading.

✔ **Remember that the basic point of publishing is to convey information.** Make sure that text is readable, that captions and headlines are informative and interesting, and that page numbers, headings, and other guideposts are easy to find and easy to read.

✔ **Invest in several fonts and use them creatively by applying effects such as small caps, colors, banner backgrounds, rotation, and skewing.**

✔ **Use clean, easy-to-read, conservative fonts in business documents.** Think of these fonts as the typographic equivalent of suits and ties.

✔ **Limit the number of fonts you use within a document.** Use variations of your core fonts, such as boldface and italics, to provide further visual and editorial contrast.

✔ **Graphics should be fairly large — lots of small images are hard to look at — and should complement the rest of the layout.**

✔ **Create visual themes.** Use a core set of fonts. If you use lines in one place, they may be effective in another. If you use boxes to separate some elements, don't use colored backgrounds to separate others — instead, pick one approach and stick with it.

✔ **Use color judiciously.** Using color is expensive and can overwhelm the content. Used well, grays can provide as much visual interest as color. In fact, in something laden with color, a gray image stands out and gains more attention than the surrounding color ones.

Chapter 14
Doing Less Work Next Time

. . . .

In This Chapter

▶ Creating master pages to automate layout

▶ Using the new multiple master pages feature

▶ Making a document template

▶ Using PageMaker's prefab templates

▶ Storing frequently used items in libraries

. . . .

*O*ne of the biggest benefits of using a program such as PageMaker is that it can automate many of your layout tasks. In earlier chapters, you discover how to use some of PageMaker's basic layout features, such as text wrap, cropping, and guides and rulers, to make your life easier. But to take full advantage of PageMaker's time- and energy-saving benefits, you need to become acquainted with the three features discussed in this chapter: master pages, templates, and libraries.

If you're unfamiliar with desktop publishing, these three concepts probably seem pretty foreign to you at first — and not nearly so exciting as such topics as, say, text wrap and special effects. But if you spend just a little time discovering these features, you'll be amazed at how many of your routine layout chores you can hoist off onto PageMaker.

Using Master Pages

You may have noticed that the far bottom-left corner of the PageMaker window has two little page icons labeled L and R (or just one icon labeled R if the document doesn't use facing pages). Those icons represent master pages.

Master pages are sort of like the basic building blocks for your pages. By placing an element on a master page, you can have PageMaker automatically place that same element on any pages you specify. For example, if you want to put a company logo at the bottom of every page in an eight-page brochure, you can place it once on a master page and tell PageMaker to automatically add that logo to all pages. You can use master pages not only to automate the placement of repeating elements, such as logos and page numbers, but also to establish column and margin settings for your pages.

In addition to saving you the time and effort of placing repeating elements over and over again throughout your document, master pages help ensure consistency. You don't have to worry about whether you're placing that logo in precisely the same spot on every page, for example — PageMaker handles that for you.

In earlier versions of PageMaker, you had access to only one pair of master pages — one master page for all left-hand pages, and one for all right-hand pages. But in Version 6, you can set up as many master pages as you want. If you're creating a long document (like this book, for example), you might create one master page to hold all the settings and repeating elements used on the first page of every chapter. You might create two more master pages for the left- and right-hand pages within chapters and create yet another set of master pages for index pages.

Creating your Document Master pages

PageMaker 6 has two basic types of master pages: Document Master pages and regular master pages. Confused yet? Hang with us, it's not as bad as it seems.

You see, every PageMaker document you create has two default Document Master pages (or just one if you're not using facing pages in your layout). Anything you place on these pages appears in all pages of your document unless you specify otherwise (which you find out how to do a little later). In addition to these Document Master pages, you can create other master pages. But these other master pages don't have any effect until you apply them to selected pages.

For the sake of convenience, we refer to the default master pages as Document Master pages. If we refer to the other type of master pages — or if we refer to both kinds of master pages — we just use the plain, lowercased term, *master pages*. Yeesh!

To set up a Document Master page, just click on either the L or R page icon, depending on whether you want to work on the left- or right-hand Document Master. Then establish columns, guides, margins, and other page settings as you normally would and place any elements that you want to appear throughout your document. To leave the Document Master page and return to your layout, just click on one of the standard page icons next to the master page icons.

After you create additional master pages for your publication, you must first select the Document Master item from the master pages pop-up menu (as explained in the section "Editing a master page") before clicking on the L or R page icon. Otherwise, you open the master page that's applied to the current document page — which may or may not be the Document Master.

Any settings you establish or elements you place on your L Document Master page appear on all left-hand pages in your document by default. Similarly, all the stuff you put on the R Document Master page appears on all the right-hand pages. If you're not using facing pages, anything you put on the R Document Master page appears on all pages in your document. However, if you apply a different master page to a page in your layout, that master overrides the Document Master page. You can also override Document Master column and guide settings by choosing new settings from the Layout menu.

Creating additional master pages

You can create additional master pages in three ways: You can create them from scratch, base them on an existing master page, or base them on an existing page on your document. In all three cases, you use the Master Pages palette, shown in Figure 14-1. To display the palette, choose Window⇨Master Pages or press ⌘+H.

Figure 14-1:
The new Master Pages palette enables you to create as many master pages as you want.

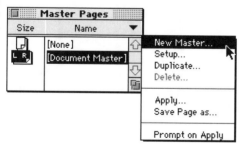

To create a master page from scratch

1. Press and hold on the triangle in the top-right corner of the palette.

Up pops the Master Pages palette menu, shown in Figure 14-1.

2. Choose New Master.

As an alternative to using the pop-up menu, you can ⌘+click on the None item in the palette.

Either way, the dialog box shown in Figure 14-2 appears. Enter a name for your master page(s) in the Name option box. If you want to create a two-page master spread, select the Two Page radio button. If you want to create just a single master page, click the One Page radio button. Then specify margin and column guide settings for your new master page or pages.

Create New Master Page

Name: | Index

○ One page
◉ Two page

Margins

Inside: | 1 | inches   Outside: | 0.75 | inches

Top: | 0.75 | inches   Bottom: | 0.75 | inches

Column Guides

Columns: | 1 | | 1 |

Space between: | 0.167 | inches | 0.167 | inches

[Cancel]   [Create]

Figure 14-2: The Create New Master Page dialog box.

3. Click on OK.

Your new master page (or two-page spread) appears in the window, and its name appears on the Master Pages palette. You can now add whatever elements or layout guides you want to your new master page(s). To return to a regular document page, just click on its page icon at the bottom of the document window.

If you want a new master page to use the same column settings, margins, or other elements that you've already established on another master page, you can save time by simply duplicating the first master page and then modifying it as necessary. To do so, choose Duplicate from the Master Pages palette menu to display the Duplicate Master Page dialog box. Choose the name of the master you want to copy from the Duplicate pop-up menu, enter a name for the new master page in the Name of New Master option box, and click on the Duplicate button. Your new master page appears in the publication window, and you can then add elements to it or remove existing elements from it.

Similarly, you can use an existing page in your layout as the basis for a new master page. Just click on the page icon for the existing page, choose Save Page As from the Master Pages palette menu, give the new master page a name, and then click on the Save button.

Applying and removing master pages

PageMaker automatically applies your Document Master pages to all the pages in your document. If you want to use one of your other master pages on a particular page, you have to apply it to the page. Any Document Master page settings or elements are then overridden for that particular page. But any other existing text or objects on the page stay put (you may need to adjust text flow or graphic positioning to account for changes in margin or column settings, though).

- ✔ To apply a master page to the page you're currently working on, just click on the master page's name in the Master Pages palette.

- ✔ If you want to determine which master page is applied to a particular page or two-page spread, just turn to the page or spread and look at the Master Pages palette. The name of the master page that's in force is highlighted in the palette.

- ✔ To apply a master page to several pages at once, choose Apply from the Master Pages palette pop-up menu to display the Apply Master dialog box, shown in Figure 14-3. Select the Set Left and Right Pages Separately check box if you want to apply one master page to the selected left-hand pages and another master page to the right-hand pages. The dialog box then displays two pop-up menus, one for selecting the left-hand master page and another for selecting the right-hand master page.

Figure 14-3:
You can choose which master page you want to apply to specific pages in this dialog box.

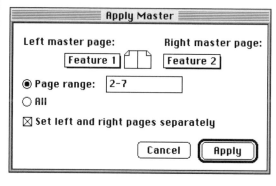

Choose the name of the master page you want to apply from the Master Pages pop-up menu(s). Select the Page Range radio button and enter the page numbers or range of pages that you want to affect in the option box. (Choose the All radio button to apply the master page to all pages in your layout.) Click on the Apply button to close the dialog box and apply the master page.

✔ To remove master page elements from a page, just apply the None master to the page, either by clicking on None in the Master Pages palette or choosing None from the pop-up menu in the Apply Master dialog box. The column and ruler guides from the master page remain. To remove elements and all guides, press Shift as you choose None in the Master Pages palette.

✔ You can prevent master page elements from displaying by turning to that page and checking Layout⇨Display Master Items. Choose the command again to redisplay the master page items. Again, the column and ruler guides from the master page remain displayed. (You can always hide them by pressing Ctrl+J.)

✔ You can override master page column and margin settings on a particular page by simply choosing new settings from the Layout menu or Document Setup dialog box (File⇨Document Setup).

✔ To delete a master page altogether, click on the master page name in the palette, choose Delete from the pop-up menu, and then click on the Delete button in the dialog box that appears. PageMaker applies the None master to all pages that had used the deleted master page. As before, column and margin guides remain, but you can override these guides by establishing new column and margin settings.

Anything on a master page appears under anything created on a standard page. So if you place a colored rectangle on a master page, for example, any text placed on a standard page in the same location appears on top of that rectangle (assuming that text wrap is turned off for the rectangle). But you can change the stacking order of the master page and standard page elements if you want; just use the Arrange⇨Send to Back and Bring to Front commands, discussed in Chapter 10.

Editing a master page

If you want to change the margins or column setup on a master page, select the master page's name from the Master Pages palette and choose the Setup command from the palette menu. Or just ⌘+click on the master page name in the palette. PageMaker displays the Master Page Setup dialog box, which offers the same margin and column guide settings as the Create New Master Page dialog box, shown back in Figure 14-2. You can also change the name of the master page in this dialog box if you want. The only thing you *can't* do in this dialog box is turn a single-page master page into a facing-pages master page or vice versa.

If you want to add or remove elements from a master page, you have to make the master page active in the publication window. You can do this in three ways:

✔ To display the master page applied to the current page of your document, click on the master page icon at the bottom of the window. If you're currently working on a spread and you have different master pages applied to the left- and right-hand pages, PageMaker displays the right-hand page master.

✔ Press and hold the mouse button on a master page icon to display a menu of master page names, shown in Figure 14-4, and choose a master page from the menu.

✔ Choose Layout⇨Go to Page (⌘+left bracket ([)) and select the master page from the pop-up menu in the Go to Page dialog box.

Figure 14-4:
Press and
hold on a
master page
icon to
display a
pop-up
menu that
lists all your
master
pages.

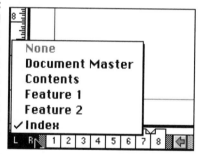

Building a Template

Although master pages go a long way toward automating the layout process, you can go even one step further by creating templates for those documents you produce on a regular basis — say, for example, a monthly newsletter. A template enables you to save all the master pages, styles, and other elements that you'll need each month as you lay out your newsletter. Then you just modify the template as needed for each issue.

What should a template contain? Following are some ideas:

- ✔ The correct number of pages for the document
- ✔ Automatic page number codes (⌘+Option+P), discussed in Chapter 8
- ✔ Styles (body text, caption, headline, and so on), as discussed in Chapter 7
- ✔ Master pages containing repeating elements and margin and column settings
- ✔ A table of contents (for magazines, reports, newsletters, and books) with dummy text
- ✔ A masthead — a list of the staff and contact information (for magazines and some newsletters)
- ✔ Postal information and mailing label text (newsletters)
- ✔ Subscription and change-of-address forms (magazines, newsletters, and some reports)
- ✔ Standing text — stories, such as *List of Benefits,* that appear in almost every issue (magazines, newsletters, some ads, and some reports)
- ✔ *Continued-on* and *continued-from* lines with dummy page numbers
- ✔ Highly formatted sidebars or tables — using dummy text, of course (magazines, newsletters, and some reports)

You can build a template in two ways: You can construct a template from scratch, or you can convert an existing layout into a template. For example, after you've laid out the first issue of your monthly newsletter, you can save the document as a template.

Building a template from scratch is the easy way, but you need to know in advance what the template should contain — which means that you have to know the requirements and look of the layouts based on the template. Converting an existing layout into a template is harder because you have to remove any elements that won't be used in all or most of your future newsletters. But this method can also be the best way to create a template because it lets you figure out what the layout should look like using a real example before finalizing the template.

Whichever method you choose, you lay out a template document the same way you lay out a regular document. To turn the document into a template, choose File⇨Save As to display the Save Publication As dialog box. Select the Template radio button and give your template a name that you'll be able to distinguish easily. Click on OK, and PageMaker saves your document as a template.

Creating a layout from a template

To start a new document based on a custom template that you've created, choose File⇨Open and choose the template from the list. PageMaker opens a copy of the template. You can then add new elements to or delete existing elements from the copy.

To start a new document based on one of PageMaker's prefab templates, choose Utilities⇨PageMaker Plug-Ins⇨Open Template. The Open Template dialog box appears, as shown in Figure 14-5. After you choose a template from the list, click on OK. PageMaker opens a copy of the template. You can then add new elements to the copy or delete existing elements, if necessary.

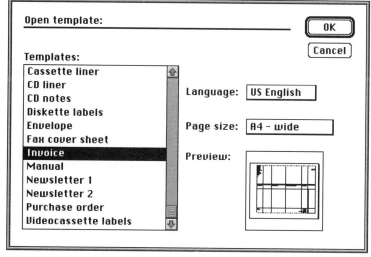

Figure 14-5:
The Open
Template
dialog box
gives you
access to
several
prefab
templates
that
PageMaker
provides.

Open template:

OK

Cancel

Templates:

Cassette liner
CD liner
CD notes
Diskette labels
Envelope
Fax cover sheet
Invoice
Manual
Newsletter 1
Newsletter 2
Purchase order
Videocassette labels

Language: US English

Page size: A4 – wide

Preview:

PageMaker's prebuilt templates contain mocked-up text and graphics as placeholders for your real text and graphics. You can delete or replace them as you would any graphic or text block. For example, to replace a graphic placeholder with your own graphic, select the placeholder and then choose Replacing Entire Graphic in the Place dialog box when you import your graphic. To replace a placeholder story, choose Replacing Entire Story.

When you're finished laying out your publication, save it as a regular publication document by choosing File⇨Save, entering a document name in the Save Publication As dialog box, and choosing the Publication radio button.

Editing a template

Over time, you'll probably need to update your custom templates to incorporate new design elements or other changes. To edit a custom template, choose File⇨Open and select the template. Select the Original radio button if you want to edit your original template. If you want to keep that template intact and work on a copy of the template instead, select the Copy radio button. When you finish updating your template, choose File⇨Save As, give the template a new name if you want, select the Template radio button, and click on OK.

You won't find PageMaker's prebuilt templates through the File⇨Open dialog box; the templates are supplied in a special format that you shouldn't try to edit. Instead, start a new document based on the template you want to edit, make the necessary changes, and then save the document as a template by choosing the Template radio button in the Save Publication As dialog box. From then on, you can edit the template as described in the preceding paragraph.

Getting Your Library Card

If you produce a lot of documents for the same client or company, you'll find that you use certain elements, such as logos, in almost every piece you create. You can keep these elements on the pasteboard — the portion of the PageMaker screen outside the page boundaries — but the pasteboard can get real cluttered real fast, and it doesn't let someone else easily access those elements for another layout, either. A better answer is to put these elements in a library.

A library is simply a holding tank for frequently used items. You can access the elements in a library — and put new elements into a library — by using the Library palette. You just drag stuff into and out of the palette, as explained a little later, in the section "Using library elements." Libraries are quick, convenient, and they keep your desktop all neat and tidy-like.

You can create as many libraries as you need. You can keep all your newsletter logos, continued lines, pull-quotes, and so on in one library, and keep elements that you use in quarterly reports in another library.

Creating libraries

To create your first library, choose WindowÍLibrary. The Open Library dialog box appears, as shown in Figure 14-6. Click on the New Library button to display the Create New Library dialog box. Type in a name for your library and choose the folder you want to store the library in. Then click on OK. PageMaker displays the Library palette, shown in Figure 14-7, which contains your new library.

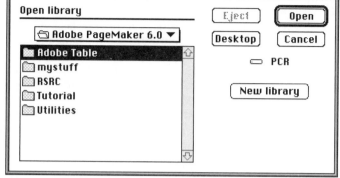

Figure 14-6:
You can create or open a library in this dialog box.

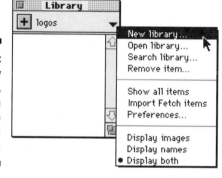

Figure 14-7:
The Library palette, shown with its pop-up menu unfurled.

✔ To create another new library, press and hold on the triangle in the upper-right corner of the Library palette. PageMaker displays the pop-up menu shown in Figure 14-7. Choose New Library to open the Create New Library dialog box and set up your library.

✔ To open an existing library, choose Open Library from the palette menu to get the Open Library dialog box. Choose the library you want from the scrolling list. You can have only one library open at a time.

✔ After you've created one or more libraries, PageMaker displays the Library palette when you choose Window⇨Library. The last library you had open is active.

Adding and deleting library elements

To add an object or text element to a library, select it with the Arrow tool and then click on the plus sign next to the library name. To add several items at once, click on the first object, Shift+click on the rest, and then click on the plus sign.

✔ Note that if you copy a text block into a library, the text block retains its text formatting but not its style names. Thus, when you place the text in another layout, formatting is correct but the text has the No Style style. So if you want to alter the text's appearance by changing the attributes of its style definition, you have to first select the text, choose Type⇨Define Styles (⌘+3) to define a new style based on that selected text, and apply that style to all text copied from the library. You can then alter the text's appearance by editing the style definition. You can use the same approach if you want to make other text in your layout match the library text's formatting; just create a style based on the library text and then apply it to the rest of the text.

✔ When you put an element into a library, PageMaker names the element *Untitled*. Because libraries are searchable — that is, you can enter the name of a library element and instruct PageMaker to hunt down that element for you — it's a good idea to give the element a name you can search, especially if you'll be creating fairly large libraries.

To name an element, double-click on it in the Library palette. PageMaker displays the Item Information dialog box, shown in Figure 14-8. You can add keywords and a description into the dialog box to make it easier to find the element in the future.

If you always want to fill in keyword and title information when you add an element to a library, choose Preferences from the Library palette pop-up menu and check the Edit Items After Adding checkbox.

✔ To delete an item from a library, select the item in the Library palette and choose Remove Item from the Library palette pop-up menu. Click on OK to confirm your decision to toss the item into the abyss.

✔ Note that you cannot use the Delete key, ⌘+X, or File⇨Cut to delete a library element. In fact, trying to do so deletes whatever is selected in your layout, not the element selected in the library. So be careful!

Figure 14-8: The Item Information dialog box lets you enter information that will help you track down library items in the future.

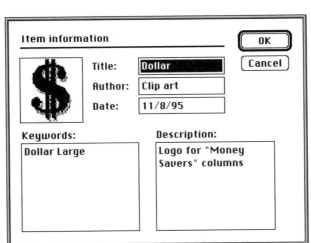

If you use Adobe Fetch, an image-cataloging program, you can copy its elements into a PageMaker library. In Fetch, select the items you want to put in the library and then choose Edit⇨Copy References⇨Include Thumbnails. Switch to PageMaker (or launch it, if it's not already running), and open the desired library. Choose Import Fetch Items from the Library palette pop-up menu to copy the elements into the library.

Finding library elements

As noted earlier, you can just scroll through the palette to find a particular element. But if the library has many elements, you'll find it easier to search for an element by its keyword, author, or name (title). To do so, choose Search Library from the Library palette pop-up menu. The Search Library dialog box, shown in Figure 14-9, appears.

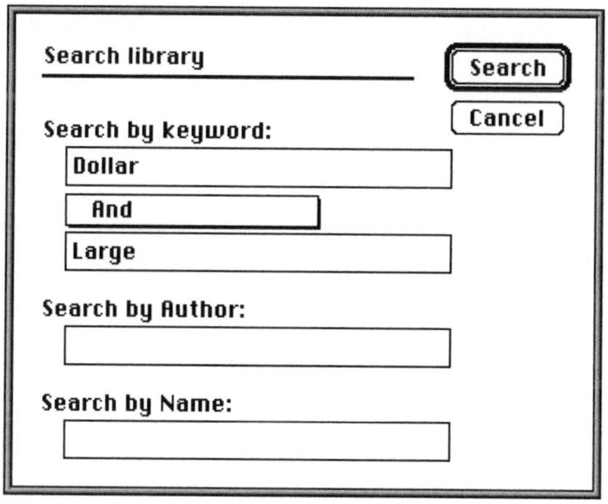

Figure 14-9:
You can search for items in your library according to keywords, authors, or titles.

> **Search library**
>
> Search | Cancel
>
> **Search by keyword:**
> Dollar
> And
> Large
>
> **Search by Author:**
>
> **Search by Name:**

✔ To search by a keyword, just enter it into the Search by Keyword option box (well, *duh*). If you want to search by two or more keywords, separate them with spaces.

✔ The search option is smart enough that exact matches are not required. For example, if the author's name is *Alexander* and you enter *Alex* as the name to search, PageMaker finds any author whose name includes the characters *a, l, e,* and *x,* in that order.

✔ Notice the pop-up menu in the Search By Keyword section. The default setting is One Keyword Only. If you choose this option, PageMaker searches for the single word (or words) in the top option box. The other options are And, Or, and But Not. If you choose And, the element must use both keywords in order for PageMaker to find it. If you choose Or, the element must use at least one of the two keywords. If you choose But Not, the element must use the first keyword but not the second keyword.

When the search is finished, PageMaker displays only those items that met the search criteria in the palette. (If it didn't find any elements that match your search request, PageMaker notifies you with a polite dialog box. Click on OK and go back to the drawing board.) To redisplay all the items in the Library palette, choose Show All Items from the palette pop-up menu.

Using library elements

This is the easiest part: To use a library element, just click on the element with the Arrow tool (the square border gets thicker) and drag the tool from the palette to anywhere in your PageMaker document. PageMaker places the element wherever you release the mouse button. Note also that PageMaker places the element at its original size, not the preview size shown in the palette. After you place the element, you can modify it just like any other element.

When you drag an element from the library into a document, the preview stays in the library — you're copying the element from the library, not actually removing it from the library.

Setting library displays

After the Library palette is displayed, you can drag its size box to make the palette wider or deeper, which lets you see more of its contents. Use the scroll bar to move through the library.

By default, the Library palette shows both a preview image and a name for each element in the open library. But you can change this display by clicking on the palette pop-up menu and selecting from the Display Images, Display Names, Display Both options. The default option — Display Both — is probably the best because you have two ways of identifying library elements. Viewing the contents according to their names, particularly when you're scrolling through a large list, can be easier.

The usefulness of Display Images is less compelling: Why not just display the name along with the image? After all, doing so takes up basically no more space in the palette. Who knows what lurks in the minds of programmers?

By default, PageMaker displays library elements in color in the palette. To display grayscale images instead, choose Preferences from the Library palette pop-up menu and then uncheck the Make Color Thumbnails box.

Setting up libraries, master pages, and templates requires some up-front time and energy. Creating a template, for example, that's exactly right takes a while. But the payoff down the road makes creating a template more than worthwhile. You not only save yourself lots of time in the long run, you end up with publications that are more consistent and professional-looking — in short, you get a heck of a lot more from your PageMaker investment.

Chapter 15

So, You Want to Be a Book Publisher?

In This Chapter

▶ Combining a series of documents into a book

▶ Adding page numbering to a booked publication

▶ Creating a table of contents and index automatically

▶ Editing and formatting an index

Way back in Chapter 1, we mention that PageMaker is particularly adept at creating long documents, such as manuals. (This very book, by the way, was laid out in PageMaker.) One of the features that makes PageMaker so great at handling long documents is its ability to automatically number your pages and create an index or table of contents for your document. Another powerful tool is the Book command, which lets you combine a series of separate documents into a single entity — known in PageMaker-speak as a *book*. After creating a book, you can generate an index and a table of contents that encompass the entire series of documents.

We know what you're thinking: "Wow, that sounds about as exciting as watching paint dry." Well, it's true that you're not likely to impress your teenagers by giving them a demonstration of features such as automatic indexing and page numbering. In fact, if you did try to show them how this stuff worked, they'd no doubt elbow each other, roll their eyes, and mutter, "What a *geek*" (or whatever term it is that teenagers use these days).

But if you've ever had to manually create an index, renumber all the chapters in a manual one by one, or compile a table of contents for a document whose contents seem to change daily, you can appreciate the nirvana of having these features around. You may not use these features every day, but when you do need them, you'll be mighty glad they're included in PageMaker's little bag of tricks.

Making Book

No, no, we're not going to tell you how to bet on a football game, or a heavy-weight fight, or anything else that may be considered illegal or immoral in your neck of the woods. (But if you already have your bookie on the line, will you put down $20 on Fool's Gold in the third race at Belmont? Honest, we're good for the loan.)

In PageMaker, bookmaking has an entirely different meaning. By using the Book feature, you can tell PageMaker to treat a series of documents as a single document. This feature has several advantages:

- ✔ You can send a whole batch of documents to the printer by issuing the Print command just once. Chapter 17 covers printing booked documents.

- ✔ You can apply automatic page numbering across several documents. For example, if you are creating a manual with 20 chapters, you can keep each chapter in a separate PageMaker document but have PageMaker number the pages as if all 20 chapters were all in the same document.

- ✔ Similarly, you can generate an index or table of contents across a series of documents.

- ✔ You can keep the size of your documents small, making them easier to work with. Imagine trying to lay out a two- or three-hundred page manual in one document! The Book command enables you to keep each chapter or section in its own document. This feature is also handy when different editors or designers need to review or edit different parts of the book at the same time.

When you create a book, you're not actually combining the files or anything — in fact, a document can be part of more than one book. You're simply giving PageMaker a list of the documents that you want to have numbered, indexed, included in a table of contents, or printed as a batch.

Also, PageMaker doesn't create any book files on your hard disk. Instead, it saves the book list information in the document that you're working on when you choose the Book command. (You don't actually see a list appear in your document; PageMaker just stores the list data in the file so that it can access it if needed later.) PageMaker also offers a feature that lets you copy the book list to other documents in the list if needed, as explained later in this chapter.

Creating a book list

Enough theory — let's get into the reality. To give PageMaker the list of documents you want to put in a book, choose Utilities⬧Book. The Book Publication List dialog box, shown in Figure 15-1, appears. On the left is a folder pop-up menu and scrolling list of folders and documents, from which you select documents to add to the book list. The buttons in the middle let you manage the book list. Buttons are grayed out if they don't apply (for example, you can't click on Insert if no document is selected to be inserted).

Figure 15-1:
The Book command allows you to create collections of documents to facilitate printing, page numbering, and indexing.

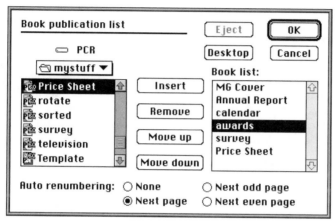

- ✔ To add a file to the book list, just double-click on it. Or select the file and then click on the Insert button. PageMaker puts the file into the Book List window, placing the file just below the currently selected document in the book list.

- ✔ Clicking on the Remove button deletes the document selected in the book list. Doing so does *not* delete the file from your hard disk.

- ✔ Clicking on the Move Up button moves the document selected in the book list up one position. Clicking on the Move Down button moves the document selected in the book list down one position. You use these buttons to reorder elements in the book list.

The order of elements is important because PageMaker paginates and prints the files according to the order they appear in the book list.

Numbering the pages in a book

That takes care of getting documents in the book list. Now for the page numbering. You use the four options at the bottom of the Book Publication List dialog box, shown in Figure 15-1, to tell PageMaker how to number the pages across booked documents.

✔ **None:** This option turns off the book page-numbering feature. Your documents use whatever page numbers you establish in the Document Setup dialog box (File⇨Document Setup), described in Chapter 3. This option is handy for documents such as manuals, where each chapter tends to have its own prefix and the page numbering restarts in each chapter. For example, Chapter 1's page numbers may be A-1 through A-49, Chapter 2's may be B-1 through B-193, and so on.

✔ **Next Page:** If you choose this option, the page numbers go consecutively from number 1, or from whatever page number you defined as the starting page number in the Document Setup dialog box for that document. For example, say that Chapter 1 is 24 pages long, Chapter 2 is 67 pages long, Chapter 3 is 41 pages long, and Chapter 4 (a supplement) is 34 pages long. In the Document Setup dialog box for Chapter 4, the Restart Page Numbering box is checked, and the Start Page # value is set at 1. With this option, Chapter 2's numbering begins at 25, Chapter 3's numbering begins at 92, and Chapter 4's numbering begins at 1.

✔ **Next Odd Page:** Each chapter (document) is forced to start on a right-hand page (and a blank left page is added at the end of the previous chapter if needed to ensure this). Using the same example as above, then, Chapter 3's numbering begins at 93 — a blank page is inserted at the end of Chapter 2 so that Chapter 3 begins on a right-hand (odd-numbered) page.

✔ **Next Even Page:** This option works like Next Odd Page except that each chapter is forced to start on a left page. In the example, then, Chapter 2's page numbering begins at 26 — a blank page is inserted before it so that the chapter starts on a left page.

If you didn't insert page number markers in your chapters, PageMaker still renumbers your pages. (The page numbers in the page icons at the bottom of the PageMaker screen reflect the new page numbering.) But when you print, you won't see page numbers. The book feature does not add page markers — it just renumbers them.

Chapter 8 covers how to insert page numbers, but here's a quick recap: Just press ⌘+Option+P in a text block where you want the page numbers to appear.

Updating page numbers

When you click on OK to leave the Book Publication List dialog box, PageMaker displays a simple dialog box asking whether you want it to do the renumbering (unless you chose the None numbering option). Select Yes if you want the renumbering to proceed. If you select No, PageMaker waits to do the renumbering until you print all documents in a book list or create an index or table of contents for the book.

If you change the number of pages in a document, PageMaker doesn't update the other documents in the book list automatically. And PageMaker doesn't offer a command to renumber the documents in the book list. To renumber the documents, you must either re-create the book list (by removing the current list's documents and inserting them back) or use a feature such as book printing, book indexing, or generating a table of contents to force PageMaker to renumber the documents. Otherwise, you have misnumbered pages — either gaps between chapters if you deleted pages in one document or duplicate page numbers if you added pages.

Copying the book list to all documents

If you press and hold the ⌘ key while choosing Utilities⇨Book, PageMaker copies the book list to all documents in the list. After you choose the command, you see a status box indicating that the copying is in progress.

The advantage of having the book list in every document is that you can then generate an index or table of contents that includes all documents in the list from within any of the book documents. You can also repaginate or print all the documents from inside any document in the list.

Creating Tables of Contents

One way to create a table of contents in PageMaker is to print your document, write down the titles and headings and their page numbers, and then create a new document in PageMaker in which you enter this information. But unless you're trying to kill some time, you don't need to go to all the trouble. PageMaker can do the job for you automatically, with very little effort on your part.

Telling PageMaker what to include

When you define styles (as explained in Chapter 7), PageMaker gives you an option called Include in Table of Contents. You find this option at the bottom of the Paragraph Specifications dialog box, as spotlighted in Figure 15-2. If you check this option for a style, any text marked with that style appears in your table of contents. For example, if you turn on the option for your Headline style, all headline text is included in the table of contents.

Typically, you enable this option for headlines and subheads. Don't turn on the option for styles that you apply to long blocks of text, such as your body text style or caption text style. If your headlines are really long, you can always edit them after the table of contents is generated — it's not like you're carving the table of contents in stone.

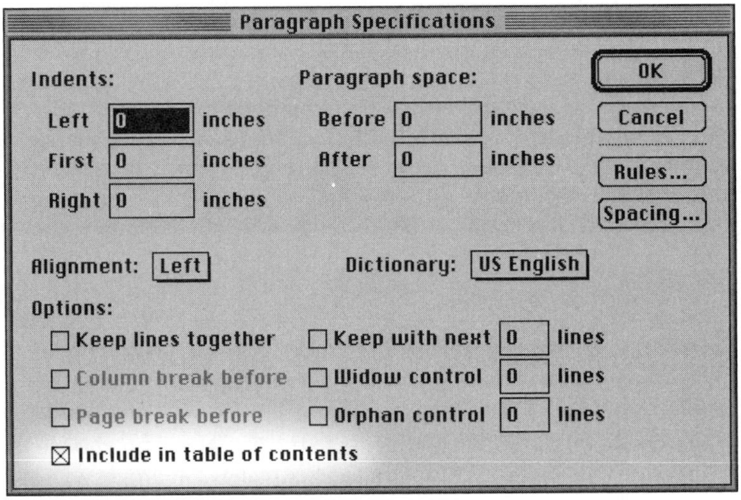

Figure 15-2:
You can tell
PageMaker
which
paragraph
styles to
include as
table-of-
contents
entries.

```
┌──────────────── Paragraph Specifications ────────────────┐
│                                                  ┌─────────┐│
│  Indents:            Paragraph space:            │   OK    ││
│                                                  └─────────┘│
│    Left  [0    ] inches   Before [0  ] inches   ┌─────────┐│
│                                                  │ Cancel  ││
│    First [0    ] inches   After  [0  ] inches   └─────────┘│
│                                                  ┌─────────┐│
│    Right [0    ] inches                          │ Rules...││
│                                                  └─────────┘│
│                                                  ┌─────────┐│
│  Alignment: [Left]       Dictionary: [US English]│Spacing..││
│                                                  └─────────┘│
│  Options:                                                  │
│    ☐ Keep lines together    ☐ Keep with next [0] lines    │
│    ☐ Column break before    ☐ Widow control  [0] lines    │
│    ☐ Page break before      ☐ Orphan control [0] lines    │
│    ☒ Include in table of contents                          │
└────────────────────────────────────────────────────────────┘
```

Generating the table of contents

After you've selected the styles that you want included in the table of contents, you're ready to generate the table. Choose Utilities⇨Create TOC to get the Create Table of Contents dialog box, shown in Figure 15-3. You can specify a title by entering one in the Title option box — *Contents* is the default. You can also tell PageMaker where to place the page numbers for each entry: before each entry or after each entry. Usually, the numbers go after each entry (see the table of contents for this book for an example). If you choose No Page Number, your table includes just the text entries and no page numbers.

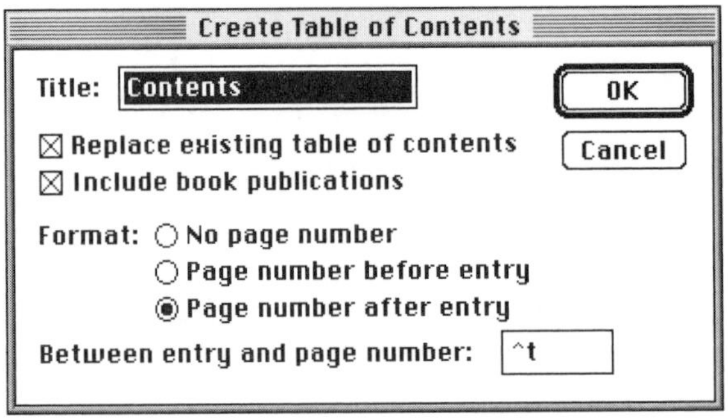

Figure 15-3:
In this dialog
box, you can
give your
table of
contents a
title and
specify how
you want
page
numbers to
appear.

```
┌──────────── Create Table of Contents ────────────┐
│                                                   │
│  Title: [Contents          ]      ┌─────────┐    │
│                                   │   OK    │    │
│  ☒ Replace existing table of contents└────────┘   │
│                                   ┌─────────┐    │
│  ☒ Include book publications      │ Cancel  │    │
│                                   └─────────┘    │
│  Format: ○ No page number                        │
│          ○ Page number before entry              │
│          ◉ Page number after entry               │
│                                                   │
│  Between entry and page number: [^t    ]         │
└───────────────────────────────────────────────────┘
```

You also have an option to put some text between the table text and the page numbers; you enter the text in the Between Entry and Page Number option box. The default is ^t, which is PageMaker's code for a tab character. (The ^ is the caret or circumflex, which you get by holding the Shift key when pressing the keyboard's 6 character.) You'll probably want to keep this default setting because by using a tab, you can have the page numbers right aligned and connected to the left-aligned contents text via a series of dots, as shown in Figure 15-4. In fact, this is the format that PageMaker automatically uses when generating your table — how nice! But you may want to use something, such as an em space (enter the code ^m) or em dash (enter ^_), between the numbers and text if, for example, you put the page numbers before the contents text. Note that you can put as many as seven characters between the text and numbers.

Two other options in the Create Table of Contents dialog box may or may not be available — the options appear when applicable to the current document. One option is Replace Existing Table of Contents, which overwrites any table of contents that you previously generated. If the current document or book doesn't have a table of contents, this option isn't available. The other option, Include Book Publications, is available if you chose the Book command and created a book list inside the current document (as explained earlier in this chapter).

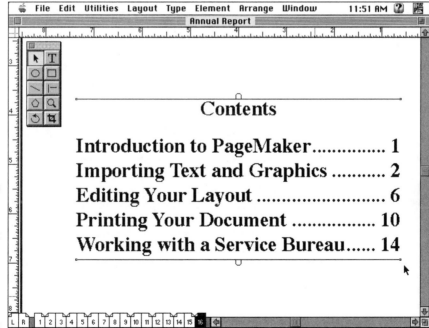

Figure 15-4: PageMaker's default settings generate a typical table of contents format.

If you want PageMaker to generate a table of contents that includes entries from all the documents in a book list, remember to copy the book list into your document (by pressing ⌘ and choosing Utilities⇨Book) before choosing the Create TOC command. Or you can simply create the book list again inside your document.

If you are working with book lists — or, for that matter, with documents — whose page numbers include a prefix, such as *A-* or *Antiques-,* make sure that you tell PageMaker to include that prefix as part of the page numbering *before* you generate the table of contents. (Assuming, of course, that you want those prefixes in the table of contents.) Just enter the prefix in the TOC and Index Prefix option box in the Page dialog box, which you get via File⇨Document Setup⇨Numbers. Make sure that whatever you type in the option box matches whatever you put in your master pages as a prefix to your page numbers — PageMaker doesn't check for you.

When you click on OK in the Create Table of Contents dialog box, PageMaker generates the table of contents and presents you with the paragraph or autoflow text placement icon. Click to place the table of contents text just as you would with imported text (as explained in Chapter 5). PageMaker also adds new styles to your style list. All begin with the word *TOC.* You get a style called *TOC Title,* which is always generated automatically. The others are *TOC* plus the names of the styles you designated for including in the table of contents. For example, if you had a style named *Headline* and you checked the Include in Table of Contents box in the Paragraph Specifications dialog box, you get a new style named *TOC Headline.*

If necessary, you can edit your table of contents just as you would any other story in PageMaker. If you want to change the formatting of your entries, you can do it easily by editing the TOC styles.

Creating a stand-alone table of contents

After PageMaker generates the table of contents, you may be tempted to insert some pages at the beginning of your document, thinking that you can place the table of contents on those new pages. *Don't.* Doing so changes all the page numbers in your document, making the table of contents outdated. Plus, chances are that you want a different numbering scheme for your contents — such as lowercase Roman numerals (i, ii, iii, iv, and so on) — and standard Arabic numbering (1, 2, 3, 4, and so on) in your main document. You may also want the page numbering in that main text to start over at 1 — you wouldn't want the contents section to end at page iv and the number of the first page of the text as page 5, right?

What to do? Use one of the following techniques:

✔ Add new pages to the end of the current document (by using File⇨Document Setup or the Layout⇨Insert Pages command) and place the table of contents there. (This way, you don't mess up the page numbering.)

✔ Use File⇨New (or ⌘+N) to create a new document and copy the text blocks containing the table of contents to that new document. (The TOC styles are copied along with the text blocks.) Unfortunately, you can't just place the contents text directly in this new document by clicking the text placement icon after you generate the table — you must first place the table in the document in which you generate the contents.

✔ *Before* generating the table of contents, create a new document and use the book list feature (Utilities⇨Book) to create a list of the documents from which you want the contents generated. Maybe the list includes just one document, but create the list anyway. This technique puts the table of contents in its own document without affecting the page numbers of the other document(s).

Insert the new pages at the beginning of your current document *only* if you want the table of contents to be part of your current document — with its pages numbered along with the rest of the pages in the document. Then be sure to regenerate the table of contents via Utilities⇨Create TOC, this time selecting the Replace Existing Table of Contents check box so that the page numbers are updated to reflect the inserted pages.

Okay, take a break. You're about to enter the woolly world of indexing — not a simple topic by any means — so you should be rested before taking the plunge.

Creating Indexes

Why is creating indexes so hard? It's not PageMaker's fault. Creating a good index means picking the right terms to track and then faithfully marking each term, including variants. For example, if you index the word *weasel,* you wouldn't want to index the term *weaseling* (as in *weaseling out of*). And if you index *deoxyribonucleic acid*, you need to index *DNA* as well and have the same index entry for both. Readers don't expect to find some entries under one term and the other entries under another term. (In fact, they may expect to find a *See DNA* cross-reference from *deoxyribonucleic acid*, assuming that they had even the remotest interest in this topic.)

Here's another complication: You can index in a word processor (PageMaker can import the index entries from Word and WordPerfect, as well as those in files saved in the RTF format, which several programs can create), or you can index in PageMaker. Where you index depends on who's doing the indexing. If all the text editing is done in the word processor, the index entries should probably be done there, too. But if extensive editing work is to be done in PageMaker, it makes sense to do the indexing there. Of course, you can index in both places, starting in your word processor and finishing in PageMaker for the text that is added or changed.

Creating index entries

In PageMaker, adding an index entry is simple — just use the Text tool to select the word or phrase you want to add to the index and press ⌘+semicolon. If you insist, you can insert an index entry the long way: via Utilities⇨Index Entry. You can add index entries either while working in Layout view or in the Story Editor.

When you insert an index entry, you get the dialog box shown in Figure 15-5. This dialog box is an all-out indexing machine, the first of a series of dialog boxes that lets you control almost every aspect of your index entry. If you're into power, you've come to the right place.

Tips for better indexing

Few of us have any professional training in indexing. The job requires familiarity with the topic being indexed — so that you know which topics are important and which text belongs in which topics. You also need to have the patience to go through an entire manuscript and correctly mark up all the index entries.

PageMaker takes some of the grunt work out of the job, but it can't do the thinking for you. Without stepping on the toes of the American Society of Indexers, whose members index for a living and probably don't want their basic secrets revealed (not that any of us can do a better job than they can), here are some basic things to keep in mind when doing your own indexing:

✔ Build a basic topic list in advance. Fortunately, you can build a list in PageMaker and then add to it as you uncover new topics or realize that some topics are too broad and need subtopics.

✔ Use multiple topics for some text. Readers may think of something with a different term than you do or perhaps from a different functional perspective. For example, in this book's index, *Place* and *Import* point to much of the same content because the terms are largely interchangeable in PageMaker parlance. Likewise, you find information on placing graphics under *Graphics, import* and *Importing, graphics* — some readers may consider importing to be a function of graphics, while others do the opposite. A good index satisfies both points of view.

✔ Use cross-references such as *See also* for related topics or just plain *See* for synonymous topics. But don't be stingy — if your document uses several different popular terms to refer to the same thing, index the item under all those different terms. Having to do the index runaround gets really annoying for the reader. The only thing more annoying is looking in the index for a particular term and not finding it.

Let's go through this dialog box of power. First, make sure that the Page Reference option is selected — this option tells PageMaker that you want your index entries to refer readers to a specific page in your publication. (The Cross-reference option is explained later in this chapter.)

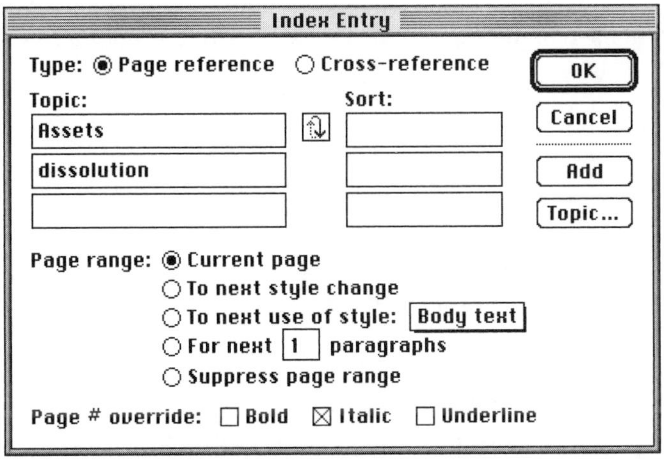

```
┌─────────────────────────────────────────────────────────────┐
│                        Index Entry                           │
│  Type: ⊙ Page reference   ○ Cross-reference    ┌──────────┐  │
│                                                │    OK    │  │
│  Topic:                       Sort:            └──────────┘  │
│  ┌──────────────────────┐ ⬍ ┌──────────────┐  ┌──────────┐  │
│  │ Assets               │   │              │  │  Cancel  │  │
│  └──────────────────────┘   └──────────────┘  └──────────┘  │
│  ┌──────────────────────┐   ┌──────────────┐                │
│  │ dissolution          │   │              │  ┌──────────┐  │
│  └──────────────────────┘   └──────────────┘  │   Add    │  │
│  ┌──────────────────────┐   ┌──────────────┐  └──────────┘  │
│  │                      │   │              │  ┌──────────┐  │
│  └──────────────────────┘   └──────────────┘  │ Topic... │  │
│                                                └──────────┘  │
│  Page range: ⊙ Current page                                  │
│              ○ To next style change                          │
│              ○ To next use of style: │ Body text │           │
│              ○ For next │1│ paragraphs                       │
│              ○ Suppress page range                           │
│  Page # override:  ☐ Bold  ☒ Italic  ☐ Underline            │
└─────────────────────────────────────────────────────────────┘
```

Figure 15-5:
Use this dialog box to create index entries.

In the dialog box, you can enter up to three levels of index information for the entry in the three Topic fields. The top field is the top-level topic (the one that is first in the index). Press Tab to move from one field to the next. In the figure, there are two levels: *Assets* is in the top level and *dissolution* is in the second level. In an index, this would usually look like:

> Assets
> dissolution, *14*

The Sort boxes to the right are tied to the Topic entries. Use the Sort boxes if you want to sort the entries differently than their spelling in the levels option. "What does that mean?" you scratch your head. Let's say that one of the index topic entries is *S. Africa* but you want it alphabetized by its full name, *South Africa.* In the Sort field corresponding to the Topic field containing *S. Africa,* type **South Africa.** Thus, when the index is created, *S. Africa* appears after *South Acton* and before *South America,* not at the top (periods are alphabetized before letters by computers).

Now look at that funny-looking icon button in the middle of the dialog box. Clicking on the icon moves topic entries around among levels. In all likelihood, you'll use this button only on rare occasions, but what the hey.

By selecting a Page Range option, you tell PageMaker how to select the page or pages that should appear with a particular index entry. Typically, you should use the default setting, Current Page. If you choose this setting, the index entry refers the reader to the page on which you clicked to add the word or phrase to the index, which is usually at the beginning of the relevant text. But you can pick any option that's appropriate to your text.

The final setting to establish is the page-number formatting, which you do by selecting from among the Page # Override check boxes. You can use any combination (including none) of boldface, italics, and underline. Whatever you select is applied to the page numbers that go with the index entries, not to the index entry text.

When you're done, click on OK or press Return. The index entry code is now inserted in your text.

You don't see index entry codes in your text when you're working in Layout view. But you can see them when working in the Story Editor. Figure 15-6 shows the diamond symbol that represents an index entry. To see or edit the entry, select the diamond character and press ⌘+semicolon or choose Utilities➪Index Entry.

Figure 15-6:
The diamond symbol in the Story Editor indicates an index entry.

Annual Report:Untitled:1

graphic freely without wreaking havoc on your layout. Multiple articles (an article is known as a ◇story in PageMaker) can fit on a page without interfering with each other. Each page is a balancing act, and columns provide the structure needed to keep it from flying apart at the seams. (And here you thought it was just because artists like to do things that the rest of us can't.)

Subhead 1 In the early days, the ability to create ◇multiple columns alone was enough reason to invest in PageMaker. Today, you can create multiple columns in a word processor. But the process is awkward, even in a powerful program such as Word or WordPerfect. You have to do a lot of formatting in dialog boxes, With all

---

Using index topics

You don't have to keep typing in the same index entry topics over and over again. Just click on the Topic button in the Index Entry dialog box to open the Select Topic dialog box, shown in Figure 15-7, and select from the existing topics. Topics are arranged by section. The sections correspond to the letter of the alphabet; a section called Symbols is for index entries that begin with symbols or numerals. You can go directly to a section via the Topic Section pop-up menu, or you can click on the Next Section button to move to the next section. When you find the section you want, select it from the list and click on OK.

That's all well and good, but where do those index topics come from in the first place? When you enter an index entry, click on the Add button in the Index Entry dialog box before clicking on OK. That adds the entry to the topic list. Pretty easy, huh?

Here's the answer to a question that may have been bothering you since you read the last section: You probably thought that one of the Page Range options in the Index Entry dialog box, Suppress Page Range, seemed a tad bit counterintuitive. Why would you have an index entry with no page range associated with it? If you're adding entries for use later, that's why — when you're building the topic list before actually applying the entry to a specific piece of text. Very likely, you won't need to use this option.

And, yes, the Text tool cursor must be inserted somewhere before you can enter index topics. The only thing you can enter with no text selected is an index cross-reference, as explained later.

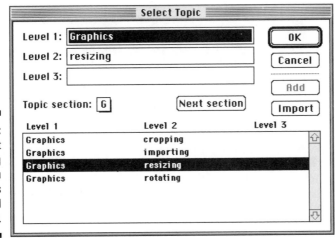

Figure 15-7:
The Select Topic dialog box lets you use topics defined earlier.

PageMaker offers another indexing time-saver in the form of the Import button in the Select Topic dialog box and the Select Cross-Reference Topic dialog box (discussed later). By clicking on this button, you can copy the topics used to index all the other publications in your book list into your current document. In addition to saving you the time of entering topics by typing them into the dialog boxes, this feature helps you to index terms consistently.

You can also copy the contents of your index topic list into all other documents in your book list. To do so, press and hold the ⌘ key as you choose Utilities⇨Book. Just be sure that the current document is not untitled — if it is, you need to save the document for this feature to work.

Shortcuts for special entries

Some index entries are basic, and using the various dialog boxes for adding index entries or selecting index topics is overkill, plain and simple. So to simplify your life, PageMaker adds several shortcuts for common index entries:

- ✔ ⌘+Shift+semicolon creates an index entry for the selected word or phrase without bothering you with the Index Entry dialog box.

- ✔ ⌘+Shift+Z formats the index entry for a proper name. For example, if you select *Homer Simpson* and press ⌘+Shift+Z, the name is indexed as *Simpson, Homer,* which is how names are usually indexed. If the name has more than two words, such as *Mary Ellen Hickey* or *John F. Kennedy* or *Ingall Bull III,* use a nonbreaking space (Option+spacebar) between all the words that go on one side of the comma. In these examples, the nonbreaking spaces go in *Mary Ellen, John F.,* and *Bull III.*

- ✔ In the Story Editor's Change dialog box (Utilities⇨Change or ⌘+H), enter a word that you want indexed in the Find What field, enter ^; in the Change To field, and select the Change All button. PageMaker doesn't replace the word with ^; but instead marks index entries throughout your document. You can also use this technique for proper names by using ^z instead of ^; as your Change To text. PageMaker formats the name specified in the Find What field as it does when you use the ⌘+Shift+Z keyboard shortcut described earlier.

In all three cases, the word or phrase is treated as a first-level topic, and the entry is *not* added to the topic list. However, for the Story Editor technique, you can search for each key word again, and as you find each occurrence, use ⌘+semicolon (or Utilities⇨Index Entry) to customize the index entry or add the entry to the topic list.

Cross-references within indexes

You'll often want to link index entries together so that readers know where to find related material or which index label is used for something that has several possible names (such as *place* and *import*).

Here's how to create a cross-reference:

1. Press ⌘+semicolon or choose Utilities⇨Index Entry.

If the Text tool was not inserted in text, you get the now-familiar Index Entry dialog box. But this time, the Page Reference option is grayed out and only the Cross-reference option is available, as shown in Figure 15-8. (If your text cursor was inserted in text, you have to select the Cross-reference option to activate it.) Also, instead of providing you with a series of Page Range radio buttons, the dialog box offers a series of Denoted By radio buttons that you use in step 4.

2. Enter the index entry topic(s).

You're entering the topic that you want the reader to look up in the index. You can enter topics — up to three levels — just as you do for a normal index entry.

3. Click on the X-Ref button and choose a cross-reference topic.

PageMaker displays the Select Cross-Reference Topic dialog box, which is similar to the Select Topic dialog box shown in Figure 15-7. But in this dialog box, you're choosing the related topic that you want the reader to look up in addition to the main entry.

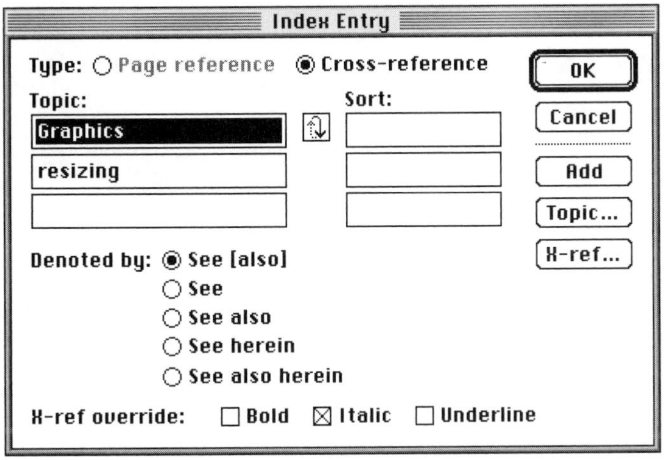

Figure 15-8: The Index Entry dialog box when you're defining a cross-reference.

```
┌─────────────────── Index Entry ───────────────────┐
│                                                     │
│ Type: ○ Page reference   ● Cross-reference  ( OK )  │
│ Topic:                    Sort:                     │
│ ┌──────────────────┐ ⇕   ┌──────────────┐ (Cancel) │
│ │ Graphics         │     │              │           │
│ └──────────────────┘     └──────────────┘ ( Add )   │
│ ┌──────────────────┐     ┌──────────────┐           │
│ │ resizing         │     │              │ (Topic...) │
│ └──────────────────┘     └──────────────┘           │
│ ┌──────────────────┐     ┌──────────────┐ (X-ref...) │
│ │                  │     │              │           │
│ └──────────────────┘     └──────────────┘           │
│ Denoted by: ● See [also]                            │
│             ○ See                                    │
│             ○ See also                               │
│             ○ See herein                             │
│             ○ See also herein                        │
│ X-ref override:  ☐ Bold  ☒ Italic  ☐ Underline      │
└─────────────────────────────────────────────────────┘
```

4. Click on OK.

You're returned to the Index Entry dialog box. Choose a Denoted By radio button to specify what text you want to use to identify a cross-reference. And, if you want to override the text formatting of the cross-reference, choose one of the X-Ref Override buttons.

5. Click on OK or Add.

If you want to create more cross-references, click on Add. Otherwise, click on OK or press Return to exit the Index Entry dialog box.

Editing an Index

When you're all done adding your index entries, it's a good idea to review all the work you did. You may find some inconsistencies (was it *S. Africa* or *South Africa*?) or misspelled words. Use Utilities⇨Show Index to display the Show Index dialog box, shown in Figure 15-9, where you can see the entire list of index topics and the page numbers they reference.

Figure 15-9:
You can
review and
edit your
index
entries in
the Show
Index dialog
box.

Show Index			
			OK
Index section: **G**	**Next section**	**Accept**	**Cancel**
Level 1	**Level 2**	**Level 3**	**Reference**
Graphics	cropping		16
Graphics	importing		16
Graphics	resizing		16
Graphics	rotating		16
Add x-ref...	**Edit...**	**Remove**	**Capitalize...**

From this dialog box, you can add cross-references, edit existing index topics, remove an index entry, and capitalize an entry by using the buttons at the bottom of the dialog box. The first two buttons — Add X-ref and Edit — open dialog boxes that you've already seen, and Remove is self-explanatory. So what's this Capitalize option? This option brings up a tiny dialog box with just three choices. Choose This Selected Topic to capitalize the first letter in the highlighted index topic; select All Level 1 Entries to capitalize the first letter of every first-level entry; and All Entries to put an initial cap on all entries. Whichever option you choose, the capitalization won't change in the Show Index dialog box; the changes are made only when you generate the index.

The Capitalize option isn't available when you're indexing multiple documents in a booked publication. To change the capitalization of entries in an index of booked documents, you have to edit each individual entry by clicking on the Edit button.

If you're indexing a booked publication and want to look at index entries for a single document in the list only, press and hold ⌘ as you choose Utilities➪Show Index. (Because you're only viewing the index for a single document, you now have access to the Capitalize button.)

Generating Indexes

After your index is all set up and corrected, you're ready to generate the index. Use Utilities➪Create Index to get the aptly named Create Index dialog box, shown in Figure 15-10.

If you want to generate an index that includes all the documents in a book, you first need to copy the book list into your index document or just re-create the book list in your index document. (Both topics are covered earlier in this chapter.)

Figure 15-10:
The dialog
box may be
small,
but it's
instrumental
in creating
an index.

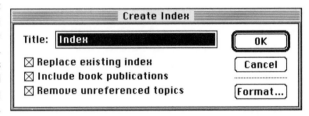

In the dialog box, you have the option of specifying a title for the index. The dialog box also has three check boxes, although the first two are often grayed out. The first is Replace Existing Index, which is available only if you previously generated an index for the current document. The second is Include Book Publications, which will index all documents in the current document's book list.

The third option is Remove Unreferenced Topics, which you should almost always check. This option removes from the generated index all topics not actually referenced in the document. The index topics aren't removed from the topic list — don't worry about that. Checking this option just ensures that if no text in the document is indexed to a topic, the topic is left out of your final index. Otherwise, you have index entries pointing nowhere.

Don't click on OK quite yet. First, check out the Index Format dialog box, which you get by clicking the Format button. Figure 15-11 shows the dialog box. These are the options:

✔ Selecting the Include Index Section Headings check box means that you want PageMaker to insert the letters for each set of index entries. For example, a big *A* appears above the index entries beginning with the letter *A*. PageMaker creates a style called Index Section for these section headings, and you can redefine the formatting as you can for any style.

✔ Selecting the Include Empty Index Sections check box means that you want PageMaker to list all the letters of the alphabet, plus *Symbols,* even if certain letters have no index entries. You usually use this option with the Include Index Section Headings option, and the result is something like:

C

    no entries

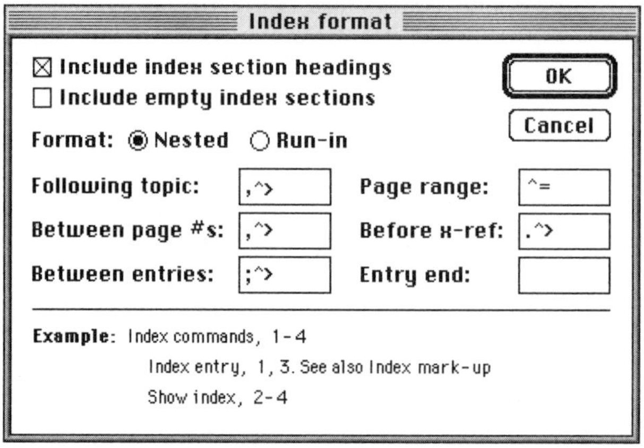

Figure 15-11:
You can
format your
index in this
dialog box.

```
┌──────────────────────────────────────────────────────┐
│                    Index format                       │
│  ┌────────────────────────────────────────────────┐  │
│  │ ☒ Include index section headings    ┌────────┐ │  │
│  │ ☐ Include empty index sections      │   OK   │ │  │
│  │                                     └────────┘ │  │
│  │ Format: ◉ Nested  ○ Run-in          ┌────────┐ │  │
│  │                                     │ Cancel │ │  │
│  │ Following topic:  [ ,^> ]   Page range:  [^=]  │  │
│  │                                                │  │
│  │ Between page #s:  [ ,^> ]   Before x-ref: [.^>]│  │
│  │                                                │  │
│  │ Between entries:  [ ;^> ]   Entry end:    [   ]│  │
│  │ ──────────────────────────────────────────────│  │
│  │ Example: Index commands, 1-4                   │  │
│  │          Index entry, 1, 3. See also Index mark-up │
│  │          Show index, 2-4                       │  │
│  └────────────────────────────────────────────────┘  │
└──────────────────────────────────────────────────────┘
```

That's hardly useful. (If you don't check Include Index Section Headings, you just get the text *no entries* where each letter of the alphabet would be.) You may want to use this option, though, if you are constructing an index piecemeal, and you want to see which areas are still missing entries.

✔ You have two choices of format: Nested and Run-in. At the bottom of the dialog box, PageMaker shows you an example of what these options look like as you select each one in turn. Basically, Nested makes the entries look like an outline, with the entry for each level on its own line and indented in from the left, while Run-in puts all the page-reference text as one block, with text for each level separated by semicolons, and then all the cross-referenced text as one block, again with text for each level separated by semicolons. The Nested option is easier to read, so unless you're really tight on space or trying to make the text hard to read (maybe for a legal brief), avoid Run-in.

✔ Finally, you get a bunch of fields for determining how the text is treated. You determine what characters follow the topic name via Following Topic; what characters separate page numbers via Between Page #s; what characters separate run-in entries via Between Entries; what characters are used to show page ranges via Page Range; what characters precede a cross-reference (via Before X-ref); and what character is put at the end of each entry via Entry End.

Here's where you get to have fun. Do you want hyphens to indicate page ranges (such as in *12-14*) or do you prefer en dashes (as in *12 – 14*)? Do you want a period and space before the *See also* text? Or how about a paragraph break? Do you want a comma or colon after the topic name? And maybe you want a tab as well (because you've defined a tab stop with a dot leader). The possibilities are almost endless. They're certainly mind-boggling. Table 15-1 lists the codes for the more common characters. You can also use standard characters, such as spaces, commas, and letters of the alphabet, plus symbols that you can access from the keyboard via Alt+key combinations. PageMaker doesn't care. But it does care that you put no more than seven characters in any field.

Table 15-1	Special Characters for Indexes	
Character	*Description*	*Code*
–	En dash	^=
—	Em dash	^_
/	Nonbreaking slash	^/
→	Tab	^t
	Nonbreaking space	^s
	Thin space	^<
	En space	^>
	Em space	^m
↵	Line break (new line)	^n
¶	Return (paragraph break)	^p

After you finish specifying your formatting, click on OK to return to the Create Index dialog box, and click on OK to begin the index generation. Let 'er rip! After PageMaker is done processing, you get the text placement icon (either the paragraph or autoflow icon, depending on how your document is set up). Go to the appropriate page and place the index text like any other text. Figure 15-12 shows the result for one document. Note that the title was changed so that it spans the width of the full page; when PageMaker created the index, it placed the title in the first column.

You'll also find five new styles in your document: Index Level 1, Index Level 2, Index Level 3, Index Section, and Index Title. As you can with any style, you can modify these styles to fit your design and layout needs.

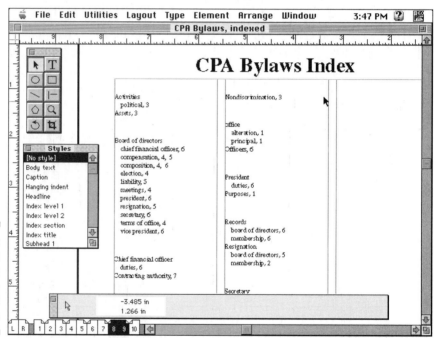

Figure 15-12:
An example of a PageMaker-generated index.

As you can see, the book feature, when combined with the page numbering, indexing, and table of contents features, can be a really powerful way to work with multidocument projects — books, manuals, reports, proposals, and magazines. These features not only handle some of the more tedious tasks associated with creating long documents, they get you out of the office a heck of a lot sooner than doing these chores manually — which leaves you scads more free time to do all those other things that your teenagers ridicule behind your back. Aren't computers wonderful?

Part V
You Mean
There's More?

The 5th Wave — By Rich Tennant

Bill and Irwin discover The Land of Lost Files

MY GOD! THIS IS A BUDGET AND ANALYSIS REPORT FOR THE MARKET-ING DEPT. OF A FORTUNE 500 COMPANY. MUST OF KILLED THE POOR BASTARD TO LOSE THIS.

In this part . . .

Layout is cool. Layout is fun. But layout is not everything. You also need to know a few other pesky details, including how to print, how to send files to a service bureau, and how to exchange files with colleagues, some of whom may work on Windows computers. This part covers all these issues plus a few others — in inimitable style, of course.

Chapter 16

What Are Links — and Why Should You Care?

• •

In This Chapter

▶ Finding out about links

▶ Deciding whether to store a copy of graphics or text in your layout

▶ Updating graphics and text files automatically

▶ Editing source files from within PageMaker

• •

*W*hen you place text or a graphic into your layout, a lot goes on behind the scenes. First, PageMaker checks the format of the file you're importing and then tries to import the file. For text, PageMaker translates the word-processor format into its own format. For graphics, it builds an image of the graphic that it will use to display the graphic on-screen (EPS drawings come with their own prebuilt screen images).

Second, PageMaker checks to see where the file resides — the disk and folder — and records that information, along with the filename and the last modification date. Third, it lets you place the file in your layout.

This second step is where *links* come into play. Links are like little electronic homing devices that tell PageMaker where to find the original file. With links, PageMaker can tell whether a graphic or text file has been modified and, if you so specify, replace it with the newer version. PageMaker also needs links when printing graphics because in many cases it substitutes the original graphic for the on-screen display image to get the best-quality output.

All of this importing and linking stuff can happen automatically if you choose, which can be good and bad. It's good if you want PageMaker to always use the latest version of a graphic, bad if you don't. It's also bad if you think that PageMaker is automatically importing the latest version of a graphic but in fact the option that tells the program to do so is turned off, or vice versa. So get in the habit of checking the link settings, as explained in this chapter.

Setting Link Defaults

The time to set your link options is when you first create a new document. To do so, use Element⇨Link Options with nothing selected. (If you establish link settings when no document is open, your settings become the defaults for all future documents.) Figure 16-1 shows the dialog box that appears. Note that the dialog box has two sets of options — one for text and one for graphics. Also note that the options are indented underneath each other — that's because in order for an option to be available, the option above it must be checked. This indentation is meant to remind you of that fact.

Figure 16-1:
Use these
options to
specify how
and when
imported
text and
graphics are
updated
from disk.

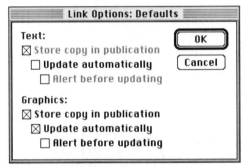

Link Options: Defaults

Text:
☒ Store copy in publication
☐ Update automatically
☐ Alert before updating

Graphics:
☒ Store copy in publication
☒ Update automatically
☐ Alert before updating

OK

Cancel

Although Figure 16-1 shows the dialog box for setting a document's defaults, you can also display a similar dialog box for a particular element and establish settings to control that element's behavior. (You don't get both the text and graphics options, just the set appropriate for the selected element.)

The same linking rules need not apply to all your elements — for example, linking a logo that never changes to its source file would be silly. And it would be equally silly not to link a graphic that changes every month (such as for a calendar) to its source file. That's why you can set link options individually.

The Store Copy in Publication option

The first Text and Graphics option in the Link Options dialog box is Store Copy in Publication. This option copies the text or graphic file into your PageMaker document. In other words, the text or graphic file is actually inserted into the PageMaker file. You'll notice that this option is checked and dimmed for text — that's because text is always stored in the publication. PageMaker gives you no choice in the matter.

For graphics, checking this option doesn't lock you into copying every graphic into PageMaker. In the More Preferences dialog box (File⇨Preferences⇨More), you can tell PageMaker to alert you, if the graphic you're importing is larger than a specified file size, by entering that value in the Alert When Storing Graphics Over value. This option is spotlighted in Figure 16-2. Setting this threshold prevents the PageMaker document from getting too big; after all, if you're linked to the original graphic, you don't really need that graphic copied in PageMaker.

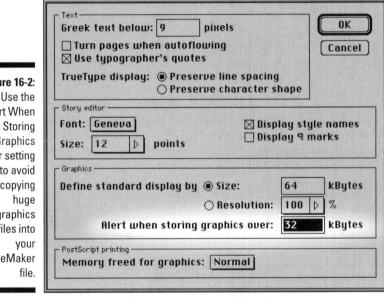

Figure 16-2:
Use the Alert When Storing Graphics Over setting to avoid copying huge graphics files into your PageMaker file.

Here's how the option works. Suppose that you set the Alert When Storing Graphics Over value at 32K, but you import a graphic that takes 67K. PageMaker displays a dialog box that lets you choose whether you want to copy the graphics file into PageMaker or not.

Should you check the Store Copy in Publication box for graphics? It depends. If you do, and the original files get lost, you still have a copy in your PageMaker layout that can be used for printing. If you don't, your PageMaker file stays smaller because the graphics don't have a duplicate inside the file. Our advice is to check the item but set a fairly low threshold in the Alert When Storing Graphics Over amount — for example, 32K. Thus, small graphics are copied in automatically while you retain the option to just link the big ones.

Files that are copied in are also linked — PageMaker still keeps a reference to the original file, for reasons that will soon become clear.

As explained in Chapter 9, Photo CD images can't be stored in a publication — the image files are just too large. So you have to relink to the Photo CD every time you open the publication. Alternatively, you can open the image in an image-editing program and save it in a format that can be stored in the publication, such as TIFF. Or you can choose the Save to CIELab TIFF File option that PageMaker offers you when you first place a Photo CD image.

The Update Automatically option

The second option in the Link Options dialog box, Update Automatically, tells PageMaker to check, every time you open the publication, whether the source files have been changed or moved. That's why PageMaker records the file information when first placing the file. Even if PageMaker previously copied a graphic or text file into the PageMaker layout file, it checks to see whether the source file has changed. If so, PageMaker replaces the old version with the updated file in your layout.

Select this option if graphics and text change frequently and you want to make sure that the latest version is used in the layout. For example, if you have a monthly newsletter with a guest columnist, you may want to save the columnist's photo under some generic filename like GUEST.TIF and simply substitute the latest photo each month. Then, when the newsletter document is opened, PageMaker loads in the latest columnist's photo. Of course, for this option to work, you need to make sure that the source file is changed only when planned — it's embarrassing to have the wrong photo for a particular columnist simply because someone changed the photo early or the newsletter was produced a little later than normal.

Note that if you decide not to copy graphics into the PageMaker file, the Update Automatically option is checked and grayed out. All such linked files are automatically updated because PageMaker must link to the source file each time you open the layout. PageMaker has no internal copy to use.

Disabling the Update Automatically option for text files is generally a good idea. If you have some text files that do change frequently, you can select this option, but understand that any editing or formatting that you did in PageMaker gets lost when the layout is updated with the new text file. And don't think that you can export your current text (via File⇨Export) to your word-processor file to get around this loss — the exporting process loses special formatting, such as tracking, kerning, drop caps, and other PageMaker-specific features not found in a word processor.

The alert box shown in Figure 16-3 is PageMaker's way of telling you that if you update the text file with the linked version, you'll lose all the changes you made in PageMaker. If that's okay with you, click on the Yes button. If you don't want to lose all the changes you've made, though, click on No.

Figure 16-3:
This box
warns you
that you're
about to
override text
that you
modified in
PageMaker
after you
imported it.

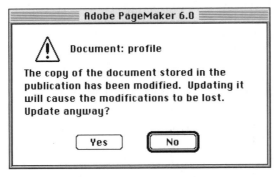

Adobe PageMaker 6.0

⚠ Document: profile

The copy of the document stored in the
publication has been modified. Updating it
will cause the modifications to be lost.
Update anyway?

Yes   No

The Alert Before Updating option

The last option, Alert Before Updating, is available only if the other two options above it are selected. This option gives you a chance to override an automatic update as the PageMaker file is being opened. We all know how smart it is to let something go off on its own without someone paying attention — the IRS, Congress, a high-school student. No, we insist that they check in with us before doing something that might affect us. That's what this option makes PageMaker do.

If you want automatic updating to catch any unplanned changes to your source files but you want to retain control over whether those updated files actually get used in PageMaker, check this option. If you are certain that you want elements to be updated automatically, with no notice to you, don't check the box.

Updating Individual Elements

After you establish your default link settings, you may want to change them for individual elements, as explained earlier. You can change the link settings for individual elements by selecting the elements and using the Link Options dialog box to set their behavior, as previously described in the section "Setting Link Defaults." But you can do more than that.

PageMaker offers a separate dialog box to manage the links themselves. The Link Options dialog box controls the behavior of the linking feature; the Links dialog box controls which element is linked to which source file. Figure 16-4 shows the Links dialog box, which you access by choosing File⇨Links or pressing ⌘+equal (=).

Figure 16-4:
Here's
where you
examine the
links for
every
imported
element in
your
publication.

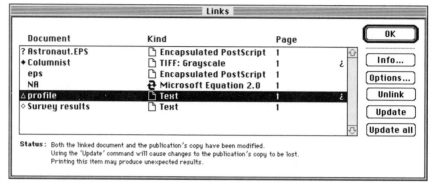

▶ Click on the Info button to get information on a current link, including the file's physical location, the date it was placed in PageMaker, its size, and the date it was created. Figure 16-5 shows the dialog box with information about an imported graphic.

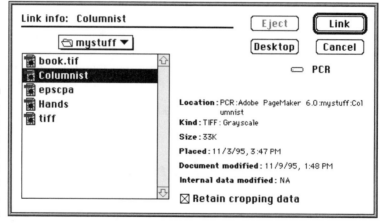

Figure 16-5:
This dialog
box shows
you
information
about a
current link.

▶ Via the Info button, you also can change the source file for an element. By selecting a new file and clicking on Link or pressing Return, you can substitute the new file for the old source file. When would you want to use this option? Well, suppose that you're doing a story on Jane Fonda. But the only picture you have of her is an old movie still from *Barbarella*. For lack of a better image, you go ahead and use it. The next day, a co-worker comes in with a copy of "Jane Fonda's Best-Selling Workout for the Dead." You rip it from said coworker's hands, throw it on the scanner — completely ignoring copyright laws — and use the Info button to link the imported *Barbarella* graphic to the new image. The old image is then replaced.

✔ Via the Options button, you can change the link behavior — this button accesses the same link options you find in the Link Options dialog box described earlier in this chapter.

✔ Use the Unlink button to break the link to a selected element. That way, the internal PageMaker copy is the only copy PageMaker uses or tracks. If no internal PageMaker copy exists, PageMaker creates one when you unlink the source file.

✔ You can update a link for an element whose source has been modified by clicking on the Update button. You only need to use this option when you turn off automatic updating for an element.

✔ If you click on Update All, PageMaker updates all links to source files that have been modified. Again, you only need to use this option if automatic updating is turned off.

Symbol shorthand

You've probably noticed all the wacky symbols that accompany element names in the Links dialog box. (See Figure 16-4.) These symbols are shorthand for link problems; if you select a filename, you get a detailed description after the word *Status* at the bottom of the dialog box. Here's a rundown of what the symbols mean:

✔ The upside-down question mark (¿) means that the text or image may not print correctly (because the linked file is missing or because some other problem has occurred with the source file).

✔ A triangle (∆) means that both the source file and the copy inside PageMaker have been modified (this applies just to text), and updating the source file overwrites changes in the PageMaker copy.

✔ A hollow diamond (◊) means that a source file has changed, but PageMaker has not updated the internal copy. You get this symbol only if the Update Automatically option is turned on for the object.

✔ A black diamond (♦) indicates that an element's source file has changed and that the element is marked for automatic updating the next time you open the PageMaker document.

✔ The right-side-up question mark (?) means that PageMaker can't find the source file.

✔ The code *NA* means that the object was pasted into your layout via the Clipboard and thus is not linked.

Using Live Links

PageMaker supports *live links*, which it calls *hotlinks*. When you have a live link, you can double-click on an element in PageMaker to open the source file and the program that created it.

Say that you're working in a layout and you notice that a graphic needs a touch-up. You know how to use Photoshop for this kind of work, so why not just fix the flaw yourself? Why not indeed. You can switch to Photoshop and load the image, or, if you want to save some effort, press and hold the Option key while double-clicking on the image in PageMaker. Presto: PageMaker launches Photoshop and opens the source image file.

Another way to do the same thing is to select the graphic in PageMaker and choose Edit⇨Edit Original. (Of course, you need to have enough RAM to have both PageMaker and Photoshop running at once — which requires about 16MB of system RAM.

If you want to edit the element in a program other than the one that created it — for example, if you want to use Fractal Design Painter to alter a TIFF image that was created in Photoshop — hold the Shift key when selecting Edit⇨Edit Original or press Option+Shift when double-clicking on the image. You can then choose which program you want to launch for your editing work.

Using the Edit Original feature can get a little tricky at times:

✔ You may still have to update the link to the modified graphic (via the Links dialog box, accessed by File⇨Links) even if you use Edit Original. PageMaker updates the graphic automatically only if Update Automatically is checked and Store Copy in Publication is *un*checked in the Link Options dialog box (Element⇨Link Options). Got that? If these options aren't exactly right, the graphic doesn't get updated.

✔ Text does not update automatically — you have to update the link manually or wait until the next time you open the publication (assuming Update Automatically is checked). This is why the best place to edit text in PageMaker is in the Story Editor (see Chapter 5). Editing in a word processor runs the risk of wiping out changes made in PageMaker — even if you don't change the words, you've likely applied formatting. So don't use Edit Original with text.

Chapter 17

The Journey to Paper

· ·

In This Chapter

▶ Setting up a PostScript printer

▶ Choosing from PageMaker's scads of printing options

▶ How to handle fonts when printing

▶ Special considerations when selecting paper size

▶ Printing thumbnails, tiled publications, and reader's spreads

▶ Creating color separations for full-color printing

▶ Using printer styles to automate printing chores

· ·

*T*he wonderful thing about computers is that they offer you so many choices. The terrible thing about computers is that they offer you so many choices. Menus full of commands, dialog boxes brimming with options — figuring out which choices will work best for you can be daunting, to say the least.

Printing your documents from PageMaker, unfortunately, requires you to make many choices, some simple, some more complicated. But never fear. This chapter helps you sort out the various decisions you need to make to get your PageMaker masterpieces from screen onto paper.

PostScript or QuickDraw?

One of the first decisions you have to make is whether to print your document on a PostScript or QuickDraw printer. *PostScript* and *QuickDraw* are computer languages that tell a printer how to print a page. (Your Mac also uses QuickDraw to display images on-screen.)

QuickDraw printers, when combined with Adobe Type Manager (a separate font-management utility) and System 7's TrueType technology, do a good job of printing text — even text that uses PostScript fonts. They can also print graphics that are created in QuickDraw graphics programs, such as MacDraw, pretty well. But if your document contains EPS (Encapsulated PostScript) graphics — for example, drawings created in programs such as Adobe Illustrator or Macromedia FreeHand — you won't be able to generate a good quality printout on a QuickDraw printer. EPS graphics turn all jagged and sad-looking when printed on a non-PostScript printer.

For professional publishing, PostScript is the format of choice. Not only do PostScript printers produce better-looking documents, most service bureaus require that documents be produced in the PostScript format. Of course, you can always proof your documents on a QuickDraw printer and then create a PostScript file for your service bureau, but you won't be able to get a very good idea of what your final graphics and text will look like.

Setting Up a Printer

Before an airplane takes off, flight mechanics and pilots do a thorough check of the plane's systems to make sure that everything's in good working order. Before you print PageMaker documents, it's a good idea to perform the same sort of preflight check on your printer. Chances are, everything's ready to go, but it never hurts to check, just the same.

Here are the preprinting steps to take for a PostScript printer:

1. Select Apple⇨Chooser.

The Chooser dialog box opens. (PageMaker 6 installs Chooser Version 7.3. The printer driver installed by PageMaker needs Chooser 7.3.)

2. Select a printer driver.

The icons in the scrolling list on the left side of the Chooser dialog box represent printer drivers, which are files that PageMaker needs in order to print your documents. Select either the PSPrinter driver or the most current LaserWriter driver.

3. Select a printer.

After you select a driver, you should see some printer options in the window in the right half of the dialog box. If the window is labeled Select a PostScript Printer and you see a list of printers (as you will if you're working in an office that uses networked printers), click on the icon for the printer you want to use. If the window is instead labeled Select a Printer Port, click on the icon for the port into which your printer cable is plugged. Usually, printers are connected to the printer port, but some folks do use the modem port.

4. Click the Setup button.

The Chooser searches for the correct PPD to match your printer.

What about QuickDraw GX?

If you're using System 7.5 or later, a little something called QuickDraw GX may be installed on your Mac. QuickDraw GX is a system extension that's supposed to make it easier for you to print documents and perform some neat tricks with type. The problem is, few programs support QuickDraw GX, including PageMaker. In fact, QuickDraw GX can really screw things up when you're trying to print from PageMaker.

To see whether QuickDraw GX is installed, open up the Extensions folder in your System folder. If you don't see an icon for QuickDraw GX, you're in good shape. But if you do see the QuickDraw GX icon, you need to do one of two things: Remove QuickDraw GX from your system entirely or disable it when you're running PageMaker. To disable QuickDraw GX, choose Apple⇨Control Panels, choose the Extensions Manager control panel, and deselect the QuickDraw GX and PrinterShare GX extensions. Then restart your system.

To remove QuickDraw GX from your system entirely, you need the QuickDraw GX Install disk that came with System 7.5. Grab it and a friendly neighborhood Mac guru, and use the Custom Remove option to wipe all the GX files from your system. (If you installed from a CD, you'll find a QuickDraw 6X folder that has the Install programs.)

If you have trouble getting your fonts to print correctly after removing or disabling QuickDraw GX, it may be because you're using PostScript Level 1 fonts (a version of PostScript that came before the current Level 2). If that's the case, you need to restore those fonts. Again, beg a Mac expert to show you how to do so.

If you can't find a Mac guru, you can get a free faxed instruction sheet from Adobe that will walk you through the process of getting rid of QuickDraw GX and restoring PostScript Level 1 fonts. Just call the FaxYI phone number found in the *Adobe PageMaker 6.0 Getting Started* booklet that came with your software.

PPD stands for *PostScript printer description* file. The information in the file tells PageMaker about your printer — what kind of fonts it has, its resolution capabilities, and so forth. PageMaker uses this information when sending your publication to your printer. You choose PPDs for your printer when you install PageMaker, as explained in this book's Appendix.

If the Chooser says it can't find a PPD for your printer, click on the Other PPD option to hunt around for the PPD file for your printer type.

If you can't get your hands on the correct PPD — or you don't have time to mess with finding one — try selecting a PPD for any Apple LaserWriter printer.

5. Click on OK twice to exit all the dialog boxes and save your printer setup information.

You'll probably be presented with a dialog box instructing you to check out the settings in the Page Setup dialog boxes in any open programs. As far as PageMaker goes, you don't need to worry about this message; just click on OK. You do all the necessary fiddling with your page setup later when you choose your print settings in PageMaker, as explained in the section "Sending Stuff to the Printer."

That's all there is to it. Unless you switch to a different printer (by selecting it from the Chooser), you don't need to go through this process again.

To set up a non-PostScript printer, the setup steps are similar: Just open the Chooser window and click on the icon for the printer you want to use. You don't have to worry about selecting a PPD with non-PostScript printers.

Checking Document Setup Options

Your printer's all set up and ready to go, your document is itching to be printed, and you're more than ready to print and call it a day. But you need to take one more step before you choose the Print command.

Choose File⇨Document Setup and check the Target Printer Resolution setting at the bottom of the dialog box. Notice the word *target* — that means the ultimate printer for the publication you're working on. That may not be the printer you're printing to at the moment.

Suppose that you're doing the company newsletter, which will be output by a service bureau at high resolution (1270 or 2540 dots per inch). Or maybe you're producing a project status report, and the target printer is a 600-dpi printer that will output pages for later photocopying. In either case, your proofing printer — the one at your desk or in your part of the building — is a humble 300-dpi laser printer. So you should set PageMaker for a 300-dpi printer, right? Wrong.

As mentioned back in Chapter 3, you need to use the resolution setting for the target printer. That lets PageMaker output the truest rendering possible of your document's bitmap images when you print to another printer, such as that 300-dpi printer used to proof the pages.

Figure 17-1 shows the Document Setup dialog box set for publishing a standard-size magazine page. The target printer resolution was set at 2540 dpi because that's standard for a graphics-intensive publication. If your document will be produced by a Linotronic or other imagesetter, but you won't be includ-ing color images, 1270 dpi is enough. (See Chapter 18 for more details on sending your document to high-end printers.)

Note that the Page Size option is set to *Magazine Narrow* — that happens to be a typical size for magazines. PageMaker includes a whole bunch of preconfigured page sizes in the Page Size pop-up menu. Again, pick the size based on the ultimate printer. If your proofing printer uses standard letter-size paper (8 1/2 x 11 inches), *don't* change the paper size to Letter unless that's the ultimate size of your document.

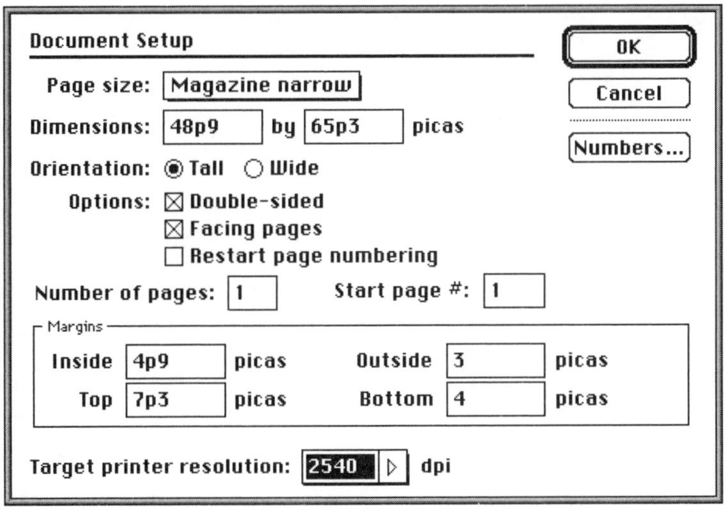

Figure 17-1:
Choose
settings
in the
Document
Setup dialog
box that
correspond
to the
printer
producing
the final
output for
your
publication.

```
┌─────────────────────────────────────────────────────────────┐
│  Document Setup _____    ┌──────────┐     │
│                                             │    OK    │     │
│   Page size:  │Magazine narrow│             └──────────┘     │
│                                             ┌──────────┐     │
│   Dimensions: │48p9│  by │65p3│  picas      │  Cancel  │     │
│                                             └──────────┘     │
│   Orientation: ● Tall  ○ Wide               ┌──────────┐     │
│        Options: ⊠ Double-sided              │Numbers...│     │
│                 ⊠ Facing pages              └──────────┘     │
│                 ☐ Restart page numbering                     │
│                                                              │
│   Number of pages: │1│    Start page #: │1│                  │
│   ┌─Margins──────────────────────────────────────────────┐  │
│   │  Inside │4p9 │ picas    Outside │3  │ picas           │  │
│   │  Top    │7p3 │ picas    Bottom  │4  │ picas           │  │
│   └──────────────────────────────────────────────────────┘  │
│                                                              │
│   Target printer resolution: │2540│ ▷ dpi                    │
└─────────────────────────────────────────────────────────────┘
```

You may see a slight effect on quality when the target printer doesn't match the current printer. For example, spacing is finer on a high-resolution printer, and fonts are more delicate. In this situation, the proof copy may appear to have awkward spacing and lighter fonts than expected. Why? Because the printer is trying to simulate a higher-resolution printer, and in so doing, it comes up against some of its own limitations. Still, overall, the spacing and look will be more accurate than if you change the target printer setting to match the proofing printer.

Note, however, that having the printer type set to something other than the printer currently being used can result in error messages while printing. If this happens, change the printer type to match that of the current printer.

Sending Stuff to the Printer

After you check the settings in the Document Setup dialog box, you're ready to give PageMaker the Print command. To do so, choose File⇨Print or just press ⌘+P. PageMaker responds by showing you the Print Document dialog box, which is the first in a series of five linked dialog boxes. You can switch from dialog box to dialog box by clicking on the buttons on the far right of the dialog box. If you're using a PostScript printer, the buttons are labeled Document, Paper, Options, Color, and Features, as shown in Figure 17-2. If you're using a non-PostScript printer, you get a Setup button instead of a Paper button.

Together, the five Print dialog boxes offer scores of printing options. Fortunately, you don't have to worry about most options most of the time. The following sections run through the options you'll use most.

```
┌─────────────────────────────────────────────────────────────┐
│▒▒▒▒▒▒▒▒▒▒▒▒▒▒▒▒▒▒▒▒▒▒▒ Print Document ▒▒▒▒▒▒▒▒▒▒▒▒▒▒▒▒▒▒▒▒▒│
│                                                    ┌─────────┐│
│  Printer:  LaserWriter                             │  Print  ││
│                                                    └─────────┘│
│  PPD:    │LaserWriter Pro 600 v2010....│  ⊠ Collate ┌─────────┐│
│                                         ☐ Reverse  │ Cancel  ││
│  Copies: │1                │           ☐ Proof     └─────────┘│
│  ┌─Pages──────────────────────────────────┐       ┌─────────┐│
│  │ ⦿ All                    Print: │Both Pages│     │Document ││
│  │                                         │       └─────────┘│
│  │ ○ Ranges │1            │  ☐ Reader's spreads    │  Paper  ││
│  │ ☐ Ignore "Non-Printing" setting ☐ Print blank pages └─────┘│
│  ┌─Book──────────────────────────┐ ┌Orientation┐  │ Options ││
│  │ ⊠ Print all publications in book│ ┌──┐┌──┐   │  └─────────┘│
│  │ ⊠ Use paper settings of each publication  │     │  Color  ││
│  └────────────────────────────────┘ └────────┘   └─────────┘│
│                                                    │Features ││
│                                                    └─────────┘│
│                                                    │ Reset   ││
└─────────────────────────────────────────────────────────────┘
```

Figure 17-2:
The Print Document dialog box for a PostScript printer.

If you're using a non-PostScript printer, the Features button doesn't do anything — well, anything useful, that is. If you click on the button, you open the Printer Features dialog box, which is empty except for a message telling you that features for your printer are accessible by clicking on the Setup button. Even if you have a PostScript printer, you may not find any features in this dialog box; it depends on your printer and the PPD file you select (as explained in the next section).

Choosing a printer and PPD

If the name of the printer you want to use doesn't appear in the Printer field at the top of the dialog box, you need to select the printer from the Chooser. Press and hold on the Apple menu, select Chooser, and then select a printer driver and printer from the Chooser dialog box. If you're selecting a PostScript printer, checking the printer setup is a good idea, as outlined in the section "Setting Up a Printer," earlier in this chapter.

If you're printing to a PostScript printer, the Print Dialog box offers a PPD pop-up menu right below the printer name. Generally, you shouldn't need to change the PPD option; the correct PPD for your printer should automatically be selected if you set up the printer properly through the Chooser. If not, choose the PPD that corresponds to your printer.

If you add memory or other upgrades to your printer (such as a second paper tray), you need to update your PPD so that PageMaker can take full advantage of your printer's new capabilities. PageMaker comes with a separate utility called Update PPD, which is designed to help you update your PPD. The process is a little complex — too complex, in fact, for this book — but your friendly neighborhood computer guru should be able to help. Alternatively, you may be able to obtain an updated PPD from your printer manufacturer or from an online bulletin board service.

Choosing how many pages print and in what order

In the Print Document dialog box, you can choose exactly which pages you want to print, in what order you want them to print, and how many copies you want:

- ✔ Enter the number of copies you want in the Copies option box. If you're printing on a non-PostScript printer and you don't see this option in the Print Document dialog box, click on the Setup button to display the Page Setup dialog box for your printer. You should find the option in the dialog box.

- ✔ Choose the All radio button to print all pages in your publication; choose the Ranges button to print only a range of pages. If you choose Ranges, enter the numbers of the pages you want to print into the Ranges option box. You can mix ranges and individual pages; if you want to print pages 1, 3, 8, 9, and 10, for example, you can type **1, 3, 8, 9, 10** into the option box or **1, 3, 8-10**.

- ✔ Select Both Pages from the Print pop-up menu if you want all pages in your specified range to print. Choose Even or Odd if you want to print only the even or odd pages, respectively.

- ✔ Check the Collate box if you are printing more than one copy of your document and you want to print each set of pages in order. If you don't check this box, PageMaker prints all copies of one page and then moves on to print all copies of the next page. Printing your document may take longer if this option is checked.

- ✔ Checking Reverse makes the last page print first, followed by the preceding page, and so on, until the first page. If your printer normally stacks pages in reverse order, you can check this option to print the pages in their correct sequential order.

- ✔ Choose Print Blank Pages if you want PageMaker to, well, print any blank pages that are in your publication. Otherwise, they don't print, even if you specify that you want to print all pages (by choosing the All radio button).

- ✔ If you're printing a booked publication (as discussed in Chapter 15), check Print All Publications in Book to print all documents in the current document's book list. The other Book printing option — Use Paper Settings of Each Publication — should generally be checked if you're printing to a PostScript printer. The option assumes that each publication may have different page sizes, orientations, or margins and that the printer can handle this. If you're printing to a non-PostScript printer or if your

PostScript printer isn't up to the task of printing different page sizes at the same time, you have to print each document in the book list separately. (Or you can create a new book list that includes just those documents that use the same page sizes, and print all those documents together using the Print All Publications in Book option.)

Printing on both sides of the paper

If you have a *duplex* printer — a printer that lets you print on both sides of the paper — you can choose from two different duplex-printing options. For non-PostScript printers, click on the Options button to access these options; for a PostScript printer, click on the Features button. If your pages will be bound along the long edge of the paper, choose the Long Edge setting; if they'll be bound along the short edge of the paper, choose Short Edge. (Note that the options available to you and the names of those options differ depending upon the type of printer you're using.)

Setting page orientation

The orientation icons in the bottom-right corner of the Print Document dialog box work the same as the ones in the Document Setup dialog box (explained in Chapter 3). If you want to print your document pages in portrait (tall) orientation, choose the left icon; if you want to print in landscape (wide) orientation, choose the right icon. Select the same icon here as you selected in the Document Setup dialog box — if you don't, some elements on your page may not print.

Printing thumbnails and reader's spreads

If your document uses facing pages, you can choose the Reader's Spreads option in the Print Document dialog box to print two facing pages on the same piece of paper. This option gives you a way to view your pages as if they were bound — which is useful for reviewing the look of your publication. Note that this option isn't available if your publication doesn't use facing pages.

The Thumbnails option is another neat little option that should come in handy for you. You access it by clicking on the Paper button for PostScript printers or the Options button for non-PostScript printers. By selecting the Thumbnails option and specifying how many thumbnails are to print on each sheet of paper, you can output small previews of each page. Thumbnails are great for showing your layout to others for comments or approval. Because the pages are miniaturized, people quickly get a feel for the document as a whole. And if you print enough thumbnails on a page, they can't read the text, so they're forced to keep focused on the overall appearance — which is what you want their comments on at this point, anyway.

Suppressing printing for selected elements

PageMaker 6 offers a feature that enables you to place text or graphics in your document but prevent them from printing. This feature can be handy for adding notations that you want everyone who works on the publication to see, for example. It can also be helpful as a troubleshooting tool. If you're having trouble printing a document and you think that the problem is a graphic — but you're not sure which graphic is to blame — you can turn printing off for one of the graphics and try to print. If you print successfully, you've found the problem graphic. If you don't print successfully, you can keep turning printing off for other graphics until you locate the problem.

To mark a text block or graphic as nonprinting, select the object in your PageMaker layout and choose Element➪Non-Printing. To hide nonprinting elements on-screen, choose Layout➪Display Non-Printing Items. Choose the command again to redisplay the elements.

If, during printing, you want the nonprinting objects to print, you don't need to go back into your layout and remove the nonprinting formatting. Just choose the Ignore "Non-Printing" Setting option in the Print Document dialog box.

Another way to suppress graphics printing is to select the Proof option in the Print Document dialog box. When this option is turned on, all graphics print as gray rectangles with Xs in them. This option can speed up your printing time because PageMaker takes less time to print the rectangles than the actual graphics. This option is great for printing rough drafts of your publication.

On PostScript printers, you can also prevent bitmap images from printing by choosing the Omit Images setting in the Print Options dialog box, as explained next.

Determining how bitmap images print

For PostScript printers, the Print Options dialog box, shown in Figure 17-3, offers a Send Image Data pop-up menu. Here, you set the resolution for bitmap images. The menu offers four options: Optimized, Low Resolution, Normal, and Omit Images. PageMaker offers you these choices because high-resolution images can take a long time to print. If you're just printing a proof copy of your publication, you can save printing time by choosing Low Resolution, which prints a low-resolution (72 dots per inch) version of your graphics, or Omit Images, which prevents bitmap images from printing. The Optimized setting sends image data to the printer according to the printer's capabilities; if you're printing a proof on a low-resolution printer, for example, Optimized sends only the image data that your printer can handle.

When you print your final copy, make sure that you select the Normal option, which sends all the image data to the printer.

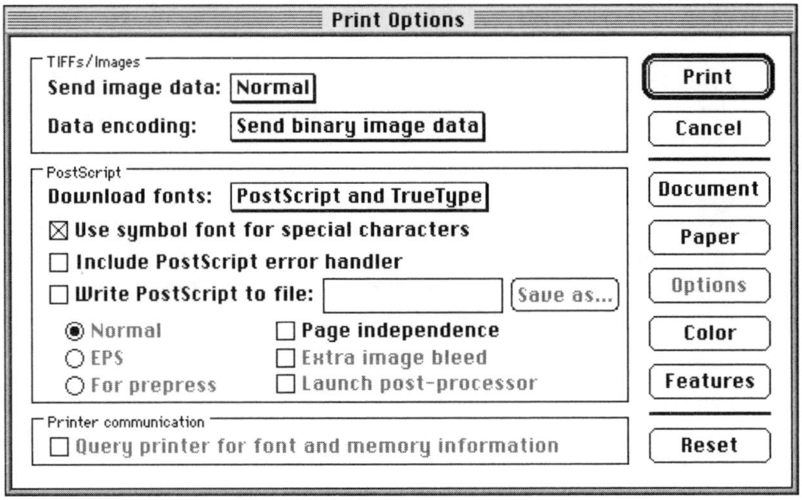

```
┌─────────────────────── Print Options ───────────────────────┐
│  ┌─ TIFFs / Images ──────────────────────────┐  ╭─────────╮  │
│  │  Send image data: │Normal│                │  │  Print  │  │
│  │  Data encoding:   │Send binary image data││  ╰─────────╯  │
│  │                                           │  ╭─────────╮  │
│  │  ┌─ PostScript ──────────────────────────┐│  │ Cancel  │  │
│  │  │ Download fonts: │PostScript and TrueType││ ╰─────────╯  │
│  │  │ ⊠ Use symbol font for special characters│ ╭─────────╮  │
│  │  │ ☐ Include PostScript error handler      │ │Document │  │
│  │  │ ☐ Write PostScript to file: │        ││ │ ╰─────────╯  │
│  │  │                              │Save as...││ ╭─────────╮  │
│  │  │  ◉ Normal      ☐ Page independence      │ │  Paper  │  │
│  │  │  ○ EPS         ☐ Extra image bleed      │ ╰─────────╯  │
│  │  │  ○ For prepress ☐ Launch post-processor │ ╭─────────╮  │
│  │                                           │  │ Options │  │
│  │  ┌─ Printer communication ───────────────┐│  ╰─────────╮  │
│  │  │ ☐ Query printer for font and memory...││  ╭─────────╮  │
│  └──────────────────────────────────────────┘  │  Color  │  │
└─────────────────────────────────────────────────╰─────────╯──┘
```

Figure 17-3:
The Print
Options
dialog box.

Printing to file

If you're printing to a PostScript printer, you can *print to file* by choosing Write PostScript to File in the Print Options dialog box. Printing to file just means that instead of sending your document to the printer, PageMaker saves the document and all the encoded printing instructions to a file on your hard disk, a floppy disk, or other storage device (such as a SyQuest cartridge). Why would you choose this option instead of just saving your document to disk as you normally would? Perhaps because you want to take the file to a service bureau, but you don't want to give it a chance to alter your print, font, or color settings.

If you don't want to print color separations, choose the Normal radio button under the Write PostScript to File option. If you do want color separations, choose For Prepress. If you intend to import your pages into another layout or program, such as to reproduce the cover in miniature on the contents page, choose EPS. If you choose the EPS setting, the Extra Image Bleed option becomes available; select this option if your document uses bleeds (images or text that go beyond the page boundaries).

After you've chosen your settings, enter a name for your PostScript file in the option box next to the Write PostScript to File option. Click on the Save As button to choose the folder or disk where you want to put the file. Then — after you've chosen all your other print settings, as explained throughout the rest of this chapter — click on the Save button to send the file to disk.

Dealing with fonts

For PostScript printers, you need to be aware of two other options in the Print Options dialog box: Page Independence and Download Fonts. To understand these two options, you first need to understand that in order to correctly print the fonts used in your document, the fonts must either be resident (installed) in your printer or downloaded (sent) from the computer to the printer's memory.

The Download Fonts option determines which nonresident fonts are downloaded to your printer's memory when you print. If you choose the TrueType and PostScript setting, PageMaker downloads TrueType and PostScript fonts. (PageMaker checks the PPD you select to find out which fonts are installed in the printer and then downloads only the nonresident fonts.) You can also choose to download TrueType fonts only or no fonts at all.

When would you *not* want to download fonts? One scenario may be when you're printing your document to file before sending it to a service bureau for final output. If the service bureau already has all your fonts installed in its printer, you don't need to send the fonts again. But in most cases, you'll want to download the fonts to the printer each time you print.

If you select Page Independence, PageMaker loads the fonts for each page into printer memory separately instead of loading all the document's fonts at the same time. If you have the same fonts on every page, checking this option slows down printing because fonts keep getting reloaded. But if each page has mostly a unique set of fonts, checking this option means that only the fonts for each page are downloaded with that page, rather than all the document fonts. This uses less printer memory per page, making output time faster. We suggest you leave this option unchecked until you know you need it.

A related option is Use Symbol Font for Special Characters, which is found right underneath the Download Fonts option in the Print Options dialog box. Generally, you should turn on this option. It tells PageMaker to use the Mac's Symbol font for some symbol characters that not all fonts support. This action ensures that the symbols — which include such common symbols as ©, ®, and ™ — will print correctly. The downside to this option is that the Macintosh Symbol font may look very different from the font you're using for the surrounding text, which can give your text an odd appearance. In addition, if you use a symbols font, such as Zapf Dingbats, PageMaker may substitute standard characters for your dingbats when you check this option. So if you're using a symbol font in your document or if you're certain that the symbol characters you're using are actually available in the standard font you're using, uncheck the option.

Choosing a paper size

To choose the size of the paper you'll be printing on, select an option from the Size pop-up menu, which you access by clicking on the Setup button for non-PostScript printers and the Paper button for PostScript printers. Figure 17-4 shows the dialog box that appears when you choose the Paper button.

The Size pop-up menu offers several predefined page sizes that vary depending on what printer you're using. The menu also offers a Custom option that enables you to create a custom page size. You can use the Custom option if you're outputting unusual page sizes — CD labels or mailing inserts for a standard envelope, for example. You also may need to create a custom page size if your document includes elements that bleed off the page or if you want to include printer's marks and page information on your document.

✔ You'll recall that a *bleed* is an image or text that intentionally runs off the page. Well, if you pick a standard page size, the image or text gets cut off right at the border of the page. So what happens if the paper slips while being printed or copied or cut? The bled image or text moves, too, and all of a sudden it may not bleed anymore. By having extra margin, PageMaker can print enough of the bleed image to account for any such variations. Add at least 0.375 inches on each side of your page to make room for the bleed.

Figure 17-4: If you're printing to a PostScript printer, you establish paper size and other page settings in the Print Paper dialog box.

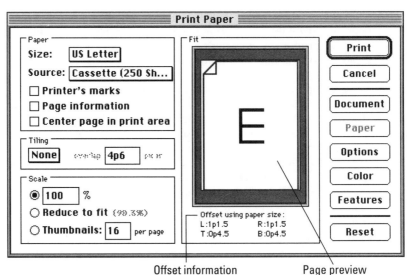

Offset information   Page preview

✔ You may also need to add to your page size if you select the Printer's Marks or Page Information options (found in the Print Paper dialog box for PostScript printers and in the Print Options dialog box for non-PostScript printers). The Printer's Marks option adds registration marks, crop marks, and other elements that a commercial printer uses when printing your document. (Some in-house artists also use crop marks to ensure that pages are cut correctly, especially if the final product is being cut down to a smaller size than the paper it's printed on.) The printer's marks consume 0.75 inches on each side of the paper.

The Page Information option prints details about the publication file, such as the name of the file and the current date, in the lower-left corner of every printed page. The page information requires 0.5 inches along the horizontal edge of your paper.

✔ Together, the page information and printer's marks take up 0.875 inches on one edge of your paper. And the printer's marks also take up space on the other side edge and along the top and bottom of the paper. So you need to add 1.625 inches to the width of your document and 1.50 inches to the depth. If your document page is 8 x 10 inches, for example, you need to define a custom paper size of 9.625 x 11.5 inches to make room for the page information and printer's marks.

✔ Some printers offer special page sizes designed to accommodate printer's marks, bleeds, and page information. The page sizes are designated by the word *Extra* after the page size.

✔ For PostScript printers, a preview in the middle of the Print Paper dialog box shows how your publication fits on your chosen paper size. If the Offset information beneath the page preview appears in red type, your publication, printer's marks, and page information won't fit on the printable area of your paper. You have two choices: Either enlarge the paper size or reduce the size of your document by using the Reduce to Fit or Scale options discussed in the next section.

✔ Some printers — PostScript and non-PostScript — can't print all the way to the edge of the paper. PageMaker takes this fact into account when displaying Offset information and figuring out how much to reduce your page to fit it on the paper.

Printing oversized publications

You just created a full-color, 21 x 28-inch poster to announce your company's grand opening. You're sending the poster to a commercial printer for final output, but your boss wants to see a full-size proof copy before you send it to the printer. Problem is, the largest paper your office printer can handle is standard legal-size pages. How in the heck are you supposed to print a full-size proof of the poster?

PageMaker offers two solutions: One possibility is to scale (reduce) the publication to a size that your printer can print. Another option is to use *tiling,* which lets you divide your page into small sections — called *tiles* — that you can print and tape together to create a mock-up of your finished poster.

The tiling and scale options are found in the Print Options dialog box if you're printing on a non-PostScript printer and in the Print Paper dialog box if you're using a PostScript printer.

Scaling your document

You have two ways to scale your publication for printing. First, you can enter a percentage in the first Scale option box. Choose a value greater than 100 percent to enlarge your publication; enter a value lower than 100 percent to reduce the document. PageMaker allows values from 5 to 1600 percent, but your printer may not be able to handle such a wide range. (Check your printer manual for specifics on your make and model.)

The Reduce to Fit option automatically scales your publication so that it fits on your selected paper size.

Neither option actually changes the size of your document in the PageMaker file — only the printed document is affected.

Tiling a publication

You can have PageMaker tile your document automatically, or you can do it manually. To create tiles automatically, select the Auto tiling option (it's a radio button for non-PostScript printers and found in the Tiling pop-up menu for PostScript printers). Then specify an overlap value in the neighboring option box. PageMaker automatically calculates the number of tiles needed to print your document and divides your document into tiles.

The *overlap* value refers to the extent to which the image on one tile overlaps the image on another when the two tiles are reassembled after printing. Make sure that this value is greater than or equal to the minimum margin value for your printer, or you'll have white gaps between tiles when you reassemble the printed tiles.

When you use the Manual tiling option, you control the exact dimension and image area for each tile. In your document, drag the ruler's zero point marker so that the zero point is placed at the upper-left corner of the tile you want to print (moving the zero point is discussed in Chapter 3). Remember to allow a little extra room for overlap. Print the tile and then repeat the process until you've created and printed all the tiles for your document.

Printing in glorious color

In the Print Color dialog box (which you access by clicking on the Color button), you can specify whether you want to print color separations or a composite of your publication. You need color separations if you're sending your document to a commercial printer for reproduction; the separations will be used to prepare plates for the printing press. (For more information on how professional printers produce color publications, see Chapter 11.)

Your other option is to print a *composite* in which all the elements and colors in your document print on one page. You can print a color composite on a color inkjet or laser printer or print a grayscale composite on a standard black-and-white printer.

Figure 17-5 shows the Print Color dialog box for a PostScript printer. The following list explains how the important options work. With the exception of the last item in the list, you'll find these same options in the Print Color dialog box for a non-PostScript printer.

✔ If you want to print color separations, select Separations and select each ink for which you want a color plate. A check mark next to the ink's name in the scrolling list beneath the Separations button means that a plate will be created for that ink. To toggle the check mark on and off, click on the Print This Ink check box or double-click on the ink name in the scrolling list. Typically, you want to select just the four process colors — cyan, magenta, yellow, and black — which you can do in one step by selecting the All to Process button. Sometimes, you may want to print a plate for a spot color in your document; your service bureau rep can advise you on this.

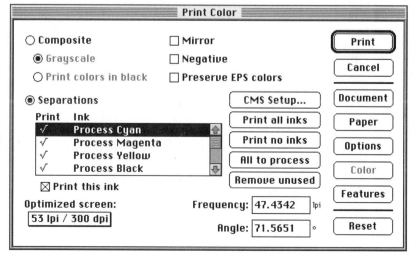

Figure 17-5:
The color printing options for a PostScript printer.

✔ If you want to print a composite instead of color separations, choose the Composite radio button.

✔ Select Print Colors in Black if you want fast printing and don't care if images appear as big blotches.

✔ For PostScript printing, select Preserve EPS Colors if your document contains a color EPS image that has its own color definitions and you want those colors to be used (rather than colors defined in PageMaker that happen to have the same names).

Saying bon voyage to your document

When you have all your print settings just so, click on the Print button (or on the Save button if you're printing to file). If you decide to make some changes to your document after printing, make your edits and then just press ⌘+P and Return to print the revised document. PageMaker retains the latest settings in the Print dialog boxes until you change them again, so you don't have to go through the trouble of setting everything up each time you print the same document.

Saving Your Printer Settings as Styles

No doubt about it — setting up your printer can be a lot of work. Fortunately, PageMaker 6 offers a feature that helps cut down on the time you spend fiddling with printing controls.

Using the Printer Styles command (File⇨Printer Styles), you can save printer settings for a particular document as a style — just as you can save paragraph and text-formatting settings as styles. The next time you want to use the same printer settings — whether for the same document or for any other document — you simply select the printer style, and PageMaker automatically applies your print settings for you.

This wonderful feature used to reside in the Utilities⇨Additions menu, which was replaced by the Utilities⇨PageMaker Plug-Ins menu in Version 6. It's now located in the File menu, where you're more likely to see — and use — it.

The Printer Styles feature comes in especially handy if you print a lot of documents that require different print setups. For example, if you print the proofs of your monthly newsletter on an office laser printer but print the final version to a high-resolution imagesetter, you can create one style for your laser-printer settings and another for your imagesetter settings.

To create a printer style

1. **From inside your PageMaker document, choose File⇨Printer Styles⇨Define.**

   You see the Define Printer Styles dialog box, shown in Figure 17-6.

2. **Click on New.**

   PageMaker displays a dialog box asking you to name your style (also shown in Figure 17-6).

3. **Enter a style name and click on OK.**

4. **Click on Edit.**

   The Print Document dialog box opens. Choose your print settings as you normally would for the document (as explained earlier in this chapter).

5. **Click on OK.**

   You're returned to the Define Printer Styles dialog box.

6. **Click on OK again.**

   You're done!

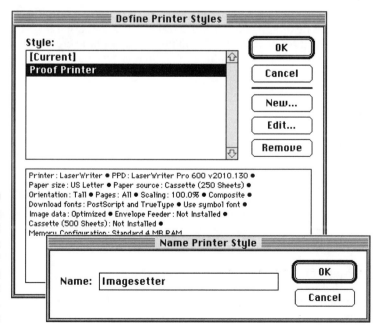

Figure 17-6: Version 6 enables you to save your print settings as styles.

To apply a printer style to a document, choose File⇨Printer Styles and then choose the style from the resulting submenu. When the Print Document dialog box appears, click Print (or Save if you're printing to file) or just press Return.

If you hold down the Shift key while you choose File⇨Printer Styles and select the style name, you can bypass the Print dialog box altogether.

If you ever need to edit your printer style, choose File⇨Printer Styles⇨Define, click on the style you want to edit, and click on Edit. When the Print Document dialog box opens, change your settings as needed and then click OK twice to close all the dialog boxes.

Whew! You never realized printing could be so complicated, right? And the truth is, we've covered only a portion of the bajillion printing options and controls that PageMaker offers. As mentioned earlier, you may want to have a PageMaker guru review your settings to make sure that you're getting the best output possible. If you're sending your publication to a service bureau or commercial printer, be sure to also go over your print settings with the technical representative; different service bureaus have different requirements, so you always need to double-check that things are set up correctly. Sending a test file to the service bureau is also a good idea anytime you change to a new version of any software used to create your documents or if you switch to a new service bureau.

Printing can be tedious (and frustrating) at times, but don't neglect this part of the publishing process. After all, you put in a lot of time creating your document, and you want the printed version to look every bit as good as the on-screen version.

The 5th Wave

By Rich Tennant

"OH, I'VE GOT IT BOOTED ALL RIGHT—JUST DON'T ASK ME TO DOUBLE KNOT IT!"

Chapter 18

Dealing with the Outside World

. . . .

In This Chapter

▶ Exchanging files with colleagues

▶ Working with Windows PageMaker users

▶ Preparing files for output by a service bureau

▶ Creating documents for electronic distribution

. . . .

*I*t's good to share — really. By working with others, you can combine your strengths and help each other out in your weaker areas. Desktop publishing is a collaborative enterprise — the folks who do the writing are usually not the folks who do the artwork, and neither of these folks usually does the layout. Even if you work in a small business and you're the one who does most or all of the work, you may still have to exchange the PageMaker document with a client or a service bureau.

PageMaker is designed for collaboration, so your efforts to share are strongly supported by the program's design. And for those areas in which PageMaker isn't quite strong enough, this chapter shows you how to get around its limitations.

Chapters 6 and 7 tell you how to collaborate with people who provide the text for your documents (text formatting and styles — remember?) In this chapter, you find out about sharing entire PageMaker documents, whether you're working with several people on the same document, passing your work on to someone else for approval or final touches, or sending your file to a service bureau for output on a high-resolution typesetting device.

Exchanging Documents with Colleagues

If several people are working on a document — whether they work collaboratively during the layout process or move the file from one person to another for specific tasks — they need to have access to all the components of the PageMaker document. However, those components can differ from document to document, depending on how you set up each document.

Sharing options

What do you do when you're ready to share PageMaker files with colleagues? First, determine the level of access people should have to your layout's elements. Here are some common file-sharing scenarios and how to handle them:

- ✔ **Scenario 1:** You want a colleague to go through the layout to make sure that elements align, everything is placed correctly, no text is overset, and other touch-up details are handled. Use the Links dialog box — File⇨Links or ⌘+equal (=) — to unlink each element from its source (by using the Unlink button for each element). Your colleague can still edit text but can't inadvertently update it with a linked text file; graphics won't be updated, either. Unlinking also tends to make the file smaller — sometimes as small as two-thirds the original size. (For a review of linking, see Chapter 16.)

- ✔ **Scenario 2:** You want a colleague to go through the layout to add elements but not to update any elements already in the layout. You may want to modify your own work when you get the document back. Use the Links dialog box — File⇨Links or ⌘+equal (=) — to disable automatic updating of links for text and graphics (for each element, use the Options button to get the Link Options dialog box and uncheck the Update Automatically option).

  Have your colleague do the same when returning the file to you. Note that either of you can use this option to override these settings if needed or use Element⇨Link Options to reestablish a link between a selected text block or graphic and an external file.

- ✔ **Scenario 3:** You've done a rough or conceptual layout, and you want a colleague to do the final layout. The graphics files may change, but you finalized the text in PageMaker's Story Editor. Unlink the text as described in Scenario 1. For graphics, open the Link Options dialog box and be sure to check Update Automatically. If the graphics files change while the other person is working on the layout, disable the Alert Before Updating check box.

- ✔ **Scenario 4:** You simply want the other person to go through your file and proofread it. Send a printout of your document, fax it, or use a program such as Common Ground, Inc.'s Common Ground or Adobe's Acrobat Exchange to e-mail an electronic version. Or open the file, unlink everything, save the file under a new name, and then send it. When you get the file back, you can compare it (probably from printouts) to your original to see what has changed.

If you're sharing PageMaker files with others on your office computer network, ask your network administrator for help in establishing file-sharing guidelines.

Images in the Kodak Photo CD format are not stored in PageMaker publications; you need to relink the image each time you open the file. So if you're going to share a publication that includes Photo CD images, be sure to pass along the image CD. Another alternative is to save the Photo CD image as a CIE Lab TIFF image when you first place it in your document or to open the image in Photoshop or another image editor and save it as a TIFF file in that program, as explained in Chapter 9. You can then store the image in your publication or copy it to a floppy disk or other removable storage device, such as a SyQuest cartridge.

You can use the new nonprinting feature to put production notes in your layout. Others who work on the layout can see the notes on-screen, but the notes don't appear in the printed document. To mark text or graphic elements as nonprinting, select them and choose Element➪Non-Printing. For more on this feature, see Chapter 17.

Fonts, libraries, and support files

When sharing files with other users, you may find that your setups differ, which can lead to unexpected results, such as bad tracking or incorrect font usage.

Sharing fonts

Everyone working on a project should have the same fonts. Many companies put directories of fonts on a network server or set of disks so that users can install them when working on the same project. If colleagues don't have a certain font used in your PageMaker document, PageMaker displays an alert box when they try to use the document. They can still work with the file, because PageMaker lets them substitute a different font temporarily. But this substitution can affect the line spacing because substituted fonts usually have different character sizes and tracking values. For more details about PageMaker's font-substitution options, skip to the section "Fonts," later in this chapter. Font substitution is more valuable for cross-platform document exchange and is thus covered in detail there.

Sharing libraries

A PageMaker document keeps a link to any libraries opened in it. If someone copies the PageMaker file, that link is retained, and the next person to open the file may get a dialog box requesting the location of the library file. If you don't need the library contents, you can just click on the Cancel button. If you do need to use the library, you have to relink it. If that library is available on your office network, great. Otherwise, you have to cancel the library relinking and get the library from your colleague by e-mail, on disk, or by some other method. (For more information about libraries, check out Chapter 14.)

Sharing dictionaries

To make sure that everyone's using the same hyphenation, spelling, and capitalization guidelines when working on text, share dictionary files. You can use the Dictionary Editor (covered in Chapter 5) to export your dictionary to other users. Just open the dictionary you want to export and then choose the Export command in the File menu. You can also print the entire contents of your dictionary by choosing File⇨Print in the Dictionary Editor.

Sharing tracking values

If you save a PageMaker file with the Files Required for Remote Printing option selected in the Save Publication dialog box, the tracking values (stored in a file named Tracking Values) for that file are copied with it. If you select any other option, the next user's copy of PageMaker uses the tracking file located in the PageMaker file's new location (if a tracking file is there) or in the RSRC folder within the Adobe PageMaker folder. Use the Files Required for Remote Printing option to ensure that the tracking files are up to date. This option also copies linked graphics not wholly loaded into the PageMaker file.

If everyone needs to use a standard set of tracking values, make sure that a master file is kept somewhere (on a disk or in a directory on the network, for example) and installed in everyone's RSRC folder. (Tracking is discussed more fully in Chapter 6.)

Working with Windows Users

In most cases, PageMaker files created on the PC can be read on the Mac, and vice versa — the file formats are the same, and most differences relate to external components. But you do need to keep a few issues in mind when you're sharing documents across platforms, as explained in the next few sections.

Platform is a techie term for the type of computer system you have. If you own a Mac, you work on the Macintosh platform. If you own a PC, you work on the PC platform. Leave it to computer folks to make the simple sound complicated!

When you're transferring files between platforms, your PageMaker document files must be saved in the same version of PageMaker that you're going to use on the new platform. For example, you can't open a Windows PageMaker Version 5 document on a Macintosh that's using PageMaker 6. You need to save the Version 5 document as a Version 6 document in Windows before trying to open it in PageMaker 6 for the Mac. In other words, you can't transfer between platforms and PageMaker software versions at the same time.

Fonts

Fonts cannot be moved across platforms. If you use custom fonts, use a font-translation program, such as Ares Software's FontMonger or Altsys's Fontographer to translate the fonts. These programs are often used to create fonts, and they can create both Mac and Windows fonts from the original font. Both programs are available in Windows and Mac versions.

Some fonts with the same names — and from the same developer — may not print exactly the same on Windows and the Mac due to minute differences in spacing. This difference can lead to reflowed text, so print a proof copy of your document after transferring it across platforms to ensure that nothing bad happened.

Some fonts have different names on different platforms. For example, Windows fonts tend not to have spaces in their names, while Mac fonts often do — thus the font Century Old Style on the Mac is known as CenturyOldStyle on the PC.

PageMaker lets you tell it which fonts have mismatched names so that it knows to rename the fonts in a transferred document in the future. The first time a mismatch occurs, PageMaker uses a tool called the *PANOSE Matching System,* which is essentially a table of fonts that indicates which fonts are the same as others with different names and which are similar, in case you need to substitute another font. Figure 18-1 shows the dialog box that the PANOSE system displays on a Mac (the dialog box is similar in the PC version of PageMaker). PANOSE recommends substitutions for you, but you can select a new name from the Substituted Font pop-up menu at the bottom of the dialog box.

Figure 18-1:
If the fonts used in a document aren't available on the computer, PageMaker displays this dialog box when you try to open the document.

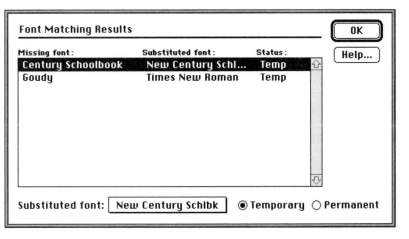

If the font really doesn't exist on the new platform, substitute a similar font and click on Temporary. When the file is transferred to a system that has the missing font, the original font is substituted for the temporary font.

But if you want to make a particular substitution permanent — whether based on PANOSE's recommendations or your own selection — click on the Permanent radio button. Doing so saves the substitution in PANOSE's database so that it knows what to do the next time it encounters the situation. You can also change or add to the PANOSE substitution table by choosing File⇨Preferences⇨ Map Fonts to display the Font Matching Preferences dialog box, shown in Figure 18-2.

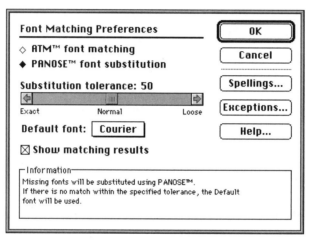

Figure 18-2:
You can edit the PANOSE font substitution table by using the options in this dialog box.

The dialog box also lets you decide the degree of substitution tolerance via a slider; the lower the tolerance value, the more exact the PANOSE system attempts to be when substituting fonts. You don't need to change the setting from its normal default value unless you have many similar fonts and want PANOSE to be more discerning in its recommendations.

Click on the Spellings button to get a list of Macintosh font names and their Windows equivalents, as shown in Figure 18-3. You can add to, modify, or remove names from this list. Notice that the names differ essentially in spacing and capitalization. Click on the Exceptions button in the Font Matching Preferences dialog box to display the dialog box shown in Figure 18-4. Here, you can make wholesale substitutions of fonts — for example, if you always want to replace Times Roman with the Times Ten font, which is not a clone but a distinct font with its own look and feel. PANOSE uses the Exceptions list for font matching.

You can use font substitution when moving files from one Macintosh system to another where their fonts differ, not just when moving between Macs and Windows systems.

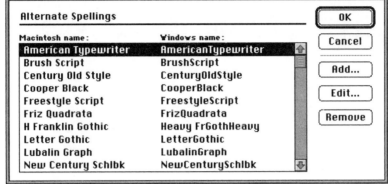

Figure 18-3:
PageMaker
gives you
a list of
Windows
and Mac
spellings for
the same
fonts.

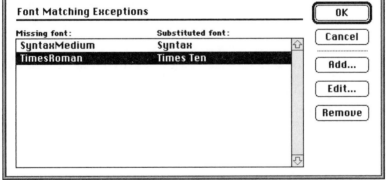

Figure 18-4:
Here's
where you
make
changes to
the default
font
substitution
table.

Filenames

On PCs running Windows 3.1 and earlier, filenames can be only eight characters long; in Windows 95, filenames can be up to 255 characters long. In both Windows 95 and earlier versions, programs add a three-letter file extension to the filename, such as .DOC and .TIF. Although Windows 95 is more flexible about filenames than older versions of Windows, it still gets persnickety if you use certain characters in your filenames. You can't use the backslash character (\), the colon (:), or quotation marks (" ") in a filename, for example.

On the Mac, files can have up to 31 characters and include any punctuation mark except a colon (:). This difference in naming conventions can easily become a source of great confusion.

When you transfer PageMaker document files across platforms and then open them, you may get a dialog box asking you whether you want to translate the filenames (Figure 18-5 shows the dialog box for Macintosh PageMaker; you get a similar dialog box in Windows PageMaker). You should answer in the affirmative by checking the Translate File Names in Links option. If you don't, the Links dialog box simply refers to linked files as *PC Text* or *PC Graphic* (or *Mac Text* or *Mac Graphic*), which doesn't help when you later try to relink to the original files. This dialog box is PageMaker's way of dealing with the differences in filenames across platforms.

Figure 18-5:
PageMaker
asks
whether you
want to
translate
filenames
to the
Macintosh
format.

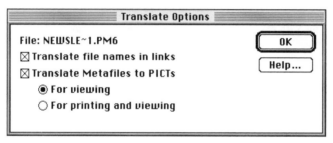

If you want to open a Macintosh PageMaker document on a PC, save it using the old-style Windows naming conventions — up to eight characters followed by a period and the three-character extension that identifies the file type. Some common extensions include .PM6 for PageMaker 6 documents; .PT6 for PageMaker 6 templates; .TIF for TIFF files; and .EPS for EPS files. Even if you're going to be opening up your document in a system that runs under Windows 95, continue to use the old, shorter filenames. Otherwise, your document names may not display properly — or appear at all — in PageMaker's Open Publication dialog box, and you will also need to relink all linked files.

Follow the same file-naming rules when you're transferring a document from Windows 95 to the Mac. Filenames longer than eight characters (plus the three-letter extension) are truncated — cut off — when transferred to the Mac, which can cause linking problems. The filename in Figure 18-5 is an example; the original filename was NEWSLETTER.PM6.

As we speak — or should we say, as we write — more and more Windows programs are being updated to run under Windows 95, and more and more Macintosh programs are being updated to accommodate the longer filenames used in Windows 95. But for now, at least, the rule to remember is to always save your documents with the shorter filenames used before Windows 95 if you want to transfer between platforms.

Note that some characters used in filenames don't transfer well across plat-forms. For example, spaces on the Mac often go away or become underscores (_) in Windows 3.1 and earlier. And filenames that contain an ampersand (&) often display with an underline in a Windows dialog box (for example, CAT&DOG.TIF appears as CAT<u>DOG</u>.TIF in a Windows dialog box). Even in Windows 95, some characters don't transfer, so avoid using symbols, spaces, and the like in your filenames.

Graphics format translation

When you transfer PC files to the Mac, PageMaker gives you the option of translating them to Windows Metafile format via the dialog box shown back in Figure 18-5. Going the other direction, you have the option of translating from Windows Metafile to PICT. Go ahead and select this option; you can't view or print the files otherwise. You have a choice of translating for viewing only or for both viewing and printing. If you plan to print the file on the new platform, make sure to choose the option for both viewing and printing.

You may lose some quality when transferring files from the Mac to Windows. That quality loss may become even worse if you move the file back to the Mac, because PageMaker translates the graphic from Windows Metafile to PICT again. Sometimes, PageMaker also produces a lower-quality version of TIFF, PCX, or other bitmap formats that are moved across platforms. This problem usually occurs for bitmap images stored within PageMaker (whether they are linked or not). In the Links dialog box, PageMaker identifies such files with an upside-down question mark, as shown in Figure 18-6. A regular question mark symbol before the filename means that PageMaker can't find the linked file.

Figure 18-6:
Open the
Links dialog
box to
check for
problems
with linked
files.

Links			
Document	**Kind**	**Page**	**OK**
Anchor.wmf	Windows Metafile	1	¿
Balloon.tif	TIFF: Grayscale	1	**Info...**
? Bio.doc	Text	1	**Options...**
Cpa9fin.eps	Encapsulated PostScript	1	
Henrick.TIF	TIFF: Grayscale	1	**Unlink**
NA	Bitmap Image	1	**Update**
pm6w1603.TIF	TIFF: Grayscale	1	**Update all**
Profile.doc	Text	1	

Status : This graphic cannot be printed in high resolution.
It may be possible to re-link the graphic using the 'Info...' dialog.

Click on the Info button to relink the file, as discussed in Chapter 16. By relinking to the original graphic, you can avoid quality loss in PICT/Windows Metafile translation and avoid quality loss for bitmap files stored internally in your PageMaker document. But if you're moving the document just one way, you may want to use a graphics format such as TIFF or EPS that requires no translation across platforms instead of using the PICT or Windows Metafile format.

Incompatible elements

Some PageMaker support files cannot be moved across platforms. One such file type is the tracking file (Tracking Values on Macs and TRAKVALS.BIN on PCs). The two platforms' font formats are different, and tracking files are font related.

Library files also cannot be moved across platforms — the formats are not compatible. If you use a library in a PageMaker file moved across platforms, PageMaker prompts you to locate the library, and you either have to select a similar library on the new platform or click on Cancel.

Working with Service Bureaus

Chapter 17 discusses how to prepare a file for output, including some of the settings of interest to a service bureau. Here, you find out what to send to a service bureau — and how to send it.

Service bureau, in this case, refers to anyone to whom you send your PageMaker layout for final output. It may be a separate company, a division of your company, or someone down the hall. Typically, a service bureau produces negatives used by a commercial printer to actually print your document; the service bureau usually uses a typesetter or imagesetter to produce these files. But a service bureau may also produce high-resolution *positives* — black ink on white paper or high-resolution color proofs. Some copy centers are, in essence, low-end service bureaus.

Before you begin, note the following:

 ✔ Remember that by copying small graphics wholly into the document (see Chapters 9 and 16 for details), you can minimize the size of your PageMaker file because it doesn't need to contain linking instructions for the graphics.

 ✔ Ask your service bureau to recommend image settings for your grayscale bitmap images. These settings are applied via the Element⇨Image⇨Image Control command.

✔ If you are doing four-color printing, make sure to check All to Process in the Color section of the Print dialog box. Ask your service bureau whether you need to create additional separations for any spot color inks you may be using.

✔ Make sure that the printer and resolution selected in the Print Document dialog box and Document Setup dialog box, respectively, match those of the target printer. Check that other print settings are appropriate for the document, as described in Chapter 17.

Now you are ready to give the service bureau what it needs: everything related to printing the document.

✔ Use PageMaker's Save Publication dialog box (File➪Save As) with the Files Required for Remote Printing option selected. Doing so ensures that any linked graphics not wholly imported into PageMaker are saved to the same folder (usually, these linked files are TIFF and EPS files). Also copied is the Tracking Values file, which ensures that the service bureau has all spacing and kerning values that you've set for your document.

✔ Depending on the size of the file and its images, copy the document and all files needed for remote printing onto a high-density (1.4MB) floppy disk or cartridge (SyQuest and Bernoulli are the most popular — check with your service bureau to see which type it uses). If your document includes Photo CD images that you haven't saved in another format and stored in the publication or on a floppy disk, provide the original Photo CD as well.

✔ Enclose a list of all the fonts your document uses. Your service bureau may have your fonts, but by enclosing the fonts on disk, you save the service bureau the time of tracking them down. At the very least, make sure that you include any custom fonts.

You can get the fonts from the Fonts folder stored inside your System Folder — for PostScript fonts, remember to include both the printer fonts and the screen font suitcase.

✔ Enclose a printout of the document so that the service bureau can check the output versus your expectations.

Going Online

VERSION 6

6

PageMaker 6 enables you to save your publications in two formats used for electronic distribution of documents: PDF and HTML.

The PDF format — which stands for *portable document format* — is used to create documents that can be opened and viewed on any computer (PC or Macintosh) that has Adobe Acrobat software installed. One common use of the PDF format is to distribute documents over office networks. You can also distribute PDF documents on the Internet.

The PageMaker 6 Deluxe CD-ROM includes a limited version of Adobe Acrobat Exchange; you get Acrobat Distiller, which converts PostScript files to PDF files, and Acrobat Reader, which lets you view and print PDF files. (The full version of Acrobat Exchange, which you can purchase separately, enables you to add interactive links, security, and other enhancements to your PDF document.)

A second option for Internet publishing is to convert your PageMaker documents to the HTML format. HTML stands for *hypertext markup language,* which is the standard format used to create pages for the Internet's World Wide Web. PageMaker 6 includes a plug-in (found in the Utilities⇨PageMaker Plug-ins submenu) called HTML Author that will translate your publication files to the HTML language.

Going through all the steps involved in creating HTML and PDF documents isn't possible in a book this size — we could fill up an entire book on the subject. In fact, IDG Books Worldwide, the publisher of this book, publishes two books on the topic: *Creating Cool Web Pages* and *HTML For Dummies.* If you're serious about creating documents for the Internet, you'll want to pick up a copy of one, or both, of those books.

If you decide to make the leap into electronic document distribution, keep in mind some of the following considerations:

✔ How your PDF documents look to the people who view them depends entirely on the capabilities of their individual systems. For example, your layout may look great on your 17-inch monitor, but to viewers whose systems have 15-inch monitors, the same layout may look cut off at the knees. And different monitors display colors differently — that lovely shade of turquoise you picked for your document may appear as a moldy green on a viewer's monitor. In other words, you can't accurately predict how your documents will appear to every user. By designing your documents so that a layout can be seen in its entirety on a small screen and by limiting colors to those that can be displayed on a monitor that has 8-bit (256 color) video capabilities, you help ensure that your layouts will look decent to most people who view them.

✔ When you're working in the HTML format, you have to specify fonts, type size, paragraph alignment, and other formatting options using special HTML style tags. The styles you apply in PageMaker won't be preserved when you save your document in the HTML format. Also, if the viewer's system doesn't have the fonts that are used in your document, your text may not display as you intended. Line lengths and spacing may be affected, for example.

✔ What looks good on the printed page may not look as good on-screen, and vice versa. You need to decide up front whether your primary audience will be printing your electronic documents and then reading the printed page or viewing the document on-screen only. Then design your layout for that format.

✔ When viewers open up your page on the Internet, all the text and graphics are downloaded over their modems. Downloading large graphics takes a long time — more time than some viewers may be willing to invest — so keep graphics simple. The smaller the graphics file, the better.

✔ HTML is still a pretty primitive language, and many of PageMaker's advanced features simply can't be re-created using HTML — and some of the standard features can't be created simply. Even the basics, such as making text boldface and centering lines of type, require you to place special style codes in your text. You can't just select text and click on a Control palette icon, as you can when creating regular PageMaker documents.

✔ With electronic documents, you can create *hypertext links* to other pages of your document. When a viewer clicks on a word or phrase that's designated as a hypertext link, the on-screen display "jumps" to a related subject or phrase elsewhere in the document. If you're going to include hypertext links, you need to format them in a way that lets viewers know what text is hypertext and what text isn't. For example, the hypertext links in PageMaker's Help system are formatted in a different color than normal text.

As you can see, creating documents for electronic distribution involves some complex design and technical issues. The PageMaker manual can get you started on the road to electronic publishing — or, should we say, on the electronic highway — but unless you're really familiar with the workings of the Internet or your office network, it's best to enlist the assistance of an electronic distribution guru when creating PDF or HTML documents.

You're Done!

Believe it or not, you now know the basics of creating and printing PageMaker documents. Up next is the Part of Tens, which is both an amusing and informative collection of wisdom, observations, and useful hints about PageMaker. Think of it as the icing on your PageMaker cake — enjoy!

Part VI
The Part of Tens

"WELL THIS HAS SURE TURNED OUT TO BE A MICKEY MOUSE SYSTEM."

In this part . . .

You know the problem with most computer books? (*Besides* the fact that their turgid prose violates all known measurements for tedium and unoriginality.) They don't offer enough sound bites. When you set the book down, you should be humming the tunes, as it were, conjuring up images of pages gone by, psyched to the gills to put a few techniques to the test. In other words, you should be raring to use PageMaker.

That's what this section is about. Now that we've discussed a few thousand issues pertinent to PageMaker in context, the rest of the book hurls factoids at you completely out of context. The idea is that if we hurl enough of them and hurl them hard enough, a few will get stuck in your brain. It is our supreme wish that on your deathbed, you say something completely meaningless to your surviving relatives like, "To create a line break, press Shift+Return." If you do, try to get someone to videotape it, will you? We may be able to use it in a marketing campaign; you never know.

Chapter 19

Ten Special Characters to Assign to Memory

- -

In This Chapter

▶ Curly quotes and the apostrophe

▶ The bullet

▶ The em space

▶ The em dash

▶ The discretionary hyphen

▶ The nonbreaking space, hyphen, and slash

▶ The line break

▶ The copyright and trademark symbols

▶ Accent marks

▶ The automatic page number

- -

*W*hen we say *characters,* we don't mean the guys down at the local bar. We're talking about the most elemental building blocks available to you in PageMaker: text characters. Some characters — a, e, i, o, u, sometimes y — are readily available to the most casual PageMaker user. But other characters lie hidden beneath PageMaker's murky surface. These special characters space text more elegantly, prevent text from breaking onto different lines at weird places, and make your words look more beautiful. Who'd have thought something so small could be so powerful?

The Curly Quotes and Apostrophe

Wouldn't that make a great title for a children's book? "The curly quotes and apostrophe all went out to tea. They sat down on a page that was as spiffy as could be." Boy, given half a chance, we could come up with something guaranteed to nauseate the most desensitized parent.

Option+left bracket ([), Option+Shift+left bracket ([)

Well, children's book or no children's book, curly quotes are the number one symbol on our hit parade. If you walk away knowing nothing else, find out how to create a curly quote. Press Option+left bracket ([ ) to get the open quote ("),Option+Shift+left bracket ([ ) to get the close quote (").

Option+right bracket (]), Option+Shift+right bracket (])

Meanwhile, press Option+right bracket(]) to get the apostrophe ('), otherwise known as the single close quote mark. Press Option+Shift+right bracket(]) to get the single open quotation mark (').

PageMaker also offers an option that automatically converts straight quotes to curly quotes; it's called Use Typographer's Quotes, and you'll find it in the More Preferences dialog box (choose File⇨Preferences and click on the More button). For more information, see Chapter 8.

⌘+Shift+left bracket ([), ⌘+Shift+right bracket (])

If you choose the Use Typographer's Quotes option and you want to be able to access the straight quotation mark — the inches symbol — press ⌘+Shift+left bracket ([). To access the single straight quote, which is the foot symbol, press ⌘+Shift+right bracket (]).

The Bullet

Option+8

Your PC provides an inexhaustible arsenal of bullets at the touch of two keys, Option+8.

Zapf Dingbats and Wingdings

If you're interested in something more lively, check out the Zapf Dingbats font. You'll find special stars, shapes, numbers, and arrows that you can use to jazz up your text. You can even access check marks similar to the ones used as bullets in this book. The Wingdings font, a TrueType font, offers an interesting assortment of symbols, too.

The Em Space

⌘+Shift+M

The em space is an alternative to the tab. But rather than creating even columns of numbers, prices, and so on, the em space results in a fixed gap between a word and the word that follows it. The gap is exactly as wide as the type size is tall. If you want to see an example of this amazing space in action, refer back to Figure 8-15. To access the em space, press ⌘+Shift+M.

The Em Dash

Option+Shift+hyphen

It's good to know where all your punctuation is. Unlike the em space, which appears only in the most highfalutin of publications — it's okay, you should be highfalutin — the em dash is as common as mud. This paragraph uses two of them, in fact. To insert an em dash into your next sentence, press Option+Shift+ hyphen.

The Discretionary Hyphen

⌘+hyphen

PageMaker is supremely talented at hyphenating text but doesn't always get it right. If PageMaker misses an opportunity to hyphenate a word, you can help it by clicking at the desired point and pressing ⌘+hyphen. If PageMaker can use the hyphen, it breaks the word according to your specifications. If it can't quite manage to squeeze even the hyphenated syllable onto the preceding line of text, no hyphen appears. That's the beauty of discretionary hyphens; they only appear when they're needed. That way, you don't have to worry that you'll be left with a bunch of hyphens that are no longer needed after you edit your text.

Nonbreaking Characters

Option+spacebar, ⌘+Option+hyphen, ⌘+Option+slash (/)

PageMaker breaks words separated by a space, a hyphen, or a slash. If you don't want PageMaker to break two words separated by one of these characters, you have to use special nonbreaking characters. The nonbreaking space is Option+spacebar; the nonbreaking hyphen is ⌘+Option+hyphen; and the nonbreaking slash is ⌘+Option+slash (/). Remember, these characters bond like Krazy Glue. (So be sure not to get any on your fingers.)

The Line Break

Shift+Return

If you don't want to deal with nonbreaking characters, you can break a line at any point without creating a new paragraph by pressing Shift+Return. Lines divided by a line break character are all part of the same happy paragraph; PageMaker doesn't insert new paragraph spacing and indents as it would if you had inserted a standard carriage return by pressing the Return key without Shift.

The Copyright and Trademark Symbols

Option+G, Option+2, Option+R

Don't like folks stealing your precious ideas? You can protect those ideas with a few commonplace symbols. The copyright symbol (©), produced by pressing Option+G, tells folks that they're looking at your original work. The trademark symbol (™), which you can create by pressing Option+2, says that this name is indicative of your product, that you own it, and that you're in the process of filing it with the proper authorities. The registered trademark (®), produced by pressing Option+R, says that the name is now registered — government authorities have accepted the name as yours — so everything's official. Together, these symbols are the *No Trespassing, Beware of Dog,* and *Protected by Neighborhood Watch* signs of typography.

Accent Marks

Option+E, Option+grave key (`)

If you want your text to have a continental flair — for example, if you want to say *Meet me at the café* instead of the more pedestrian *Meet me at the cafe* — PageMaker can provide all the accent marks you need. To create an accent acute (as in *café*), press and release Option+E and then type the letter that gets the accent mark. To create an accent grave (as in *très jolie*), press and release Option+grave key (`) and then type the letter that gets the accent mark.

Option+U, Option+N, Option+C

To top a letter with a dieresis (as in *naïve*), press and release Option+U and then type the letter. To put a tilde on a letter (as in *piña colada*), press and release Option+N and type the letter. But to create a C cedilla, (as in *français*), just press Option+C.

The Automatic Page Number

⌘+Option+P

To tag any page with its page number automatically, press ⌘+Option+P.
Even if you later renumber your pages, the page number character will
update automatically.

Chapter 20

The Ten Shortcuts You'll Always Use

• •

In This Chapter

▶ Choosing commands in the File menu

▶ Zooming in and out on the page

▶ Scrolling and changing pages

▶ Displaying PageMaker's palettes

▶ Activating tools from the keyboard

▶ Choosing the Undo command

▶ Choosing Clipboard commands

▶ Using PageMaker's word processor, the Story Editor

▶ Applying formatting attributes

▶ Creating and editing styles and colors

• •

*T*he amount of money we spend on computers and other hardware that operate faster than our previous hardware is amazing. For a mere thousand dollars, you can shave seconds off your working day. But while your computer pushes new frontiers in speed, you're working at the same pace as always. Imagine this scenario from your computer's perspective: Here it is stuck with this same old-model user with no chance to update, *ever*.

The point is that you'll get a lot more work done a lot more quickly without spending a single penny if you find out how to work more efficiently. And the best way to save time is to discover the essential shortcuts, which are laid at your feet in this one-of-a-kind, efficiency-building chapter. No seminars, no weight lifting, no pyramid schemes. Just a few moments of your time, and you'll witness the most amazing transformation your computer has ever seen.

Opening, Saving, and Quitting

⌘+N, Return

To create a new one-page, letter-sized document (assuming default settings), press ⌘+N and then press Return. Don't even bother to look at the dialog box. If you want to customize the document a little, press ⌘+N and change the settings in the dialog box as desired.

⌘+O

To open a document that you created previously and saved to disk, press ⌘+O.

⌘+S

To save your document to disk, press ⌘+S. Do this early and do it often.

⌘+Q

To escape the generous clutches of PageMaker, press ⌘+Q. If you haven't saved your most recent changes, press Return to do so.

Zooming with Keyboard and Clicks

⌘+0, ⌘+1, ⌘+2, ⌘+5

To switch to Fit in Window view size, press ⌘+0. Press ⌘+1 to access the Actual Size view; ⌘+2 for 200 percent view size; and ⌘+5 for 50 percent view size.

⌘+Option+click, ⌘+Option+Shift+click

Press ⌘+Option+click to toggle between Fit in Window view and Actual Size view. Press ⌘+Option+Shift+click to toggle between Actual Size view and 200 percent size. The spot where you click becomes centered in the document window.

Zoom tool tricks

Click on an area of the page with the Zoom tool to zoom in on that area. To zoom out, press Option+click. Keep clicking to zoom in or out further. You can also drag around an area to zoom in on it.

To temporarily access the Zoom tool while you're working with another tool, press ⌘+spacebar to magnify and ⌘+spacebar+Option to zoom out. Click or drag to marquee (surround) an area when you see the zoom in or zoom out cursor.

Navigating inside Your Document

Option+drag

To move the page inside the window, Option+drag with any tool except the Zoom tool. Your cursor changes to the cute little grabber hand for the duration of your drag.

⌘+Tab, ⌘+Shift+Tab

Press ⌘+Tab to move to the next page or set of facing pages. To move back a page, press ⌘+Shift+Tab.

⌘+left bracket ([), p#, Return

If you want to go to a specific page, press ⌘+left bracket ([), enter the page number, and press the Return key. To go to a master page, press ⌘+left bracket ([), select the Master Page radio button, choose a master page from the pop-up menu, and press Return.

Shift+choose Layout⇨Go to Page

To peruse every page of your document, press the Shift key while choosing Layout⇨Go to Page. After you release the Shift key, PageMaker shows the next page spread, waits a few seconds, and then shows the page spread after that. PageMaker continues cycling, displaying the first page after the last page, until you click your mouse button. Give it a try!

Displaying Palettes

⌘+apostrophe, ⌘+Y, ⌘+K, ⌘+backslash (\), ⌘+H

You can display five palettes by pressing key combinations. Press ⌘+apostrophe to hide and show the Control palette. To access the Styles and Colors palettes, press ⌘+Y and ⌘+K, respectively. ⌘+backslash (\) displays and hides the Scripts palette, and ⌘+H accesses the Master Pages palette. Sadly, a keyboard shortcut for displaying and hiding the toolbox no longer exists.

Selecting Tools

If you work on a 13-inch screen, you're going to love this tip. Hide the toolbox by clicking on its Close button and access tools from the keyboard. The function keys correspond to the tools in the order that they appear in the toolbox. The Arrow tool is Shift+F1, the Text tool is Shift+F2, the Ellipse tool is Shift+F3, and so on, down to the Crop tool, which is Shift+F10.

Shift+F1, Shift+F2

The main tools to remember are the Arrow tool, Shift+F1, and the Text tool, Shift+F2. These two tools are far and away the most commonly used tools in PageMaker.

Shift+F3, Shift+F4, Shift+F5

Of secondary interest are the Ellipse tool, Shift+F3; the Rectangle tool, Shift+F4; and the Line tool, Shift+F5. These tools are useful for drawing rules and borders and simple shapes.

Shift+F6, Shift+F7, Shift+F8

You don't really need to memorize the shortcut for the Perpendicular Line tool, Shift+F6; if you want to draw perpendicular lines, just Shift+drag with the regular Line tool. But the new Polygon tool, Shift+F7, comes in handy for drawing shapes with more than four sides. And the Zoom tool, Shift+F8, is useful for quickly zooming in and out on your page.

Shift+F9, Shift+F10

Every once in a while, you may need the Rotate tool, Shift+F9, or the Crop tool, Shift+F10.

⌘+spacebar

To toggle between the Arrow tool and the currently selected tool, press ⌘+spacebar. For example, if the Text tool is selected, pressing ⌘+spacebar selects the Arrow tool. Pressing ⌘+spacebar again takes you back to the Arrow tool. Go ahead, give it a try. You'll fall in love all over again.

Note that ⌘+spacebar is also the shortcut to temporarily access the Zoom tool. If you press and hold the two keys, you get the Zoom tool cursor; you can then click or drag to zoom in on your document. If you just press and release the two keys, you get the Arrow tool. Fancy that, two shortcuts for the price of one!

Undoing Mistakes

⌘+Z

If you want to eliminate the last action you performed, press ⌘+Z. Unfortunately, PageMaker can't undo as many operations as it should — it can't undo text formatting, for example — and it can't undo any action except the very last one, but sometimes the Undo feature comes in handy. For example, if you delete an entire text block, ⌘+Z brings it back to life.

Making Copies

⌘+X, ⌘+C, ⌘+V

To cut some selected text or a selected graphic and transfer it to the Clipboard, press ⌘+X. To copy a selection, press ⌘+C. And to paste the contents of the Clipboard into your PageMaker document, press ⌘+V.

Editing Text in the Story Editor

⌘+E

To enter the Story Editor, select some text with either the Arrow or Text tool and press ⌘+E. Pressing ⌘+E again takes you back to the Layout view.

⌘+L, Return

Inside the Story Editor, you can press ⌘+L and then Return to check the spelling of your text. (The Return key activates the Start button inside the Spelling dialog box.)

⌘+H, text, Return

To search for some text while working in the Story Editor, press ⌘+H, enter the text, and press Return. To search for one bit of text and replace it with another, press ⌘+H, enter the text you want to search for, press Tab, enter the text you want PageMaker to substitute, and press Return.

⌘+A

To select all text, press ⌘+A. If you choose this shortcut in Layout view when the Text tool is inside a text block, all text in the story is selected. If the Arrow tool is selected, PageMaker selects everything in your document.

Formatting Text

PageMaker provides lots of ways to change the formatting of text from the keyboard. Here are just a few of the most popular shortcuts.

⌘+Shift+period, ⌘+Shift+comma, ⌘+Option+Shift+period, ⌘+Option+Shift+comma

To increase the type size to the next menu size — 10, 11, 12, 14, 18, and so on — press ⌘+Shift+period. Press ⌘+Shift+comma to reduce the type size. Both shortcuts are applicable only to characters selected with the Text tool. Press

⌘+Option+Shift+period to increase the size by one point; press ⌘+Option+Shift+comma to decrease the text one point size.

⌘+Delete, ⌘+Shift+Delete, Option+Delete, Option+Shift+Delete

To kern two letters closer together by $^1/_{25}$ em space, click between them with the Text tool and then press ⌘+Delete. Press ⌘+Shift+Delete to kern the letters apart by the same amount. To kern characters together by $^1/_{100}$ em space, press Option+Delete; press Option+Shift+Delete to kern characters apart by the same amount (on some keyboards, the Delete key is labeled Backspace). These shortcuts are also applicable to multiple selected characters, enabling you to kern several letters at a time.

⌘+Shift+L, ⌘+Shift+C, ⌘+Shift+R, ⌘+Shift+J, ⌘+Shift+F

To change the alignment of a paragraph selected with the Text tool, press ⌘ and Shift plus the first letter of the alignment; left is ⌘+Shift+L, for example. Centered is ⌘+Shift+C. Right is ⌘+Shift+R, and justified is ⌘+Shift+J. To make fully justified text — in which the last line of the paragraph is also justified — press ⌘+Shift+F.

⌘+T, ⌘+M, ⌘+I

These shortcuts access PageMaker's tried-and-true dialog boxes of formatting options. To display the Type Specifications dialog box — which controls the formatting of selected characters — press ⌘+T. To format entire paragraphs, press ⌘+M to display the Paragraph Specifications dialog box. (PageMaker adopted this keyboard equivalent from Microsoft Word, but where Microsoft got it is anyone's guess.) To set tabs, press ⌘+I to display the Indents/Tabs dialog box.

Making Styles and Colors

⌘+click

With the Styles palette on-screen, you can edit styles and create new ones by ⌘+clicking. ⌘+click on any style name to edit it. ⌘+click on No Style at the top of the palette to create a new style sheet.

This same technique allows you to edit and create colors in the Colors palette. ⌘+click on any color name to edit it. To create a new color, ⌘+click on the Black or Registration color.

Chapter 21

Ten Typefaces Everyone
Should Have

· ·

In This Chapter

▶ Helvetica

▶ Antique Olive

▶ New Baskerville

▶ Garamond

▶ Palatino

▶ Bodoni

▶ American Typewriter

▶ Mistral and other scripts

▶ Herculaneum and other display faces

▶ Zapf Dingbats

· ·

*1*f you're a new PageMaker user, one of your first questions probably will be, "What typefaces should I use?"

The answer, of course, is, "Why, whatever you think looks good."

"But," you say, "I have no taste."

"Yes, you do," we respond. "You just need to have more faith in yourself. Try experimenting with a few fonts to see how they look together and build your library based on that."

"No, you don't understand," you protest. "I still wear leisure suits, and I drive a Gremlin."

"Uh-oh, this is worse than we thought."

For those of you who need a little help — taste or no taste — we offer this chapter. Keep in mind, however, that selecting typefaces is an incredibly subjective task. So rather than throwing out a hit parade of favorites, we steer you toward a few tried-and-true solutions that have been around long enough to find mainstream acceptance.

These fonts were selected from the Adobe Typeface Library, because Adobe is probably the most established. Adobe also licenses its fonts from the source, meaning that you get the font as it was originally designed. See, you can't copyright typefaces, only their names. So if other font manufacturers see a typeface they like, they can feel free to copy it as long as they name it something different, like Missive instead of Mistral. As your grandpappy told you, life ain't always fair.

The upshot of all this is that Adobe's fonts are of the absolute highest quality. They are also readily available at your local service bureau or commercial printer. But they're expensive — roughly $100 to $200 per family of four typestyles. For that same price, you can get 100 fonts from a knockoff vendor. Either way, you get basically the same font.

Whether you decide to ante up for authentic Adobe fonts or opt for knockoffs, following are ten choices you'll want to keep in your collection.

Helvetica

If you were to conduct a scientific survey to determine the most legible font at all type sizes, Helvetica would probably come out the winner. Sure, Helvetica is kind of boring, and it appears in just about every desktop-published document in the Western world, but it absolutely epitomizes stability and flexibility.

Its no-nonsense approach seems to provide type designers with constant inspiration. Helvetica is sort of the Meryl Streep of fonts, a blank canvas that lends itself well to one makeover after another. Since its debut in 1957, Helvetica has been the subject of countless stylistic variations, just a few of which are shown in Figure 21-1. The Adobe Type Library alone contains nearly 100 different styles of the font, including outline, condensed, expanded, and rounded. Our recommendation: Buy all the Helveticas you can get your hands on.

Helvetica

Helvetica Light

**Helvetica
Black Oblique**

Helvetica Condensed

*Helvetica Condensed
Bold Oblique*

Helvetica Compressed Extra

Helvetica Inserat

Figure 21-1:
These are
but a few of
the half-
billion
variations
on
Helvetica.

Antique Olive

If you're looking for a sans serif face with a little more flair than Helvetica, you can't go wrong with Antique Olive. Although its name may conjure up images of Popeye's girlfriend in a retirement home, Antique Olive is actually a highly distinctive font, sporting angular *terminals* (the ends of the characters) and variable-weight strokes, as demonstrated by the variations shown in Figure 21-2.

Don't you just love this font talk? Well, the practical upshot is, if you want to add a little attitude to your sans serif text, use Antique Olive. And if Antique Olive isn't quite your cup of tea, try out Optima, Kabel, or Eras, each of which is equally distinctive and offers its own unique flair. They all prove that sans serif fonts don't have to be as boring or dated as the PostScript standard, Avant Garde Gothic.

Antique Olive

Antique Olive Italic

Antique Olive Light

Antique Olive Black

Antique Olive Nord

Antique Olive Compact

Antique Olive Condensed Bold

Figure 21-2: Antique Olive shows that sans serif fonts can be as individual and stylish as their serifed cousins.

New Baskerville

Ultimately a conservative and symmetrical face, New Baskerville is at the same time stylish and versatile, as shown in Figure 21-3. Though named after 18th-century book designer John Baskerville, New Baskerville bears only passing resemblance to Baskerville's specimens. If you want to get a little closer to his roots, look to Berthold Baskerville Book from the venerable Berlin-based foundry.

New Baskerville

New Baskerville Italic

New Baskerville Bold

New Baskerville Bold Italic

Figure 21-3:
The four basic styles of New Baskerville.

Garamond

Claude Garamond designed type back in the 16th century and is considered by many to be the father of modern typography. His primary legacy is a font that's named for him but is actually based on a recutting made by contemporary Jean Jannon and wrongly ascribed to Garamond around the turn of our century. Meanwhile, the italics came from Robert Granjon, a friend of Garamond, who helped to divide the labor. Still, the modern font looks a lot like the stuff Claude used to carve, so the name stuck.

After that introduction, you'd expect Garamond to be a dusty relic, of interest only to type historians and wholly illegible by modern standards. But as Figure 21-4 shows, this assumption is anything but the case. Garamond is perhaps the most widely available, modified and remodified typeface short of Helvetica. And unlike Helvetica, the font is the absolute picture of grace and elegance, almost soft in appearance and full of little flourishes that keep it interesting after many years of use.

For other typefaces with historic appeal, try out Bembo (based on the first roman typeface designed by Aldus Manutius), Granjon, Galliard, and Caslon. The last of these is based on the 18th-century designs of William Caslon and was, according to type historian Douglas C. McMurtrie, "as good a book type as has ever been produced." He wrote that in 1938, before most of the fonts in this chapter had been produced, but it's still one heck of a recommendation.

Garamond Light

Garamond Book Italic

Garamond Bold

Garamond Ultra

Garamond Three Regular

Garamond Three
Bold Italic

Berthold Garamond

Berthold Garamond
Medium Italic

Berthold Garamond
Condensed

Figure 21-4:
Garamond and its many variations are based on some of the oldest roman type designs in existence.

Palatino

All this history making you thirsty for something a little more modern? Well, then, look no further than Palatino. Created by modern type wiz Hermann Zapf, Palatino is a modernization of the age-old designs of Garamond and the gang. The font features chiseled terminals, sculpted transitional strokes, and calligraphic italics, all of which appear in Figure 21-5.

The best news about Palatino is that it's built into virtually all PostScript printers. If you want to add to your Palatino collection, more styles are available. Ironically, Zapf created Palatino exclusively for headlines and logos, but it caught on for body text as well. To complement Palatino, Zapf created a lighter font called Aldus that looks better at very small type sizes, such as 9 points and smaller.

Figure 21-5:
The four styles of Palatino built into most PostScript printers.

Palatino

Palatino Italic

Palatino Bold

Palatino
Bold Italic

Bodoni

The Didots were an illustrious family of French printers from the late 18th century. It is said that François Ambroise Didot tutored Benjamin Franklin's grandson in the art of typography. Ironically, however, the most famous creator of so-called Didone fonts was an Italian named Giambattista Bodoni. Some say he got in cheap by lifting Didot's style. Some say he *perfected* it. Either way, he ended up creating something along the lines of the styles shown in Figure 21-6.

Like all Didone styles, Bodoni features very thick vertical strokes and hairline horizontal strokes. This radical contrast between neighboring stems makes for a highly stylized font that works well at larger sizes, say, 12 points and up. Other Didone styles include New Caledonia and, to a lesser extent, New Century Schoolbook, the font built into most PostScript laser printers.

Bodoni

Bodoni Italic

Bodoni Book

Bodoni Bold Italic

Bodoni Poster

Bodoni Condensed Bold

Bodoni Compressed Poster

Figure 21-6:
The Bodoni family includes dozens of variations, including the ultra-heavy Bodoni Poster.

American Typewriter

If you want to impart a typewriter look to your pages, avoid Courier and instead try out American Typewriter, shown in Figure 21-7. American Typewriter is just the thing for that "Extra, extra, read all about it!" look.

American Typewriter falls into a category of type called *slab serifs,* which gained momentum during the Industrial Revolution of the 1800s. (They're called slab serifs because the serifs are so big and slabby.) The difference between Typewriter and other slab serifs — such as Clarendon and Melior — is that the stroke weight of Typewriter characters is uniform throughout. In other words, the serifs are just as thick as the stems, perfect for hearty text that reproduces well even at small sizes.

American
Typewriter Light

American
Typewriter
Medium

**American
Typewriter Bold**

American Typewriter
Condensed

Figure 21-7:
American
Typewriter
reproduces
well,
regardless
of how
many times
you
photocopy
it.

Script Faces

Having the gang over for a few hands of pinochle? Thinking of getting hitched, and you want to create your own invites? Well, then, you need some script faces. As shown in Figure 21-8, characters set in script faces typically join together, just like they do in cursive handwriting. This means that you can't kern them or change the letter spacing, as in a justified paragraph. If you do, you change the amount of space between neighboring characters, and the letters no longer join correctly.

> *Mistral*
>
> **Brush Script**
>
> *Shelley Allegro*
>
> *Shelley Volante*
>
> *Snell Roundhand*
>
> ***Snell Roundhand Black***

Figure 21-8:
Text set in
script faces
generally
looks like it
was written
in one
continuous
stroke.

Display Faces

One thing you may have noticed about the fonts discussed so far is that they're not very wacky. That's because wacky fonts — like the ones shown in Figure 21-9 — aren't particularly legible at small sizes. For example, can you imagine reading a whole paragraph set in Arnold Böcklin? Only a unicorn could put up with that font for more than a few words. But although they aren't suitable for body text, these so-called display fonts are great for headlines, logos, and other large type (18 points or larger).

It's good to have an arsenal of these fonts at your fingertips. Why? Because you can't use them very often. They're so unique that your readers will notice if you use them over and over. For example, you might set the headline for a monthly column about World War I paraphernalia in the font Wilhelm Klingspor Gotisch. But if you did, you wouldn't want to use that font anywhere else in your newsletter. It's just too obvious.

Zapf Dingbats

The last font on the hit parade, illustrated in Figure 21-10, is Zapf Dingbats, another font built into most laser printers. Rather than being composed of letters, Dingbats comprises more than 250 symbols. You'll find check marks, crosses, stars, flowers, arrows, and a bunch of other doohickeys. Some of them are a little dated — Hermann Zapf created the font in the '70s — but you can find all sorts of useful stuff if you search around.

Other useful symbol fonts include Symbol (built into all PostScript printers), Wingdings, Carta, Bundesbahn Pi, and Lucida Math.

More Fonts!

By limiting this list to ten (or so) fonts, we can't even begin to scrape the surface of what's out there. If you're feeling ambitious, following are some other faces that we suggest you look into:

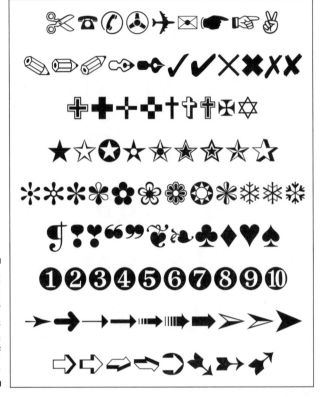

Figure 21-10: A smattering of the many symbols available in Zapf Dingbats.

✔ **Melior:** This font's squarish forms make it highly readable at very small sizes. The screen font is especially nice when you're working on long blocks of text.

✔ **Berkeley Oldstyle:** Armed with unusual diagonal crossbars, angled vowels, and calligraphic italics, this face harkens back to the first roman typefaces. Based on a design for the University of California Press created by the father of American typography, Frederic W. Goudy, this font is another favorite.

✔ **Souvenir:** Okay, Souvenir's been called the "happy face of type," but the sloping letterforms and plastic transitions of Souvenir are hard not to like. The designer of this font is Ed Benguiat, who also created Korinna, Tiffany, and, of course, Benguiat.

✔ **Tekton:** Invented by Adobe's type staff, this face is based on the meticulous hand lettering of architect Francis Ching, complete with little balls at the terminals of the letters.

✔ **Lithos:** Available only in capital letters, these chiseled letterforms are available in a variety of weights. Also check out Trajan and Charlemagne.

Tons more fonts are available, but if we continue like this, you'll think that we're total type dweebs (a label that we wear proudly, thank you very much). So, to finish things off, how about if we stop telling you which fonts we like and focus a moment's attention on the ones we *don't* like?

- **Wood Type:** These display typefaces harken back to the woodcut letters of the Old West. They're kind of fun, but honestly, how many "Wanted!" posters are you going to typeset?

- **Zapf Chancery:** This font has become synonymous with cheesy restaurant menus. Thanks to the fact that it's installed in nearly all PostScript laser printers, Zapf Chancery is absolutely the most overused script in existence. And — with all due respect to Mr. Zapf — Zapf Chancery is ugly to boot.

- **Courier:** Your Mac is not a typewriter.

- **Futura:** Perhaps the least interesting sans serif font on the planet, Futura features miserable little lowercase letters and overly geometric letterforms. Futura Condensed is a marked improvement; at large sizes, it can even look stylish.

Of course, these are just personal peeves. You may love all these fonts. But if you use them, keep in mind that at least two snooty typeface aficionados out there are looking at your document and saying, "Yuck." And it's likely that we're not alone. So if you're tempted to use one of these rather clichéd fonts, try experimenting with something more sophisticated instead. It's a pretty sure bet that you'll get a better response from readers. At the least, you'll make us very proud.

Appendix

How to (Re)Install PageMaker

●●

*I*nstalling PageMaker is an easy, straightforward process. But just in case you're a novice at installing programs, this chapter walks you through the basics.

If You're Upgrading from Version 5

If you're upgrading from PageMaker Version 5, be aware that many of your custom settings, such as tracking values and custom dictionaries, aren't automatically available to you after you install Version 6. If you want to use these custom settings in Version 6, you have to copy the Version 5 custom setting files, which are stored in the Aldus folder, into the RSRC folder in the Adobe PageMaker 6 folder. PageMaker 6 provides a utility called Use PM5 Custom Settings that helps you accomplish the same task; for complete information, see the *Getting Started* guide that came with your copy of PageMaker.

Installing Version 6

Before you begin installing PageMaker, turn off any virus-checking programs that may be running on your computer, because these programs can interfere with the installation process. (You can usually turn off virus-checking programs via the Apple menu's Control Panel.) Because PageMaker may need to restart your Mac after installation, you should also save and close any open documents.

If you're installing from floppy disks, you may want to turn off all extensions on your Mac by pressing the Shift key as you choose Special⇨Restart. Hold down the Shift key until you see the notice that all extensions are turned off. If you're installing from CD-ROM, however, *don't* use this procedure; you'll disable some extensions that PageMaker needs during installation. Instead, if you're running System 7.5, choose the Control Panel item from the Apple menu, and then select the Extensions Manager item. Then choose the System 7.5 Only option from the Sets menu.

PageMaker does not support QuickDraw GX. If you have QuickDraw GX installed and active on your Mac, you need to either remove or disable it before installing PageMaker. For more information, see the sidebar, "What about QuickDraw GX?" in Chapter 17.

With those little issues out of the way, you're now ready to move ahead with the installation process:

1. **Put the PageMaker CD-ROM into your CD-ROM drive.**

   (Or, if you're installing from floppy disks, insert Disk 1 and skip to step 4.) After your Mac mounts the CD-ROM, you should see a window containing various items related to PageMaker.

2. **Double-click on the Adobe PageMaker 6 folder.**

   A new window opens, this time containing an Install folder.

3. **Double-click on the Install folder.**

   The Install window opens.

4. **Double-click on the PageMaker 6 Installer/Utility icon.**

   You see a PageMaker 6 Installer opening screen, which offers three language option buttons: U.S. English, Canadian English, and International English. Your choice here determines the spellings and lingo used in PageMaker's dialog boxes, menus, and such. For example, instead of a Colors palette menu item, you see a Colours palette menu item. Your choice of language here *doesn't* affect the internal dictionary that PageMaker uses when spell-checking your document; you choose that language later in the installation process.

   The Quit button at the bottom of the Installer screen is provided just in case you're overwhelmed by the prospect of choosing which language version you want to install. If you click on it, the Installer program politely closes (although it's probably snickering behind your back just a little).

5. **Click on Continue.**

   That is, click on Continue if you followed the instructions and saved any open documents and turned off QuickDraw GX. If you didn't follow those instructions, click on Quit and go back and read the paragraphs at the beginning of this section. And this time, heed our advice, okay?

6. **Choose an installation type.**

   After you select a language, PageMaker displays a dialog box asking you to choose an installation mode:

   ✔ If you select the Easy Install option, all of PageMaker's bells and whistles are installed. This option requires from 32MB to more than 40MB of disk space.

✔ If you're short on disk space, you can choose the Minimum install option, which installs only those components that are absolutely required to run PageMaker. This option requires 20 to 30MB of disk space. Or you can choose Custom install and pick and choose which components you want to install. For example, you may want to turn off the option that installs PageMaker's built-in tutorial guide.

✔ If you choose Custom install, you're presented with a list of options to install. Check those options that you want to install. Adobe PageMaker 6 is checked by default; you need to keep it checked to install the files necessary to run the program. If you're not sure whether you'll need a particular option, go ahead and select it just to be safe. Keep in mind, too, that you can always return to the setup program and install additional components later, if needed.

7. Click on Install.

PageMaker displays a dialog box asking for your personal information. Do as you're told and enter your name, company name, and the PageMaker serial number. (Actually, if you're feeling rebellious, you don't have to enter a company name.) The serial number should be printed on Disk 2 if you're installing from floppies. You can also find the number on your product registration card. If you're upgrading from an earlier version of PageMaker, use the serial number for that version.

After you enter the requested information, click on OK and then click on OK again when PageMaker asks you to confirm that you entered everything correctly.

8. Choose the version of PageMaker that matches your Mac.

If you're installing on a Power Macintosh, choose the Power Macintosh button. Otherwise, click on the Macintosh button.

9. Select a dictionary language.

Your next decision is which dictionary you want to install. PageMaker uses these dictionaries when performing spell-checking and hyphenation functions. You can choose one or all of the following dictionaries: U.S. English, U.K. English, and French-Canadian (français-canadien). If you won't be creating publications for the French-Canadian or U.K. market, don't select those dictionaries — remember that every component you install eats up more precious hard disk space.

10. Click on OK.

The dialog box you see next depends on whether you chose the Easy Install, Minimum Install, or Custom option in step 6. If you chose Easy Install or Minimum Install, PageMaker asks you to select the PPDs you want to install. If you'll be printing to a PostScript printer, click on the PPD for that printer. Shift+click to install additional PPDs (you can install as many as you need). Don't forget to install any printers that your service bureau uses to output your documents. (For a more in-depth discussion of PPDs, see Chapter 17.)

If you don't see a PPD that matches your printer, you can usually obtain one from your printer manufacturer. You can also try installing a PPD for any of the Apple LaserWriters; these printers have been the standard for PostScript printing for a long time, and many other PostScript printers can use LaserWriter PPDs.

If you're doing an Easy Install, move to step 11. If you're doing a Minimum Install, skip to step 12.

If you chose Custom in step 6, you're asked to select various components related to the options you chose to install. For example, if you checked the Color Libraries option, you get the chance to select the specific color libraries you want to install. To choose one item, click on it; to choose additional items, Shift+click on them. If you want to select all the components in a dialog box, click on the Select All button. Click on OK to move on to the next dialog box and select additional items to install. When you've worked your way through all the custom install dialog boxes, skip to step 12.

11. **Click on OK and ignore the next dialog box.**

After you exit the PPD dialog box, PageMaker asks you to choose Kodak Precision CMS Device Profiles. This is PageMaker's obtuse way of asking you to tell it which pieces of hardware you use to create and print your documents — your brand of scanner, monitor, printer, and so on. PageMaker uses this information if you opt to use the Kodak Color Management System, which is included with PageMaker 6.

As explained in Chapter 9, you need to worry about color-management issues only if you're dealing with very high-end color publishing. So don't worry about selecting any CMS device profiles (you can always come back and install them later if you find that you need them). Just click on OK to exit the dialog box and move on.

12. **Specify where you want to store the PageMaker files.**

When you see the Install Files dialog box, make sure that your hard drive appears in the Folder pop-up menu above the scrolling list of folders. By default, PageMaker installs itself in a folder called Adobe PageMaker 6.0. You have the option of renaming this folder if you want, but it's a good idea just to let things be.

13. **Click on Install.**

You should see an installer dialog box with a progress bar showing you how many files PageMaker has installed and how many more it has yet to copy. If you're installing from floppy disks, just insert the proper disk when you're prompted to do so.

14. **Register your copy of the program — or not.**

When the installation process is complete, you see a screen that invites you to register your copy of the program by modem. If you have a modem and want to register, click on the Continue button and follow the on-screen prompts. Otherwise, click on Cancel. When PageMaker asks you whether you really and truly want to exit out of the registration process, respond in the affirmative.

When the installation process is complete, PageMaker displays an installation screen that says that everything was installed properly. You may also be asked to restart your computer. If so, click on the Restart button.

What about This Other Stuff on the CD?

If you bought the Deluxe CD-ROM version of PageMaker, you also get a bunch of goodies in addition to the main PageMaker program, including demonstration versions of other Adobe programs, such as Adobe Photoshop and Illustrator; an assortment of Photo CD images that you can place in your PageMaker documents; examples of PageMaker layouts created by some leading design firms; and an interactive multimedia guide to PageMaker 6.

You also get these additional programs, which you can install if you like:

✔ Adobe Acrobat Distiller: You need this program to create PDF files for electronic distribution of your PageMaker documents, as explained in Chapter 18. To install it, double-click on the Acrobat Distiller Install icon in the Adobe PageMaker Deluxe window. (To open the window, put the PageMaker CD in your CD-ROM drive and then double-click on the CD-ROM icon on the Finder desktop.) When the Acrobat Distiller Install window appears, double-click on the Disk 1 folder icon, and when the Disk 1 window opens, double-click on the Installer icon. Then just follow the on-screen prompts. (If you're unsure of which options to choose during installation, just accept the default settings, which are usually the best settings anyway.)

✔ Adobe Acrobat Reader: Install this program if you want to be able to view PDF files, including the technical notes files and other text documents on the PageMaker CD-ROM. Double-click on the Acrobat Reader Install folder in the Adobe PageMaker Deluxe window, double-click on the Acro-Read.mac item in the Acrobat Reader Install window, and then follow the on-screen prompts to install the program.

Even if you don't care about viewing PDF files, you may want to install the Acrobat Reader program anyway, because Adobe Type Manager (ATM) 3.8.3 is installed along with it. If you don't already have this version of

ATM (or later) on your system, we highly recommend that you install it. Among other things, ATM enables you to print PostScript fonts on a non-PostScript printer.

✔ QuickTime 2.0: You need QuickTime 2.0 and the Apple Multimedia Tuner installed if you want to view the movies provided in the Welcome to PageMaker 6.0 multimedia guide on the PageMaker CD. To install them, double-click on the Apple QuickTime & Extensions folder in the Adobe PageMaker 6.0 Deluxe window. Then copy the Apple Multimedia Tuner and QuickTime items to your System Folder. If you're working on a Power Macintosh, also copy the QuickTime PowerPlug item. If you're using System 7.1, you need to copy the four extensions in the For System 7.1 Users folder to the System Folder as well and then enable the extensions. After copying the necessary stuff to your System Folder, restart your Mac.

Reinstalling PageMaker

After you've installed PageMaker, you can always return to the installation program to add a PPD file, CMS device profile, or any other component. Just follow the PageMaker installation instructions given earlier in this chapter, but choose Custom as your installation type. You can then select those components that you want to install.

Index

(continued)

(continued)

Notes

Notes

Notes

The Fun & Easy Way™ to learn about computers and more!

Windows® 3.11 For Dummies,® 3rd Edition
by Andy Rathbone

ISBN: 1-56884-370-4
$16.95 USA/
$22.95 Canada

Mutual Funds For Dummies™
by Eric Tyson

ISBN: 1-56884-226-0
$16.99 USA/
$22.99 Canada

DOS For Dummies,® 2nd Edition
by Dan Gookin

ISBN: 1-878058-75-4
$16.95 USA/
$22.95 Canada

The Internet For Dummies,® 2nd Edition
by John Levine & Carol Baroudi

ISBN: 1-56884-222-8
$19.99 USA/
$26.99 Canada

Personal Finance For Dummies™
by Eric Tyson

ISBN: 1-56884-150-7
$16.95 USA/
$22.95 Canada

PCs For Dummies,® 3rd Edition
by Dan Gookin & Andy Rathbone

ISBN: 1-56884-904-4
$16.99 USA/
$22.99 Canada

Macs® For Dummies,® 3rd Edition
by David Pogue

ISBN: 1-56884-239-2
$19.99 USA/
$26.99 Canada

The SAT® I For Dummies™
by Suzee Vlk

ISBN: 1-56884-213-9
$14.99 USA/
$20.99 Canada

Here's a complete listing of IDG Books' ...For Dummies® titles

Title	Author	ISBN	Price
DATABASE			
Access 2 For Dummies®	by Scott Palmer	ISBN: 1-56884-090-X	$19.95 USA/$26.95 Canada
Access Programming For Dummies®	by Rob Krumm	ISBN: 1-56884-091-8	$19.95 USA/$26.95 Canada
Approach 3 For Windows® For Dummies®	by Doug Lowe	ISBN: 1-56884-233-3	$19.99 USA/$26.99 Canada
dBASE For DOS For Dummies®	by Scott Palmer & Michael Stabler	ISBN: 1-56884-188-4	$19.95 USA/$26.95 Canada
dBASE For Windows® For Dummies®	by Scott Palmer	ISBN: 1-56884-179-5	$19.95 USA/$26.95 Canada
dBASE 5 For Windows® Programming For Dummies®	by Ted Coombs & Jason Coombs	ISBN: 1-56884-215-5	$19.99 USA/$26.99 Canada
FoxPro 2.6 For Windows® For Dummies®	by John Kaufeld	ISBN: 1-56884-187-6	$19.95 USA/$26.95 Canada
Paradox 5 For Windows® For Dummies®	by John Kaufeld	ISBN: 1-56884-185-X	$19.95 USA/$26.95 Canada
DESKTOP PUBLISHING/ILLUSTRATION/GRAPHICS			
CorelDRAW! 5 For Dummies®	by Deke McClelland	ISBN: 1-56884-157-4	$19.95 USA/$26.95 Canada
CorelDRAW! For Dummies®	by Deke McClelland	ISBN: 1-56884-042-X	$19.95 USA/$26.95 Canada
Desktop Publishing & Design For Dummies®	by Roger C. Parker	ISBN: 1-56884-234-1	$19.99 USA/$26.99 Canada
Harvard Graphics 2 For Windows® For Dummies®	by Roger C. Parker	ISBN: 1-56884-092-6	$19.95 USA/$26.95 Canada
PageMaker 5 For Macs® For Dummies®	by Galen Gruman & Deke McClelland	ISBN: 1-56884-178-7	$19.95 USA/$26.95 Canada
PageMaker 5 For Windows® For Dummies®	by Deke McClelland & Galen Gruman	ISBN: 1-56884-160-4	$19.95 USA/$26.95 Canada
Photoshop 3 For Macs® For Dummies®	by Deke McClelland	ISBN: 1-56884-208-2	$19.99 USA/$26.99 Canada
QuarkXPress 3.3 For Dummies®	by Galen Gruman & Barbara Assadi	ISBN: 1-56884-217-1	$19.99 USA/$26.99 Canada
FINANCE/PERSONAL FINANCE/TEST TAKING REFERENCE			
Everyday Math For Dummies™	by Charles Seiter	ISBN: 1-56884-248-1	$14.99 USA/$22.99 Canada
Personal Finance For Dummies™ For Canadians	by Eric Tyson & Tony Martin	ISBN: 1-56884-378-X	$18.99 USA/$24.99 Canada
QuickBooks 3 For Dummies®	by Stephen L. Nelson	ISBN: 1-56884-227-9	$19.99 USA/$26.99 Canada
Quicken 8 For DOS For Dummies,® 2nd Edition	by Stephen L. Nelson	ISBN: 1-56884-210-4	$19.95 USA/$26.95 Canada
Quicken 5 For Macs® For Dummies®	by Stephen L. Nelson	ISBN: 1-56884-211-2	$19.95 USA/$26.95 Canada
Quicken 4 For Windows® For Dummies,® 2nd Edition	by Stephen L. Nelson	ISBN: 1-56884-209-0	$19.95 USA/$26.95 Canada
Taxes For Dummies,™ 1995 Edition	by Eric Tyson & David J. Silverman	ISBN: 1-56884-220-1	$14.99 USA/$20.99 Canada
The GMAT® For Dummies™	by Suzee Vlk, Series Editor	ISBN: 1-56884-376-3	$14.99 USA/$20.99 Canada
The GRE® For Dummies™	by Suzee Vlk, Series Editor	ISBN: 1-56884-375-5	$14.99 USA/$20.99 Canada
Time Management For Dummies™	by Jeffrey J. Mayer	ISBN: 1-56884-360-7	$16.99 USA/$22.99 Canada
TurboTax For Windows® For Dummies®	by Gail A. Helsel, CPA	ISBN: 1-56884-228-7	$19.99 USA/$26.99 Canada
GROUPWARE/INTEGRATED			
ClarisWorks For Macs® For Dummies®	by Frank Higgins	ISBN: 1-56884-363-1	$19.99 USA/$26.99 Canada
Lotus Notes For Dummies®	by Pat Freeland & Stephen Londergan	ISBN: 1-56884-212-0	$19.95 USA/$26.95 Canada
Microsoft® Office 4 For Windows® For Dummies®	by Roger C. Parker	ISBN: 1-56884-183-3	$19.95 USA/$26.95 Canada
Microsoft® Works 3 For Windows® For Dummies®	by David C. Kay	ISBN: 1-56884-214-7	$19.99 USA/$26.99 Canada
SmartSuite 3 For Dummies®	by Jan Weingarten & John Weingarten	ISBN: 1-56884-367-4	$19.99 USA/$26.99 Canada
INTERNET/COMMUNICATIONS/NETWORKING			
America Online® For Dummies,® 2nd Edition	by John Kaufeld	ISBN: 1-56884-933-8	$19.99 USA/$26.99 Canada
CompuServe For Dummies,® 2nd Edition	by Wallace Wang	ISBN: 1-56884-937-0	$19.99 USA/$26.99 Canada
Modems For Dummies,® 2nd Edition	by Tina Rathbone	ISBN: 1-56884-223-6	$19.99 USA/$26.99 Canada
MORE Internet For Dummies®	by John R. Levine & Margaret Levine Young	ISBN: 1-56884-164-7	$19.95 USA/$26.95 Canada
MORE Modems & On-line Services For Dummies®	by Tina Rathbone	ISBN: 1-56884-365-8	$19.99 USA/$26.99 Canada
Mosaic For Dummies,® Windows Edition	by David Angell & Brent Heslop	ISBN: 1-56884-242-2	$19.99 USA/$26.99 Canada
NetWare For Dummies,® 2nd Edition	by Ed Tittel, Deni Connor & Earl Follis	ISBN: 1-56884-369-0	$19.99 USA/$26.99 Canada
Networking For Dummies®	by Doug Lowe	ISBN: 1-56884-079-9	$19.95 USA/$26.95 Canada
PROCOMM PLUS 2 For Windows® For Dummies®	by Wallace Wang	ISBN: 1-56884-219-8	$19.99 USA/$26.99 Canada
TCP/IP For Dummies®	by Marshall Wilensky & Candace Leiden	ISBN: 1-56884-241-4	$19.99 USA/$26.99 Canada

Microsoft and Windows are registered trademarks of Microsoft Corporation. Mac is a registered trademark of Apple Computer. SAT is a registered trademark of the College Entrance Examination Board. GMAT is a registered trademark of the Graduate Management Admission Council. GRE is a registered trademark of the Educational Testing Service. America Online is a registered trademark of America Online, Inc. The "...For Dummies Book Series" logo, the IDG Books Worldwide logos, Dummies Press, and The Fun & Easy Way are trademarks, and ---- For Dummies and ... For Dummies are registered trademarks under exclusive license to IDG Books Worldwide, Inc., from International Data Group, Inc.

For scholastic requests & educational orders please Educational Sales at 1. 800. 434. 2086

FOR MORE INFO OR TO ORDER, PLEASE CALL ▶ 800. 762. 2974

For volume discounts & special orders please call Tony Real, Special Sales, at 415. 655. 3048

Title	Author	ISBN	Price
The Internet For Macs® For Dummies® 2nd Edition	by Charles Seiter	ISBN: 1-56884-371-2	$19.99 USA/$26.99 Canada
The Internet For Macs® For Dummies® Starter Kit	by Charles Seiter	ISBN: 1-56884-244-9	$29.99 USA/$39.99 Canada
The Internet For Macs® For Dummies® Starter Kit Bestseller Edition	by Charles Seiter	ISBN: 1-56884-245-7	$39.99 USA/$54.99 Canada
The Internet For Windows® For Dummies® Starter Kit	by John R. Levine & Margaret Levine Young	ISBN: 1-56884-237-6	$34.99 USA/$44.99 Canada
The Internet For Windows® For Dummies® Starter Kit, Bestseller Edition	by John R. Levine & Margaret Levine Young	ISBN: 1-56884-246-5	$39.99 USA/$54.99 Canada

MACINTOSH

Title	Author	ISBN	Price
Mac® Programming For Dummies®	by Dan Parks Sydow	ISBN: 1-56884-173-6	$19.95 USA/$26.95 Canada
Macintosh® System 7.5 For Dummies®	by Bob LeVitus	ISBN: 1-56884-197-3	$19.95 USA/$26.95 Canada
MORE Macs® For Dummies®	by David Pogue	ISBN: 1-56884-087-X	$19.95 USA/$26.95 Canada
PageMaker 5 For Macs® For Dummies®	by Galen Gruman & Deke McClelland	ISBN: 1-56884-178-7	$19.95 USA/$26.95 Canada
QuarkXPress 3.3 For Dummies®	by Galen Gruman & Barbara Assadi	ISBN: 1-56884-217-1	$19.99 USA/$26.99 Canada
Upgrading and Fixing Macs® For Dummies®	by Kearney Rietmann & Frank Higgins	ISBN: 1-56884-189-2	$19.95 USA/$26.95 Canada

MULTIMEDIA

Title	Author	ISBN	Price
Multimedia & CD-ROMs For Dummies® 2nd Edition	by Andy Rathbone	ISBN: 1-56884-907-9	$19.99 USA/$26.99 Canada
Multimedia & CD-ROMs For Dummies®, Interactive Multimedia Value Pack, 2nd Edition	by Andy Rathbone	ISBN: 1-56884-909-5	$29.99 USA/$39.99 Canada

OPERATING SYSTEMS:

DOS

Title	Author	ISBN	Price
MORE DOS For Dummies®	by Dan Gookin	ISBN: 1-56884-046-2	$19.95 USA/$26.95 Canada
OS/2® Warp For Dummies® 2nd Edition	by Andy Rathbone	ISBN: 1-56884-205-8	$19.99 USA/$26.99 Canada

UNIX

Title	Author	ISBN	Price
MORE UNIX® For Dummies®	by John R. Levine & Margaret Levine Young	ISBN: 1-56884-361-5	$19.99 USA/$26.99 Canada
UNIX® For Dummies®	by John R. Levine & Margaret Levine Young	ISBN: 1-878058-58-4	$19.95 USA/$26.95 Canada

WINDOWS

Title	Author	ISBN	Price
MORE Windows® For Dummies® 2nd Edition	by Andy Rathbone	ISBN: 1-56884-048-9	$19.95 USA/$26.95 Canada
Windows® 95 For Dummies®	by Andy Rathbone	ISBN: 1-56884-240-6	$19.99 USA/$26.99 Canada

PCS/HARDWARE

Title	Author	ISBN	Price
Illustrated Computer Dictionary For Dummies® 2nd Edition	by Dan Gookin & Wallace Wang	ISBN: 1-56884-218-X	$12.95 USA/$16.95 Canada
Upgrading and Fixing PCs For Dummies® 2nd Edition	by Andy Rathbone	ISBN: 1-56884-903-6	$19.99 USA/$26.99 Canada

PRESENTATION/AUTOCAD

Title	Author	ISBN	Price
AutoCAD For Dummies®	by Bud Smith	ISBN: 1-56884-191-4	$19.95 USA/$26.95 Canada
PowerPoint 4 For Windows® For Dummies®	by Doug Lowe	ISBN: 1-56884-161-2	$16.99 USA/$22.99 Canada

PROGRAMMING

Title	Author	ISBN	Price
Borland C++ For Dummies®	by Michael Hyman	ISBN: 1-56884-162-0	$19.95 USA/$26.95 Canada
C For Dummies® Volume 1	by Dan Gookin	ISBN: 1-878058-78-9	$19.95 USA/$26.95 Canada
C++ For Dummies®	by Stephen R. Davis	ISBN: 1-56884-163-9	$19.95 USA/$26.95 Canada
Delphi Programming For Dummies®	by Neil Rubenking	ISBN: 1-56884-200-7	$19.99 USA/$26.99 Canada
Mac® Programming For Dummies®	by Dan Parks Sydow	ISBN: 1-56884-173-6	$19.95 USA/$26.95 Canada
PowerBuilder 4 Programming For Dummies®	by Ted Coombs & Jason Coombs	ISBN: 1-56884-325-9	$19.99 USA/$26.99 Canada
QBasic Programming For Dummies®	by Douglas Hergert	ISBN: 1-56884-093-4	$19.95 USA/$26.95 Canada
Visual Basic 3 For Dummies®	by Wallace Wang	ISBN: 1-56884-076-4	$19.95 USA/$26.95 Canada
Visual Basic "X" For Dummies®	by Wallace Wang	ISBN: 1-56884-230-9	$19.99 USA/$26.99 Canada
Visual C++ 2 For Dummies®	by Michael Hyman & Bob Arnson	ISBN: 1-56884-328-3	$19.99 USA/$26.99 Canada
Windows® 95 Programming For Dummies®	by S. Randy Davis	ISBN: 1-56884-327-5	$19.99 USA/$26.99 Canada

SPREADSHEET

Title	Author	ISBN	Price
1-2-3 For Dummies®	by Greg Harvey	ISBN: 1-878058-60-6	$16.95 USA/$22.95 Canada
1-2-3 For Windows® 5 For Dummies® 2nd Edition	by John Walkenbach	ISBN: 1-56884-216-3	$16.95 USA/$22.95 Canada
Excel 5 For Macs® For Dummies®	by Greg Harvey	ISBN: 1-56884-186-8	$19.95 USA/$26.95 Canada
Excel For Dummies® 2nd Edition	by Greg Harvey	ISBN: 1-56884-050-0	$16.95 USA/$22.95 Canada
MORE 1-2-3 For DOS For Dummies®	by John Weingarten	ISBN: 1-56884-224-4	$19.99 USA/$26.99 Canada
MORE Excel 5 For Windows® For Dummies®	by Greg Harvey	ISBN: 1-56884-207-4	$19.95 USA/$26.95 Canada
Quattro Pro 6 For Windows® For Dummies®	by John Walkenbach	ISBN: 1-56884-174-4	$19.95 USA/$26.95 Canada
Quattro Pro For DOS For Dummies®	by John Walkenbach	ISBN: 1-56884-023-3	$16.95 USA/$22.95 Canada

UTILITIES

Title	Author	ISBN	Price
Norton Utilities 8 For Dummies®	by Beth Slick	ISBN: 1-56884-166-3	$19.95 USA/$26.95 Canada

VCRS/CAMCORDERS

Title	Author	ISBN	Price
VCRs & Camcorders For Dummies™	by Gordon McComb & Andy Rathbone	ISBN: 1-56884-229-5	$14.99 USA/$20.99 Canada

WORD PROCESSING

Title	Author	ISBN	Price
Ami Pro For Dummies®	by Jim Meade	ISBN: 1-56884-049-7	$19.95 USA/$26.95 Canada
MORE Word For Windows® 6 For Dummies®	by Doug Lowe	ISBN: 1-56884-165-5	$19.95 USA/$26.95 Canada
MORE WordPerfect® 6 For Windows® For Dummies®	by Margaret Levine Young & David C. Kay	ISBN: 1-56884-206-6	$19.95 USA/$26.95 Canada
MORE WordPerfect® 6 For DOS For Dummies®	by Wallace Wang, edited by Dan Gookin	ISBN: 1-56884-047-0	$19.95 USA/$26.95 Canada
Word 6 For Macs® For Dummies®	by Dan Gookin	ISBN: 1-56884-190-6	$19.95 USA/$26.95 Canada
Word For Windows® 6 For Dummies®	by Dan Gookin	ISBN: 1-56884-075-6	$16.95 USA/$22.95 Canada
Word For Windows® For Dummies®	by Dan Gookin & Ray Werner	ISBN: 1-878058-86-X	$16.95 USA/$22.95 Canada
WordPerfect® 6 For DOS For Dummies®	by Dan Gookin	ISBN: 1-878058-77-0	$16.95 USA/$22.95 Canada
WordPerfect® 6.1 For Windows® For Dummies® 2nd Edition	by Margaret Levine Young & David Kay	ISBN: 1-56884-243-0	$16.95 USA/$22.95 Canada
WordPerfect® For Dummies®	by Dan Gookin	ISBN: 1-878058-52-5	$16.95 USA/$22.95 Canada

Fun, Fast, & Cheap!™

The Internet For Macs® For Dummies® Quick Reference
by Charles Seiter

ISBN:1-56884-967-2
$9.99 USA/$12.99 Canada

Windows® 95 For Dummies® Quick Reference
by Greg Harvey

ISBN: 1-56884-964-8
$9.99 USA/$12.99 Canada

Photoshop 3 For Macs® For Dummies® Quick Reference
by Deke McClelland

ISBN: 1-56884-968-0
$9.99 USA/$12.99 Canada

WordPerfect® For DOS For Dummies® Quick Reference
by Greg Harvey

ISBN: 1-56884-009-8
$8.95 USA/$12.95 Canada

Title	Author	ISBN	Price
DATABASE			
Access 2 For Dummies® Quick Reference	by Stuart J. Stuple	ISBN: 1-56884-167-1	$8.95 USA/$11.95 Canada
dBASE 5 For DOS For Dummies® Quick Reference	by Barrie Sosinsky	ISBN: 1-56884-954-0	$9.99 USA/$12.99 Canada
dBASE 5 For Windows® For Dummies® Quick Reference	by Stuart J. Stuple	ISBN: 1-56884-953-2	$9.99 USA/$12.99 Canada
Paradox 5 For Windows® For Dummies® Quick Reference	by Scott Palmer	ISBN: 1-56884-960-5	$9.99 USA/$12.99 Canada
DESKTOP PUBLISHING/ILLUSTRATION/GRAPHICS			
CorelDRAW! 5 For Dummies® Quick Reference	by Raymond E. Werner	ISBN: 1-56884-952-4	$9.99 USA/$12.99 Canada
Harvard Graphics For Windows® For Dummies® Quick Reference	by Raymond E. Werner	ISBN: 1-56884-962-1	$9.99 USA/$12.99 Canada
Photoshop 3 For Macs® For Dummies® Quick Reference	by Deke McClelland	ISBN: 1-56884-968-0	$9.99 USA/$12.99 Canada
FINANCE/PERSONAL FINANCE			
Quicken 4 For Windows® For Dummies® Quick Reference	by Stephen L. Nelson	ISBN: 1-56884-950-8	$9.95 USA/$12.95 Canada
GROUPWARE/INTEGRATED			
Microsoft® Office 4 For Windows® For Dummies® Quick Reference	by Doug Lowe	ISBN: 1-56884-958-3	$9.99 USA/$12.99 Canada
Microsoft® Works 3 For Windows® For Dummies® Quick Reference	by Michael Partington	ISBN: 1-56884-959-1	$9.99 USA/$12.99 Canada
INTERNET/COMMUNICATIONS/NETWORKING			
The Internet For Dummies® Quick Reference	by John R. Levine & Margaret Levine Young	ISBN: 1-56884-168-X	$8.95 USA/$11.95 Canada
MACINTOSH			
Macintosh® System 7.5 For Dummies® Quick Reference	by Stuart J. Stuple	ISBN: 1-56884-956-7	$9.99 USA/$12.99 Canada
OPERATING SYSTEMS:			
DOS			
DOS For Dummies® Quick Reference	by Greg Harvey	ISBN: 1-56884-007-1	$8.95 USA/$11.95 Canada
UNIX			
UNIX® For Dummies® Quick Reference	by John R. Levine & Margaret Levine Young	ISBN: 1-56884-094-2	$8.95 USA/$11.95 Canada
WINDOWS			
Windows® 3.1 For Dummies® Quick Reference, 2nd Edition	by Greg Harvey	ISBN: 1-56884-951-6	$8.95 USA/$11.95 Canada
PCs/HARDWARE			
Memory Management For Dummies® Quick Reference	by Doug Lowe	ISBN: 1-56884-362-3	$9.99 USA/$12.99 Canada
PRESENTATION/AUTOCAD			
AutoCAD For Dummies® Quick Reference	by Ellen Finkelstein	ISBN: 1-56884-198-1	$9.95 USA/$12.95 Canada
SPREADSHEET			
1-2-3 For Dummies® Quick Reference	by John Walkenbach	ISBN: 1-56884-027-6	$8.95 USA/$11.95 Canada
1-2-3 For Windows® 5 For Dummies® Quick Reference	by John Walkenbach	ISBN: 1-56884-957-5	$9.99 USA/$12.95 Canada
Excel For Windows® For Dummies® Quick Reference, 2nd Edition	by John Walkenbach	ISBN: 1-56884-096-9	$8.95 USA/$11.95 Canada
Quattro Pro 6 For Windows® For Dummies® Quick Reference	by Stuart J. Stuple	ISBN: 1-56884-172-8	$9.95 USA/$12.95 Canada
WORD PROCESSING			
Word For Windows® 6 For Dummies® Quick Reference	by George Lynch	ISBN: 1-56884-095-0	$8.95 USA/$11.95 Canada
Word For Windows® For Dummies® Quick Reference	by George Lynch	ISBN: 1-56884-029-2	$8.95 USA/$11.95 Canada
WordPerfect® 6.1 For Windows® For Dummies® Quick Reference, 2nd Edition	by Greg Harvey	ISBN: 1-56884-966-4	$9.99 USA/$12.99/Canada

scholastic requests & educational orders please Educational Sales at 1. 800. 434. 2086

FOR MORE INFO OR TO ORDER, PLEASE CALL ▶ **800. 762. 2974**

For volume discounts & special orders please call Tony Real, Special Sales, at 415. 655. 3048

Windows® 3.1 SECRETS™
by Brian Livingston

ISBN: 1-878058-43-6
$39.95 USA/$52.95 Canada
Includes software.

MORE Windows® 3.1 SECRETS™
by Brian Livingston

ISBN: 1-56884-019-5
$39.95 USA/$52.95 Canada
Includes software.

Windows® GIZMOS™
by Brian Livingston & Margie Livingston

ISBN: 1-878058-66-5
$39.95 USA/$52.95 Canada
Includes software.

Windows® 3.1 Connectivity SECRETS™
by Runnoe Connally, David Rorabaugh, & Sheldon Hall

ISBN: 1-56884-030-6
$49.95 USA/$64.95 Canada
Includes software.

Windows® 3.1 Configuration SECRETS™
by Valda Hilley & James Blakely

ISBN: 1-56884-026-8
$49.95 USA/$64.95 Canada
Includes software.

Internet SECRETS™
by John Levine & Carol Baroudi

ISBN: 1-56884-452-2
$39.99 USA/$54.99 Canada
Includes software.

Internet GIZMOS™ For Windows®
by Joel Diamond, Howard Sobel, & Valda Hilley

ISBN: 1-56884-451-4
$39.99 USA/$54.99 Canada
Includes software.

Network Security SECRETS™
by David Stang & Sylvia Moon

ISBN: 1-56884-021-7
Int'l. ISBN: 1-56884-151-5
$49.95 USA/$64.95 Canada
Includes software.

PC SECRETS™
by Caroline M. Halliday

ISBN: 1-878058-49-5
$39.95 USA/$52.95 Canada
Includes software.

WordPerfect® 6 SECRETS™
by Roger C. Parker & David A. Holzgang

ISBN: 1-56884-040-3
$39.95 USA/$52.95 Canada
Includes software.

DOS 6 SECRETS™
by Robert D. Ainsbury

ISBN: 1-878058-70-3
$39.95 USA/$52.95 Canada
Includes software.

Paradox 4 Power Programming SECRETS™, 2nd Edition
by Gregory B. Salcedo & Martin W. Rudy

ISBN: 1-878058-54-1
$44.95 USA/$59.95 Canada
Includes software.

Paradox 5 For Windows® Power Programming SECRETS™
by Gregory B. Salcedo & Martin W. Rudy

ISBN: 1-56884-085-3
$44.95 USA/$59.95 Canada
Includes software.

Hard Disk SECRETS™
by John M. Goodman, Ph.D.

ISBN: 1-878058-64-9
$39.95 USA/$52.95 Canada
Includes software.

WordPerfect® 6 For Windows® Tips & Techniques Revealed
by David A. Holzgang & Roger C. Parker

ISBN: 1-56884-202-3
$39.95 USA/$52.95 Canada
Includes software.

Excel 5 For Windows® Power Programming Techniques
by John Walkenbach

ISBN: 1-56884-303-8
$39.95 USA/$52.95 Canada
Includes software.

...SECRETS®

INFO WORLD TECHNICAL BOOKS

For scholastic requests & educational orders please call Educational Sales, at 1. 800. 434. 2086

FOR MORE INFO OR TO ORDER, PLEASE CALL ▶ 800 762 2974

For volume discounts & special orders please Tony Real, Special Sales, at 415. 655. 3048

"A lot easier to use than the book Excel gives you!"

Lisa Schmeckpeper, New Berlin, WI, on PC World Excel 5 For Windows Handbook

Official Hayes Modem Communications Companion
by Caroline M. Halliday

ISBN: 1-56884-072-1
$29.95 USA/$39.95 Canada
Includes software.

1,001 Komputer Answers from Kim Komando
by Kim Komando

ISBN: 1-56884-460-3
$29.99 USA/$39.99 Canada
Includes software.

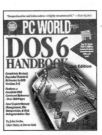

PC World DOS 6 Handbook, 2nd Edition
by John Socha, Clint Hicks, & Devra Hall

ISBN: 1-878058-79-7
$34.95 USA/$44.95 Canada
Includes software.

PC World Word For Windows® 6 Handbook
by Brent Heslop & David Angell

ISBN: 1-56884-054-3
$34.95 USA/$44.95 Canada
Includes software.

PC World Microsoft® Access 2 Bible, 2nd Edition
by Cary N. Prague & Michael R. Irwin

ISBN: 1-56884-086-1
$39.95 USA/$52.95 Canada
Includes software.

PC World Excel 5 For Windows® Handbook, 2nd Edition
by John Walkenbach & Dave Maguiness

ISBN: 1-56884-056-X
$34.95 USA/$44.95 Canada
Includes software.

PC World WordPerfect® 6 Handbook
by Greg Harvey

ISBN: 1-878058-80-0
$34.95 USA/$44.95 Canada
Includes software.

QuarkXPress For Windows® Designer Handbook
by Barbara Assadi & Galen Gruman

ISBN: 1-878058-45-2
$29.95 USA/$39.95 Canada

Official XTree Companion, 3rd Edition
by Beth Slick

ISBN: 1-878058-57-6
$19.95 USA/$26.95 Canada

PC World DOS 6 Command Reference and Problem Solver
by John Socha & Devra Hall

ISBN: 1-56884-055-1
$24.95 USA/$32.95 Canada

Client/Server Strategies™: A Survival Guide for Corporate Reengineers
by David Vaskevitch

ISBN: 1-56884-064-0
$29.95 USA/$39.95 Canada

"PC World Word For Windows 6 Handbook is very easy to follow with lots of 'hands on' examples. The 'Task at a Glance' is very helpful!"

Jacqueline Martens, Tacoma, WA

"Thanks for publishing this book! It's the best money I've spent this year!"

Robert D. Templeton, Ft. Worth, TX, on MORE Windows 3.1 SECRETS

scholastic requests & educational orders please Educational Sales, at 1. 800. 434. 2086

FOR MORE INFO OR TO ORDER, PLEASE CALL ▶ 800 762 2974

For volume discounts & special orders please call Tony Real, Special Sales, at 415. 655. 3048

"*Macworld Complete Mac Handbook Plus CD* covered everything I could think of and more!"

Peter Tsakiris, New York, NY

"Very useful for PageMaker beginners and veterans alike— contains a wealth of tips and tricks to make you a faster, more powerful PageMaker user."

Paul Brainerd, President and founder, Aldus Corporation

"Thanks for the best computer book I've ever read—*Photoshop 2.5 Bible*. Best $30 I ever spent. I *love* the detailed index....Yours blows them all out of the water. This is a great book. We must enlighten the masses!"

Kevin Lisankie, Chicago, Illinois

"*Macworld Guide to ClarisWorks 2* is the easiest computer book to read that I have ever found!"

Steven Hanson, Lutz, FL

"...thanks to the *Macworld Excel 5 Companion*, 2nd Edition occupying a permanent position next to my computer, I'll be able to tap more of Excel's power."

Lauren Black, Lab Director, Macworld Magazine

Macworld® QuarkXPress 3.2/3.3 Bible
by Barbara Assadi & Galen Gruman
ISBN: 1-878058-85-1
$39.95 USA/$52.95 Canada
Includes disk with QuarkXPress XTensions and scripts.

Macworld® PageMaker 5 Bible
by Craig Danuloff
ISBN: 1-878058-84-3
$39.95 USA/$52.95 Canada
Includes 2 disks with PageMaker utilities, clip art, and more.

Macworld® FileMaker Pro 2.0/2.1 Bible
by Steven A. Schwartz
ISBN: 1-56884-201-5
$34.95 USA/$46.95 Canada
Includes disk with ready-to-run data bases.

Macworld® Word 6 Companion, 2nd Edition
by Jim Heid
ISBN: 1-56884-082-9
$24.95 USA/$34.95 Canada

NEWBRIDGE BOOK CLUB SELECTION

Macworld® Guide To Microsoft® Word 5/5.1
by Jim Heid
ISBN: 1-878058-39-8
$22.95 USA/$29.95 Canada

Macworld® ClarisWorks 2.0/2.1 Companion, 2nd Edition
by Steven A. Schwartz
ISBN: 1-56884-180-9
$24.95 USA/$34.95 Canada

Macworld® Guide To Microsoft® Works 3
by Barrie Sosinsky
ISBN: 1-878058-42-8
$22.95 USA/$29.95 Canada

Macworld® Excel 5 Companion, 2nd Edition
by Chris Van Buren & David Maguiness
ISBN: 1-56884-081-0
$24.95 USA/$34.95 Canada

NEWBRIDGE BOOK CLUB SELECTION

Macworld® Guide To Microsoft® Excel 4
by David Maguiness
ISBN: 1-878058-40-1
$22.95 USA/$29.95 Canada

Microsoft is a registered trademark of Microsoft Corporation. Macworld is a registered trademark of International Data Group, Inc.

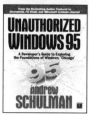

Unauthorized Windows® 95: A Developer's Guide to Exploring the Foundations of Windows "Chicago"
by Andrew Schulman

ISBN: 1-56884-169-8
$29.99 USA/$39.99 Canada

Unauthorized Windows® 95 Developer's Resource Kit
by Andrew Schulman

ISBN: 1-56884-305-4
$39.99 USA/$54.99 Canada

Best of the Net
by Seth Godin

ISBN: 1-56884-313-5
$22.99 USA/$32.99 Canada

Detour: The Truth About the Information Superhighway
by Michael Sullivan-Trainor

ISBN: 1-56884-307-0
$22.99 USA/$32.99 Canada

PowerPC Programming For Intel Programmers
by Kip McClanahan

ISBN: 1-56884-306-2
$49.99 USA/$64.99 Canada

Foundations™ of Visual C++ Programming For Windows® 95
by Paul Yao & Joseph Yao

ISBN: 1-56884-321-6
$39.99 USA/$54.99 Canada

Heavy Metal™ Visual C++ Programming
by Steve Holzner

ISBN: 1-56884-196-5
$39.95 USA/$54.95 Canada

Heavy Metal™ OLE 2.0 Programming
by Steve Holzner

ISBN: 1-56884-301-1
$39.95 USA/$54.95 Canada

Lotus Notes Application Development Handbook
by Erica Kerwien

ISBN: 1-56884-308-9
$39.99 USA/$54.99 Canada

The Internet Direct Connect Kit
by Peter John Harrison

ISBN: 1-56884-135-3
$29.95 USA/$39.95 Canada

Macworld® Ultimate Mac® Programming
by Dave Mark

ISBN: 1-56884-195-7
$39.95 USA/$54.95 Canada

The UNIX®-Haters Handbook
by Simson Garfinkel, Daniel Weise, & Steven Strassmann

ISBN: 1-56884-203-1
$16.95 USA/$22.95 Canada

Learn C++ Today!
by Martin Rinehart

ISBN: 1-56884-310-0
34.99 USA/$44.99 Canada

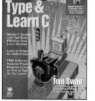

Type & Learn™ C
by Tom Swan

ISBN: 1-56884-073-X
34.95 USA/$44.95 Canada

Type & Learn™ Windows® Programming
by Tom Swan

ISBN: 1-56884-071-3
34.95 USA/$44.95 Canada

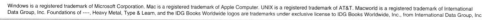

For scholastic requests & educational orders please call Educational Sales, at 1. 800. 434. 2086

FOR MORE INFO OR TO ORDER, PLEASE CALL ▶ 800. 762. 2974

For volume discounts & special orders please Tony Real, Special Sales, at 415. 655. 3048

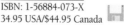

Order Center: **(800) 762-2974** *(8 a.m.–6 p.m., EST, weekdays)*

Quantity	ISBN	Title	Price	Total

Shipping & Handling Charges

	Description	First book	Each additional book	Total
Domestic	Normal	$4.50	$1.50	$
	Two Day Air	$8.50	$2.50	$
	Overnight	$18.00	$3.00	$
International	Surface	$8.00	$8.00	$
	Airmail	$16.00	$16.00	$
	DHL Air	$17.00	$17.00	$

*For large quantities call for shipping & handling charges.
**Prices are subject to change without notice.

Ship to:

Name _____

Company _____

Address _____

City/State/Zip _____

Daytime Phone _____

Payment: ☐ Check to IDG Books Worldwide (US Funds Only)

☐ VISA   ☐ MasterCard   ☐ American Express

Card # _____ Expires _____

Signature _____

Subtotal _____

CA residents add
applicable sales tax _____

IN, MA, and MD
residents add
5% sales tax _____

IL residents add
6.25% sales tax _____

RI residents add
7% sales tax _____

TX residents add
8.25% sales tax _____

Shipping _____

Total _____

Please send this order form to:
IDG Books Worldwide, Inc.
7260 Shadeland Station, Suite 100
Indianapolis, IN 46256

Allow up to 3 weeks for delivery.
Thank you!

IDG BOOKS WORLDWIDE REGISTRATION CARD

RETURN THIS REGISTRATION CARD FOR FREE CATALOG

Title of this book: PageMaker 6 For Macs For Dummies 2E

My overall rating of this book: ❏ Very good [1] ❏ Good [2] ❏ Satisfactory [3] ❏ Fair [4] ❏ Poor [5]

How I first heard about this book:

❏ Found in bookstore; name: [6]

❏ Advertisement: [8]

❏ Word of mouth; heard about book from friend, co-worker, etc.: [10]

❏ Book review: [7]

❏ Catalog: [9]

❏ Other: [11]

What I liked most about this book:

What I would change, add, delete, etc., in future editions of this book:

Other comments:

Number of computer books I purchase in a year: ❏ 1 [12] ❏ 2-5 [13] ❏ 6-10 [14] ❏ More than 10 [15]

I would characterize my computer skills as: ❏ Beginner [16] ❏ Intermediate [17] ❏ Advanced [18] ❏ Professional [19]

I use ❏ DOS [20] ❏ Windows [21] ❏ OS/2 [22] ❏ Unix [23] ❏ Macintosh [24] ❏ Other: [25]_____

(please specify)

I would be interested in new books on the following subjects:
(please check all that apply, and use the spaces provided to identify specific software)

❏ Word processing: [26]

❏ Data bases: [28]

❏ File Utilities: [30]

❏ Networking: [32]

❏ Other: [34]

❏ Spreadsheets: [27]

❏ Desktop publishing: [29]

❏ Money management: [31]

❏ Programming languages: [33]

I use a PC at (please check all that apply): ❏ home [35] ❏ work [36] ❏ school [37] ❏ other: [38] _____

The disks I prefer to use are ❏ 5.25 [39] ❏ 3.5 [40] ❏ other: [41]_____

I have a CD ROM: ❏ yes [42] ❏ no [43]

I plan to buy or upgrade computer hardware this year: ❏ yes [44] ❏ no [45]

I plan to buy or upgrade computer software this year: ❏ yes [46] ❏ no [47]

Name: _____ Business title: [48] _____ Type of Business: [49] _____

Address (❏ home [50] ❏ work [51]/Company name: _____)

Street/Suite# _____

City [52]/State [53]/Zipcode [54]: _____ Country [55] _____

❏ **I liked this book!** You may quote me by name in future IDG Books Worldwide promotional materials.

My daytime phone number is _____

IDG BOOKS

THE WORLD OF COMPUTER KNOWLEDGE

❑ YES!

Please keep me informed about IDG's World of Computer Knowledge.
Send me the latest IDG Books catalog.